Grenada

Carriacou • Petite Martinique

the Bradt Travel Guide

Paul Crask

www.bradt

Bradt Travel
The Globe Pe

edition
2

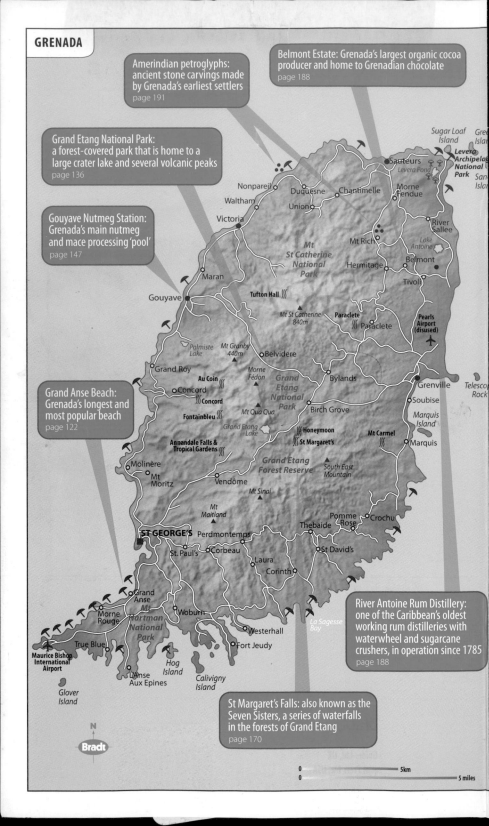

GRENADA

Amerindian petroglyphs: ancient stone carvings made by Grenada's earliest settlers
page 191

Belmont Estate: Grenada's largest organic cocoa producer and home to Grenadian chocolate
page 188

Grand Etang National Park: a forest-covered park that is home to a large crater lake and several volcanic peaks
page 136

Gouyave Nutmeg Station: Grenada's main nutmeg and mace processing 'pool'
page 147

Grand Anse Beach: Grenada's longest and most popular beach
page 122

River Antoine Rum Distillery: one of the Caribbean's oldest working rum distilleries with waterwheel and sugarcane crushers, in operation since 1785
page 188

St Margaret's Falls: also known as the Seven Sisters, a series of waterfalls in the forests of Grand Etang
page 170

Sugar Loaf Island
Gre Isla
Levera Archipela National Park
San Isla
Sauteurs
Levera Pond
Morne Fendue
Nonpareil
Duquesne
Chantimelle
Waltham
Union
Victoria
River Sallee
Mt Rich
Lake Antoine
Mt St Catherine National Park
Hermitage
Belmont
Maran
Tivoli
Gouyave
Tufton Hall
Mt St Catherine 840m
Paraclete
Paraclete
Pearls Airport (disused)
Palmiste Lake
Mt Granby 440m
Belvidere
Grand Roy
Morne Fédon
Bylands
Grenville
Telesco Rock
Au Coin
Concord
Grand Etang National Park
Soubise
Concord
Fontainbleu
Mt Qua Qua
Birch Grove
Marquis Island
Grand Etang Lake
Honeymoon
St Margaret's
Mt Carmel
Marquis
Annandale Falls & Tropical Gardens
Molinère
Grand Etang Forest Reserve
South East Mountain
Mt Moritz
Vendôme
Mt Sinai
Mt Maitland
Pomme Rose
Crochu
Thebaide
ST GEORGE'S
Perdmontemps
St David's
St. Paul's
Corbeau
Laura
Corinth
La Sagesse Bay
Grand Anse
Mt Hartman National Park
Woburn
Westerhall
Morne Rouge
Fort Jeudy
Maurice Bishop International Airport
True Blue
Hog Island
L'Anse Aux Epines
Calivigny Island
Glover Island

N

Bradt

0   5km
0   5 miles

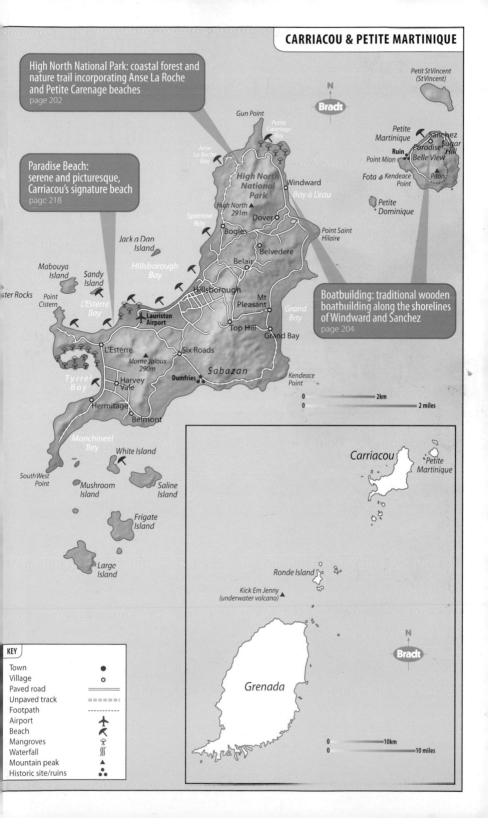

CARRIACOU & PETITE MARTINIQUE

High North National Park: coastal forest and nature trail incorporating Anse La Roche and Petite Carenage beaches
page 202

Paradise Beach: serene and picturesque, Carriacou's signature beach
page 218

Boatbuilding: traditional wooden boatbuilding along the shorelines of Windward and Sanchez
page 204

Bradt

Petit St Vincent (St Vincent)

Gun Point

Petite Carenage Bay

Anse La Roche Bay

High North National Park

High North 291m

Sparrow Bay

Jack a Dan Island

Mabouya Island

Sandy Island

ster Rocks

Point Cistern

L'Esterre Bay

Hillsborough Bay

Bogles

Belvedere

Belair

Hillsborough

Mt Pleasant

Top Hill

L'Esterre

Morne Jaloux 290m

Six Roads

Harvey Vale

Tyrrel Bay

Hermitage

Belmont

Manchineel Bay

White Island

South West Point

Mushroom Island

Saline Island

Frigate Island

Large Island

Windward

Bay à L'eau

Dover

Point Saint Hilaire

Grand Bay

Grand Bay

Sabazan

Dumfries

Kendeace Point

Lauriston Airport

Petite Martinique

Point Mion

Ruin

Fota

Kendeace Point

Sanchez

Paradise Belle View

Sugar Hill

Piton

Petite Dominique

0 ———— 2km
0 ———— 2 miles

Carriacou

Petite Martinique

Ronde Island

Kick Em Jenny (underwater volcano)

Grenada

Bradt

0 ———— 10km
0 ———— 10 miles

KEY

Town	●
Village	○
Paved road	——
Unpaved track	======
Footpath	-------
Airport	✈
Beach	☂
Mangroves	♨
Waterfall	)))
Mountain peak	▲
Historic site/ruins	∴

Grenada, Carriacou and Petite Martinique

Spices and cocoa
Known as the 'Spice Island of the Caribbean', Grenada is home to a range of exotic flavours. Pictured here, harvesting organic cocoa in the parish of St Patrick
(PC) page 20

Stunning beaches and bays
The secluded Anse La Roche is one of Carriacou's finest spots (CS) page 225

Tropical forests, mountains and waterfalls
A hike through Grenada's lush interior brings you to St Margaret's Falls, a series of alluring cascades and pools
(CS) page 170

St George's
Built around a large natural harbour, St George's is often described as the Caribbean's prettiest capital
(EU/A) page 91

Cultural heritage and traditions
At the River Antoine Rum Distillery sugar cane is converted into rum in the same way it was over 200 years ago (CS) page 188

above Lining St George's harbour, the Carenage is home to some of Grenada's most impressive Georgian architecture (EG) page 100

below The 3km-long Grand Anse Beach is popular amongst visitors and locals alike (CS) page 122

above   Visitors can take a tour around the fascinating old waterwheels and machine works at the Westerhall Estate (PC) page 168

right   Visit Grenada's nutmeg stations, or 'pools', to see how this traditional spice is collected and prepared for export. Here, the Dougaldston Estate (PC) page 140

below   The high mountain ridges of the Grand Etang National Park offer unsurpassed panoramic views of the islands (PC) page 136

THE Caribbean Airline

Discover our Day Trips

Leave in the AM, return in the PM.

With over 120 daily departures and high-frequency, inter-island service, you can take advantage of morning and evening departures to any of our 21 island destinations.

You can follow your favourite team, see your favourite artiste live, explore a new destination or just getaway to relaxation.

Log on to liat.com and book while you are in Grenada and the Grenadines and find out more about our fares and specials. Now you can also book your accommodation, car rentals, activities and travel insurance whatever your destination.

From Grenada

DESTINATION	DEPARTURE TIME*	RETURN TIME*
Barbados	6:25am	7:00pm
St. Lucia	6:25am	6:05pm
St. Vincent	6:25am	5:10pm

Flight times subject to change

ANGUILLA • ANTIGUA • BARBADOS • CANOUAN • CURAÇAO
DOMINICA • DOMINICAN REPUBLIC • GRENADA • GUADELOUPE
GUYANA • MARTINIQUE • NEVIS • PUERTO RICO • ST. CROIX
ST. KITTS • ST. LUCIA • ST.MAARTEN • ST. THOMAS
ST. VINCENT • TORTOLA • TRINIDAD

liat.com

AUTHOR

Born in England, Paul Crask grew up in Yorkshire and graduated from Leeds University in 1988 with a Bachelor of Arts degree. He also spent time in former East Germany, studying at what was once the Karl Marx University of Leipzig. After graduating he travelled to Japan where he lived and worked as a teacher for two years before backpacking around the world from the Far East back to Europe via North America. He worked in London for ten years before dropping out and embarking on a radical lifestyle change with his wife, Celia. They moved to her native Dominica in 2005.

Paul works as a writer and photographer. Specialising in life, nature and travel in the eastern Caribbean, he has been published in a number of books, newspapers and magazines. He is also the author of *Dominica: the Bradt Travel Guide.*

AUTHOR'S STORY

It was the 10th birthday of the Grenada Chocolate Factory and I had been invited by founder Mott Green and Belmont Estate owner Shadel Nyack Compton to celebrate with them on Bathway Beach. Everyone seemed to want to come and chat. I can't recall ever feeling so at home with people I had only just met. The same happened when Philip and Annie invited me to lunch at Petite Anse, and also when I went up to see DJ at The Heights – it was as if I had known them all my life. On my first night back in Gouyave, Gurry came to see me. He and I had spent the best part of ten hours cutting our way through landslides and fallen trees to get to the top of Morne Fédon and back down again from Belvidere in 2007. He showed me some of his archives – he collects photographs and other memorabilia from the parish of St John. Although I had only spent a few days with him when I was writing the first edition, it felt like we were old friends. In Carriacou I spent all morning with museum curator Clemencia talking about her dad, the artist Canute Caliste, and when I returned to Belair to see Becca and Michael, it seemed like I had never been away. If the experience of writing the first edition of this book had been about discovering new places then the second was certainly about meeting people and making friends. It is the dimension of travel that I think we often neglect, but it enriches our journeys and makes them far more rewarding.

And I think about the people who used the first edition of this guide for their Grenada travels. I received quite a few complimentary and funny emails: 'Your description of the hike around Grand Etang Lake was spot on. We got stuck in the mud too!' and 'You would have been amused by the daily "Is Paul Crask in the car?", "Where is Paul Crask?", "What does Paul Crask say about that?"'. When Shadel from Belmont told me her visitors' book was crammed with references to this guide I realised I was connecting with a lot of people, and so writing the second edition began to mean much more. And as for places, well I did retrace my steps around Grand Etang, of course, and I got stuck in the mud again. I laughed out loud and thought of you. I hope you enjoy these islands and their people as much as I do.

PUBLISHER'S FOREWORD
Adrian Phillips, Managing Director

What I love about Paul Crask's guidebooks is that they reveal a textured side to the Caribbean that you rarely find in other writing about the place. We've all read travel magazines pronouncing the best resorts and the newest honeymoon spots.

But in this book Paul reveals where to find Grenada's most haunting shipwrecks, where to learn about the making of rum and chocolate, and how to avoid mischievous spirits. There are white-sand beaches, of course, but somehow I can't imagine Paul spending all his time sunbathing when there are rainforest-covered mountains to explore…

Reprinted September 2015
Second edition published July 2012 First published January 2009
Bradt Travel Guides Ltd
IDC House, The Vale, Chalfont St Peter, Bucks SL9 9RZ, England
www.bradtguides.com
Published in the USA by The Globe Pequot Press Inc,
PO Box 480, Guilford, Connecticut 06437-0480

Text copyright © 2012 Paul Crask
Maps copyright © 2012 Bradt Travel Guides Ltd
Photographs copyright © 2012 Individual photographers (see below)
Project Manager: Greg Dickinson

ISBN: 978 1 84162 401 3

British Library Cataloguing in Publication Data
A catalogue record for this book is available from the British Library

Photographs Alamy: Bill Bachmann (BB/A); Eye Ubiquitous (EU/A); Brenda S/Duncan Kirkby/Dive Grenada (BS/DK/DG); Paul Crask (PC); Ethan Gordon (EG); Grenada Board of Tourism (GBT); Bob Hall (BH); Anthony Jeremiah (AJ); Michael J Pazzani/New Jersey Birds (MJP/NJB); Shutterstock: R Gombarik (RG/S), RJ Lerich (RJL/S), Pawel Kazmierczak (PK/S); Celia Sorhaindo (CS); St George's University/Joshua Yetman (SGU/JY)
Front cover Mardi Gras parade, St George's (SS)
Back cover Antillean-crested hummingbird (MJP/NJB), Levera Beach (CS)
Title page Roucou plant (CS), Fiddler in St George's (PC), Concord Falls (CS)

Maps David McCutcheon; colour map relief base by Nick Rowland FRGS

Typeset from the author's disc by D & N Publishing, Baydon, Wiltshire
Production managed by Jellyfish Print Solutions; printed in India

INTRODUCTION

Grenada is a scenic and interesting island. It has picture-postcard beaches where you can while away the hours by a turquoise sea, watching sailboats passing by, dreaming, relaxing with a book. There are plenty of comfortable resort hotels and self-catering villas to choose from and most are located along the shoreline or have ocean views. Restaurants are plentiful and the choice of cuisine is varied.

Inland the island is mountainous and forest-covered. Nature-lovers and hikers can explore trails to waterfalls, mountain peaks, and secret coves. The tropical countryside has lush rainforest, colourful plants, diverse fauna, and farmlands growing root crops, citrus, nutmegs and other spices for which this island has become famous.

Watersports enthusiasts can scuba-dive to interesting shipwrecks and colourful coral reef systems. Sailing is big here. The islands host several international regattas each year, there are operators offering a range of day charters and tours, and well-equipped marinas and haul-out facilities are located in many of the natural anchorages, bays and inlets of Grenada's south coast.

Cultural heritage comes alive in the form of historic rum distilleries, cocoa estates, nutmeg processing stations, plantation ruins, and village feasts. On next-door Carriacou the string band and maroon festivals, Big Drum Dance, traditional boat launchings, Amerindian artefacts, and community *saracas* offer a potent and intoxicating link to the past.

Carriacou and Petite Martinique should not be missed, and you should try to visit for longer than just a day. These magical islands of the southern Grenadines are not only steeped in history and tradition, they are also beautiful, remote, romantic and, in many senses, very carefree. When I am not there, I miss them.

People travel for many reasons and you may want to do as little as possible and recharge. In this day and age, it is understandable. Nevertheless I do urge you to explore beyond the loungers and the beaches if you can, to discover more of these three alluring islands and to engage with their friendly and interesting people. Have a memorable journey.

ACKNOWLEDGEMENTS

For their friendship, help, encouragement and support: Becca and Michael, Shadel, Vernessa, Mott, Philip and Annie, Lisette and Jimmy, Gurry, Clemencia, Tim, Jonas, Kitty and Russ, Lucille, Folayan, Edlyn, Kendra, Karen, Sunkey, and my lovely wife Celia.

DEDICATION

In loving memory of my Grandad Ray and my pal Zoe. Love you and miss you.

Contents

UPDATES WEBSITE AND FEEDBACK REQUEST

Things change over time; a restaurant opens or closes, a new hotel appears, perhaps someone even discovers a new waterfall or a secret beach. Just after the second edition of my Dominica guide was published a whole lake disappeared; the dam wall collapsed and it was gone overnight. I suppose I should have expected something like that from a place called Miracle Lake! Hopefully nothing quite as dramatic as that will occur in Grenada, but you never know. If you do spot something new, or if indeed something does disappear, let me know. I will post any updates at www.bradtupdates.com/grenada. You can contact me with comments, feedback or updates via e info@bradtguides.com or alternatively via my website www.paulcrask.com, and you can follow @paulcrask on Twitter.

LIST OF MAPS

KEY TO SYMBOLS

═══	Main road (regional)		🏺	Museum/gallery
───	Other road (regional)		✿	Park/garden
■	Capital		🏛	Historic/important building
●	Town		🏰	Historic castle/fortification
○	Village		✈	Beach
✈	Airport (international)		⚓	Swimming
✝	Airstrip		🏃	Stadium
🚌	Bus station		⚓	Marina
🅿	Car park		⚑	Golf course
🚗	Taxi rank		⚱	Monument/statue
⛽	Filling station/garage		≈	Waterfall
✚	Hospital/clinic		❋	Scenic viewpoint
✚	Pharmacy		➤	Birdwatching/nesting sites
✉	Post office		∴	Historic site/ruins
$	Bank		⚓	Shipwreck
ℹ	Tourist information		⚘	Mangroves
✝	Church/cathedral		○	Hot spring
⌂	Hotel/guest house		⌂	Cave
❶	Restaurant		▲	Summit
⚲	Bar		⬚	Market
			⬚	National park/nature reserve
			▦	Shopping mall

Part One

GENERAL INFORMATION

Location Grenada 12°07'N, 61°40'W, Carriacou 12°29'N, 61°27'W, Petite Martinique 12°31'N, 61°23'W. The tri-island state of Grenada is located at the southernmost tip of the Windward Islands in the West Indies between St Vincent and the Grenadines and Trinidad and Tobago.

Size Tri-island state of Grenada: 344km²

Climate Tropical: average daytime 25°C winter, 31°C summer

Population c100,000

Capital St George's

Other main towns Gouyave, Grenville, Sauteurs (Grenada), Hillsborough (Carriacou)

Economy Tourism and agriculture

Language English

Main religions Roman Catholic, Anglican

Currency East Caribbean dollar (XCD or EC$)

Exchange rate US$1 = EC$2.7 fixed, £1 = EC$4.36 variable, €1 = EC$3.51 variable (May 2012)

Airports Maurice Bishop International Airport (Grenada), Lauriston Airport (Carriacou).

International dialling code +1 473

Time GMT −4 hours

Electricity supply 220V, 50Hz with UK-style three-pin sockets. Many hotels and self-catering cottages and villas also have a 110v supply with two-pin sockets.

Flag Four triangles of yellow (top and bottom) and green (left and right) form a rectangle against a red background with a line of three gold stars above and below. At the centre is a red circle with a seventh gold star. On the left-hand green triangle is a nutmeg pod.

National bird Grenada dove (*Leptolia wellsi*)

National flower Bougainvillea (*Bougainvillea spectablis*)

Public holidays See page 60

Background Information

GEOGRAPHY

Grenada is an independent tri-island nation located at the southern tip of the Windward Islands in the West Indies at 12°07'N and 61°40'W. To the north are St Vincent and the Grenadines, and to the south are Trinidad and Tobago from where it is just a short hop to Venezuela and the South American continent.

Grenada is the main island of the three and is approximately 34km long and 18km wide. The Atlantic Ocean is to the east and the Caribbean Sea to the west. Located in the southwest of the island, on a natural harbour, is the nation's capital, St George's, which is also its major sea port. Grenada's interior consists of a mountainous terrain that is testament to its volcanic origin. High, narrow, forest-covered ridges create a vertiginous environment of steep slopes and deep valleys that are home to small farming communities. Located in the north is Mt St Catherine, Grenada's tallest peak at an elevation of 840m. The island's coastline combines precipitous cliffs and a rugged volcanic environment with numerous sheltered bays and eye-catching beaches of both powder white and rich black sand. The beaches and natural anchorages of Grenada's southwest peninsula attract the majority of the island's visitors, with the 3km-long Grand Anse Beach one of its most popular.

Carriacou is the second largest of the three islands and is located approximately 37km north of Grenada at 12°29'N and 61°27'W. It is about 11km long, 5km wide and covers an area of 34km². Carriacou's main town is Hillsborough, which is located on the west coast of the island. It has a hilly interior that is predominantly covered in farmland and dry scrub forest. The two highest points are High North at 291m and Morne Jaloux in the south at 290m. An exposed eastern coastline faces the wind and weather from the Atlantic and consists of a rocky shoreline with both black- and white-sand beaches. The more leeward-facing coastlines on the west of the island have a number of sheltered bays, natural anchorages, turquoise seas and picture-postcard white-sand beaches.

Petite Martinique is located approximately 5km to the northeast of Carriacou at 12°31'N and 61°23'W. This diminutive island has an area of just 2km² and largely consists of a single conical peak, called Piton, which rises to 225m. Most of the island's residents live around its western shoreline with the remainder of it uninhabited, save for sheep, cattle, mules and goats. Petite Martinique's closest neighbour is the private resort island of Petit St Vincent (PSV), which is just a short boat ride to the northwest, and the southernmost point of the St Vincent Grenadines.

The **Grenadines** are a chain of more than 125 islands and islets located at 12°30'N and 61°30'W that belong to both Grenada and St Vincent. The Grenada Grenadines meet the St Vincent Grenadines at a partition between Petit St Vincent and Petite Martinique. Carriacou, Petite Martinique, Île de Ronde (commonly known as Ronde Island) and around 30 islets and rocky pinnacles form Grenada's dependencies and therefore part of the state of Grenada.

CLIMATE

Grenada, Carriacou and Petite Martinique have a tropical climate with average daytime temperatures ranging from around 25°C in January and February, which are the coolest months, to 31°C in July and August. Grenada is usually at its wettest between the months of July and December, the **rainy season**, when unsettled weather arrives with the Atlantic trade winds. Average rainfall is around 250cm with most of it falling on the windward east coasts and the mountainous interior of Grenada. There can be frequent showers and some heavy, prolonged bouts of rainfall throughout this period, especially at higher elevations. July to November is also the time when the West Indies becomes vulnerable to tropical storms and Atlantic hurricanes.

The driest and sunniest months tend to be from January to June, the **dry season**, but visitors to Grenada should always anticipate showers and be prepared for excursions into the interior to be wet occasionally and almost always humid. Throughout the islands, and especially along the sheltered leeward coasts, it is usually very hot and sunny during these months. Higher elevations as well as the windward-facing coastlines usually benefit from a cooling breeze which helps to make the tropical climate a little more comfortable.

Hurricanes that have the potential to affect Grenada tend to develop from tropical depressions in the Atlantic Ocean south of the Cape Verde Islands. The season for hurricanes and tropical storms usually begins in July and lasts until November, with August and September being the months when the risk is often greatest. Though it is situated to the south of most hurricanes' tracks, Grenada was hit in 1955 (Hurricane Janet), 1999 (Hurricane Lenny), 2004 (Hurricane Ivan) and 2005 (Hurricane Emily). Although Hurricane Janet was devastating, Hurricane Ivan is generally considered to have been the worst hurricane to hit Grenada in recent memory.

NATURAL HISTORY AND CONSERVATION

HABITATS Though all three islands of the state of Grenada are relatively small, they contain a variety of natural habitats with a surprising diversity of vegetation and wildlife. The impact of the 2004 and 2005 hurricanes is still visible, particularly in the high mountain elevations and along windward-facing slopes. These areas were exposed to the full force of the storms and there was considerable damage to tall, mature trees as well as vulnerable, shallow-rooted vegetation. The condition of these interior habitats remains one of flux. Because most of the mature trees were toppled by storms, vegetation that is accustomed to a dark, shady and very wet rainforest environment now finds itself exposed to sunlight, wind and a drier habitat than it prefers. Though these habitats are recovering well, some species will require a much longer period of time to re-establish themselves properly.

The highest mountain peaks, pinnacles and ridges of Grenada's interior will often be hidden by a blanket of cloud. The rain-laden weather that arrives with the prevailing winds across the Atlantic Ocean tends to reach the island's eastern shoreline and then sit over the high elevations of the interior. These areas can therefore be quite cold and wet for much of the year and their vegetation reflects this moist and exposed environment. Habitats of this type are usually referred to as **elfin woodland** or cloud forest and tend to consist of low-growing species of trees such as the regionally endemic *Clusia mangle*. The Clusia has thick, ovate leaves, dark red hard-skinned fruit, and small white flowers. Look out for a wide selection of ferns, mountain palms (*Prestoea montana*), moss, lichens and grasses such as *Scleria*, also known for very good reason as razor grass. Anyone exploring Grenada's interior will certainly encounter elfin woodland habitats at the summit of peaks such as Mt St Catherine, which is the island's tallest mountain, and Morne Fédon (Fédon's Camp).

Located just below elfin woodland is a habitat usually referred to as **montane forest**, sometimes also called montane thicket. The vegetation found here is similar to that of the rainforest though its growth tends to be a little more stunted. Below the montane thicket is the **rainforest**. It is here that some of the largest and most impressive trees are found. They include the gommier, or gum tree (*Dacryodes excelsa*), also known regionally as the *tabonuco* or *candlewood* because of the flammable gum-like sap that oozes from its bark; the maruba (*Simarouba amara*); mahogany (*Swietenia mahogani*); and the small- and large-leaf santai (*Sloanea caribaea* and *Sloanea truncata*). A species of Caribbean pine (*Pinus caribaea*), introduced to Grenada in an effort to reduce the country's need for wood imports, can be found in the Grand Etang region. The rainforest habitat is also where you will see a wide variety of ferns and epiphytes, including tree ferns, bromeliads and orchids.

Grenada's extensive **coastal woodland** is a fairly dry forest habitat that receives much less rainfall than the heights of the interior. Carriacou and Petite Martinique are predominantly coastal or dry scrub woodland environments where trees are usually semi-deciduous, shedding some of their leaves during the dry season to conserve moisture and survive. Trees found in this habitat include the white cedar (*Tabebuia heterophylla*), the campeche or dogwood (*Haematoxylum campechianum*), acacia (*Acacia*), black sage (*Cordia curassavica*) and the blackthorn (*Pisonia aculeata*). Along the fringes of sandy beaches you may come across torchwood (*Jacquinia armillaris*), sea grape (*Coccoloba uvifera*), sea almond (*Terminalia catappa*), the poisonous manchineel (*Hippomane mancinella*) and, of course, the prolific coconut palm (*Cocos nucifera*).

Grenada and Carriacou have a number of inland and coastal **mangrove forests** and **swamps**. Here you will find black mangrove (*Avicennia germinans*), red mangrove (*Rhizophora mangle*) and, around the margins of the Grand Etang Lake, the arum lily (*Montrichardia arborescens*).

See page 8 for information on the islands' marine environment.

PLANTS AND FLOWERS The national flower of Grenada, Carriacou and Petite Martinique is the **bougainvillea** (*Bougainvillea spectabilis*) which grows all over the three islands and is often found in the carefully tended gardens of many private homes. Visitors to Grenada will also see many other varieties of colourful flowers and plants including ginger (*Alpinia purpurata*), heliconia (*Heliconia*), hibiscus (*Hibiscus*), ixora (*Ixora*), allamanda (*Allamanda cathartica*), angel's trumpet (*Datura candida*), anthurium (*Anthurium andraeanum*), bird of paradise flower (*Strelitzia reginae*) and several varieties of orchid. Endemic to Grenada is the bois agouti (*Maytenus grenadensis*), a tree with simple leaves and small white flowers. Also endemic are *Rhytidophyllum caribaeum*, a small shrub with cream or orange flowers, *Lonchocarpus broadwayi* and *Cyathea elliotii*. Flowering trees such as the flamboyant (*Delonix regia*) are usually seen growing along coastlines and are very bright and colourful when in full bloom.

Fruits and vegetables In addition to a wonderful range of fresh aromatic spices (see pages 22–23), Grenada's farmers grow a wide variety of interesting and delicious fruits and vegetables. Most families own a piece of land of some shape or size that allows them to plant their own produce. They tend to grow traditional subsistence crops such as yams, calalou, sweet potatoes and pigeon peas. Vegetable crops such as beans, carrots, cabbage and potatoes are also common. Banana plantations are small though quite widespread on the main island. In addition to the bananas that most visitors recognise from supermarkets back home, Grenadians also cultivate plantain and *bluggo* as well as unripe bananas, known as 'green bananas' or 'figs', which are boiled in soups, stews and the national dish, 'oil-down' (see page 57). In addition to pigeon peas, corn is a traditional crop which is still commonly cultivated in dry areas. Fruits you will see growing in the wild, as well as on managed farms, include mango, grapefruit, lime, pawpaw (also known as papaya), guava, passionfruit, sapodilla, pineapple, watermelon and breadfruit.

BIRDS Grenada's forests, coastal woodlands, bays, estuaries, rugged coastlines and floral gardens combine to create habitats for birds of all kinds. The national bird is the **Grenada dove** (*Leptotila wellsi*), which is thought to be endemic to Grenada and very rare. The dove has been observed mainly in the southwest of Grenada, within the Mt Hartman National Park and Clarke's Court Bay areas. It has also been recorded around Perseverance, Beauséjour, Black Bay and Halifax Harbour. Little is known about the dove though its numbers are believed to be small. Also considered endemic to Grenada is the endangered **hook-billed kite** (*Chondrohierax uncinatus*), which is one of the smallest species of hawks. Like the Grenada dove, it has been observed in the dry scrubland habitat of the southwest.

Grenada has three nesting species of **hummingbird**. The rufous-breasted hermit (*Glaucis hirsuta*), also known as the hairy hermit, is thought to be endemic to Grenada and Trinidad and Tobago. It has a brown-coloured head, a bronze and green upper body, and a rufous underbelly. It prefers the habitat of the elevated rainforest, feeding on the nectar of heliconia and ginger lilies, but is rarely seen. More common is the emerald-throated hummingbird (*Eulampis holosericeus*), also known as the green-throated carib. Its very distinct colouration includes a covering of shimmering emerald and a vivid, violet-blue breast. This hummingbird can be seen all around Grenada. The third hummingbird is the Antillean-crested hummingbird (*Orthorhyncus cristatus*), also known locally as the *colibri*, a name thought to have Amerindian origins. Said to be the smallest bird found in the islands, it is brightly coloured with an emerald green and blue crest, and is found throughout Grenada.

Bird enthusiasts will enjoy sightings of the magnificent **frigatebird** (*Fregata magnificens*), which is seen circling and diving along inshore waters, as well as boobies, terns, herons and egrets. Woodland and mangrove birds to see and hear in Grenada include the unmistakable **bananaquit** (*Coereba flaveola*), the **Grenada flycatcher** (*Myiarchus nugator*), the **southern mockingbird** (*Mimus gilvus antillarum*), the **smooth-billed ani** (*Crotophaga ani*) and the **mangrove cuckoo** (*Coccyzus minor grenadensis*). Birds of prey include the **barn owl** (*Tyto alba*), also known as the *jumbie* bird because it is thought to contain evil spirits, the **osprey** (*Pandion haliaetus*), which is rarely seen, and the **broad-winged hawk** (*Buteo platypterus*), also known as the chicken hawk, which is more commonly sighted.

MAMMALS The **mona monkey** (*Cercopithecus mona*) is also known as the macaque and was probably brought from west Africa to Grenada by slave traders in the 18th century. The population is thought to have developed from very small numbers though studies have suggested it is healthy and lives off fruits, leaves and insects in Grenada's mountainous, forested interior. Though hurricanes and hunters continue to threaten its existence, it seems to survive well and in relatively high numbers.

The **small Asian mongoose** (*Herpestes auropunctatus*) was introduced to Grenada in the late 19th century in an attempt to control rodents in sugarcane plantations. Its impact on pests is thought to have been extremely negligible and it was soon considered a pest itself. In the second half of the 20th century it was discovered that the mongoose carried the rabies virus and an island-wide vaccination and eradication programme commenced. Though rabies still exists in the mongoose population it is not considered a serious problem. Visitors to Grenada should nevertheless avoid contact with this animal if it is encountered (see page 41 for advice on rabies).

The **nine-banded long-nosed armadillo** (*Dasypus novemcinctus hoplites*) is a small mammal with a bony, armour-like shell. It was probably introduced by the island's original settlers and is known locally by its Amerindian name, *tatu*. Though it is classified as rare, it is also considered a game animal, which seems very contradictory. It lives in the forests of Grand Etang, feeding on insects, small animals, vegetables and decaying flesh. Interesting facts about this particular species of armadillo are that it produces four identical offspring, it can inflate its intestine, making it buoyant enough to float or swim across rivers, and, if swimming is an unattractive proposition, it can hold its breath long enough to be able to walk along riverbeds instead.

Manicou is the name given to two species of opossum that live in Grenada. They are Robinson's mouse opossum (*Marmosa robinsoni*) and the large opossum (*Didelphis marsupialis insularis*). The rare mouse opossum lives in Grenada's interior, feeding on fruits and insects. Like the armadillo, the large opossum is hunted for Grenada's bush meat market, yet is also considered a rare species.

Eleven species of bat have been recorded in Grenada. With the exception of the greater fishing bat, all species feed on insects, hunt at night and are most commonly observed in forest habitats.

REPTILES AND AMPHIBIANS There are thought to be around ten species of lizard living in the tri-island state. The most common is the **bronze anole** (*Anolis aeneus*), also known locally as the *zandoli*, which grows to around 20cm in length and has the ability to change colour according to its environment. The male green lizard has a distinctive colourful throat fan that it uses in courtship and also as a territorial warning. Slightly larger than the green lizard, and also quite commonly sighted, is the **tree lizard** (*Anolis richardii*), which is either green or brown and has a distinctive crest running the length of its head and neck. The **ground lizard** (*Ameiva ameiva*), also known as the *zagada*, does not climb trees and prefers to live in dry undergrowth or to sit stock-still, sunning itself on a rock. The male is usually a bluish colour and the female brown with lighter stripes along her flanks. Grenada's largest lizard is the very colourful **green iguana** (*Iguana iguana*), which has been known to grow as large as 1.5m in length. It is herbivorous and usually lives in trees where it feeds on leaves and flowers. The iguana is considered a threatened species in Grenada due to loss of habitat and hunting.

Four snake species are recorded as still living in Grenada, although exact numbers are unknown. The largest snake is the **tree boa** (*Corallus enydris*), also known locally as the *serpent*. As its name suggests, it is usually found living in trees where it feeds on lizards, rodents and birds. The **cribo** (*Clelia clelia*) is a large snake that has its home in the forest, often close to water, and is said to have the appearance of a sizeable eel. It is thought to be endemic and extremely rare. The two other snakes found in Grenada are the **grass snake** (*Mastigodryas bruesi*) and the **blind worm snake** (*Typhlops tasymicris*). An encounter with a snake should be considered fortunate as they are rarely sighted. None of Grenada's snakes are venomous, though the cribo is rumoured to have a bad temper if it is annoyed. So don't go calling it an eel.

The **red-legged tortoise** (*Geochelone carbonaria*), or *morocoy*, is rare because it was once hunted for its meat and shell. On the brink of extinction, captive animals were reintroduced to the wild to supplement native populations that had managed to survive. It is doing much better. You can see the morocoy at Belmont Estate on Grenada and in the wild on Carriacou. I bumped into one on a hike from Belair to Limlair. It is said they also live on the diminutive Frigate Island.

The **giant toad** (*Bufo marinus*), or *crapaud*, is the only toad found in Grenada. Also known as the giant cane toad, this large amphibian was introduced in the early 19th century in an attempt to control pests in the sugarcane fields of the island's estates and plantations. It is a rather ugly beast that uses a milky secretion called bufotalin as a defence measure. Following the decline of the estates, the crapaud now finds its home by water in forested areas of the island. In addition to the cane toad, Grenada has three species of frog that include **Garman's woodland frog** (*Leptodactylus validus*), which is found in the forest and is also quite rare. The two remaining species are responsible for the chorus of sound that you hear at night if you are staying near woodland areas, especially during the rainy season. They are **Johnstone's whistling frog** (*Eleutherodactylus johnstonei*) and the **highland piping frog** (*Eleutherodactylus urichi*). Both are tiny, nocturnal and feed on small insects.

Tête chien is the local name often given to a boa or a serpent, because the broad head of the snake is said to resemble that of a dog. In this case, however, the creature is not a snake but the rather shy and elusive **marbled swamp eel** (*Synbranchus marmoratus*). This eel can grow up to 1.5m in length and is an aggressive predator that eats fish and invertebrates. During the day it lives buried in the silt and sand of brackish water environments, but at night it emerges to feed and has been known to travel long distances over land.

MARINE ENVIRONMENT Along the rugged windward coastlines of Grenada, Carriacou and Petite Martinique, formidable seas roll in from the Atlantic Ocean, crashing against impenetrable rocky volcanic outcrops and cliffs, and stretches of isolated black- and white-sand beaches. In these areas the marine environment is wild and unforgiving with strong currents, powerful surges and tall plumes of white spray. On the southern and southeastern coastlines there are numerous beaches and bays, inshore reefs and natural harbours that provide a peaceful haven for sun-seekers, sailors and fishermen.

In the channels of the Grenada Grenadines the waters are deep, clear and unpredictable. Where Caribbean Sea and Atlantic Ocean merge, strong currents rip around rocky barren outcrops and carry nutrient-rich waters that attract large shoals of fish and preying pelagics. The active submarine volcano of Kick-Em-Jenny (see box on page 4), located off the north coast of Grenada, adds a certain aquatic spice to this challenging environment.

Along the leeward coastlines of the three islands the difference is stark. The calm seas of the Caribbean lap gently against tall cliffs, rocky peninsulas, secluded bays and powder-white sandy beaches. As well as idyllic escapes for beach lovers and sun worshippers, the calmer Caribbean Sea offers a marine environment that is much safer to explore. Its waters contain an exuberance of aquatic life that includes whales and dolphins, sharks, turtles, colourful fish and coral reefs. Also within these more sheltered waters are shipwrecks and underwater sculptures that have become artificial reefs and home to a wide variety of interesting marine creatures.

Coral reefs Grenada's reef topography includes long, undulating ledges and steep drop-offs. From sandy shorelines, reefs along leeward coastlines tend to develop in deeper waters and sometimes contain quite a high degree of turbidity. The reefs and waters in the channels and around the islets and pinnacles of more exposed waters tend to be much clearer and have a far more dramatic marine topography. Here, shallow reefs quickly end in breathtaking drop-offs and deep blue water. Grenada's marine environment is a healthy one and its reefs contain an interesting mixture of hard and soft corals, sponges and gorgonians. Stony coral varieties include finger coral, sheet coral and large brain coral. Gorgonians are widespread, particularly along the reefs of Grenada's southwest, and include sea fans and sea whips.

Fish Large numbers of fish live in and around Grenada's reef systems, and migratory pelagics and predators are also common visitors. Shoals of Napoleon and Creole wrasse patrol expansive reefs where shelter and food are available to a wide variety of other brightly coloured fish, including damselfish, angelfish and butterflyfish. Within the nooks and crannies of the reef system itself live both green and spotted varieties of moray eel together with lobster, crab and octopus. Parrotfish, cowfish, trunkfish and trumpetfish add further interest to the reef environment.

It is common to see nurse sharks resting on the sand between reef formations or beneath the natural shelters provided by hard corals. Reef sharks are also occasional visitors, especially in and around some of the deeper shipwrecks and reef systems of the Atlantic channels. Stingrays and large eagle rays are frequently sighted along Grenada's reefs together with patrolling barracuda, predatory jacks and mackerel.

Whales and dolphins Around 15 species of whale have been recorded in Grenada's waters, many of which are regularly sighted between December and April, though some can be seen all year round. They include humpback whales (*Megaptera novaeangliae*), sperm whales (*Physeter macrocephalus*), Bryde's whales (*Balaenoptera brydei*) and pilot whales (*Globicephala melaena*).

Large pods of dolphins are frequently encountered offshore, and varieties include spinner dolphin (*Stenella longirostris*), bottlenose dolphin (*Tursiops truncatus*), Fraser's dolphin (*Lagenodelphis hosei*) and common dolphin (*Delphinus delphis*).

Other marine creatures From March each year, along the coasts of Grenada and Carriacou, in particular the beaches of the Levera Archipelago National Park and High North National Park, giant **leatherback turtles** (*Dermochelys coriacea*) return to lay their clusters of eggs. The giant leatherback is the largest of all living sea turtles and is a protected species. The **hawksbill turtle** (*Eretmochelys imbriocota*) is the most common species of turtle sighted in Grenada's waters along with the **green turtle** (*Chelonia mydas*). The **loggerhead turtle** (*Caretta caretta*) is also observed, though more rarely. Other interesting creatures that can be found in Grenada's diverse marine environment include **echinoderms** such as the sea cucumber, long-spined sea urchins, crinoids and sea eggs.

CONSERVATION In an effort to protect areas of both natural and cultural significance, the government of Grenada implemented a national park and forestry management system. As part of the plan, selected areas and landmarks were aligned to management and conservation categories that included national parks, natural landmarks, cultural landmarks, and protected seascapes.

Forest reserves As part of the country's forestry management policy, Grenada has a number of forest reserves. Designating areas as forest reserves means that resources of land, timber and important water catchments can be properly managed and protected and soil erosion prevented. Grenada's forest reserves include the **Mt St Catherine Forest Reserve**, the **Grand Etang Forest Reserve** and, in Carriacou, the **Belair Forest Reserve** (also known as Belair Park).

National parks Grenada's national parks take conservation one step further. Within the boundaries of the park, all flora and fauna are protected all year round.

To the northwest of the Grand Etang Forest Reserve is the 1,000ha **Grand Etang National Park**. The park is located in the central mountain range in the middle of Grenada and covers several high peaks including Mt Granby, Mt Qua Qua and Morne Fédon. Also within the park is the Grand Etang crater lake and the three Concord waterfalls: Concord, Au Coin and Fontainbleu. In Grenada's northern interior, to the west of the Mt St Catherine Forest Reserve, is the 580ha **Mt St Catherine National Park**. The park encompasses Grenada's highest peak, Mt St Catherine, at 840m. Along Grenada's northeastern coastline is the 182ha **Levera Archipelago National Park**. Located within this park are the 259m-high Levera Hill, Levera Pond, Levera Bay, Sugar Loaf Island, Green Island and Sandy Island. The park contains marine reef systems, giant leatherback turtle nesting sites and a bird sanctuary. The **Mt Hartman National Park** in Grenada's southwest contains a bird sanctuary and is one of the main habitats for the endangered Grenada dove. The 276ha **High North National Park** is located in the north of Carriacou. It encompasses deciduous forest, mangrove forest, the 291m High North Peak, the L'Appelle bird sanctuary, turtle nesting sites, Anse La Roche Beach and Petite Carenage Beach.

Natural landmarks Designating a natural landmark means that the area should be protected and developed as a natural attraction for both Grenadians and visitors. In some cases, these landmarks are located on private property which means that the government commits to working with the landowner to facilitate access to and provide visitor facilities for these areas. Designated natural landmarks include Lake Antoine, Concord waterfalls, Annandale Waterfall, Quarantine Point and Mt Carmel Waterfall.

Cultural landmarks In a similar vein to natural landmarks, cultural landmarks have been identified as sites of historic significance that should be preserved and developed with government assistance as attractions for Grenadians and for visitors. Designated cultural landmarks include the River Antoine Rum Distillery, the Westerhall Rum Distillery, Carib's Leap (Leaper's Hill), Mt Rich Amerindian petroglyphs, Marquis village, Fort George and Fort Frederick. In Carriacou they include the Dover ruins, the La Pointe ruins and Belair Estate.

Protected seascapes Protected seascapes include those stretches of coastline, beaches, mangrove forests and swamps, oyster beds and coral reefs that are considered to be of significant natural interest and should therefore become the subject of conservation efforts. Designated protected seascapes include Molinère Reef, North East Seascape (Bathway Beach to Telescope Rock), Southern Seascape (the peninsulas of Grenada's southwest) and La Sagesse Bay. In Carriacou they include the Sandy Island/Oyster Bed Marine Protected Area and Sabazan.

Organisations Organisations involved with the management and conservation of Grenada's wildlife and natural environment include the following:

KIDO Ecological Research Station Carriacou
☎473 443 7936; e marina.fastigi@gmail.com; www.kido-projects.com. A non-profit NGO that aims to preserve natural resources & ecosystems, promote sustainable development & provide environmental education. It is involved in a number of conservation efforts that include sea turtle protection, monitoring, rescuing & rehabilitating wildlife, & facilitating educational & research programmes especially for young people.

Ministry of Agriculture, Forestry & Fisheries
☎473 440 2708; e agriculture@gov.gd. Government ministry with divisions responsible for the management of forests & national parks. **Ocean Spirits** e info@oceanspirits.org; www. oceanspirits.org. An NGO focused primarily on the protection of Grenada's marine turtles. Research, school trips & volunteer programmes are also part of the project.

A BRIEF HISTORY

EARLY SETTLERS The first people to arrive in Grenada would have been Amerindian adventurers from South America somewhere between 5000BC and 3000BC. Very little is known about these people as their lineage has long since died out, although we can assume they were hunter-gatherers who lived off plants, fish and shellfish, and used stones for basic hand-held tools. Some historians refer to these first people as **Ortoiroid people** based on archaeological findings at Ortoire in Trinidad, which lies very close to the continental mainland. A common misconception is that they were Ciboneys. The Ciboney were indeed an ancient people but they are believed to have settled in the area around present-day Cuba, in a different age. Archaeological finds suggest the Ortoiroid people gradually moved northwards through the Lesser Antilles island chain and reached as far as the island of Puerto Rico.

Sometime between 1000BC and 500BC, a new group of people made their way northwards from the Amazon Basin. These people are often referred to as **Arawaks**, a term derived from a family of languages spoken by Amerindian tribes of that region. These Arawakan-speaking people travelled from the Orinoco region of South America and, as they established themselves in both the Lesser and Greater Antilles, they developed their own identity, culture and variations in language over the next 2,000 years or so.

In the Greater Antilles, the dominant group of Amerindians were the **Taino** who settled in Cuba, Jamaica, the Bahamas, Puerto Rico, the Virgin Islands and Antigua. Their counterparts in the Windward Islands were the **Igneri** who, it is believed, occupied Guadeloupe, Dominica, Martinique, St Lucia, St Vincent and Grenada.

The Igneri would have lived in thatched huts made from wood and woven leaves and slept in traditional hammocks. It is thought they lived in relatively small communities with a single headman, or chief, who was in charge of affairs and who also provided guidance. They hunted with spears and bows and arrows, and carved canoes from single tree trunks for fishing. These boats provided them with a vital lifeline. In addition to fishing, their canoes were also a means of transportation between islands, enabling them to trade with other migratory groups, including the Taino of the north. The Igneri were also farmers. They cultivated cassava, yam, maize, sweet potato, calabash, pawpaw, cotton and annatto. They were accomplished potters too, creating very ornate ceramics, and they worshipped nature spirits which were often represented by three-cornered *zemi* stones. In relative peace and harmony with each other, their neighbours and with nature, the Igneri are believed to have lived in this region until about AD1200.

Around this time, another group of people from the South American mainland, called the **Kalinago**, had begun to make forays, in their own very impressive dugout canoes, to the Greater and Lesser Antilles island chain. Over time, they too began to establish settlements, gradually displacing the Igneri as they did so. They were said to be a more warfaring people whose chiefs were selected on their virtues as brave fighting men. Records indicate that the men of the village all lived together in a large central house which was called a *carbet*, and the women and children lived in surrounding family huts. The Kalinago were also skilful fishermen, basket weavers and excellent boat makers. According to Father Raymond Breton, a Dominican priest who lived with the Kalinago of Dominica for many years, the name they gave to the island that we now call Grenada was **Camàhogne**. This name is recorded in Father Breton's famous *Dictionnaire Français–Cariabe* and, although some scholars believe it translates to 'those people', its meaning is really not at all clear.

The Kalinago probably completely displaced the Igneri in Grenada somewhere between AD1000 and AD1300 and from this point onwards the Igneri seem to have disappeared. The Kalinago traded with the Taino people of the Greater Antilles but, it seems, more often fought with them and created great notoriety for themselves which has often been misinterpreted and misrepresented as cannibalism. It was not from Kalinago raids that the Taino faced their greatest threat, however. This was to come from an entirely different people altogether.

NEW ARRIVALS On his third voyage to the region in 1498, Christopher Columbus sighted Grenada and named it **La Concepción** in honour of the Virgin Mary. It is said he may actually have named it Assumption – no-one can be sure, as he is believed to have sighted what are now Grenada and Tobago from a distance and named them both at the same time. However, history has accepted that it was Tobago he named Assumption and La Concepción was the name he gave to the island we now call Grenada. But it didn't end there. In 1499, the Italian explorer Amerigo Vespucci travelled through the region with the Spanish explorer Alonso de Ojeda and mapmaker Juan de la Cosa. Vespucci is reported to have renamed the island **Mayo**, which is how it appeared on maps for around the next 20 years. In the 1520s the Spanish named the islands to the north of Mayo as Los Granadillos

(Little Granadas), presumably after the mainland Spanish town. Shortly after this, Mayo disappeared from Spanish maps and an island called **Granada** took its place. Although it was deemed the property of the King of Spain, there are no records to suggest the Spanish ever landed or settled on the island.

The Kalinago were referred to as **Caribs** by the European explorers of the time. Today they are also referred to as 'Island Caribs' in an effort by scholars to distinguish them from the 'Caribs' of mainland South America. The reason for this distinction is that it is thought the Caribs who settled in the Greater and Lesser Antilles developed a cultural identity of their own. The name *Carib* finds its roots in some rather dubious and very questionable assumptions of 15th-century European explorers. Described by the Europeans as a warfaring people, the Kalinago, it is said, would capture brides, kill menfolk and take a limb from the body of a victim as a prize. This trophy was taken back to their village as proof of victory and a symbol of bravery and manhood. As part of the celebration ritual, it was noted that 'a warrior may take a mouthful of his victim's flesh, chew it and spit it out in a display of ferocity and malice'. The Europeans also recorded that the Kalinago preserved the bones of their ancestors within their houses in the belief that the spirits of their forefathers were protecting them. These two aspects of Kalinago culture were interpreted as cannibalism – a word that itself finds its roots in the names used by both the Igneri and Taino, and then subsequently by the Europeans, for the Kalinago people. In Columbus's journal of 1492 he records that the people he encountered were frightened of those of *caniba* or *canima*, actually seeming to refer to the name of a place rather than the name of a people. From there the word took on several variations including *caribi, caribe, carib* and, in Spanish text, *canibal*. Descendants of the Kalinago strongly refute any suggestion that their ancestors were cannibals.

Granada, as it was then called, was left undisturbed by Europeans until 1609 when a group of British merchants landed there and tried to establish a settlement which they called Megrin Town, which was located in the present-day parish of St David. Finding themselves under constant attack and harassment by the island's Kalinago, they ultimately abandoned their venture and sailed back to London the very same year. Thirty years later a group of Frenchmen tried their luck as fishermen but were also forcibly removed.

In 1650, under the leadership of Jacques Dyel du Parquet, then Governor of Martinique, another group of French settlers arrived in a different area of the island. They landed on the spit of land that is known today as the Ballast Ground, on the western side of the Lagoon in St George's where the Port Louis Marina is now located, and they were met by the Kalinago chief, Kaierouanne. Du Parquet offered the chief gifts and then set about establishing a settlement which, very significantly, included a barricade and a fort with mounted cannons. It was named **Fort Louis** after the reigning French monarch. The settlers clearly meant business and, in a very short period of time, they had felled trees and begun cultivating a large tobacco plantation. Following its introduction to Europe, tobacco was a much sought-after product and there was a great deal of money to be made from it. After a period of only eight months, the settlers had harvested their first crop and du Parquet returned to Martinique naming his cousin, Jean Le Compte, the island's new governor.

Realising their European visitors were here to stay, the disgruntled Kalinago mounted a number of isolated attacks on individuals though they resisted the temptation to attack the fortification itself. In response, Le Compte attempted an attack on a large Kalinago village but he failed and many Frenchmen were killed. Du Parquet then decided to send 300 soldiers as reinforcements to Le Compte from Martinique, instructing the governor to drive the Kalinago out of the island altogether. As the French were reinforcing their numbers, so too were the Kalinago, welcoming brothers-in-arms from the nearby islands of Dominica and St Vincent.

In 1652, the French learned of a planned attack on Fort Louis and, when it occurred, they launched a devastating counter-attack, killing many Kalinago and forcing them into retreat. Some Kalinago escaped over the mountains to the east of the island, while others fled to the north. It is recorded that around 40 Kalinago reached a rocky peninsula in the very north of the island and, realising their situation was completely hopeless, threw themselves from the cliffs, choosing certain death in favour of capture and humiliation. This is the area that is known today as Leapers' Hill or Carib's Leap and is located in the northern village of Sauteurs (which is in fact French for 'leapers').

This battle proved to be a defining moment for the Kalinago. Though a number remained, mostly in the less accessible east, their fight for survival was essentially over. Nevertheless they still managed to organise themselves into small bands and launched sporadic guerrilla-style attacks, instilling fear and panic into French settlements. Governor Le Compte moved to quell this threat once and for all with a push of 150 soldiers over the mountains to the east. The soldiers killed every Kalinago man, woman and child they encountered and burned their villages to the ground. By the end of the campaign, the Kalinago were almost entirely wiped out. A few survived but eventually they too disappeared. For the next 100 years, **La Grenade** became a colony of the French Crown.

During French rule La Grenade was divided into six parishes: Basseterre (now St George), Gouyave (St John), Grand Pauvre (St Mark), Sauteurs (St Patrick), Megrin (St David) and Marquis (St Andrew). Churches were constructed and the main town was moved north from Fort Louis to its current location and was renamed **Fort Royal** after a fortification built by French engineer Monsieur de Caillus in 1706. Plantations were established by the French throughout the island and west African slaves were brought to work them.

CONFLICT AND REBELLION On 10 February 1763 the island of La Grenade was ceded to the British under the Treaty of Paris. The British renamed it **Grenada** and set about thoroughly anglicising everything the French had established. Fort Royal was renamed **St George's** and its main fortification was renamed Fort George. The French owners of around 80 sugar and 200 coffee plantations, which were the new cash crops of the time, found themselves under British colonial rule and it was not long before Anglo-French conflict started to surface. Protestant British planters began plotting against their Catholic French counterparts, attempting to coerce them into subscribing to the Test Act which was, in essence, a rejection of their religion. During this period of British rule the island's economy thrived. In the year 1772, there were over 300 plantations in total, of which around 140 were run by French settlers and 170 by British planters. There was a total of 125 sugar estates and Grenada had become the largest coffee and cocoa producer in the British West Indies.

In 1776, war broke out between Britain and France once again, this time over the latter's assistance to the British colonies in America and their attempt at independence. In 1779, under the command of the Count d'Estang from Martinique, the French recaptured Grenada from the British with a force of 25 ships and 6,500 soldiers. Over the next four years of French rule, the island was governed in an equally despotic manner, this time with a focus on suppressing the British population of planters and their families. On 3 September 1783, Grenada was once again ceded to the British, on this occasion under the Treaty of Versailles.

SLAVERY IN GRENADA

It is estimated that around 20 million people were taken from west Africa in ships to work as slaves in the Americas. Records indicate that British-controlled islands of the West Indies received approximately two million slaves and the French-controlled islands some 1.5 million slaves from the mid 17th century up to the abolition of the slave trade in British colonies in the early 1800s. In Grenada the years between 1735 and 1780 witnessed the highest number of slave arrivals – a time when planters were reaping the financial benefits of a highly lucrative sugar trade. In the 30 years between 1750 and 1780 the slave population of Grenada jumped from around 10,000 to approximately 35,000, the highest that slave numbers would reach until emancipation in 1838.

It was an entirely miserable and unforgivably inhumane existence. From the moment of capture and sale in west Africa, they were crammed into ships for the Atlantic crossing. Many died *en route* and many others killed themselves. For those who made it to the other side, the tragedy was only just unfolding.

The French planters felt the wrath of the British after living for four years under an oppressive regime, particularly by ultra-Protestant leaders such as Governor Ninian Home. Many French residents found it unbearable and left the island, taking their slaves with them. Catholic churches were seized and transferred to the Protestants, and marriages, baptisms and burials were considered illegal unless they were celebrated in Anglican churches. A further act was passed which stated that French Catholics were required to submit to the Test Act before they could hold any form of political office. Similar legislation also effectively excluded French Catholics from holding public office and from voting in elections.

With such rising levels of discrimination and dissatisfaction, everything inevitably came to a head. In 1795 a free, black, estate owner from Martinique named Julien Fédon, together with hundreds of other free, black, French ex-slaves and French planters, staged a rebellion that was supported by French commanders in Guadeloupe. The **Fédon Rebellion** lasted from March 1795 to June 1796. Inspired by the French Revolution, Fédon led a bloody and destructive island-wide revolt against British rule, liberating slaves, ransacking estates and killing British planters. At the height of the rebellion Fédon controlled most of the island but he was unable to drive home his superiority by taking the capital, St George's. It was this failing that eventually allowed the British to regroup and strengthen their numbers until they were successful in quelling the insurgency and either killing or capturing the rebels. During the rebellion Fédon infamously executed 43 prisoners at his headquarters at the Belvidere Estate, including Ninian Home. No-one knows what became of Julien Fédon after he was routed from his mountain stronghold, though many believe he drowned trying to escape to Trinidad. The rebellion brought ruin to Grenada's economy. It is estimated to have destroyed property to the tune of £2.5million and brought about the death of some 7,000 slaves. See box on page 142 for more information.

EMANCIPATION AND INDEPENDENCE Following the Treaty of Versailles the French threat disappeared and, despite Fédon's rebellion, the island's plantation system recovered and continued to prosper under British rule. In

1833, however, things began to change. Together with years of resistance from the victims themselves, the British anti-slavery movement finally succeeded in forcing the British Parliament to end slavery in its colonies. The **Imperial Act of Emancipation** was passed in 1833, abolishing slavery and the slave trade on 1 August 1834. There was a great deal of resistance to this Act, in particular from the plantation and estate owners who relied on enforced labour for their businesses and for their personal wealth. Although it is recorded that almost 24,000 slaves were freed in Grenada on 31 July 1834, their liberation was unfortunately far from realised. In order to appease colonial plantocracy, the British Parliament agreed to set up a system called **compulsory apprenticeship** which required liberated slaves to continue working for their former masters for a designated period of time. This meant that field slaves were bound to work for six years and other slaves up to four years, without pay. In return for their labour, the apprenticed workforce would be given food rations and granted time to tend and sell produce from their own kitchen gardens. It was hardly liberation. It was a system that was doomed to failure, however. Many estate and plantation owners simply used it as a means to further exploit their workforce. Apprentices protested bravely against great odds and in an environment of very real physical danger. By 1838, four years after the Emancipation Act had been passed, the apprenticeship system was abolished formally through legislation. On 31 July that year Grenada's slaves were finally free.

Because they no longer enjoyed the fruits of an enslaved workforce, many estates and plantations simply failed and were ultimately abandoned. Freed slaves built houses and established smallholdings around former estate lands, creating the rural communities and villages that exist today. The estates that continued to operate switched production from sugar to cocoa during the mid 19th century and then to nutmeg during the 1900s. In Carriacou, corn and pigeon peas became the main crops following the collapse of the sugar industry there.

In order to compensate for the refusal of many former slaves to continue working on the surviving estates following the abolition of apprenticeship, Grenada introduced **indentured immigration** programmes which involved importing a cheap labour force from west African nations, India, Malta and Madeira. The scheme was largely a failure with the majority of early immigrants migrating to Trinidad. It is recorded that in the latter half of the 19th century just over 3,200 immigrants arrived from India and over half of them remained. They settled in communities both in the interior and in the east of the island and they gradually became absorbed into the emerging post-emancipation Grenadian culture and society. The Indo-Grenadian population that still lives in Grenada is relatively small yet very influential. There have been and still are a number of extremely successful Indo-Grenadian families, businesses and entrepreneurs.

Following a succession of failed attempts at federating a number of islands belonging to the British colonies in the West Indies during the mid 20th century, the British government announced on 3 March 1967 that Grenada would be granted self-rule under a system of **associated statehood** through the 1967 West Indies Act. **Eric Gairy**, leader of the Grenada United Labour Party (GULP), became Grenada's premier and his extremely controversial leadership sparked a period of unrest and political conflict that is still hotly debated today. One point that everyone agrees on, however, is that Gairy was absolutely determined to be rid of associated statehood, which he considered a 'farce', and he sought nothing less than complete independence from Britain. Despite strong opposition to his policies and his questionable regime, mounting civil unrest, and incidents of violence and brutality that infamously took place on 'Bloody Sunday' (18 November 1973) and 'Bloody Monday' (21 January 1974), the British government granted full **independence** to the state of Grenada on 7 February 1974. Some commentators suggest it was almost as if Britain was finally relieved to wash its hands of what had become an economic and political burden.

REVOLUTION AND INTERVENTION The Gairy regime had been accused by its opponents of financial irregularities, brutality and unconstitutional power-mongering prior to and following independence. Though he had begun his political life as the voice of ordinary Grenadians, it seemed Gairy had become an authoritarian figure who has been described by some respected commentators as nothing short of a dictator. Disenfranchised from ordinary people, in particular the young, growing opposition to his right-wing leadership manifested itself in the organisation of strikes, riots and public protests, and ultimately in the creation of a socialist opposition party calling itself the **New Jewel Movement**. Formed in March 1973 by the amalgamation of two opposition groups, the Movement for Assemblies of the People (MAP) and the Joint Endeavour for Welfare, Education and Liberation (JEWEL), the New Jewel Movement (NJM) was led by the charismatic **Maurice Bishop**. In November 1973, Bishop had been one of six NJM members who were brutally beaten, allegedly by members of Gairy's secret police, at a meeting in Grenville. Known as 'Bloody Sunday' this inhumane act was one that would return to haunt Grenada's premier in the years to come. The NJM's manifesto 'Power to the People' voiced a left-wing ideology that demanded a fundamental change to the nation's governance, and was influenced by contemporary movements such as Castro's Cuban Revolution. The party appealed to the young, the trade unions, and those who had become disillusioned with the Gairy administration.

On 13 March 1979, Gairy's GULP government was overthrown in an armed coup d'état. The constitution was suspended and 63 People's Laws were implemented by the newly established **People's Revolutionary Government** (PRG). The PRG was a non-elected government that administered the country through a Central Committee. Maurice Bishop became prime minister and his comrade Bernard Coard became deputy prime minister. The new regime received financial and political support from Cuba and the former Soviet Union and, under People's Law No 7, the PRG created the **People's Revolutionary Army** (PRA). From 1979 Cuba began supplying the PRA with arms and ammunition. Grenada thus became a one-party, military state pursuing a socialist programme that promised one day to develop a revised and more appropriate 'people's constitution'.

The period that followed is one that still generates strong emotions in Grenada, with few agreeing on the rights and the wrongs that were committed, and fewer still able to forgive and to forget. Economic pressures mounted on the PRG regime and deep ideological conflict took hold within the Central Committee itself. It was also a time of brutality and oppression. Despite the nation's deeply entrenched religious beliefs, the church became a target of the PRG. It is said priests were spied upon and church meetings monitored for 'counter-revolutionary activities'. It is also claimed that there were a series of human rights abuses including the torture, murder and execution of innocents during the PRG's rule. A power struggle emerged within the Central Committee between Coard and Bishop which ultimately culminated in the house arrest of Bishop on Wednesday, 12 October 1983. Ideological disagreements became extremely bitter with little hope for a positive outcome to the conflict and the revolution was in danger of collapsing.

On 19 October 1983, known later as **Bloody Wednesday**, a mass demonstration of thousands of Grenadians released Bishop from his captors and then escorted him to Fort George (at the time renamed Fort Rupert in memory of Bishop's father who was murdered in 1974), which was the military headquarters of the PRG. Coard and his supporters appeared to have a choice of either risking possible incarceration themselves due to mounting support for Bishop, or taking a course of action that would deal with the threat once and for all. The outcome of these deliberations was an armed assault by the PRA on the fort and on the people within it. Some of Bishop's supporters tried to escape by throwing themselves over the fort's 20m-high walls, while others faced the bullets. Bishop and a core of his supporters were captured and taken to the fort's upper courtyard. Once there, they were lined up against a wall and executed. Their bodies are said to have been taken to the site of Fédon's Camp where they were burned and never recovered. The PRA announced the formation of a **Revolutionary Military Council** that would govern the country until further notice.

The left-wing ideologies of Castro's Cuba and Bishop's Grenada had certainly made some leaders in the region very uncomfortable. And so it was that the events of Bloody Wednesday gave the Reagan administration in the United States sufficient reason, they felt, for an intervention which would remove Grenada's Cuban-backed military regime and restore a more 'Western' democracy. With the support of some, though by no means all, Caribbean countries, **Operation Urgent Fury** was implemented. On the morning of 25 October 1983, just six days after Bloody Wednesday, 1,900 US troops, together with a force of over 300 soldiers from six Caribbean countries, collectively referred to as the Caribbean Multinational Force, landed in Grenada and engaged in armed conflict with Cuban and Grenadian PRA militia. By 31 October, the combined forces had secured the island and, on 2 November, Carriacou and Petite Martinique were taken without conflict. The US-led intervention drew a great deal of international criticism, with the British Parliament condemning the invasion of one of its Commonwealth nation members as illegal. Following the operation, those who were accused of being responsible for the acts of Bloody Wednesday were tried and, after initially being sentenced to death, were imprisoned for life. This trial, sentencing and subsequent incarceration was the subject of much debate, including questions over fair trials and human rights. For those who were involved on both sides, their families, friends and supporters, the events and outcomes of 1983 remain emotional and sensitive subjects.

An interim **Advisory Council** was set up after the intervention with the mandate of restoring the country's constitution and preparing it for free elections which were held a year later on 3 December 1984. Herbert Blaize of the New National Party (NNP) became Prime Minister of Grenada for the next five years. The NNP and the National Democratic Congress (NDC) became Grenada's two main political parties and have governed the country in turn up to the present day. The longest-serving prime minister was Keith Mitchell of the NNP who led Grenada from 1995 to 2008. Tillman Thomas of the NDC became prime minister on 9 July 2008. In 1996, his notoriety somewhat forgotten in light of subsequent events, Eric Gairy was celebrated as Grenada's 'Father of the Nation' during the country's independence celebrations. He died the same year and, in 2008, he was declared Grenada's first National Hero. Bernard Coard, who, following a 2007 Privvy Council review, was given a 30-year sentence for ordering the murder of Maurice Bishop and his comrades at Fort George, was released from prison on 5 September 2009.

HURRICANE IVAN Hurricane Ivan struck Grenada a near-fatal blow on 7 September 2004. By the time it hit, Ivan had strengthened to a category three hurricane and it ravaged the island with sustained 193km/h winds for over eight hours. Until that fateful day, it had been Hurricane Janet that most Grenadians remembered and considered the worst storm to ever hit the island. In 1955, Janet had blasted northern Grenada and Carriacou with winds of up to 260km/h, destroying everything in its path and leaving 120 people dead in its wake. The nation's agricultural economy was severely damaged by Janet and many structures were destroyed, including the already weakening St George's harbour jetty and buildings.

The eye of Hurricane Ivan passed approximately 10km south of Point Salines and thoroughly ransacked the island. It either completely levelled or damaged around 90% of residences and other buildings, leaving countless Grenadians homeless. It ravaged the island's forests and farmlands, destroying the majority of the nation's crops, including nutmeg, and it crippled the island's infrastructure. Schools, churches, hospitals, roads, water and electricity supplies, homes, hotels, businesses, farms and orchards were left in complete tatters. Immediately after the hurricane there followed some very frightening days of lawlessness with widespread looting and violence. The Grenadian people were in a state of immeasurable shock and altogether fearful for their very existence.

The world came to Grenada's assistance in the weeks and months following Ivan. A programme of donor and loan aid commenced and plans were initiated to reconstruct schools and hospitals, to clear and replant crops, and to repair and rebuild homes. The estimated cost of Ivan's fury was put at around US$1 billion and it was clearly going to take a long time to completely recover. The island's tourism industry, which was beginning to thrive, together with nutmeg and cocoa crops, suffered an unmitigated setback. Before Ivan, Grenada was the world's second-largest producer of nutmeg, after Indonesia. With only 10% of nutmeg trees still standing, and a period of seven to ten years for a seedling to reach maturity, it is no wonder that very many livelihoods were in serious jeopardy.

After picking themselves up from the rubble and the despair, Grenadians would be forgiven for feeling entirely desperate when just one year later Emily passed over their island as a category one hurricane. Though not as devastating as Ivan, Emily caused an estimated US$100 million worth of damage to the island as well as untold psychological harm to its people.

Grenada is recovering, yet its agriculture sector still has a long way to go and, though many new nutmegs were planted, it appears highly unlikely that this industry will ever thrive as it once did. New nutmeg trees are bearing fruit, but in smaller numbers, and only one of three processing plants is currently operating. Visitors to Grenada will no doubt come across some of Ivan's legacy when travelling around the island. Many buildings, such as the Anglican church in St George's, are still awaiting repair, skeletons of abandoned domestic residences can be seen in some villages, and tours of nutmeg stations tell their own sad tale of the storm's impact on this once significant spice crop.

GOVERNMENT AND POLITICS

Grenada is a parliamentary democracy within the Commonwealth of Nations, with Queen Elizabeth II represented by a governor general who is appointed as head of parliament on the advice of Grenada's prime minister.

The country's political and legal systems closely mirror those of the United Kingdom. Parliament consists of two chambers, the House of Representatives and the Senate. There are 15 members of the House of Representatives who represent single-seat constituencies in Grenada, Carriacou and Petite Martinique. They are elected by democratic vote for a period of up to five years. The Senate has 13 members who are appointed by the ruling government (10) and by the leader of the opposition (3). The prime minister is head of government, which represents the country's executive branch. Grenada's legislative power resides within parliament.

Grenada has seven administrative divisions, which consist of dependencies and parishes. They are Carriacou and Petite Martinique, St George, St David, St Andrew, St Patrick, St Mark and St John.

There are two major political parties: the New National Party (NNP) and the National Democratic Congress (NDC). Minor parties include the Grenada United Labour Party (GULP), which is Grenada's oldest political party, and the Maurice Bishop Patriotic Movement (MBPM), which was founded by survivors of the Bloody Wednesday coup.

LAW Grenada's legal system is based on English common law. It upholds freedom of speech and freedom of religion, and it prohibits discrimination based on race, gender, place of origin, colour and creed. Grenada's law is enforced by the Royal Grenada Police Force (RGPF), a paramilitary Special Services Unit (SSU) and the Grenada Coast Guard.

ECONOMY

Grenada is a member of CARIFORUM (Caribbean Forum of African, Caribbean and Pacific States), CARICOM (Caribbean Community and Common Market) and the OECS (Organisation of Eastern Caribbean States). Together with other OECS members, Grenada is committed to the free movement of goods, services and labour across participating countries within the region.

Grenada's GDP contracted in 2009 (–7.65%) and 2010 (–1.405%). A huge decline in the construction sector (–52.4% in 2009) contributed significantly to this. The tourism industry also contracted by some –20% during this period. The global economic downturn is of course the main cause. The NDC government of Tillman Thomas has placed a greater emphasis on agriculture, and economic activity in this sector rose by over 9% when others were on the decline. St George's University also made, and continues to make, positive contributions to the country's economy.

In 2011 the economy showed signs of recovery with GDP at 1%. The country's borrowings and loan repayments remain a concern and, at the time of writing, the Maurice Bishop International Airport had come under serious threat of closure due to pressure exerted by Taiwan in its efforts to recover debt.

In the International Human Development Index, Grenada is ranked 67 out of 187 countries (USA 4, France 20, UK 28, Barbados 47, Jamaica 79, Dominica 81, St Lucia 82, St Vincent & Grenadines 89), which is slightly above the regional average.

AGRICULTURE Grenada is affectionately known as the **Spice Island of the Caribbean** and, wherever you travel, you will see vendors selling spices, you will encounter numerous references to spice and, at some point or other, you will probably find yourself on a spice tour. Grenada's spice heritage is succeeding in bridging the divide between agriculture and tourism, creating a new **agro-tourism** (sometimes written as 'agri-tourism') product that now constitutes a small part of the country's economic development and provides a potential area of wealth generation for some of the island's rural people.

Grenada's principal agricultural exports are nutmeg, cocoa, mace, spices, citrus and various fruits and vegetables.

Natural disasters such as hurricanes have had a detrimental impact on Grenada's agriculture and the inability to attract young people is contributing to an uncertain future. The average age of farmers is estimated to be around 54 years.

Cocoa In the 18th and 19th centuries cocoa was grown alongside sugar as a secondary crop and, from the 1880s, following the decline of the sugar industry, it became the mainstay of Grenada's economy. Native to the Amazon region of South America, the **cacao** tree (*Theobroma cacao*) is believed to have been introduced to Grenada in the late 17th century where it was cultivated on the elevated hillsides of the island's interior. It is a small evergreen tree that grows to between 4m and 8m in height and produces ovoid pods up to 30cm long. Within each pod there are between 20 and 50 seeds, commonly called beans, that are embedded in a thick white pulp. Each seed contains up to 50% fat which is referred to as 'cocoa butter'.

Though yields are possible after three years, cocoa trees usually bear their fruit in their fourth or fifth year. Once ripe, the cocoa is harvested and the mix of pulp and beans removed from their pods. The pods are discarded and the bean and pulp mixture is stored in a large bin or container where it undergoes a natural fermentation process, removing the beans' bitterness and enriching their flavour. The pulp can reach temperatures of up to 50°C during the fermentation process. After several days naturally fermenting, the beans are removed and dried. This is done by spreading the beans on large trays and leaving them out in the tropical sunshine, turning them at regular intervals. Cocoa drying sheds, known as *boucans*, contain numerous drying trays that can be rolled out or retracted under cover along purpose-built steel rails. Turning the beans was traditionally undertaken by a method called 'walking the beans' where estate workers, usually women, would walk through the trays of beans, turning them with their bare feet (see Belmont Estate on page 188). After drying, the beans are graded and packed in large sacks ready for consumption and export.

At the turn of the 20th century, at the industry's peak, Grenada was producing as much as 4,500 tonnes of cocoa. In 1955, Hurricane Janet uprooted many mature cocoa trees, causing a significant decline. Younger trees were planted and, though

WHAT'S THE POINT OF SAND FLIES?

Most of us have been pestered by biting midges such as sand flies during our travels and may have questioned where on earth these irritating pests fit into the grand scheme of things. They make mincemeat of your ankles, and boy do they itch.

Sand flies belong to the dipterous family *Ceratopogonidae*, commonly known as biting midges, and the females are the principal pollinators of cocoa. Each cocoa tree produces tiny flowers that grow all over its trunk, and these flowers, if pollinated by *Ceratopogonidae*, will eventually grow into pods. If the flowers are not pollinated by these midges they die within 24 hours. For cocoa farmers it is therefore very important to ensure they create habitats in cocoa plantations that *Ceratopogonidae* will enjoy (humid shade, often with decaying matter on the ground).

What price chocolate.

cocoa production increased, it never regained pre-war levels, and when Hurricane Ivan struck in 2004, the industry was dealt another shattering blow. Today Grenada still produces cocoa for export as well as for domestic consumption. The main export markets are Belgium and Switzerland. Cocoa grown at the Belmont Estate in St Andrew is used for the production of organic chocolate by the **Grenada Chocolate Company** (see page 190 for more information).

Nutmeg It is said that nutmeg trees were first planted as an experiment on the Belvidere Estate in 1843 from seeds brought from the **Banda Islands** of Indonesia by a man called Frank Gurney. It is believed commercial planting of nutmegs began in the 1850s on the Bellevue and Capitol estates in the parish of St Andrew. Until the 19th century, the Banda Islands were the only place in the world where this particular species of nutmeg tree could be found.

The nutmeg (*Myristica fragrans*) is an evergreen tree that grows well in the elevated hillsides of Grenada's interior. The seed of the tree, the nutmeg, grows inside a tough shell which in turn resides within a roundish yellow pod. Surrounding the nutmeg shell is a lacy, reddish coating known as **mace**. Nutmegs have a wide variety of applications. Most commonly, when ground into a fine powder, nutmegs are used as a food and drink flavouring, notably in desserts, potato dishes and soups. Nutmegs also produce an essential oil that is used in the cosmetic and pharmaceutical industries and is an ingredient in some perfumes, toothpastes and cough syrups. It is also used in medicinal massage and pain-relieving oils and sprays. The nutmeg pod that surrounds the seed is used to make delicious jams and jellies, and the brittle shells that are removed to expose the nutmeg seed are recycled as a very effective garden mulch or path covering. Mace is also used in cooking and is especially well known as a natural meat preservative.

In the 1880s, following the decline of the sugar industry and the subsequent search for new economic crops, which included cocoa, Grenada began exporting nutmegs and mace for the first time. Production increased and by 1910 Grenada was responsible for 14% of world nutmeg exports. By the 1990s Grenada was exporting around 23% of the world's nutmegs, and was the second-largest producer in the world, behind Indonesia.

In 1955, the devastation wreaked by Hurricane Janet culled Grenada's nutmeg production by around 80% and it was not until the mid 1970s, around 20 years later, that pre-Janet levels were regained. In 2004, Hurricane Ivan destroyed 90% of Grenada's nutmeg crop as well as around EC$11 million of nutmegs that were

NUT-MED

Nut-Med is a pain-relieving spray and cream that is made from a combination of nutmeg oil and plant extracts. Nutmeg has been used for centuries to improve health and relieve muscle pain through its natural analgesic properties, and is a key ingredient in several mainstream pharmaceutical products. Created by Dr Denis Noel, a man whose family have been associated with the nutmeg industry for years, Nut-Med is a real Grenadian success story. Those who have used it swear by it, and his company, Noelville Ltd, appears to be going from strength to strength.

Nut-Med is available from pharmacies island-wide. You can also find it for sale at the Gouyave Nutmeg Station. For more information and to buy online, go to www.nut-med.com.

sitting in stock. Numerous livelihoods were either entirely lost or at the very least put on long-term hold. Many receiving stations around the island were closed and of the three main operating plants (or 'pools') at Gouyave, Victoria and Grenville, it would only be the one at Gouyave which would continue processing the surviving crop. Based on the experiences of Hurricane Janet, and despite efforts to plant faster-growing species, it is the view of most experts that it will take at least two decades for Grenada's nutmeg industry to recover properly. Whether it will ever get back to pre-Ivan levels is the subject of debate. A further factor that will inevitably influence the recovery of the nutmeg industry is the younger generation's apparent lack of interest in pursuing careers in agriculture. Many see it as high-risk, hard, unattractive and unrewarding work compared with the trappings of alternative, more 'fashionable' lifestyles. With an ageing farming population and a reluctance of younger people to get involved, the outlook for the industry is far from bright.

Around 30% of nutmeg exports are to Holland, and around 40% to the USA and Canada. These markets require standards and certification which add further cost and complexity to the work on the ground. Despite these difficulties and set-backs, this sub-sector is seen as critical to Grenada's economic welfare and development.

Cinnamon (*Cinnamonum verum*)
An evergreen tree that grows to around 15m in height, cinnamon is native to parts of Asia and the Indian subcontinent. The tree is pruned, or coppiced, every two years to produce a number of new branches which are harvested for the inner skin of their bark. The bark is removed from the branch and left to dry. The thin inner bark is removed from the outer bark which is discarded. This inner bark curls up into cinnamon sticks or 'quills' which are then prepared for sale either whole or by grinding into a powder. Cinnamon is commonly used as a spice to flavour desserts and beverages.

Clove (*Syzygium aromaticum*)
An evergreen tree, clove produces aromatic flower buds that are dried and used as a spice in cooking. Cloves are also said to have medicinal uses and their essential oil is frequently applied as a herbal painkiller, particularly for toothache. It is also said to be an effective remedy for upset stomachs. Grenada is a minor clove producer with over 80% of the world's output coming from Indonesia.

Turmeric (*Curcuma longa*)
A member of the ginger family, turmeric is a perennial plant that is native to south Asia. It is cultivated for its rhizome, or underground stem, which is boiled, dried and then ground into an orange-yellow powder that is commonly used as a spice in curry dishes. In recent times turmeric has been cited for its medicinal qualities, in particular regarding prostate cancer.

Allspice (*Pimenta dioica*)
Allspice is a tree similar in appearance to bay laurel. Its small, unripe fruit is harvested and dried in the sun before either being ground or sold whole as a spice. Also known as **pimento**, allspice has a variety of culinary applications that vary around the world. In the Caribbean, in particular Jamaica, it is used as a key ingredient of jerk seasoning. Though it is not harvested in huge quantities, allspice is an important part of Grenada's spice-island make-up.

Bananas (*Musa*)
Bananas are grown all around Grenada, from plantations in the island's interior to the vegetable gardens of resorts in the south. The crop is no longer a significant export, however, and is largely consumed by the domestic market, in particular the hotel industry. In the face of world trade practices and large-scale

food production, small Caribbean islands just cannot compete. In Grenada's case, the natural disasters of recent years have simply added to the mix of what many perceive as insurmountable hurdles. Though some islands' banana producers are now successfully fighting back thanks to the assistance of the Fairtrade Foundation, many of Grenada's large-scale banana farmers have left the industry. Visitors to Grenada will still see plenty of banana plants growing alongside rural roads, hiking trails and dotted around the island's interior, but these plantations are relatively small-scale in comparison with the past. Visitors will also come across **plantain** and **bluggo**, varieties of banana that are usually cooked before eating and are a traditional staple in Caribbean cuisine.

Corn (*Zea mays*) and pigeon peas (*Cajanus cajan*) Both crops are very commonly grown in Carriacou, though you will also find them on the main island, Grenada. They are usually inter-cropped, rotated and farmed together. Again, they are primarily grown on subsistence farms for local consumption and are staples of the Grenadian diet. Pigeon peas are usually eaten in pea soup and rice and pea dishes, and corn is most commonly used in very traditional dishes such as *conkie* and *cou-cou*.

FISHERIES Many Grenadians make their living in the fishing industry which, like agriculture, is becoming inextricably intertwined with the growing tourism industry. Grenadian fishermen can make a manageable living selling their catch to the island's restaurants and hotels as well as to luxury island resorts located in the St Vincent Grenadines, where prices are said to be very high indeed. Though a controlled, seasonal catch, the tourism industry's insatiable desire for fresh lobster is where many fishermen are able to make some money. Other more lucrative catches include queen conch (*Strombus gigas*), commonly known as lambie, and sea turtles, in particular the hawksbill (*Dermochelys coriacea*), which are only protected from May to September.

Fishing practices include long-line fishing, hand-lining and the use of seine nets. The most common fish caught and consumed include yellow-fin tuna (*Thunnus albacares*), black-fin tuna (*Thunnus altantivus*) and blue marlin (*Makaira nigrican*). A very popular catch is dorado, or *mahi-mahi* (*Coryphaena hippurus*), which is locally, and somewhat confusingly, known as 'dolphin'.

Visitors to Grenada will see many colourful wooden fishing boats along the shoreline all around the three islands, as well as a number of larger long-liners tied up in St George's Carenage. If you are lucky, you may get to see locals helping to haul in seine nets near villages such as Gouyave, Duquesne, or in the bays of the southeast.

TOURISM The main focus of Grenada's tourism, despite what the brochures may say, has been on the beaches and bays of the south. Thanks to an international airport, natural anchorages, powder-white sand, and two decades of considerable overseas investment, the southern tourism product has developed organically. Beaches, sailing, luxury resort and boutique hotels, high-class restaurants, and tour operators are all concentrated in this part of the island. So much so, in fact, that sometimes it feels like the rest of Grenada simply isn't there. (But it is, and hopefully this book will help you enjoy some of it.)

The stimulus created by overseas investors has brought about successful home-grown tourism businesses with a range of ancillary services and sub-sectors, such as tour operators, supermarkets, yacht provisioning and haul-out, holiday weddings, and agro-tourism products. Coupled with a seasonal cruise ship market and the spending power of St George's University and its students, Grenada's tourism sector has become a key contributor to the country's economic development.

Tourism beyond Grenada's south is diverse but far less concentrated. It is the domain of those who like to explore and get off the beaten track: hikers, culture vultures and eco tourists. Carriacou and Petite Martinique are usually marketed as day-trips, yet they deserve much more than this. Steeped in tradition and culture, and with stunning scenery, they have considerable appeal to independent travellers and sailors.

Yachting has become an important market for Grenada and the island has experienced significant overseas investment in this area. The Port Louis Marina in St George's Lagoon, owned and developed by entrepreneur Peter de Savary and Camper & Nicholsons Marinas Ltd, along with other marina projects such as Le Phare Bleu, have made Grenada one of the eastern Caribbean's primary ports of call for both private and charter sailboats, and annual sailing regattas are a draw for regional and international enthusiasts.

Grenada receives around 300,000 visitors annually with roughly two-thirds arriving by cruise ship and staying for just a day. Visitors from the UK, USA and Canada account for more than half of all stay-over visitors, with a further quarter arriving from other Caribbean countries.

PEOPLE

Although it is a generalisation, in my experience Grenadians are warm and friendly people. They are very approachable and genuine. Indeed if you spend your holiday

CUTLASS AND MACHETE

Sailors and pirates of the Caribbean in the 17th and 18th centuries would carry a cutlass as their main weapon. It was a short sabre with a broad curved blade and was especially effective in close combat on ship and shore, as well as for cutting rope and wood. On land it was also occasionally used as an agricultural tool, especially for cutting through rainforest or even for harvesting sugarcane.

Also used both as a weapon and an agricultural tool was the machete. Very similar in shape and length to a cutlass, the machete also has a broad blade with a very thin, sharp cutting edge. It is however much less elegant in design than the cutlass, and is sometimes referred to as the 'poor man's sword'. Variations of the machete exist in many countries. The *parang*, *golok* and *bolo* are very similar long knives used in Malaysia, Indonesia and the Philippines; in Nepal it is the *kukri* and in China the *dao*.

In Grenada today the machete is commonly used as an agricultural tool and most households will possess at least one. Often referred to as a cutlass, it is in fact a basic machete, rather than its upmarket relative. Visitors to Grenada may see both men and women walking along the roadside carrying a machete. This should not cause alarm, although it almost certainly will at first. It is used by Grenadians for cutting overgrown bush, pruning trees, weeding and for getting the refreshing water out of a young coconut.

holed-up in an all-inclusive resort, never giving yourself the opportunity to interact with local people, you will most certainly have missed out.

Many Grenadians lead a tough life and are relatively poor by Western standards, often living in conditions that contrast starkly with the luxury residences of the south. In spite of hardship and a history of conflict, setbacks and rebellion, Grenadians are predominantly a quiet and reserved people who are very polite and genuinely warm towards visitors. If you plan on visiting Carriacou and Petite Martinique (which you absolutely should) you may notice a difference between these islanders and those on Grenada. Also extremely friendly and hardworking, they are a very independent people with a strong sense of identity with their island home, with their cultural heritage and with their historical roots, which – you may be surprised to learn – are as diverse as Africa and Scotland.

POPULATION The population of Grenada is estimated to be approximately 100,000, with roughly a third of the nation's people living in or around the capital St George's.

ETHNICITY The majority of Grenadians (approximately 80%) are descendants of slaves brought to the island by both the French and the British from west Africa. There are also a small number of people (around 5%) of East Indian origin who are descendants of the indentured workforce that was introduced following the abolition of slavery during the mid 19th century.

LANGUAGE

The official language of Grenada is English, which is spoken throughout the island. French Patois (also called French Creole, Kwéyòl, Patwa or Patois) is still spoken in some communities, such as L'Esterre in Carriacou for example, though it is becoming very rare.

The English spoken by Grenadians can occasionally be heavily accented and illustrated with colourful expressions that have their origins in both French and English Creole. These dialects were born during slavery and combined the grammar and syntax of their captors' languages with those of their native Africa. Some 'Grenadianisms' are also influenced by expressions and words that reflect the East Indian origins of the island's former indentured workforce. It may take a little time to tune in to the accent if you are not accustomed to it.

Listen out for some of the following words and expressions that add a distinct linguistic spice to the English spoken on all three islands:

Wa gwan/W'ap'nin?	What's going on/happening? (usually a greeting)
One time	All at once
Oh shrimps man!	Oh goodness!
He went out to come back	He'll be back soon
Saraca	Feast (usually related to a ceremony)

RELIGION

Despite the dominance of the British in colonial times, the majority of Grenadians (approximately 53%) follow the Roman Catholic faith. It is thought that the British Protestant plantocracy behaved so badly towards the slave population that, once liberated and allowed to worship in churches, the freed slave population rejected their former masters' faith in an act of defiance and became Roman Catholics instead. Approximately 14% of Grenadians are practising Anglicans. A number of other Christian denominations are present in Grenada including Methodists, Pentecostals, Seventh-Day Adventists, Baptists and Jehovah's Witnesses. Minority faiths include Islam, Baha'i, Rastafarianism and Scientology.

EDUCATION

Grenada's education system is based to a large extent on that of Britain. Education is free and compulsory for children between the ages of five and 16. Primary education in Grenada lasts for seven years and secondary education for five years.

Grenada's further education institutions include the T. A. Marryshow Community College, which is located near the Lagoon in the capital, St George's. Students wishing to pursue degree courses travel abroad to study and are usually reliant on scholarships or bursaries to pay for their tuition. In True Blue there is a large, private American further education institution called the St George's University Medical School which was founded in 1977. The school provides training for veterinary and medical students from 140 overseas countries. St George's is affiliated with higher education institutions worldwide and makes an important economic contribution to Grenada. For more information see www.sgu.edu.

CULTURE

Although they inhabited the islands for longer than any of their successors, the cultural influences of the original Amerindian settlers have sadly been lost. Grenada's cultural heritage is largely the result of African, French, British and, to a certain extent, East Indian and Latin American influences. African tribal traditions including music, dance, dress and belief systems merged with the culture of the island's French settlers, and then later on with those of the British plantocracy. Unlike some Caribbean nations whose culture continued to be strongly influenced by the proximity of islands that were governed by France, Grenada's **French Creole** began to wane once the country became a British Crown Colony. Nevertheless, despite the dominance of the British and the Anglican and Roman Catholic churches, French influence still managed to survive in the form of dress, language and also in many of Grenada's place names. Stronger still were the residual influences of the liberated population's African heritage, which can still be enjoyed today in the form of music, dance, festivals, folklore and cooking. East Indian cultural influences originally stem from the island's indentured labour force of the mid 19th century and more recently from the neighbouring island of Trinidad. These tend to show themselves primarily in local cuisine and also in music.

MUSIC AND DANCE Traditional music and dance finds its roots deep within the island's history. From the slaves of west Africa, the influences of their European masters, and the more contemporary sway of neighbouring islands such as Trinidad and Tobago, Grenada's instruments, songs, music and dance have evolved as heady concoctions of past and present that are still used, performed and enjoyed today.

Central to most traditional music and dance festivals, especially in Carriacou, is usually the goatskin drum, or *la peau cabrit*, providing the celebration with an unmistakable rhythm of Africa that harks back to the Akan tribes of the former Gold Coast and the Igbo and Mandingo of Nigeria. Interestingly, the lyric of many traditional songs is sung in French Creole, creating what is often a haunting yet ebullient fusion of cultures. Grenada's most celebrated music and dance expression is the **Big Drum Dance**, which is performed in Carriacou. Big Drum is also occasionally known as the African Nation Dance and is a central feature of many festivals and ceremonies in Carriacou, such as maroons, boat launchings, weddings and so on. It consists of three drums, the *cot* and two *bula*, plus an assortment of simple percussion accompaniments such as the *shak-shak* and the *old hoe*. Many types of dancing accompany the drumming, which is led by the cot, all of which combine African and Creole influences. Singing is traditionally in Creole, and its lyric usually tells of a time of slavery and a longing for a return to the homeland of Africa.

The *bélé*, or *belair*, is a Creole dance of African origin. Again, the drum is the centrepiece of the dance which traditionally reflects a courtship between a man and a woman. The dancers move in turn towards the drum and, by the time the dance reaches its conclusion, the drum is beating ever louder and the man and woman are dancing together with quick steps and vigorous body movements that symbolise their union.

The *quadrille* is a more formal square dance that has its origins in the French court of the 19th century. The style is aristocratic, graceful and elegant, with four couples dancing together and usually accompanied by a four-instrument ensemble.

Couples dancing the *quadrille*, the bélé and Big Drum are likely to have worn colourful outfits that were in stark contrast to the drab uniforms they were forced to wear when they were in servitude. These outfits may have included white chemises, flowing skirts and a colourful material known as *madras*. This material is an East Indian cotton that was made by the Kalabari people in the vicinity of Chennai (formerly Madras, India) and still known by them as *injiri*. Though it became an essential part of traditional French Creole wear, it was originally traded by Portuguese merchants in west Africa where it was worn by the Igbo of southern Nigeria. After arriving in the West Indies as slaves, the Igbo are thought to have continued to wear madras whenever they could, especially on Sundays or feast days. Although Grenada's French Creole heritage is not as strong today as it is on other islands, dancers continue to wear brightly coloured skirts and chemises, adding to the ancestral spirit of Africa that prevails throughout the nation's music and dance festivals.

Parang is a traditional form of Latin American music that probably arrived in Grenada from Trinidad, where it is also very common today. A parang music ensemble usually consists of string instruments, drum and percussion, who accompany a singer. The lyric is either impromptu or rehearsed, and its theme reflects a story, perhaps a scandal, a rumour or a critique of something or someone from the local community. In Carriacou, parang festivals usually take place at Christmas time and can be lively, raucous affairs, depending on the subject, the humour and the skill of the lyric.

Calypso is very similar to parang in that its lyric usually comprises a social commentary of some kind. This music form evolved as part of the preparations for carnival (see opposite) and was traditionally performed by women who sang short, cutting ballads that ridiculed members of the plantocracy, administrators or overseers, and in particular perpetrators of bad deeds. Today calypso songs are much longer and usually performed in competitions at carnival time. The lyric still contains at least a hint of irony or some kind of political comment.

Grenada's popular music scene finds its roots in calypso and the **steel pan** music of the 1960s. Strongly influenced by neighbouring islands, in particular Trinidad and Tobago, music forms such as *soca* became very prominent from the 1980s. Soca is essentially a fusion of calypso and Trinidad's Indian music, sometimes called *chutney* music. Other contemporary music influences from neighbouring islands include **zouk** and **bouyon**, which have emerged as popular music genres in Guadeloupe, Dominica and Martinique, and, of course, **reggae** and **dancehall** music from Jamaica.

FESTIVALS Grenada celebrates a number of festivals that have a very interesting blend of traditional influences. The annual Carriacou **Maroon & String Band Music Festival** has its roots in Africa, Scotland and in the emergent communities of liberated African slaves who provided each other with assistance, celebrated bountiful harvests, and prayed for newly planted crops. Essential components of each village maroon are good-humoured people, lots of great food and usually a Big Drum Dance (see page 206 for more information).

Carnival is traditionally celebrated on the Monday and Tuesday before Ash Wednesday. This is still the case in Carriacou, though the Grenada Carnival is now celebrated in August. Known as the *Spice Mas*, Grenada's carnival has its origins in the masquerade balls of the French court, though it was liberated African slaves who added rhythm, vibrancy, colour and a strong sense of rebellion.

Contemporary carnival is a mix of both the traditional and the modern. Booming amplifiers on flatbed trucks mix with vivacious costumes and colourful traditional figures such as the *jab-jabs*, *wild Indians*, *shortknees*, *moko jumbies* and *tamboo-bamboo* bands, as well as the *paywo* or *Shakespeare mas* of Carriacou. (For more information on Grenada's carnivals go to www.spicemasgrenada.com.)

ART AND SCULPTURE Grenada has some very talented homegrown and resident artists and sculptors. Perhaps one of the nation's most celebrated artists is **Canute Caliste**, from L'Esterre in Carriacou. Born in 1914, Caliste became a revered Carriacouan artist and musician who was known for his simple style of painting, capturing the everyday life and vivid natural beauty of his island home. He worked mainly with acrylics on hardboard and canvas and, it is said, he could 'knock-out' 20 paintings a day when the mood caught him. Mermaids appeared as a motif in many of his works, reflecting an experience he claimed to have had as a child when a mermaid appeared to him in a vision, telling him that if he followed the Bible he could achieve anything. When he was not painting, Caliste was a boatbuilder and quadrille dance musician, playing both guitar and fiddle. Caliste's paintings have been exhibited in North America and Europe. Visitors to Grenada can view some of his artwork at the **Yellow Poui Gallery** on Young Street in St George's, and reproductions can be found at the Grenada National Museum in St George's and the Carriacou Museum in Hillsborough (see page 218). *The Mermaid Wakes* was a book published in 1989 showcasing many of his works. Canute Caliste died in 2005. His daughter, Clemencia, is a curator at the Carriacou Museum and is always happy to talk about her father's work.

Elinus Cato was born in St Patrick in 1933 and rose to prominence as a very popular painter. His works of town and rural Grenadian life depict bright and colourful scenes and one such piece, *People at Work*, was presented to Queen Elizabeth II when she visited the island in 1985. Some of Cato's work can be seen at the Yellow Poui Gallery in St George's. The Yellow Poui Gallery was set up by Jim Rudin and his wife in 1968 and it exhibits and sells paintings, sculptures and carvings by artists either from, working in or inspired by the Caribbean.

Jackie Miller is a celebrated Grenadian artist, producing paintings and drawings in a variety of media including watercolour, acrylic and charcoal. Miller's works can also be found on display at the Yellow Poui Gallery.

Susan Mains is a self-taught artist from the United States who is also a citizen of Grenada. Susan works in both acrylic and oil on canvas and her works depict beautiful, colourful images of Caribbean life, landscapes and people. Her subjects include traditional boatbuilding and launching, farming, coastal and countryside scenes, portraits and tropical flora. In Grenada her artwork is on display at a number of hotels including the Flamboyant and Mount Cinnamon at the western tip of Grand Anse Beach. You will find them both on display and for sale at the Art & Soul gallery in the Spiceland Mall, also in Grand Anse. For more information go to www.susanmains.com.

Judith Jarvis grew up in Iraq and then lived and studied in England. She moved to Grenada with her husband in 2007, and she paints colourful scenery, still life and portraits. Her work is a particular favourite of mine and you can see more of it at www.judithjarvis.com.

Freddy Paul is a Grenada-born painter who specialises in very colourful landscape and traditional scenes. His paintings of Big Drum dancers and crowded markets are especially beautiful. Freddy has a gallery on Halifax Street in St George's and his website is www.freddysartgallery.com.

Although finding original artwork in Grenada can be quite tricky, great places to begin are the Yellow Poui Gallery and the **Grenada Arts Council Gallery** on Young Street in St George's. In addition to those mentioned above, visitors should look out for artists and sculptors such as **Trish Bethany, Frankie Francis, Michael Paryag, Joseph Rome, Joseph Browne, Rene Froehlich, Ivan Godfrey** and **Stanley Coutain**, to name just a few.

LITERATURE Grenada has produced no real literary giants, although many of its more contemporary writers, poets and playwrights are definitely worth seeking out. **Merle Collins** has published poetry and short-story collections such as *Because the Dawn Breaks!* and *Rain Darling*, as well as novels such as *Angel* and *The Colour of Forgetting*. **Jacob Ross** is a Grenadian-born writer who has published acclaimed short-story collections such as *Song for Simone* and *A Way to Catch the Dust*. Children's writer **Verna Allette Wilkins** has written a number of charming and popular books such as *Dave and the Tooth Fairy*, *Toyin Fay* and *Kim's Magic Tree*. **Joan Anim-Addo** is a Grenadian poet and publisher of *Haunted by History*, a collection of poems that explore history and its effect on individuals. She is also the author of works that study African-Caribbean women's writing, such as *Touching the Body* and *Framing the Word*. **Jean Buffong**'s novels *Under the Silk Cotton Tree*, *Jump Up and Kiss Me* and *Snowflakes in the Sun* are colourful portrayals of Grenadian life from the perspectives of young and old. **Claude J Douglas** has published interesting books about the history and development of Grenada such as *When the Village was an Extended Family in Grenada* and *The Battle for Grenada's Black Gold* which is a fascinating study of the island's turbulent nutmeg industry. Anyone interested in Grenada's history should definitely own a copy of *Grenada: Island of Conflict* by historian and former prime minister **George Brizan**.

FOLKLORE Grenada's folkloric heritage originates in the fascinating myths, legends, spirit tales and rites of west African tribal traditions. For many Grenadians this lore still goes beyond mere superstition and is inextricably bound with the island's more contemporary practices and belief systems.

Obeah, a kind of magic or witchcraft, is still practised by some Grenadians, though it is rare. It is a combination of superstition, medicine and divination whose rituals included the sacrifice of animals and the use of symbols or amulets to call upon or quell evil spirits. Traditionally an *obeahman* or *obeahwoman* would be hired to help you with advice, protection, potions or spells in your efforts to satisfy a particular ambition or desire.

The **soucouyant** is a night spirit of west African origin who sheds her skin and flies through the forest in the form of a ball of fire. She is continuously on the lookout for innocents and for the blood of people and animals. In order to catch a soucouyant you must find her skin after she has shed it (usually she hides it in a mortar or beneath a stone) and then rub it with salt before she can put it on and transform herself back into a human being. Alternatively you can place a bowl of peas or grain next to her skin which she must count before transforming herself again. The **ligarou** is a male version of the soucouyant and is equally unpleasant. **La Diablesse** (or 'Lajabless') is a beautiful woman who walks through the forest by the light of the moon and lures unsuspecting men deeper and deeper into the woods until they are lost. Once there, she reveals herself as a she-devil who causes her victims either to go mad or to die. In some variations of the myth she wears a large hat to hide her skeletal face, or she walks in long grass to disguise both the appearance and sound of her cloven hooves. **Mama Glo** is a female spirit of lakes and rivers who may take the form of a beautiful young woman or a mermaid. It is said that she will command you to perform menial tasks such as scratching her back or collecting leaves. If you ignore or disobey her she becomes extremely angry and may strangle or drown you. Mama Glo is worshipped by believers of Shango (see page 184).

Staying indoors, not walking in the forest, avoiding water and hiding beneath your bed covers does not necessarily guarantee your safety, however. A **jumbie** (or *jombie*) is the spirit of a dead person who brings you bad luck or ill health if it discovers you sleeping, and **Mama Maladie** is the angry spirit of a woman who has died in childbirth and who walks back and forth between her grave and her former home. She may also linger, waiting for unsuspecting mothers to open their doors and let her inside. You will know she is in your home because you will hear the voice of a crying child, and with it comes a plague of disease. It is said that cursing the spirit in French Creole may help to make her disappear. The **baccoo** is a temperamental spirit who lives in a bottle, rather similar to a genie, and who can bring both wealth and happiness as well as financial ruin and even death. Usually a baccoo is viewed as simply an unattractive, mischievous spirit who may be returned to its bottle by beating a drum. So if you return to find your hotel room a mess, it may not be that room service forgot about you; it could be that someone has sent a baccoo to cause you trouble. So you'd better go buy a drum.

2

Practical Information

Whether you are travelling with friends, a young family, or perhaps arriving by sailing boat, Grenada, Carriacou and Petite Martinique are certainly fun and fascinating places to visit. The tri-island state caters for a diverse range of interests and activities. You can hike to waterfalls, explore rainforest-covered mountains, see how rum and chocolate are made, experience cultural activities and events like boat-launching or drumming, scuba-dive evocative shipwrecks and wonderful reef systems, learn about Grenada's long tradition of spice cultivation, or simply chill out and enjoy the tranquil waters and powder-white sands of some of the Caribbean's most beautiful beaches.

WHEN TO VISIT

For both stay-over and cruise ship visitors the most popular time to visit Grenada is between November and June. Although there is always the chance of a passing shower and the peaks of the interior may be damp and hidden by clouds, this is the dry season and sunny days are practically guaranteed. The islands are busier, accommodation more expensive, and restaurants are quite crowded, but it is a lively time and there is usually a lot going on. By May and June the cruise-ship season has petered out, popular attractions are less busy, and the skies are usually clear and blue. If you prefer less hustle and bustle, but still crave back-to-back sunny days, then this is a good time for you.

If festivities are your thing then the carnival seasons (February in Carriacou and August in Grenada) offer around the clock parties, street parades, traditional 'jump-up', carnival queen and calypso competitions (see pages 29 and 61 for more information on carnival). The Carriacou Maroon & String Band Festival (see page 207) and numerous sailing regattas (see page 81) attract plenty of culture vultures and boating enthusiasts.

The wet season runs from July to December and the Atlantic hurricane season usually peaks in early September. A common misconception of the hurricane season is that Caribbean islands are constantly bombarded by them. Fortunately this isn't true, but the threat of occasional tropical depressions, storms and hurricanes is real enough from July all the way through to the end of October. For much of the time the weather is hot and humid. Rainfall usually comes in short but heavy waves and can be expected on a daily basis. At this time of the year accommodation prices are much lower and the island is very quiet. Some hotels may close during September. The low season can actually be a nice time to explore the islands but you have to be prepared, both physically and mentally, for rainstorms to disrupt your plans.

HIGHLIGHTS

Naturally everyone has different ideas about travelling and you may well want to simply sit in the sun and do as little as possible for a week or so. I can manage just about 20 minutes of that before I'm ready to do something else – so for those of you who also get the fidgets, here are some of things I recommend you try to see and do during your stay. And, by the way, go to Carriacou.

BEACHES For many visitors to Grenada and Carriacou the highlights will be the beaches. **Grand Anse Beach** (see page 122) is one of the best known and is also where you will find some of Grenada's most popular resorts. On Grenada, my favourite is **Magazine Beach** (see page 123), closely followed by **Bathway Beach** (see page 183) in the northeast. For families with small children, I think the best beach on Grenada is probably **Morne Rouge Beach** (see page 122). Carriacou has gorgeous beaches too. **Paradise Beach** (see page 218) is the best known but you should try to get to **Anse La Roche** (see page 225) if you can. My favourite beach on Carriacou is **Petite Carenage** (see page 226).

CULTURE AND HERITAGE Don't miss **Belmont Estate** (see page 188). Follow the journey from tree to bar, enjoy lunch, and indulge yourself with some of the best organic chocolate in the world. You could easily combine a trip to Belmont with a visit to the **River Antoine Rum Distillery** (see page 188). This amazing place has been making rum with the same methods and machinery since the 1700s. Try to avoid large group tours if you can as the guides tend to go into 'auto-pilot' (you can't blame them – they do several tours a day in the high season). Fewer people means you can discreetly let your guide know he/she can drop the script and just be him/herself; it makes all the difference.

Support and learn about Grenada's nutmeg industry with a tour of the **Gouyave Nutmeg Pool** (see page 147) and the **Grenville Receiving Station** (see page 166). If you are in the Gouyave area then take a look at the cocoa boucans at **Dougaldston Estate** (see page 140) and be sure to sample the seafood at **Fish Friday** (see page 146).

When on Carriacou you should pass by the boatyards at **Windward** (see page 221) to see if there is a wooden sloop in progress. Don't miss the Amerindian artefacts collected from the beautiful Grand Bay and Sabazan coastlines on display at the **Carriacou Museum** in Hillsborough (see page 218), and try to catch a **Big Drum Dance** or the **Maroon Festival** (see pages 206 and 207).

FORESTS, LAKES AND WATERFALLS Visit the **Grand Etang National Park** (see page 136). The visitor centre is very informative and the views from the **Mt Qua Qua** trail (even if you don't go all the way to the top) are worth the walk. Take the short hike to **St Margaret's Falls** (see page 170) and the second waterfall at **Concord (Au Coin)** (see page 152). The adventurous should try to find a guide to the top of **Morne Fédon** (see page 150) if the trail has been cleared sufficiently. It is both a historic and very scenic place. I also enjoy the serenity and the walk around the margins of **Lake Antoine** (see page 196), which you can do by yourself.

SUGGESTED ITINERARIES

ONE WEEK
Days 1–3 Accommodation in the north of Grenada. From there visit Belmont

Estate, River Antoine Rum Distillery, Levera Archipelago, Bathway Beach, Gouyave Nutmeg Pool, Dougaldston Estate and Fish Friday.

Days 4–7 Accommodation in the south of Grenada. From there take a day trip to Carriacou, visit Concord Falls, the Grand Etang National Park and St Margaret's Falls. Relax on Grand Anse Beach, Morne Rouge Beach and Magazine Beach.

TWO WEEKS
Days 1–4 Accommodation in the north of Grenada. From there visit Belmont Estate, River Antoine Rum Distillery, Levera Archipelago, Bathway Beach, Gouyave Nutmeg Pool, Dougaldston Estate and Fish Friday.

Days 5–9 Accommodation on Carriacou. Visit Paradise Beach, Anse La Roche Beach and Petite Carenage Beach. Seek out boatbuilding projects at Windward and Petite Martinique (take a day trip or overnight), call in at the Carriacou Museum, charter a water taxi to Sandy Island or perhaps the Tobago Cays, and enjoy a coastal walk from Mt Pleasant to Sabazan.

DAY TRIPS

Here are six days out you may like to try:

1 River Antoine Rum Distillery followed by the Belmont Estate and lunch. Head up to Levera Beach and then back down to Bathway. Call in at Aggie's for a drink or dinner. Other good dining options are The Heights and Petite Anse (see page 178).

2 Concord Waterfall (first and second falls) followed by the Dougaldston Estate and a tour of the Gouyave Nutmeg Pool. Plan properly and dine on seafood at Gouyave's Fish Friday (see page 146).

3 Grand Etang Forest Reserve Visitor Centre, lake and forest views, then a hike to St Margaret's Falls. Call in at the Spice Basket for refreshments (see page 145).

4 Take a tour of the De La Grenade Nutmeg Garden followed by the Bay Gardens. Alternatively take a gardens tour with Sunsation or Caribbean Horizons (see page 74). Head down to the Poolside Restaurant at Le Phare Bleu for a late lunch and then spend the afternoon on a beach – Grand Anse or Magazine, where you could sidle off for refreshments at Umbrellas or the Aquarium.

5 Hop on the Osprey ferry to Carriacou and then take an island tour. Relax for a while on Paradise Beach, call in at the Carriacou Museum, and buy some original souvenirs from Fidel Productions, Simply Carriacou or Kato Charles Folk Art (see page 215).

6 Stroll around St George's (see the self-guided tour on page 106), take in some local art on Young St, visit the Grenada Museum and have some lunch at the Museum Bistro. Take a water taxi from the Carenage to Grand Anse Beach.

2

Days 10–14 Accommodation in the south of Grenada. Visit Concord Falls (including Au Coin – the second waterfall), the Grand Etang National Park and St Margaret's Falls. Relax on Grand Anse Beach, Morne Rouge Beach, and Magazine Beach. Indulge yourself with watersports, scuba-diving, chartered sailing or some wellness therapy, and enjoy fine dining at a wide selection of restaurants.

TOUR OPERATORS

A number of international tour operators offer flight and accommodation packages to Grenada, though very few include Carriacou and Petite Martinique. These operators tend to offer accommodation in the large resort hotels and villas of Grenada's southwest peninsula. Here is a selection of the travel operators offering flights, accommodation, villa lettings and all-inclusive packages:

UK
Blue Lizard Travel 01798 861935; www.bluelizardtravel.com
British Airways 0844 493 0787; www.britishairways.com
Carib Tours 020 3131 0172; www.caribtours.co.uk
Caribbean Unpackaged 020 8446 8122; www.caribbean-unpackaged.com
Dial A Flight 0844 811 4444; www.dialaflight.com
Holiday Lettings www.holidaylettings.co.uk
Holiday Rentals www.holiday-rentals.co.uk
Just Caribbean 0800 327 7322; www.justcaribbean.com
Just Grenada 01373 814214; www.justgrenada.co.uk

Kenwood Travel 020 7749 9245; www.kenwoodtravel.com
Kuoni 0844 448 0474; www.kuoni.co.uk
Monarch 08719 405040; www.monarch.co.uk
Newmont Travel 020 8920 1155; www.newmont.co.uk
Responsible Travel 01273 600030; www.responsibletravel.com
Sovereign 0844 415 1984; www.sovereign.com
The Holiday Place 020 7644 1755; www.theholidayplace.co.uk
Thomson 0844 050 2828; www.thomsonworldwide.com
Trailfinders 020 7368 1200; www.trailfinders.com
Tropical Sky 0844 332 9371; www.tropicalsky.co.uk

GETTING MARRIED IN GRENADA

Here is a selection of planners and hotels offering full wedding packages in Grenada:

Caribbean Horizons 473 444 1555; e info@caribbeanhorizons; www.caribbeanhorizons.com
Flamboyant Hotel & Villas 473 444 4247; e flambo@spiceisle.com; www.flamboyant.com
Grenada Wedding 473 420 2878; e grenadawedding@spiceisle.com; www.grenadawedding.com/www.karibikhochzeit.net
Petite Anse 473 442 5252; e info@petiteanse.com; www.petiteanse.com
Simply Weddings 473 442 6943; e weddingsgnd@yahoo.com
True Blue Bay Resort 473 443 8783; e mail@truebluebay.com; www.truebluebay.com

If you are planning on getting married in Grenada you must satisfy a number of statutory requirements and also provide the relevant documentation. These are outlined below. In practice, if you engage a local wedding planner, they will assist you with all this.

Turquoise Holidays 📞01494 678400; www.
turquoiseholidays.co.uk
Virgin Holidays 📞0844 573 0088; www.
virginholidays.co.uk

Caribbean Journey 📞1 866 236 1924; www.
caribbeanjourney.com

Caribbean Way 📞1 877 953 7400; www.
caribbeanway.com
Classic Vacations 📞1 800 635 1333; www.
classicvacations.com
Expedia Vacations 📞1 877 787 7186; www.
expedia.com
Funjet Vacations 📞1 888 558 6654; www.
funjet.com

TOURIST OFFICES

Grenada Grenada Board of Tourism, PO Box 293,
St George's; 📞473 440 2279/2001; f 473 440
6637; e gbt@spiceisle.com; www.
grenadagrenadines.com
Carriacou Grenada Board of Tourism, Main
Street, Hillsborough; 📞473 443 7948; f 473 443
6127; e carrgbt@spiceisle.com
Canada 439 University Av, Suite 920, Toronto,
Ontario M5G 1Y8; 📞+1 416 595 1339; f +1 416
595 8278; e tourism@grenadaconsulate.com

Germany Schenkendorfstrasse 1, 65187
Wiesbaden; 📞0611 267 6720; f 0611 267 6760;
e grenada@discover-fra.com
UK 1 Lyric Square, London W6 0NB; 📞020 8328
0644; f 0870 199 2626; e grenada@eyes2market.
co.uk
US PO Box 1668, Lake Worth, FL 33460; 📞+1 561
588 8176, toll free 📞+1 1 800 927 9554; f +1
561 588 7267; e cnoel@grenadagrenadines.com

RED TAPE

ENTRY REQUIREMENTS All visitors to Grenada must be able to present a valid
passport and a return or an onward ticket. Visitors from the UK, US, Canada,
Commonwealth countries, EU countries, Caribbean countries, Japan, Norway, and
Israel do not need a visa. Eastern European and Asian countries are required to
purchase a tourist visa on arrival in Grenada at a cost of EC$100 for single entry
and EC$250 for multiple entry. For information and requests regarding visas
e immigrationgnd@spiceisle.org.

- You must be resident on the island for at least three working days (excluding
weekends) before you may apply for a licence.

- Your application for a marriage licence is made at the Prime Minister's Office
after the requisite stamp duty and marriage licence fees have been paid.
(Though this sounds quite daunting, it actually only takes about two days and
is something your wedding planning service will do for you.)

- Documents you must have with you when you marry in Grenada are: valid
passports; birth certificates; proof of a decree absolute, if either party is
divorced; proof of single status (this is usually in the form of a letter from a
lawyer or clergyman stating that neither of you has previously been married);
proof of a name change, if relevant; a death certificate, if either of you have
been widowed; evidence of parental consent if either of you is under 21 years
of age.

Practical Information   RED TAPE

2

DEPARTURE TAXES There is no longer a requirement to pay departure tax on leaving Grenada's Maurice Bishop International Airport. The tax has been built in to your ticket. Travellers departing Lauriston Airport in Carriacou and connecting to an international flight the same day must pay a departure tax of EC$60. If you are flying from Lauriston and staying in Grenada then you must pay a departure tax of EC$10.

CONSULATES AND EMBASSIES

British High Commission (located in Barbados) ✆246 730 7800
Chinese Embassy ✆473 440 3054
Cuban Embassy ✆473 444 1884
French Consulate ✆473 405 9090
German Consulate ✆473 440 7260
Guyanese Consulate ✆473 440 2031

Jamaican Consulate ✆473 444 5210
Netherlands Consulate ✆473 459 0712
Spanish Consulate ✆473 440 2087
Swedish Consulate ✆473 440 2765
US Embassy ✆473 444 1173
Venezuelan Embassy ✆473 440 1721

GETTING THERE AND AWAY

BY AIR Grenada's **Maurice Bishop International Airport** services flights to and from the United Kingdom, the United States, Canada and the Caribbean. The airport is located in the southwest of Grenada and is very close to the large resorts and beaches of Grand Anse.

Flights from the UK
British Airways ✆0844 493 0787; www.britishairways.com. Direct flights & holidays to Grenada from London.
Monarch ✆08719 405040; www.monarch.co.uk. Direct flights & holidays from London to Grenada.
Virgin Atlantic ✆0844 811 0000; www.virgin-atlantic.com. Direct flights & holidays from London to Grenada.

Flights from the US and Canada
Air Canada toll free ✆1 888 247 2262; www.aircanada.com. Direct flights to Grenada from Toronto.
American Airlines & American Eagle toll free ✆1 800 433 7300; www.aa.com. Flights from US cities to San Juan, Puerto Rico, with connecting American Eagle flights to Grenada. Direct American Airline flights to Grenada from Miami.
Caribbean Airlines toll free ✆1 800 920 4225; www.caribbean-airlines.com. Direct flights to

Grenada from New York. Flights from New York, Miami, Fort Lauderdale & Toronto to Trinidad with connections on Liat Airlines to Grenada (see below).
Delta Airlines ✆1 800 241 4141; www.delta.com. Weekly direct flights from New York to Grenada.

Inter-island flight services and connections
Liat toll free ✆1 800 444 5428; www.liatairline.com. With connections throughout the eastern Caribbean, Liat flies to Grenada's Maurice Bishop International Airport.
SVG Air toll free ✆784 457 5124/5777; Grenada ✆473 444 3549; Carriacou ✆473 443 8519, f 473 444 2898; www.svgair.com. SVG Air operates both scheduled and charter flights throughout the Caribbean as well as North and South America. SVG Air also has daily domestic charter flights between Grenada & Carriacou.

Checked-baggage allowances The standard allowance for checked baggage on international flights is two pieces together totalling no more than 23kg (50 pounds). On Liat it is one piece weighing no more than 23kg (50 pounds) and on SVG Air it is 18kg (40 pounds). Check with your airline prior to travelling for up-to-date information on baggage allowances, charges, and restricted cabin items. Airlines have become rather strict with baggage allowances of late and, where once they turned a blind eye to a bag that was a little overweight, now they issue an excess fee or ask you to lighten your load at check-in.

Maurice Bishop International Airport
Formerly Point Salines International Airport, but renamed in honour of the murdered revolutionary leader in 2009, it is located on the southwest peninsula of the island, some 11km from the capital St George's and 5km from the popular resorts of Grand Anse. The airport is simple to navigate and has a small number of air-conditioned restaurants, cafés, bars and souvenir shops. The information desk is located between the departures and arrivals halls next to the flight information screens. There is also an ATM located here. You will find taxis and limousine buses directly opposite the exit near the clearly marked passenger pick-up area.

Taxi drivers work to fixed tariffs for journeys from the airport. For an idea of taxi fares from Point Salines International Airport: EC$50 to St George's, EC$40 to Grand Anse, EC$35 to True Blue, EC$40 to L'Anse Aux Epines, EC$110 to Gouyave and EC$150 to Sauteurs (the furthest point from the airport at 45km). A minimum fare of EC$25 is charged for short distances. An additional charge of EC$5 per person is levied when passenger numbers exceed four persons per taxi.

Once outside the airport, the road to the right leads away from the southwest peninsula to the capital. The airport car park is also located a short walk to the right on the opposite side of the road. Opposite the car park you will see a memorial to the soldiers who lost their lives during the US military intervention of 1983. Dedicated by US president Ronald Reagan in 1986, the concrete arches and epitaphs cite dedications and thanks to the soldiers of 'Operation Urgent Fury'. For more information on the US military intervention of 1983, see page 18.

Follow the road to a traffic island. To the right is True Blue and straight ahead is the main road heading north. The main road north to St George's widens and passes an industrial estate before reaching a second traffic island. To the right is the road to the east (Grenville, La Sagesse, Westerhall, L'Anse Aux Epines), and the road to the left leads to St George's, Grand Anse and the west coast.

BY SEA
Ferry and mail boat
Osprey Lines ✆473 440 8126; e ospreylines@ gmail.com; www.ospreylines.com. Osprey lines operates a daily high-speed ferry service between Grenada, Carriacou & Petite Martinique. The journey between Grenada & Carriacou takes around 90mins. It is a further 30mins to Petite Martinique.
BEDY Ocean Line www.bedytravel.com. Not yet launched at the time of writing though it promises to offer a regional high-speed ferry

service (including vehicle transportation) between Barbados, St Lucia, Trinidad, St Vincent and Grenada.
Mail Boat The mail boat is a cheap way to travel between Grenada and Carriacou. The journey time is somewhere between 3 to 4 hours and the price as low as EC$25pp each way. Catch the mail boat from St George's Careneage on Tue, Wed, Fri & Sat at 10.00 and from Hillsborough jetty on Mon, Wed, Thu & Sun at 14.00.

Cruise ship Grenada is visited by several cruise lines. The cruise-ship terminal is located in the capital, St George's, where two ships are able to put in at the same time. Additional ships either berth at the port or in St George's Harbour where passengers are transported by tender to the cruise-ship terminal. Cruise prices vary according to time of year and cabin type, and schedules are also subject to change. When booking cruises, you have the option of choosing shore excursions in advance. Here are just a few cruise lines that visit Grenada:

Celebrity Cruises www.celebritycruises.com
Cunard www.cunard.com

Princess Cruises www.princess.com
Windstar Cruises www.windstarcruises.com

Private yacht Visitors to Grenada, Carriacou and Petite Martinique arriving by private or charter vessel should notify authorities within two hours of arrival at one of the following ports of entry: Grenada Marine, Grenada Yacht Club, Grenville Harbour, Hillsborough (Carriacou), Le Phare Bleu, or Prickly Bay Marina. A clearance form can be downloaded from the internet (*www.grenadagrenadines. com*) and you must purchase a cruising permit which is valid for a month and allows you to sail Grenada's waters unrestricted. Other documentation requirements include: three crew and/or passenger lists; immigration cards for crew members and passengers landing; ships, stores and health declaration; a port clearance from the last port of call; a valid passport for all crew and passengers. Grenada uses the Red Light Returning Rule.

Marinas

Carriacou Yacht Club Tyrrel Bay, Carriacou; 473 443 6292; VHF 16; e carriyacht@spiceisle.com. Facilities include wireless internet, accommodation, restaurant, mini-market, ice & water, showers & dinghy dock.

Clarke's Court Bay Marina Clarke's Court Bay, Woburn; 473 439 2593; VHF 16 & 74; e office@clarkescourtbaymarina.com; www.clarkescourtbaymarina.com; 06.00–18.00 (office). Finger slip & swing moorings available. Facilities include water & electricity, laundry, showers, wireless internet access, bar & restaurant, 24hr security.

Grenada Yacht Club Lagoon, St George's; 473 440 6826; VHF 16 call sign GYC; e gyc@spiceisle.com; www.grenadayachtclub.com. The marina offers high-class facilities including docking for 44 yachts, customs & immigration, water & electricity, garbage disposal, fuel, laundry, showers & ice, bar & restaurant, 24hr security, Wi-Fi.

Le Phare Bleu Marina Petite Calivigny Bay; 473 444 2400; e marina@leipharebleu.com; www.leipharebleu.com. Located in the beautiful Petite Calivigny Bay, Le Phare Bleu offers 65 berths for vessels up to 90 feet, clearing, customs & immigration, water & electricity, fuel, laundry, ice, mini-mart, wireless internet access, boutique hotel, pool, restaurant & bar, & fine dining on a retired lighthouse boat.

Martin's Marina (Secret Harbour) L'Anse Aux Epines; 473 444 4449; VHF 16 & 71;

e martinsmarina@caribsurf.com; www. secretharbourgrenada.com. 53-slip concrete marina, 42 stern-to slips, 11 alongside slips & 32 swing moorings. Services include fuel, storage, dockage, showers, waste disposal, bar, wireless internet access, cottage rental, 24hr security.

Port Louis Marina Lagoon, St George's; 473 435 7431; e info@cnportlouismarina.com; www.cnportlouismarina.com. Marina with 160 berths for yachts up to 300 feet. Facilities include fresh water, Wi-Fi, shower & laundry, waste disposal, grey & black water pump out, 24hr security. Marina village has restaurant & bar, yacht services & provisioning, shops.

Prickly Bay Marina Prickly Bay, L'Anse Aux Epines; 473 439 5265; e info@pricklybaymarina.com; www.pricklybaymarina.com. Berths for vessels up to 180 feet. Services include clearing, customs & immigration, fresh water, electricity, fuel, marine services, mini market, laundry, internet access, restaurant & bar.

True Blue Bay Marina True Blue; 473 439 1000; e horizonyachts@caribsurf.com; www. truebluebay.com. Located at the True Blue Bay Resort & close to Spice Island Marine for chandlery & haul-out services. There are 18 slips for boats up to 30 feet. Facilities include hotel, bar, restaurant, fuel, electricity, ice, showers, wireless internet, swimming pool, gift shop.

Whisper Cove Marina Clarke's Court Bay; 473 444 5296; e info@whispercovemarina.gd; www. whispercovemarina.gd. 12 berths for boats up to

60 feet. Services include fresh water, electricity, laundry, waste disposal, butcher & deli shop, restaurant & bar, workshop, Wi-Fi.

Marine, haul-out and boatyard services

Grenada Marine St David's Harbour, Corinth;

☎473 443 1667; e info@grenadamarine.com; www.grenadamarine.com
Spice Island Marine Services Prickly Bay; ☎473 444 4342; VHF 16; e simsco@spiceisle. com; www.spiceislandmarine.com
Tyrrel Bay Haul-Out Tyrrel Bay, Carriacou; ☎473 443 8175; VHF 16; e tbyh@usa.net

HEALTH With Dr Felicity Nicholson

BEFORE YOU GO The only immunisation requirement for visitors to Grenada over one year of age is a yellow fever vaccination certificate if you are arriving from a yellow fever infected area. The vaccine is not suitable for everyone so this should be discussed with a health care professional experienced in giving it. Grenada does not have malaria and the water is usually safe to drink, however, it is still wise to drink bottled water and avoid ice. It is recommended that standard vaccinations such as tetanus, diphtheria and polio, which comes as an all-in-one vaccine (Revaxis), are up to date, and travellers may also wish to consider protecting themselves from hepatitis A. **Rabies** is endemic in Grenada but is only usually a problem for those staying for extended periods or working with animals. It may be present in any warm-blooded mammal and is spread through the transfer of saliva from a bite, a scratch or a lick over broken skin. It is more commonly found in the mongoose population (see page 7). You will see this animal quite often in rural areas – it was introduced here and has no natural predators – but it is a shy creature and will usually run away. Beware of those that are not shy, that stand their ground or demonstrate aggressive behaviour. If you are likely to be living or working in rural areas for a long period you should consider getting a pre-exposure rabies vaccine which consists of three doses given over a minimum of 21 days. Whether or not you have had the vaccine you should scrub the wound with soap and running water, apply an antiseptic and get yourself to medical help as soon as possible. Visitors requiring health care in Grenada are required to pay upfront for treatment. Medical insurance is usually a good idea, particularly if you will be participating in activities such as hiking or scuba-diving.

INSECT BITES

Mosquitoes Although there is no risk of malaria in Grenada, mosquito bites can still spoil your trip, especially if you react badly to them. It is definitely worth bringing insect repellent. You should opt for one containing DEET (50–55%), which is very effective. Other natural options are available but are likely to be less effective and should at least be applied more often. Be sure to apply repellent day and night. Dengue fever is common in Grenada and this unpleasant flu-like viral infection is transmitted by day-biting mosquitoes – see below. Though it is difficult, try to remember that scratching your mosquito bites can result in open wounds and infections, especially in Grenada's tropical climate. Anti-itch remedies containing ammonia work well where your repellent may have failed. Most hotels will have either mosquito screens or bed nets if mosquitoes are a problem. Stand-up and ceiling fans usually deter mosquitoes at night when you are sleeping.

If you are walking in dark, damp areas of forest or beside mangrove swamps wear long, loose clothes in addition to the repellents. These days you can purchase clothes that are impregnated with permethrin, which kill mosquitoes on contact, though they can be quite expensive.

Dengue fever has been a global problem in recent times and the Caribbean has seen high levels of infection come and go in waves. Dengue is caused by a day-biting mosquito (*Aedes aegypti*). There are known to be four strains of the disease, which in most cases causes a week or two of acute unpleasantness including high fever, severe headache, and joint and muscle pains. The only way to prevent dengue fever, as there are no vaccines or tablets against the virus, is to use insect repellents containing DEET. Second or subsequent doses of dengue fever with a different strain can lead to a more serious illness called dengue haemorrhagic fever so it is best to avoid it in the first place.

Sand flies (sometimes called biting midges or no-see-ums) are members of the subfamily *Phlebotominae* and are tiny blood-sucking insects. They are attracted to warm-blooded animals and can be a nuisance on some beaches and in areas of mangrove. The small bites of the female can irritate and become inflamed if you rub or itch them. Sand flies are often roused by digging up the damp sand where the female may have laid eggs. Insect repellent containing DEET or neem helps to deter them (see box on page 21 for something you may not know about sand flies).

Biting ants Biting ants can catch the unaware traveller by very unpleasant surprise. This is usually the result of either standing and pausing on a nest accidentally or by brushing against or holding on to branches or foliage where ants are going about their business. Take care where you put your feet and hands and, if you have placed clothes or shoes on the ground, give them a good shake before putting them back on again. Ants do not usually cause or leave any permanent damage, but their bites are quite painful.

Chiggers (*Trombicula alfreddugesi*). Chiggers are known locally as *bête wouj*, and are the parasitic larvae of the harvest mite that move to the tips of leaves and grasses. When you brush against them, they migrate to your body and then spend a while rummaging around, trying to find a nice protected warm spot (often beneath the waistband of underwear or in other places you would really rather they not venture) where they pierce your skin and suck up the tissue. An extremely irritating rash appears which is caused by an allergic reaction to the

---

ROUCOU

Roucou (*Bixa orellana*), also known as annatto, rocou, ruku or uruku – depending on which part of Central America, South America or the Caribbean you come from – is a plant with a diversity of applications and an interesting history. It is a fruiting tree that grows to around 5m in height and produces prickly, heart-shaped pods each containing around 50 seeds. These seeds are coated in a reddish pigment that produces a vibrant dye. Grenada's early Amerindian settlers used this dye as a body paint and to colour crafts and fabrics. For centuries it has also been used as a medicinal plant, treating skin problems, fevers, dysentery, liver disease and even hepatitis. The plant's leaves can be used to calm the stomach and as an antiseptic. Today roucou is still used worldwide as a food colouring – often as an alternative to saffron – as well as a herbal remedy and an ingredient in skin and hair-care products.

salivary secretions of the larvae, which drop off the skin once they have had their fill of you. They leave you with the rash as a memento of their visit, however, which can develop into severe welts if you scratch them a lot or if you are particularly sensitive to having insects partying in your nether regions. Insect repellents containing DEET help to prevent them hopping aboard your body in the first place. I have also used coconut oil. It works well and is a natural alternative to the chemicals.

HARMFUL PLANTS

Manchineel The manchineel (*Hippomane mancinella*) is native to the Caribbean and Central America. Its name is derived from the Spanish word *manzanilla*, meaning 'little apple' in reference to the similarity of this tree and its fruit to an apple tree. The full Spanish name, however, is *manzanilla de la muerte*, meaning 'little apple of death'. It is a very poisonous tree and common along beaches and coastlines in the Caribbean. Growing to around 15m high, the manchineel provides natural shade from the hot sun and helps to prevent sand and soil from erosion by the sea. Unfortunately, it contains toxins which, in wet or damp weather, can cause severe skin irritation or worse. Avoid standing beneath one in the rain and please do not mistake it for an apple – it can be fatal. So long as it is dry and you do not touch the tree or its leaves, then you should be fine using it as a shade from the sun.

Zoutie The stinging or devil's nettle (*Laportea aestuans*), known locally as *zoutie*, has broad palmate leaves with tiny hairs. Touching the plant and its leaves causes inflammation, pain and severe irritation of the skin which can last a very long time. I have seen the zoutie more often on Carriacou trails than on those in Grenada, but that doesn't mean they are not there. If you are planning on doing a lot of hiking, perhaps heading off the beaten path, I suggest looking it up on Google so you can identify it.

Cow-itch Cow-itch (*Mucuna pruriens*), also known as *pwa-gaté*, is a plant that grows in dense bush and can be very difficult to spot. The plant has pods which, when dry and brown, are covered with tiny hairs that are extremely irritating if they come in contact with the skin. Again, Google it if you plan on being in the bush.

TRAVELLERS' DIARRHOEA A bout of travellers' diarrhoea can spoil a holiday so it is always wise to take basic precautions. Try to be sure water is safe to drink (tap water is usually fine in Grenada) but it is easier to use bottled water both for drinking and cleaning teeth as the mineral content of tap water alone can be enough to upset your system. Avoid food that has been left around or looks like it has been reheated – buffet meals are often the worst culprits. Food should be thoroughly cooked and served piping hot. Remember to wash your hands before eating. Avoid ice cubes and ice cream and ensure you peel any fruit yourself. If you do get diarrhoea, in most cases it will settle down after 24 hours with rest, drinking plenty of fluids and taking rehydration salts (such as Electrolade). However, if the diarrhoea comes with a fever and/or blood and/or slime then you should seek medical help immediately as antibiotics may be needed. That said, by taking sensible precautions you can minimise your chances of getting diarrhoea while still being able to eat and enjoy local foods.

PRICKLY HEAT A very itchy red skin rash known as *miliaria*, or prickly heat, is caused by sweating a lot in humid weather. In high levels of humidity, particularly in Grenada's forest interior, this can be a problem for visitors who are not used to such conditions. Dead skin cells and bacteria block sweat glands and the skin becomes inflamed. Air conditioning, cold showers, calamine lotion or, in severe cases, steroid creams can bring some relief. Aloe also helps. People suffering from prickly heat should try to avoid exerting themselves for a couple of days in order to reduce sweating and give their skin a chance to recover.

DEHYDRATION, HEAT EXHAUSTION AND HEATSTROKE A combination of high temperatures, humidity, exertion and a lack of fluids will inevitably result in dehydration, heat exhaustion and possibly even heatstroke. It is incredibly easy to become dehydrated in a tropical climate and most people do not even realise that their irritability, weariness, headaches and dizziness are actually due to a lack of water. Travellers to tropical climates frequently underestimate the volume of water they should consume to remain hydrated and healthy. It is said that exertion in the tropics requires replenishment of around three litres a day. When out walking take as much water as you can comfortably carry – at least one to two litres per person. Drink plenty of water before hiking and try to drink at regular intervals, regardless of whether you actually feel thirsty or not. Beer and carbonated soft drinks are no substitute for water when it comes to rehydrating your body.

Heat exhaustion occurs when the body's cooling system hits overdrive. Profuse sweating, pale clammy skin, fast shallow breathing, nausea, headaches, rapid weak pulse and stomach cramps are all signs of heat exhaustion. It is important to counter heat exhaustion as quickly as possible by trying to cool your body down by finding shade, taking a dip in a river or pool, drinking plenty of water and relaxing.

Heatstroke can be fatal. This occurs when the body's cooling system has collapsed completely. Skin becomes hot and red, breathing slows and confusion and dizziness can ultimately lead to unconsciousness. Cooling the body down as quickly and as effectively as possible is absolutely essential and you should seek immediate medical assistance.

SUN DAMAGE In a very short period of time the hot Caribbean sun will redden and burn your skin. Try to stay in the shade as much as you can, wear a hat, protect your skin with a sunscreen (at least SPF 15) and wear good-quality sunglasses to protect your eyes. Sun reflecting on the water can be especially damaging if you are exposed to it for too long without adequate protection. If your skin is not used to the sun, limit direct exposure as much as possible. Wearing a T-shirt to protect your back when snorkelling is also a good idea. If you absolutely must sunbathe (I know, you can't go back to work looking pale), try to limit direct exposure to 20–30 minutes and stay out of the sun during the hottest part of the day. That will easily be enough. If you can't tell if your skin is turning red, ask someone. Sunburn is not only harmful to your skin, it is very painful and can upset your holiday plans. Wearing light-coloured, loose shirts, skirts and trousers made from cotton is the best solution.

SCUBA-DIVING INJURIES Certified scuba-divers should always dive conservatively and within recreational dive limits. If you do not know what they are, or have forgotten, check with your certifying organisation. It is usually a maximum depth of 20m for up to 45 minutes. Do not dive beyond your training and avoid alcohol and strenuous activities before and immediately after dives.

Diving in Grenada is mostly easy, though some shipwrecks are in deep water and islets such as Île de Ronde have strong currents and are therefore for

LONG-HAUL FLIGHTS, CLOTS AND DVT

Any prolonged immobility including travel by land or air can result in deep vein thrombosis (DVT) with the risk of an embolus going to the lungs. Certain factors can increase the risk and these include:

- Previous clot or close relative with a history
- People over 40 but increased risk over 80 years
- Recent major operation or varicose veins surgery
- Cancer
- Stroke
- Heart disease
- Obesity
- Pregnancy
- Hormone therapy
- Heavy smokers
- Severe varicose veins
- People who are very tall (over 6ft/1.8m) or short (under 5ft/1.5m)

A deep vein thrombosis causes painful swelling and redness of the calf or sometimes the thigh. It is only dangerous if a clot travels to the lungs (pulmonary embolus). Symptoms of a pulmonary embolus (PE) include chest pain, shortness of breath, and sometimes coughing up small amounts of blood, and commonly start three to ten days after a long flight. Anyone who thinks that they might have a DVT needs to see a doctor immediately.

PREVENTION OF DVT
- Keep mobile before and during the flight; move around every couple of hours
- Drink plenty of fluids during the flight
- Avoid taking sleeping pills and drinking excessive tea, coffee and alcohol
- Consider wearing flight socks or support stockings (see www.legshealth.com)

If you think you are at increased risk of a clot, ask your doctor if it is safe to travel.

experienced divers only. Be sure to dive with a reputable operation, stay with your buddy or the dive master, maintain good buoyancy and always check depth and no-decompression limits.

Decompression sickness can be avoided by ensuring you always dive conservative profiles, ascending slowly, looking and listening for boat traffic, and making safety stops at 5m. Signs and symptoms of decompression sickness include tingling or numbness in extremities, aching joints, rashes, headaches, dizziness and nausea. Request 100% pure oxygen and seek medical assistance. Decompression sickness can be fatal and, while the most severe symptoms become apparent within the first two hours of surfacing, problems can emerge up to 24 hours after diving. Allow dive crew to help and advise you as they are trained in dive emergencies.

Grenada does not have its own recompression chamber. Should a diver require emergency recompression treatment, he or she will be evacuated by a

30-minute low-level flight to either Trinidad or Barbados. It is always a sensible precaution to take out dive insurance to cover the cost of any evacuation and emergency recompression treatments that may be required. They can be very expensive.

St George's General Hospital ☎ 473 440 2051. Ambulance crews are trained in dealing with emergencies.

Divers Alert Network (DAN) Americas ☎ +1 919 684 9111 for diving emergencies. For information go to www.diversalertnetwork.org.

AQUATIC-LIFE INJURIES Whether scuba-diving, snorkelling or just having fun in the sea, it is always possible to pick up an injury from aquatic life. Grenada's seas are safe, though there are sharks patrolling the formations and shipwrecks that lie in deeper waters. Most aquatic injuries tend to come from contact with sea urchins or small jellyfish. Sea urchins are bottom-dwellers, usually found around rocks in the shallows. They have sharp spines that can pierce the skin of a foot that stands on them or arms that brush against them. Typically the tips of the spines break off and embed themselves under the skin. This can be very painful and if not treated may cause an infection. It is prudent to seek medical assistance if you are unsure. Contact with small jellyfish can result in a small but painful sting. Rubbing makes it worse. If possible remove any visible traces of tentacles with tweezers (not with your fingers, as the tentacles still retain their sting) and douse the affected area with white vinegar.

SEXUALLY TRANSMITTED DISEASES Unprotected sex is risky in any part of the world and Grenada is no exception. The official incidence of HIV infection is relatively low, however, discrimination and the stigma attached to the disease may mean that reported cases do not reflect the true picture. Common sense and caution is the best advice. If you must indulge, use condoms or femidoms, which help reduce the risk of transmission – these are best bought from home to ensure the quality. If you notice any genital ulcers or discharge, get treatment promptly since these increase the risk of acquiring HIV. If you do have unprotected sex, visit a clinic as soon as possible; this should be within 24 hours, or no later than 72 hours, for post-exposure prophylaxis.

TRAVEL CLINICS AND HEALTH INFORMATION A full list of current travel clinic websites worldwide is available on www.istm.org. For other journey preparation information, consult www.nathnac.org/ds/map_world.aspx. Information about various medications may be found on www.netdoctor.co.uk/travel.

UK
Berkeley Travel Clinic 32 Berkeley St, London W1J 8EL (near Green Park tube station); ☎ 020 7629 6233; ⊕ 10.00–18.00 Mon–Fri, 10.00–15.00 Sat.
CityDoc 42 Wimpole St, London W1G 8YF; ☎ 0207 935 6260; 16 City Rd, London EC1Y 2AA; ☎ 0207 256 8668; www.moorgatemd.co.uk; both clinics ⊕ 09.00–18.00 Mon–Fri, 10.00–15.00 Sat. Walk in or same day travel clinic appointments. Vaccinations & travel advice.

The Travel Clinic Ltd, Cambridge 41 Hills Rd, Cambridge CB2 1NT; ☎ 01223 367362; e enquiries@travelclinic.ltd.uk; www.travelcliniccambridge.co.uk; ⊕ 10.00–16.30 Mon & Fri, 10.00–16.00 Tue & Sat, 12.00–18.30 Wed & Thu.
The Travel Clinic Ltd, Ipswich Gilmour Piper, 10 Fonnereau Rd, Ipswich IP1 3JP; ☎ 01223 367362; ⊕ 09.00–16.30 Mon, 09.00–17.30 Wed, 10.00–17.30 Fri.
Edinburgh Travel Health Clinic 14 East Preston St, Newington, Edinburgh EH8 9QA; ☎ 0131 667

1030; www.edinburghtravelhealthclinic.co.uk; ☺ Extended hours including some evenings. Travel vaccinations.

Fleet Street Travel Clinic 29 Fleet St, London EC4Y 1AA; ☎020 7353 5678; e info@ fleetstreetclinic.com; www.fleetstreetclinic.com; ☺ 08.45–20.00 Mon–Thu, 08.45–17.30 Fri. Vaccinations & travel products.

Hospital for Tropical Diseases Travel Clinic Mortimer Market, Capper St (off Tottenham Ct Rd), London WC1E 6JB; ☎020 7387 4411; www.thehtd.org; ☺ 13.00–17.00 Wed & 09.00–13.00 Fri. Consultations are by appointment only & are only offered to those with more complex problems. Check the website for inclusions. Runs a Travellers' Healthline Advisory Service (☎020 7950 7799) for country-specific information & health hazards. Also stocks nets, water purification equipment & personal protection measures. Travellers who have returned from the tropics & are unwell, with fever or bloody diarrhoea, can attend the walk-in emergency clinic at the hospital without an appointment.

InterHealth Travel Clinic 111 Westminster Bridge Rd, London SE1 7HR; ☎020 7902 9000; e info@interhealth.org.uk; www.interhealth.org. uk; ☺ 08.30–17.30 Mon–Fri. Competitively priced, one-stop travel health service by appointment only.

MASTA pre-travel clinics ☎01276 685040; www.masta-travel-health.com/travel-clinic. aspx. Call or check the website for the nearest clinic; there are currently 50 in Britain. They also sell memory cards, treatment kits, bednets, net treatment kits, etc.

NHS travel websites www.fitfortravel.nhs.uk or www.fitfortravel.scot.nhs.uk. Provide country-by-country advice on immunisation, plus details of recent developments, & a list of relevant health organisations.

Nomad Travel Clinics Flagship store: 3–4 Wellington Terrace, Turnpike Lane, London N8 0PX; ☎020 8889 7014; e turnpike@ nomadtravel.co.uk; www.nomadtravel.co.uk; walk in or appointments ☺ 09.15–18.00 Mon, Tue, Wed & Fri, 11.45–19.30 Thu, 09.15–18.00 Sat. See website for clinics in southwest & central London, Bishops Stortford, Bristol, Loughton, Manchester & Southampton. As well as dispensing health advice, Nomad stocks mosquito nets & other anti-bug devices, & an excellent range of adventure travel gear.

Trailfinders Immunisation Centre 194 Kensington High St, London W8 7RG; ☎020 7938 3999; www.trailfinders.com/travelessentials/ travelclinic.htm; ☺ 09.00–17.00 Mon, Tue, Wed & Fri, 10.00–18.00 Thu, 10.00–17.15 Sat. No appointment necessary.

Travelpharm www.travelpharm.com. The Travelpharm website offers up-to-date guidance on travel-related health & has a range of medication & equipment available through their online store.

IRISH REPUBLIC

Tropical Medical Bureau 54 Grafton St, Dublin 2; ☎01 2715272; e graftonstreet@tmb.ie; www.tmb.ie; ☺ until 20.00 Mon–Fri & Sat mornings. For other clinic locations, & useful information specific to tropical destinations, check their website.

USA

Centers for Disease Control 1600 Clifton Rd, Atlanta, GA 30333; ☎800 232 4636 or (800) 232 6348; e cdcinfo@cdc.gov; www.cdc.gov/travel; ☺ 08.00–20.00 Mon–Fri. The central source of travel information in the USA. Each summer they publish the invaluable *Health Information for International Travel*.

IAMAT (International Association for Medical Assistance to Travelers) 1623 Military Rd #279, Niagara Falls, NY 14304-1745; ☎716 754 4883; e info@iamat.org; www.iamat.org. A non-profit organisation with free membership that provides lists of English-speaking doctors abroad.

CANADA

IAMAT 67 Mowat Ave, Suite 036, Toronto, Ontario M6K 3E3; ☎416 652 0137; www.iamat.org

TMVC Suite 106, 4180 Lougheed Hwy, Burnaby BC, V5C 6A7; ☎604 681 5656; e vancouver@tmvc. com; www.tmvc.com. One-stop medical clinic for all your international travel health & vaccination needs.

AUSTRALIA AND NEW ZEALAND

TMVC (Travel Doctors Group) ☎1300 65 88 44; www.tmvc.com.au. 30 clinics in Australia & New Zealand, including: *Auckland* Canterbury Arcade, 174 Queen St, Auckland 1010, New Zealand;

\(64) 9 373 3531; e auckland@traveldoctor.co.nz;
Brisbane 75a Astor Terrace, Spring Hill, Brisbane,
QLD 4000, Australia; \07 3815 6900; e brisbane@
traveldoctor.com.au; *Melbourne* 393 Little Bourke
St, Melbourne, Vic 3000, Australia; \(03) 9935
8100; e melbourne@traveldoctor.com.au; *Sydney*
428 George St, Sydney, NSW 2000, Australia;
\(2) 9221 7133; e sydney@traveldoctor.com.au
IAMAT 206 Papanui Rd, Christchurch 5, New
Zealand; www.iamat.org

SOUTH AFRICA
Netcare Travel Clinics \011 802 0059;
e travelinfo@netcare.co.za; www.travelclinic.
co.za. 11 clinics throughout South Africa.
TMVC NHC Health Centre, cnr Beyers Naude Dr &
Waugh Ave, Northcliff 2195; \0861 300 911;
e info@traveldoctor.co.za; www.traveldoctor.co.
za. Consult the website for clinic locations.

SAFETY

Grenada is a safe country for visitors and precautions you should take when visiting Grenada, Carriacou and Petite Martinique are no different from those you would take travelling anywhere else in the world. It is usually very safe to walk around, both by day and by night. Most people are very friendly and helpful. There are few reported incidents of visitors experiencing crime though you should apply common-sense precautions such as not flaunting wealth openly, dressing conservatively, and avoiding conflict. If approached by people asking for money, either give them a dollar or two, or politely decline and walk on. Do not lose your temper or decide to give someone a lecture. It is simply not worth it and it will ruin your day. It is not uncommon for locals to admonish people they see hounding visitors for money. If you do find yourself in a threatening situation your focus should be on getting through it as peacefully as possible and not fighting back.

If I think I may be in a spot (I have been in a few), my method is to strike first with a big smile and a hearty 'Hello! How are you doing?' I talk a lot, smile and joke. It has worked so far. If it doesn't:

Police Emergencies \911

WOMEN TRAVELLERS

Inevitably as a visitor you will attract attention – whatever your gender. You are the subject of possible friendship, a link to the world beyond the confines of life on the islands, and a potential source of income – however short term. This attention should not, however, be misinterpreted as a threat. As mentioned, Grenada is a very safe place and women travelling alone need only take the same, common-sense precautions they would at home. Certainly women travellers are generally more vulnerable to theft or unwanted attention than men, but this should not prevent you from exploring and enjoying the freedom of these beautiful islands. If you can, you should avoid going to remote places alone, both by day and by night, try to dress as conservatively as your taste in fashion will allow, and do not sunbathe topless. You could consider carrying a flashlight at night and trying to blend in as much as you can. Wearing similar clothing to local people is one way of doing this, as is not wearing ostentatious jewellery. If you do attract unwanted attention from amorous men, be as polite and good humoured as possible in the way you express your wish to be left alone. Try to extract yourself from the situation as quickly as you can, avoid conflict, resist becoming angry and do not try to humiliate or belittle those you feel are harassing you. Some recommend wearing dark sunglasses as this helps you to avoid eye contact and may also enhance your confidence.

DISABLED TRAVELLERS

Grenada is not especially disabled-traveller friendly. Many hotels do not make special provision for wheelchair access, some are located on steep slopes and have lots of steps, and public buses are predominantly the small minibus type. Nevertheless, with a little research and planning, it is possible to work your way around these obstacles.

Several of the hotels along Grand Anse Beach have hotel rooms and self-catering facilities on ground-floor level, and access to the resorts themselves is flat and just a short distance from the main road. The Grenada Grand Beach Resort, the Coyaba Beach Resort and the Spice Island Beach Resort are three examples. The Calabash at L'Anse Aux Epines is also a good option, as is Lance Epines Cottages. In terms of sightseeing, there are many private bus- and taxi-tour operators (see page 70 for a small selection) and your hotel may also be able to arrange something specific to your needs. In addition to driving tours, sites and attractions that are accessible by wheelchair include: River Antoine Rum Distillery (most parts), Belmont Estate (there is a slope, but the immediate area around the boucan, drying sheds and museum should all be fine), Concord Waterfall (viewing the first waterfall), Annandale Waterfall (the path is flat and paved most of the way) and Gouyave Fish Friday (though the streets are narrow and can be crowded). Boarding and disembarking the Osprey ferry between Grenada, Carriacou and Petite Martinique is certainly not wheelchair friendly; indeed anyone with significant manoeuvrability challenges will probably find this very difficult.

TRAVELLING WITH CHILDREN

Travelling with children is certainly not a problem in Grenada and most hotels and self-catering accommodations welcome families. Nice beaches with calm waters include Morne Rouge, L'Anse Aux Epines and Paradise Beach on Carriacou. The Grenada Grand Beach Resort is located on Grand Anse Beach and has excellent facilities for family holidays including a large 'fantasy pool', man-made waterfalls and a wide selection of adventure packages such as snorkelling, boating and kayaking. Children will enjoy the natural waterfalls at Concord and Annandale, both of which are easily accessible, and the Belmont Estate should provide lots of interest for cocoa and chocolate lovers. Other outdoor activities that are fun for families include river tubing (check minimum age limits with operators), turtle watching and hiking – the St Margaret's Falls (sometimes referred to as the Seven Sisters Falls) is a good pick and an adventure you are sure to talk about into the evening.

If you are travelling with infants you will find baby products in the Spiceland Mall in Grand Anse as well as the pharmacies in St George's (see page 99). As they are imported, they can be quite expensive, however, so you will need to balance cost with convenience when planning your trip and deciding what to bring with you from home.

GAY TRAVELLERS

The Roman Catholic church is the predominant religion on the islands and so majority views on homosexuality are in accord with church doctrine. Like many of the Caribbean islands, homosexuality in Grenada has not been decriminalised though in recent times there has been increasing international pressure to do so with aid funding tied to human rights. Grenada's homosexuals are therefore forced

2

to maintain a low profile and are unable to express their sexuality openly and without prejudice. However you choose to deal with this is your choice, of course. But you should be aware that overt displays of your sexuality will certainly draw attention, and responses will be unpredictable in nature.

WHAT TO TAKE

Grenada is only 12° from the equator and it has a hot and humid climate. Carriacou and Petite Martinique can feel particularly hot and are considerably more exposed to the sun than mainland Grenada.

You will need to bring shorts, light skirts and tops, and at least one swimming costume. Bring a hat to protect your head and sunglasses to protect your eyes from the sun. For hiking, a pair of training shoes is fine but if you prefer proper hiking footwear then try to find something that has a good grip in the wet. Hard plastic soles are not very good for this. Some hikes require river crossings or scrambles over rocks, so your choice of footwear is quite important (see box on page 78). Bring a light rain jacket. If you are staying in the interior, on the east coast or at a high elevation, take a sweater too, as it can become cool in the evenings. Lightweight trousers are also good for the evenings when mosquitoes are on the prowl.

You will need a small backpack for day trips – a waterproof one is best. Take a small first-aid kit, sunscreen, after-sun and mosquito repellent.

If you are a photographer, it is always worth bringing sufficient digital storage media with you as well as a supply of extra batteries. A waterproof bag to protect your gear in the rainforest, at waterfalls, when you are crossing rivers and on charter boats is also prudent.

The supermarkets and pharmacies of St George's and Grand Anse have a good selection of toiletries and medicines, but if you are taking prescription drugs please ensure you bring them with you.

You should not have too many difficulties with electrical appliances. The supply is 220V, 50Hz with UK-style three-pin plugs and sockets, but many hotels and self-catering accommodations have dual voltage systems, and so 110V with two-pin sockets is quite common these days. It is worth checking in advance whether your choice of accommodation offers the supply you need. With regards to electrical appliances, please remember that you are travelling to a tropical climate where heat, exposure to direct sunlight, and high levels of humidity may have a detrimental effect on sensitive equipment if it is not adequately protected. Moisture-absorbing sachets are quite inexpensive and can be placed in camera bags, backpacks and so on during your trip.

MONEY AND BUDGETING

CURRENCY Grenada's currency is the East Caribbean dollar (commonly written EC$ though officially XCD) and it has been fixed to the US dollar at a rate of US$1 = EC$2.7 since 1979. Notes come in denominations of EC$100, EC$50, EC$20, EC$10 and EC$5. Coins come in denominations of EC$1, EC$2, and then 50, 25, 10, 5, 2 and 1 cents. In addition to Grenada's dependencies, the East Caribbean dollar is also the official currency of Anguilla, Antigua and Barbuda, Dominica, St Kitts and Nevis, St Lucia, Montserrat, and St Vincent. It is issued by the Eastern Caribbean Central Bank, which is based in St Kitts and Nevis.

US dollars are widely accepted throughout Grenada and visitors will usually be quoted prices in both EC and US dollars.

Travellers' cheques can be exchanged at the main banks and in most of the larger hotels. ATMs can be found at Maurice Bishop International Airport, in St George's, Grand Anse, Grenville, Gouyave and Sauteurs. You will also find ATMs in Hillsborough and Tyrrel Bay, Carriacou. Most stores, hotels, restaurants and tour operators accept all major credit cards though some do not accept American Express. Market vendors, independent guides, taxi drivers, water taxis and ferries will all expect to be paid in cash.

BANKS Banks are open 08.00–14.00 Monday to Thursday and 08.00–16.00 Friday. They are closed on Saturdays, Sundays and public holidays. You will find banks with ATMs in most of the following locations:

First Caribbean International Bank
Carriacou Main St, Hillsborough; ✆473 443 7232
Grand Anse Grand Anse Rd ✆473 444 1184
Grenville Victoria St; ✆473 442 7220
St George's Church St; ✆473 440 3232

Grenada Co-operative Bank
Carriacou Main St, Hillsborough; ✆473 443 6385
Grand Anse Spiceland Mall; ✆473 440 2111
Grenville Victoria St; ✆473 442 7748
Sauteurs Main St; ✆473 442 9247
St George's Church St; ✆473 440 2111

RBTT Bank
Grand Anse Grand Anse Rd ✆473 444 4919

Grenville Victoria St; ✆473 438 0880
St George's Halifax St; ✆473 440 3521

Republic Bank
Carriacou Main St, Hillsborough; ✆473 443 7289
Grand Anse Maurice Bishop Highway; ✆473 444 2265
Gouyave Central Depradine St; ✆473 444 8353
Grenville Victoria St; ✆473 442 7618
Sauteurs Main St; ✆473 442 1045
St George's Melville St; ✆473 440 3566

Scotiabank
Grand Anse Grand Anse Rd ✆473 444 1917
Grenville Victoria St; ✆473 442 5507
St George's Halifax St; ✆473 440 3274

MONEY TRANSFERS There are **Western Union** and **Moneygram** agents in St George's (Bruce St and Carenage), Grand Anse, Gouyave, Grenville, Sauteurs, and Hillsborough on Carriacou.

BUDGETING As Grenada's southwest peninsula is the hub of tourist activity, accommodation and dining, this region tends to be a little more expensive than elsewhere. Nevertheless, Grenada offers a wide variety of options and, with a bit of planning, you should easily find something that suits your taste and budget. Outlined below are some basic tips for two people.

Low budget You can find guesthouse or self-catering accommodation for as little as US$50–75 per night, even in the more touristy south. For dining, you should eat local, heading for the snackettes and local eateries that serve traditional Grenadian dishes. Here you can get a decent meal for US$10–15. For around US$5–10, fish, vegetable or chicken roti is always a great filler if your stomach is beginning to rumble. To see the sights, avoid organised excursions and be independent. The bus system is excellent and great value for money (see pages 52–3).

Medium budget For between US$75 and US$150 per night, your options are plentiful; there are some comfortable places to stay both on mainland Grenada as well as on Carriacou. You should still try to eat at local eateries whenever you can, though you could splash out on the occasional meal in one of the fancier international restaurants. Blend organised tours with independent travel and combine buses with car rental. Try to include Carriacou in your plans. The Osprey ferry is quite cheap, the mail boat even more so (see page 39), as is no-frills bed-and-breakfast accommodation.

High budget Many of Grenada's mid- to high-end hotels and self-catering villas charge between US$150 and US$250 per night in the peak season, based on double occupancy. Sit back and enjoy an organised excursion, splash out on a nice meal or two, or rent a vehicle for a more independent holiday. Villa accommodation is a good option. Consider a yachting day charter and be sure to include Carriacou in your plans.

Luxury budget Grenada has some extremely luxurious hotels, resorts and private villas and the amount of money you could spend would appear almost limitless. If you don't flinch at rates from US$500-$2,000 per night, you should certainly consider staying at the Spice Island Beach Resort, Maca Bana Villas, Laluna, Mount Cinnamon, or the lavish La Source where you can treat yourself to an all-inclusive

CATCHING THE RIGHT BUS

On the windscreen of each bus you will see a number and a list of some of the places the bus will pass along the route. Each number refers to a designated zone. Within each zone there may be slight variations to the routes. The names on the windscreen help you to understand which route the bus will take so check them to ensure your bus is going where you want to go. If in doubt, simply ask. The route designations are as follows, with the final destination (and therefore turnaround point) in italic:

Zone 1 St George's–Lagoon Road–Grand Anse–*Calliste*–Grand Anse–Lagoon Road–St George's

Zone 1 St George's–Belmont–Grand Anse–*Calliste*–Grand Anse–Belmont–St George's

Zone 2 St George's–Springs–Woodlands–*Woburn*–Woodlands–Springs–St George's

Zone 2 St George's–Calivigny–Westerhall–*Grenville*–Westerhall–Calivigny–St George's

Zone 3 St George's–Richmond Hill–Morne Jaloux–*Marian*–Morne Jaloux–Richmond Hill–St George's

Zone 4 St George's–St Paul's–Perdmontemps–*Vincennes*–Perdmontemps–St Paul's–St George's

Zone 4 St George's–Beaton–La Tante–Pomme Rose–*Grenville*–Pomme Rose–La Tante–Beaton–St George's

Zone 4 St George's–St Paul's–*Mardigras*–St Paul's–St George's

Zone 4 St George's–St Paul's–*La Borie*–St Paul's–St George's

Zone 5 St George's–Grand Roy–Gouyave–*Victoria*–Gouyave–Grand Roy–St George's

and riotously self-indulgent pampering. Dine out at Rhodes', Oliver's, the Beach House, and Laluna, and charter a sailing boat for a few days' cruising around Carriacou and the southern Grenadines.

GETTING AROUND

Getting around Grenada, Carriacou and Petite Martinique is relatively straightforward. The public transport system of buses is very efficient and inexpensive and taxis are widely available. Without doubt the most convenient and flexible way to explore the islands, however, is by rental car. Both Grenada and Carriacou have a good selection of car-hire firms.

BY BUS Grenada has an excellent bus system. It is very convenient, affordable and extremely reliable. The only real downside is that many buses tend to stop operating after around 19.00 on most days and are very scarce on Sundays.

The bus system is straightforward. Almost all bus routes start and finish at the bus terminus on Melville Street. The terminus is very easy to find. It is a busy

Zone 5 St George's–Gouyave–Victoria–*Sauteurs*–Victoria–Gouyave–St George's

Zone 5 St George's–Concord–Grand Roy–*Gouyave*–Grand Roy–Concord–St George's

Zone 6 St George's–Grand Etang–Birch Grove–*Grenville*–Birch Grove–Grand Etang–St George's

Zone 7 St George's–Annandale–New Hampshire–*Willis*–New Hampshire–Annandale–St George's

Zone 7 St George's–Beaulieu–Boca–*Vendôme*–Boca–Beaulieu–St George's

Zone 7 St George's–River Road–Tempe–*Mt Parnassus*–Tempe–River Road–St George's

Zone 8 St George's–Cherry Hill–Fontenoy–*Happy Hill*–Fontenoy–Cherry Hill–St George's

Zone 8 St George's–Cherry Hill–Fontenoy–*Mt Moritz*–Fontenoy–Cherry Hill–St George's

Zone 8 St George's–Happy Hill–Beauséjour–*Brizan*–Beauséjour–Happy Hill–St George's

Zone 9 Sauteurs–Rose Hill–Mt Rose–River Sallee–*Grenville*–River Sallee–Mt Rose–Rose Hill–Sauteurs

Zone 9 Sauteurs–Hermitage–Tivoli–*Grenville*–Tivoli–Hermitage–Sauteurs

Zone 10 Hillsborough–Lauriston–L'Esterre–Harvey Vale–*Belmont*–Harvey Vale–L'Esterre–Lauriston–Hillsborough

Zone 11 Hillsborough–Bogles–Dover–*Windward*–Dover–Bogles–Hillsborough

Zone 12 Hillsborough–Top Hill–Mt Pleasant–*Grand Bay*–Mt Pleasant–Top Hill–Hillsborough

and noisy place, yet deceptively well organised, with droves of buses seeming to arrive and depart in an orderly fashion. The buses are the minibus variety and can be identified by the prefix H on their number plate as well as the route number and destinations printed on the front windscreen (see box on page 52 for route details). Many drivers also have their own colourful slogans, nicknames or mottos plastered on both front and rear windows. Some bus drivers may be accompanied by a 'conductor' who makes appeals to potential passengers and collects money. Where there is no conductor simply pay the driver at the end of your trip. Catching a bus is great value for money and fares will rarely top EC$10. Here is a sample of typical adult bus fares: St George's to Grenville EC$6.50; St George's to La Sagesse EC$4; St George's to Grand Etang EC$5; St George's to Crochu EC$4.50; St George's to Gouyave EC$6; Grenville to Sauteurs EC$4.50, Hillsborough to L'Esterre EC$2.50.

There is an 'off-route' system that takes in the beaches, hotels and bays of the southwest peninsula and is a little more expensive. For example, the bus fare from St George's to La Source or the Aquarium restaurant is EC$15; to True Blue, L'Anse aux Epines and Point Salines International Airport the fare is EC$10.

In Carriacou, the buses follow the same system, beginning and ending their routes at the terminus in Hillsborough. There are no buses on Petite Martinique.

BY TAXI Grenada's taxi drivers are licensed by the government and should prominently display their official credentials. The price of journeys from Maurice Bishop International Airport are fixed but in other places you should agree the fare before getting into the taxi. Many taxi drivers will also offer island tours, and fares are negotiable. Be sure you are clear on the fare before you set off and that you know whether the dollar price quoted is US or EC. If you have any complaints regarding taxi services in Grenada, or if you would like more information, please contact the **Grenada Taxi Association** office (℡ 473 440 6850) located on Wharf Road on the southeastern tip of the Carenage in St George's.

CAR HIRE You have a good choice of car-hire companies in Grenada and Carriacou. The most common cars are small 4x4 vehicles. Prices vary according to car type and season but are on average between US$50 and US$70 per day with discounted rates usually offered for longer periods. Collision damage waiver is often an additional cost – please ask. Many hire companies offer free drop-off and pick-up at the airport and hotels. Check the car over very carefully before signing your rental agreement. Look for scratches and bumps, test lights and brakes, examine tyre tread and make sure any bodywork defects are properly recorded. If the vehicle has poor tyre tread, request replacements. If the car handles poorly when driven, return it and request a replacement straight away. Do not settle for something that feels or looks wrong. Grenada has very steep and winding roads, some along high cliffs. If you are exploring the interior, you may also have to drive along rough, perhaps muddy vehicle tracks. Be sure you are happy with your car before driving off.

The Grenada government requires the purchase of a visitor's temporary driving licence. This costs EC$30 or US$12 for a three-month licence and is either obtained from the car-hire company itself or from a local police station (if the latter is the case the rental company will take you there). In order to hire a car and purchase a visitor's licence, you must be able to present either your domestic or international driving licence, so make sure you bring it on holiday with you.

Here is a selection of car-hire companies. This list is by no means comprehensive.

Grenada

Archies Auto Rental ✆473 439 0086; www.archierentals.com

Azar's Auto Rentals ✆473 439 2911; www.azarsrentals.com

B-Parkey's Car Rental ✆473 439 4311; www.b-parkeyscarrental.com

B Thomas & Sons ✆473 439 3309; www.bthomasandsons.com

Dabs Car Rentals ✆473 444 4116; www.dabscarrentals.com

David's Car Rental ✆473 444 4091; www.davidscars.com

Gabriel's Rental & Taxi Service ✆473 443 2304; www.gabrental.com

Grenada Car Rental ✆473 443 0600; www.drivegrenada.com

Indigo Car Rentals Ltd ✆473 439 3300; www.indigocarsgrenada.com

J&B Auto Rentals ✆473 405 4889; www.jandbautorentals.com

Maitlands Car & Jeep Rentals ✆473 444 4022; www.maitlandsrentals.com

Reggie's Car Rental ✆473 440 6374; www.reggierental.com

Sanvics Jeep & Car Rentals Ltd St George's; ✆473 439 4123; www.sanvics.com

Vista Rentals ✆473 439 8105; www.vistarentalsgnd.com

Y&R Car Rentals ✆473 444 4448; www.carrentalgrenada.com

Carriacou

Ade's Dream ✆473 443 7317; e adesdea@ spiceisle.com; www.adesdream.com

Carriacou Auto Rentals & Sales (CARS) ✆473 443 8307; e info@carsgrenada.com; www.carsgrenada.com

Sunkey's Auto Rentals ✆473 443 8382; e sunkeywp@yahoo.com; www.sandx.net

Waynes Auto Rentals ✆473 443 6120; e waynesautorentals@yahoo.com

Driving in Grenada, Carriacou and Petite Martinique

Driving in Grenada, Carriacou and Petite Martinique is on the left. Roads are generally good, though they are occasionally narrow with sharp, blind corners and very steep precipices. Exercise caution and keep your speed low. If you are approaching a blind corner on a narrow road be sure to hit your horn to let anyone coming the other way know you are there. Do not be shy about it. Beeping horns is like a language in Grenada (you will have fun trying to figure it out) and it may prevent a nasty surprise. There are not too many pot-holes on Grenada's roads, but look out for them just in case. During your stay there will inevitably be a vehicle (or several) right up against your rear bumper trying to pass. Usually this will be a bus. Let vehicles pass you rather than allow them to influence your speed, even if it means slowing down and pulling over. Do not race or be stubborn or macho about it. Keep it slow and relaxed, be alert for the unexpected, breathe deeply and leave your road rage at home. There is no point in letting a silly driving incident spoil your holiday.

WATER TAXI An interesting, fun and often quite wet way to either explore or simply get from A to B is to take a water taxi. A ride on one of these colourfully painted wooden motorboats can cost as little as US$2 or as much as US$100; it all depends on where and how far you would like to go. During the cruise-ship season water taxis make frequent runs between the cruise-ship terminal and Grand Anse Beach. Simply follow the signs to the water taxis in the Esplanade shopping mall. Prices are usually on a per-person basis. They also operate from the Carenage in St George's.

Water taxis may also take you further afield to other beaches or to offshore islands. Some of these trips may include a spot of fishing and a barbecue on the beach. They can be great fun. Many hotels can set you up with water taxis that they recommend. Alternatively you can simply look for one and negotiate. Very few actually advertise, however.

In Carriacou water taxis can take you to Sandy Island, White Island, Petite

Martinique, or even further afield to places like the Tobago Cays, five beautiful desert islands that belong to St Vincent and which were a location for the film *Pirates of the Caribbean*.

HITCHING Hitching a ride is common in Grenada and, if your budget is very tight, or if buses do not operate along your planned route, it is an inexpensive way to get around. You will often see people trying to get a ride, especially on Sundays and in the evenings when fewer buses operate. Hitching may involve long waits, of course, sometimes in heavy downpours, but together with travelling by bus, it is a nice way to meet local people and experience a part of their lives and their island that may not be possible in other circumstances.

ACCOMMODATION

The accommodation available in Grenada, Carriacou and Petite Martinique reflects the diversity of the country's visitors. For those seeking comfort and elegance, there are a number of excellent, award-winning luxury resorts and boutique hotels that offer extremely high-quality accommodation, dining and services. Many offer all-inclusive packages that include meals, excursions and a range of activities such as golf and watersports. If you are travelling in a little less luxury, mid-range hotels are numerous, conveniently located and usually of a very high standard. For the budget traveller, there are plenty of guesthouses and moderately priced hotels. You may also wish to consider homestays (see box above).

Grenada also has a wide range of self-catering options, from stylish, luxury villas, to beachside apartments, cottages and summer homes. There are currently no campsites on any of the three islands.

All accommodation charges are subject to a government tax of 10% and many establishments may also add their own 10–15% service charge. Before booking your accommodation, be sure you understand whether rates quoted include or exclude these taxes.

Much of Grenada's accommodation is located on the southern coastlines of the main island. If you plan on seeing and experiencing more of Grenada than the beautiful white-sand beach outside your room, you may wish to consider staying in two or three places during your holiday, including Carriacou which is well worth visiting for more than just a day.

Note: the accommodation listed in this guide is deliberately selective and by no means comprehensive. Price codes quoted are current at the time of writing and are based on double occupancy per room per night during the peak season, or roughly the equivalent for self-catering accommodation with weekly rates, unless stated otherwise. Please be aware that these price codes are meant as guides only and are subject to change, see box above for details.

✗ EATING AND DRINKING

Archaeologists and anthropologists believe Grenada's original settlers would have survived on a diet of local seafood and animals they brought with them in their canoes as they moved north along the Lesser Antillean island chain from South America. As time passed they would have cultivated crops such as sweet potatoes, yams and cassava. European settlers brought bananas, breadfruit, mangoes, plantain, cocoa, sugar and spices, and their west African slaves would have combined all these ingredients to make simple one-pot soups or stews that were heavily seasoned and cooked over open fires.

Caribbean Creole is a culinary style that emerged from the heritage of islands during European occupation and the slave trade. Those islands that continued to have a strong French influence after emancipation would have developed French Creole cuisine. Other islands, such as Grenada, where stronger influences came from indentured East Indian immigrants, Trinidad and Tobago, and the British plantocracy, would have taken a slightly different path and developed their own unique style of Caribbean Creole cooking.

Today, traditional Grenadian cuisine still includes many customary ingredients and is often cooked outside, over an open fire, and in a single pot. You will find authentic, great tasting and very reasonably priced local dishes in many of the islands' smaller and sometimes more remote eateries and roadside snackettes. World-class international dining has become a by-product of Grenada's burgeoning tourism industry, with its luxury resorts, hotels and sailing regattas. Visitors will find a good selection of restaurants offering various culinary styles and fine-dining experiences that suit all pockets and tastes, including, of course, traditional Grenadian.

LOCAL DISHES Grenada's national dish is called **oil-down**. It is a simple, one-pot dish that is often cooked over an open fire or on a traditional coal pot. Typically its ingredients include a combination of provisions such as breadfruit, yams, tannia, green bananas and dasheen, flavoured with meat such as pork or beef, and then cooked in coconut milk and spices until the liquid boils right down to leave only an oily residue remaining. Both international and local restaurants offer oil-down occasionally on the menu, though it is usually eaten as a picnic or festival dish

Some of the exotic fresh fruits and vegetables you may come across on your visit to Grenada:

Ackee Related to the lychee and toxic when immature or overripe, the ackee is commonly grown and eaten in Jamaica, often fried with salt fish.

Bluggo Related to the banana and plantain, usually cooked before it is eaten.

Breadfruit A large round fruit with white flesh that is sometimes fried in butter or served in a salad.

Calalou/Dasheen A small, starchy tuber, usually eaten like a potato. The leaves, known as calalou, are eaten like spinach or made into a soup.

Carambola Also called star fruit or 'five finger'; it is usually eaten as a fruit or blended as a juice.

Christophene A pear-like green-skinned squash, usually eaten boiled or fried as a vegetable.

Golden apple (*pomme-sité*) A very common fruit in Grenada, either eaten as a fruit, pickled when still green or, more commonly, blended to make a very refreshing juice.

Green banana Confusingly referred to as 'figs', but actually unripe bananas, usually boiled and eaten as a provision. They are a common ingredient in oil-down.

Guava The original Arawakan name for this scented fruit which is eaten raw, turned into jam or blended as a juice.

Noni A fruit with a very pungent odour when ripe (hence the name 'vomit fruit' in some countries). Considered medicinal, it is either eaten as a fruit or blended as a drink.

Okra Long, crisp green pods, often used as a flavouring for stews and soups. Also eaten parboiled and fried.

Passionfruit A round yellow fruit with soft sweet pulp, usually blended for juice.

Pawpaw Also called papaya, with an elongated shape, yellow when ripe and eaten as a fruit. Green, unripe pawpaw is sometimes used in salads or pickles.

Plantain A type of banana that is either fried or boiled and eaten as a provision.

Sapodilla A round fruit with reddish brown skin, its fleshy pulp is often used to make custard or ice cream.

Sorrell A member of the hibiscus family, it is a plant with edible flowers which are usually brewed as a tea or blended for juice, traditionally at Christmas time.

Soursop A large green ovoid fruit with soft spines and tart, white flesh which is sweetened to make juice or ice cream. A sweet version (sweetsop) can be eaten as a fruit.

Sweet potato Not a yam, and not a potato. Actually belonging to the bindweed family, this elongated vegetable has a sweet flavour and is often boiled, roasted or mashed.

Tamarind (*Tambrand*) This tree has a segmented pod with a reddish brown shell. The inner pulp is very bitter and is mixed with sugar to make tamarind balls, a popular confectionery.

Tannia A small, starchy tuber, usually eaten like a potato.

Yam A large tuber which is boiled, fried or roasted as a provision. It is a common ingredient in oil-down.

Average price of a main course:

$$$	Fine dining	Often more than EC$75
$$	Mid-priced and casual	Somewhere between EC$25 and EC$75
$	Cheap as chips	Less than or around EC$25

outdoors. Another very traditional dish with coconut as a key ingredient is **cou-cou**. This dish is thought to have its roots in west Africa and is made from cornmeal flour, seasonings and coconut milk. The ingredients are mixed in a large pot over a stove or open fire and continuously stirred, or 'turned', until the mixture thickens. It is often eaten with fish and in Carriacou traditionally blended with pigeon peas.

Calalou is frequently used to describe dasheen, a ground provision whose young leaves are cooked as a vegetable similar to spinach, or alternatively as the basis of calalou soup, a very common Caribbean Creole dish. Calalou soup is often served with crab and is a seasonal speciality. Land crabs are also used in the preparation of another favourite dish, **crab backs**. The crab's flesh is mixed with a combination of spices and seasonings and then stuffed back into the shell, sprinkled with breadcrumbs and baked in a hot oven.

Given Grenada's strong fishing heritage, seafood features prominently in local cuisine. **Lambie** is the queen conch (*Strombus gigas*) and has been eaten in Grenada ever since the first settlers landed there. It is a seasonal dish and is usually served stewed, fried, curried, or in a Creole sauce. The discarded, cleaned and polished conch shell is often sold in souvenir and gift shops and is also traditionally blown by fish vendors to let people know their catch is for sale. Conch is found in shallow waters with sandy beds and caught by free divers. According to conservationists, conch is the victim of overfishing throughout the Caribbean. **Titiwi** is a juvenile goby that is caught in nets at the mouths of rivers at certain times of the year. The fish are eaten whole, usually in a seasoned fritter, often known as a titiwi cake or titiwi ackra. Fish caught by local fishermen and also common in local cuisine are tuna, bonito, marlin (known locally as *ocean gar*), flying fish, jacks, and dorado, also known by many as *mahi-mahi* or *dolphin fish*, and by locals simply as *dolphin*. Lobster is a seasonal catch and many restaurants will offer it on their menus. A great place to try out some lobster or other delicious local fish dishes is at **Gouyave's Fish Friday** which is held every Friday evening from around 19.00 in the heart of the town (see page 146).

The influence of East India is evident in curried food, such as curried goat, as well as the very popular **roti**. The latter is a dish made of a flat bread that is stuffed with a mixture of curried vegetables, chicken or fish. It is an inexpensive and tasty dish that is very filling. Roti connoisseurs should note that quite a number of local eateries in Grenada may serve chicken rotis with bones. You may therefore wish to ask before you order.

Vegetarians should have few problems finding good food to eat in Grenada. As well as a number of vegetarian eateries, many restaurants will have vegetarian options on the menu. Rice and peas, fried plantain, roasted breadfruit, boiled or stewed provisions, grilled corn, pumpkin soup and calalou are all common local dishes.

LOCAL DRINKS
Non-alcoholic Tap water is safe to drink on all three islands though most supermarkets, convenience stores and hotels will sell bottled water. **Glenelg Natural**

2

The high tourist season also coincides with the hunting season. This is why you see so many lobsters offered on restaurant menus. What you may not see quite so often, but which you may come across in more rural areas of Grenada, are 'bush meats', which are animals that have been hunted during this season and are considered delicacies by much of the local population. Bush meat can include the armadillo, also known as *tatu* (see page 7), the manicou (see page 7), iguana (see page 8), and even the mona monkey (see page 7). Other animals eaten only during the official hunting season include crayfish and sea turtles.

Spring Water is Grenada's local product, and is available island-wide. **Mauby** is the name of a drink that is made from the bark of the mauby tree (*Colubrina elliptica*). The bark is boiled with spices and sweetened with sugar to produce a concentrated syrup that is diluted with cold water. The drink is an acquired taste and can be a little bitter.

Freshly made **fruit juices** are widely available in Grenada and your choice is usually based on what is in season. Golden apple, mango, pineapple, guava, passionfruit, orange and grapefruit are all common juices and are very refreshing.

Alcoholic The signature drinks of the Caribbean are **rum** and **rum punch**, and Grenada is no exception. With three distilleries producing a range of high-quality rums, connoisseurs are quite spoiled for choice. **Clarke's Court Estate** produces a great range of blended rums and rum punches including the very popular Old Grog. **Westerhall Estate** also has a nice selection of blended rums, including its fabled Jack Iron. The **River Antoine Estate** is an amazing place. One of the oldest distilleries in the Caribbean, it claims to have been working non-stop since the 18th century and is still using the same machinery and processes. Pure cane rum is produced from the sugarcane that is cultivated on its own estate. Its Rivers rums are also a very popular range (see page 188 for more on the River Antoine Estate). **Carib** is Grenada's local lager beer and is brewed in the southwest, near Grand Anse.

EATING OUT Grenada has a wide selection of dining options ranging from cheap-and-cheerful roadside snackettes to high-class restaurants offering haute international and Caribbean Creole cuisine. Most snackettes and local eateries are very similarly priced as are the majority of restaurants. Instead of including sample dinner prices in this guide, I have used a simple code that you can use as a broad guide to eating out. Check menus to see if prices include government sales tax (15%) and an optional service charge.

Most restaurants are open daily and you can usually just turn up. Some are very popular, however, and I recommend you either pass by or call in advance to avoid disappointment, especially in the high season. Save for roadside snackettes, you can pay by credit or debit cards at most restaurants.

PUBLIC HOLIDAYS AND EVENTS

January New Year's Day (1 January). Also taking place during this month are the Port Louis Grenada Sailing Festival (see page 81) and the Spice Island Billfish Tournament (see page 74).

On your travels through the islands you will undoubtedly come across snackettes and rum shops. Either along a main road or hidden away in village backstreets these colourful establishments can be found throughout the Caribbean. Often fairly makeshift affairs and frequented by local men rather than women, snackettes and rum shops sell cheap eats such as bakes, fried chicken and fish, roasted plantain or corn. They are usually licensed to sell alcohol and most will have a good selection of rum. In remote villages a snackette frequently doubles as a general store selling rudimentary foodstuffs and household essentials. Your presence at one will no doubt create a surprise and you may find yourself engaged in all kinds of interesting conversations, but they will usually be very friendly, warm and welcoming, if perhaps a little drunken. Snackettes are a good place to get a cheap bite to eat and a drink along with an opportunity to engage with local people.

February Independence Day (7 February). The Carriacou Carnival takes place on the Monday and Tuesday before Ash Wednesday. The South Grenada Regatta (see page 81) is hosted by Le Phare Bleu Marina.

March If Ash Wednesday falls in March, look out for the Carriacou Carnival during this month.

April Good Friday and Easter Monday. The Carriacou Maroon Festival takes place during the month of April (see page 207).

May Labour Day (1 May) and Whit Monday.

June Corpus Christi and Whit Monday. Fisherman's Birthday is celebrated in Gouyave on 29 June (see page 141).

July This month sees the build-up to Grenada's carnival celebrations and is also when the Carriacou Regatta takes place (see page 81).

August Emancipation Day is celebrated on the first Monday of August. This is also the month of the Grenada Carnival with Carnival Monday (J'Ouvert and Carnival Pageant) and Carnival Tuesday (Parade of Bands), both public holidays. Carnival celebrations also encompass the National Soca Monarch final, the Miss Spicy Grenada Queen Show, and the Rainbow City Festival, which takes place in Grenville.

September Most people spend September recovering from carnival celebrations but, if you are still in the mood, you can check out the Grenada Culinary Fest.

October Thanksgiving Day is on 25 October and celebrates the US and Caribbean military intervention of 1983 (see page 18).

November No public events.

December Christmas Day (25 December) and Boxing Day (26 December). Also taking place around Christmas time is the Carriacou Parang Festival (see page 207).

SHOPPING

The majority of shops in Grenada are located in the capital, St George's, and in the southwest peninsula around Grand Anse where there are two popular shopping malls. You should be able to find what you are looking for as most of the shops and pharmacies in St George's and Grand Anse are well stocked and diverse. This includes essentials such as baby foods, nappies and sanitary products as well as toiletries, medicines and prescription drugs. You will also find a number of shops

Practical Information SHOPPING

2

When visiting new places it is always nice, and extremely worthwhile, to support small businesses, artisans and cottage industries through the purchase of original products that are made locally, often by hand. Here is a small selection of some of Grenada's excellent local products. Please look out for them.

Amba Kaila Excellent homemade jams, jellies, hot pepper sauce, essences and concentrates. Look out for the Amba Kaila craftshop in Constantine, just south of the turn-off to Annandale Waterfall.

Arawak Islands (*www.arawak-islands.com*) Perfumes, sweets, gifts, soaps, body oils, candles, balms and much more.

Barguna Enterprises Ltd Alcoholic wines flavoured with *bois bandé*, ginger, lemon grass, almond and spice (cinnamon). Try the Tibli Grog, known as the 'under-the-counter rum'. Also look out for Kay, Spice Isle herbal and fruit tea.

Belinde Crafts Very original hand-made stuffed dolls.

Belzeb (*www.belzeb.net*) A cottage industry producing body and bath oils, lotions and scrubs, soaps, neem insect repellents, and teas – all from natural ingredients.

De La Grenade Industries Ltd (*www.delagrenade.com*) Award-winning nutmeg products containing no colours or artificial preservatives, including De La Grenade liqueur, Morne Delice nutmeg jam and jelly, Morne Delice nutmeg syrup, De La Grenade guava jam and jelly, hot pepper sauce, pepper jelly, orange and grapefruit marmalade, seamoss, rum punch and mauby syrup (see also page 168).

Fidel Productions (*www.fidelproductions.com*) Excellent original T-shirts, *mojo* jewellery, and other crafts from Paradise Beach (L'Esterre), Carriacou. You will find Fidel products in various craft and souvenir stores in St George's, Port Louis Marina, and Grand Anse.

Grenada Chocolate Company (*www.grenadachocolate.com*) From tree to bar, delicious organic chocolate from Hermitage and Belmont. Available island-wide. See page 190 for more information

Kato Charles Folk Art (*www.facebook.com/katocharlesart*) Carriacou-based artisan producing original fabric wall art, friendship bracelets and Rasta rag baskets. See box on page 215.

Moses Essences A range of essences for cakes and ice cream including pear, aniseed, pineapple and vanilla. Produced in La Fortune, St Patrick's.

Noelville Ltd (*www.nut-med.com*) A Grenville-based company producing Nut-Med, Spice Island noni juice and Noel's lemon grass tea. Look out for their products in the Gouyave Nutmeg Pool. The Nut-Med painkilling spray and lotion are extremely popular and very effective after those long hikes!

Spice Isle Plantations Handmade soaps from St George's.

Veronica's Visions (*www.grenadaspicecloth.com*) Original painted fabric designs from Concord. Look out for Spicewear and jola bags with a nutmeg theme. For more information see box on page 140.

White Cane Industries Workshop for the blind and disabled located on the Carenage in St George's, near BB's Crabback restaurant, producing excellent white-cane basketware. See box on page 101.

Visitors to Grenada may come across the term 'provisions' or 'ground provisions' when eating local food. Provisions may refer to any one or a collection of root crops such as yam, eddoe, dasheen, sweet potato or tannia. The term is occasionally stretched to include breadfruit, plantain and unripe bananas (also known as figs). Provisions are usually boiled and served with a main meat dish. They also feature in traditional soups or one-pot brafs (broths) such as 'oil-down' (see the section on local dishes, below). Provisions are very filling and high in carbohydrates. Grown and eaten by slaves working plantations and estates, they are still a staple food across the Caribbean, especially for those whose work involves a lot of physical activity.

selling crafts and souvenirs. In towns such as Gouyave, Grenville and Sauteurs you will find small supermarkets, chemists and convenience stores selling basic items.

Hillsborough is Carriacou's main town and has small supermarkets, convenience stores, pharmacies and a variety of other small shops and boutiques. Both St George's and Hillsborough have markets and street vendors selling fruits, vegetables and spices. They also have fish markets.

Shopping in Petite Martinique may be more of a challenge, though it does have a few small convenience stores selling groceries and other essential items, and a very pleasant gift shop and boutique.

OPENING HOURS Inevitably there are variations to the rule but, generally speaking, you should aim to do your shopping within the following opening hours: 08.00–16.00 Monday to Friday and 08.00–13.00 Saturday. Expect most shops to be closed on Sundays and Saturday afternoons. Exceptions include some shops in Grand Anse which may stay open later. Supermarkets also often stay open a little later. Shopping centres may open all day on Saturday as do most stores in Grenville. Spiceland Mall in Grand Anse is open until late and also on Sundays.

ARTS AND ENTERTAINMENT

THEATRE The Spice Basket Cultural Village has a large theatre and concert hall (see page 145 for more details). Other than this, there is no other permanent theatre in Grenada. From time to time there will be events at community centres, schools, or sometimes in parks. Check newspapers, listen to the radio, or ask at your hotel to find out about any performances or events that may be taking place during your stay.

ART GALLERIES AND MUSEUMS If you are interested in seeking out both local and regional art and cultural exhibits then the following places are definitely worth a visit:

Art & Soul Spiceland Mall, Grand Anse. An art gallery with a collection of works for sale by Susan Mains (see page 30).
Carriacou Museum Hillsborough, Carriacou. Contains a wonderful collection of Amerindian artefacts & ceramics from archaeological sites around the island. There are also informative exhibits of African heritage, European occupation & Carriacouan culture, illustrated by the Big Drum and Maroon festivals. Often the museum also exhibits artworks; traditional, such as those by Canute Caliste, or perhaps more contemporary displays by local schoolchildren. For more information see page 218.

Freddy Paul Halifax St, St George's. Small art gallery & workshop of talented Grenada-born painter Freddy Paul (see page 30).

Grenada Arts Council Young St, St George's. The Arts Council hosts regular exhibitions by local artists.

Grenada National Museum Monckton St, St George's. The museum has a number of fascinating exhibits & displays including a collection of Amerindian & Yoruba artefacts, plantation machinery & tools, & antique firearms & cannons. The museum also has an exhibition room for contemporary displays. For more information see page 101.

Yellow Poui Art Gallery Young St, St George's. A gallery of paintings, sculptures & carvings by artists from, working in, or inspired by the Caribbean region.

MEDIA AND COMMUNICATIONS

MEDIA Grenada has several weekly newspapers and a selection of online sources (see *Appendix 3*). In addition to local and regional news and information, cable television channels are predominantly American. Radio stations are a good source of information as well as a great way to find out about local events. Stations include the Grenada Broadcasting Network (GBN) broadcasting **Hott FM** (105.5FM) and **Klassic 535** (535AM); **Voice of Grenada** (95.7FM and 103.3FM); **CRFM** (89.5FM); **City Sound** (97.5FM); **WeeFM** (93.9FM) and Carriacou's own **Kayak 106 FM** (106FM).

POST Grenada's postal service is called the Grenada Postal Corporation. The main office is located on the southern tip of the Carenage in St George's. You will also find small post offices and stations in most villages. The main post office in Carriacou is located in Hillsborough next to the jetty. Post office opening hours are usually 08.00–16.00 Monday to Thursday and until 16.30 on Friday. The post office is closed at the weekends and on public holidays. A stamp for a postcard to either the UK or the US costs around EC$1.

TELEPHONE

International calls The international dialling code for Grenada, Carriacou and Petite Martinique is +1 473 followed by a number consisting of seven digits. A sample of international direct-dialling codes from Grenada is as follows:

Belgium ✆ 011 + 32 + number
Canada ✆ 1 + area code + number
Caribbean ✆ 1 + area code + number
People's Republic of China ✆ 011 + 86 + number
Cuba ✆ 011 + 53 + number
France ✆ 011 + 33 + number
Germany ✆ 011 + 49 + number

Guyana ✆ 011 + 592 + number
Netherlands ✆ 011 + 31 + number
Norway ✆ 011 + 47 + number
Spain ✆ 011 + 34 + number
Sweden ✆ 011 + 46 + number
UK ✆ 011 + 44 + number
US ✆ 1 + area code + number
Venezuela ✆ 011 + 58 + number

Mobile phones Mobile-phone providers in Grenada include Digicel and LIME. If you do not bring a mobile phone and wish to have one during your stay, it is possible to purchase an inexpensive pay-as-you-go phone for as little as EC$60–70 from either of these providers. You will find both a LIME and a Digicel store located near to the Esplanade Shopping Mall in the capital, St George's. A number of hotels either rent or loan out pay-as-you-go mobile phones to their guests, and some car rental companies have also begun this practice.

The amount and quality of camera equipment you carry will be determined by both your budget and your enthusiasm for photography. Serious photographers should bring along a digital SLR with several lenses; the scenery is worth it and conditions can occasionally demand it. Amateur photographers can capture great images with a good quality digital camera or even an iPhone. iPhone photography is becoming very popular due to the excellent balance of image quality and device portability, and if all you want to do is upload pictures to Facebook or Twitter, then a device such as this is just what you need.

Whatever you bring you should be aware that Grenada's climate is tropical and humidity can be very high (often higher than the safe operating limits quoted in your camera's instruction manual!). Protecting your equipment as much as possible from heat, direct sunlight, high humidity, heavy rains, salt spray and sand is therefore very important. This is where a good camera bag comes in. If you are planning on hiking or going out on the water with your camera, then your bag ought to be either waterproof or splash proof. Even with a good bag, I always make a point of wiping my camera down after a day out. It's amazing how far salt spray travels and how sand somehow manages to get everywhere.

If your battery (or phone) charger requires a 110V supply, check to see if your hotel has dual voltage; many do. And remember to bring it, of course. If your digital camera runs on disposable AA type batteries then carry a supply of spares with you. It can be difficult to find shops selling batteries that have not expired or drained themselves in the heat. Cheap imitations are also plentiful and hard to identify.

When it comes to photographing people you must weigh up the situation carefully and always ask for permission. For more on this subject see the Cultural Etiquette section on page 66.

SOME BASIC TIPS FOR AMATEUR PHOTOGRAPHERS The best time to take photographs is either early morning or late afternoon when the light creates shadows and contrast. Try to avoid taking photographs in the midday sun if you can. The light at this time is very strong and your photographs may lack depth. An ISO setting of 80-100 is just about all you will need here, except in the forest where you may have to use ISO 200. Think about your position relative to the sun and your subject. As a general rule of thumb you should try to keep the sun either behind or to the side of you. Be sure to focus on your main subject, but try to position them a little off-centre rather than directly in the middle of your photograph. Also experiment with different angles; try crouching down or standing on something to gain a little height. Sometimes minor adjustments such as these can really transform photos. If you want to experiment with settings, try AV mode and set your aperture to f8 or more for scenery, and for subjects such as people, flowers or animals, set the aperture at f5 or lower to blur the background a little and make the subject stand out more. Have fun.

Practical Information MEDIA AND COMMUNICATIONS

2

Internet Many hotels will provide either hard-wired or wireless high-speed internet access. Most offer free wireless services, though some charge by the day or half-day. Maurice Bishop International Airport is also a wireless internet zone. Many of Grenada's restaurants, bars and cafés, and marinas have free Wi-Fi.

BUSINESS

Hours of business vary although most will begin around 08.00. On weekday mornings expect traffic to be busy in and around the capital St George's from 07.30 onwards. Some businesses seem to take a little longer to get warmed up in the mornings with their shutters making half-hearted efforts at opening any time between 08.00 and 10.00, though they eventually make it. Everything gets rather busy around the Esplanade Shopping Mall and the bus terminal in St George's when cruise ships are calling and also in the streets around St George's marketplace. Carriacou and Petite Martinique never really get busy although there is always a good deal of activity around the jetty when supply boats, the mail boat, and the Osprey ferry arrive and depart.

Most businesses end their working day between 16.00 and 17.30. Again, expect heavy traffic in and around St George's at this time. A five-day week is standard, though more and more businesses also open on Saturday mornings.

If you are dealing with government-related services you will need to be aware that processes and working practices may be very different from what you are accustomed to back home. It is not uncommon to have to make several trips between different offices or departments, and they may not always be located in the same building. Patience and a generous allocation of your time are essential ingredients for keeping your cool and making progress. Government offices are usually open from 08.00–16.00 Monday to Friday.

CULTURAL ETIQUETTE

DRESS When walking around Sr George's, Grand Anse, or any other town or village for that matter, please wear a top. You should also dress appropriately when entering churches and people's homes; bikinis, swimming costumes or no shirt will certainly offend and embarrass, though it is unlikely anyone will actually challenge you about it. Sunbathing topless is not permitted.

DRUGS AND ALCOHOL Please confine your consumption to bars and do not walk around the streets drinking alcohol, unless it is Carnival, of course! Although you may well encounter someone smoking marijuana somewhere, and may even be offered some, please remember it is actually illegal and penalties are severe.

DEALING WITH BEGGARS At some point in time you are likely to be asked by a beggar for money, especially in towns or near popular tourism sites. Some are drug addicts or alcoholics, but many are simply destitute and have no family or friends to care for them. Few will harass you – they will simply ask for help. The decision whether to give or not has to be yours alone. Please be polite and resist lecturing and being rude. If you do feel you are being harassed then simply walk away.

TAKING PHOTOGRAPHS OF PEOPLE In recent times local people have become very sensitive about photography. The reasons are not clear but it may have something to do with hoards of cruise-ship visitors pointing cameras everywhere when they come ashore. It therefore seems understandable that locals have become a little fed up with it, or have decided to ask for money in exchange for permission. Markets are perhaps the most difficult places to photograph because of this. Once a fisherman instructed me not to photograph his boat. Take nothing for granted.

Please do not assume it is OK to take photographs of people. If you do wish to take a photograph of someone, try the following:

- Ask for permission. Some photographers suggest taking the photograph first – when the subject is more natural – and then asking permission. I can certainly understand this from an artistic perspective, but it carries risks.
- Offer to share by email the photograph you wish to take, and then actually email that photograph to the person as soon as possible (if you do not email it, people will eventually consider this type of offer an empty promise).
- Offer a 'contribution'. Some people will accept a few dollars in return for allowing you to take their photograph. At the market, why not buy some produce or some spices? Try having a conversation with the vendor first.
- If your request is declined, please respect that decision and, however tempting, do not try to take the photograph candidly.

If you are genuinely taking photographs of scenery that just happens to have people in it, there is not much you can do; take the photograph. If anyone challenges you, simply tell them you are photographing the beautiful scenery (it is always a good idea to emphasise how beautiful you think Grenada is), and perhaps offer to show and share with them some of the photographs you have taken.

TRAVELLING POSITIVELY

Throughout this guide I encourage you to look out for and try to support local businesses, farmers, artists and so on. Grenada, Carriacou and Petite Martinique have many practical problems that a number of NGOs and local groups of volunteers try to resolve or improve upon. Grenadians living abroad are continually a great source of assistance to these organisations by sending materials and helping with fundraising. Visitors to the three islands can also make a difference. Think about contacting one of these organisations before or during your visit and asking how you might be able to support them.

STUFF YOUR RUCKSACK – AND MAKE A DIFFERENCE

www.stuffyourrucksack.com is a website set up by UK TV's Kate Humble that enables travellers to give direct help to small charities, schools or other organisations in the country they are visiting. Maybe a local school needs books, a map or pencils, or an orphanage needs children's clothes or toys – all things that can easily be 'stuffed in a rucksack' before departure. The charities get exactly what they need and travellers have the chance to meet local people and see how and where their gifts will be used.

The website describes organisations that need your help and lists the items they most need. Check what's needed in Grenada, Petite Martinique and Carriacou, contact the organisation to say you're coming and bring not only the much-needed goods but an extra dimension to your travels and the knowledge that, in a small way, you have made a difference.

www.stuffyourrucksack.com
Responsible tourism in action

Bel Air Children's Home St George's; ☎473 444 5100; e belairhome@spiceisle.com; www.belairchildrenshome.com. Located between Grand Anse & the Maurice Bishop International Airport, the Bel Air Children's Home accommodates & cares for over 30 children – from babies to adolescents – who have either been orphaned, neglected, or who have been living in poverty.

Carriacou Children's Education Fund Carriacou; e ccefinfo@gmail.com. Raising money for children's education, school uniforms, books, etc in Carriacou.

Carriacou Historic Society Hillsborough, Carriacou; e carriacoumuseum@gmail.com; www.carriacoumuseum.org. Support the Carriacou Museum, cultural events, & even archaeological digs by becoming a member, friend, patron or sponsor of the Carriacou Historic Society.

Grenada Society for the Prevention of Cruelty to Animals St George's, Grenada & Hillsborough, Carriacou; www.grenadaspca.org

Hearts and Hands Belmont Estate; ☎473 442 9524; e heartsandhandsgrenada@gmail.com; www.heartsandhandsgrenada.com. Helping people to rebuild their lives after natural disaster, & improving the living conditions of the less fortunate. Hearts and Hands provides school books & uniforms & also helps with exam fees.

Jason Roberts Foundation London (UK) & St George's; ☎473 409 9442 & UK ☎0208 963 9179; www.jasonrobertsfoundation. Professional soccer player Jason Roberts' foundation provides opportunities for children to develop in sporting activities, health & fitness programmes in the UK and Grenada.

J.J. Robinson Trust www.jjrtrust.com. Provides financial assistance for further education for those who are unable to afford it. Also provides financial support for the School for Pregnant & Adolescent Mothers.

Queen Elizabeth Home for Children ☎473 440 2327; e qehchildren@spiceisle.com; www.facebook.com/queen-elizabeth-home-for-children. Caring for children who are orphaned or who need help.

3

Activities and Special Interests

There are many ways to enjoy the culture and the natural environment of Grenada, Carriacou and Petite Martinique. Visitors to the islands will find a diverse choice of activities that suit a wide range of interests, ages and abilities. Here are a few suggestions.

BEACHES

For those lazy days – yes, you are allowed one or two – here are some ideas.

BEACHES WITH BARS AND RESTAURANTS

Grand Anse Grenada (page 122). Grenada's most popular beach with resort hotels such as Spice Island Beach Resort (Oliver's restaurant), Coyaba Beach Resort (Arawakabana restaurant), Flamboyant Hotel & Villas (Beachside Terrace restaurant), and Allamanda Beach Resort (Ali Baba Grill). Beachside bars and restaurants include Umbrellas, Garfield's, Coconut Beach, and Oasis.

Morne Rouge Grenada (page 122). Sublimely tranquil, making it an ideal beach for families with small children, Morne Rouge has the Fedelis Restaurant & Bar at the Kalinago Beach Resort, and the Sur La Mer beachside cabana bar and restaurant.

Magazine Grenada (page 123). My favourite beach on the main island, Magazine has the Aquarium Restaurant and La Sirena Beach Bar at its southern end.

Dr Groom's Grenada (page 123). Usually a very quiet beach, Dr Groom's is home to the excellent Beach House Restaurant & Bar.

La Sagesse Grenada (page 165). Located in Grenada's southeast, this very quiet crescent-shaped beach is where you can also enjoy food and refreshments at La Sagesse Nature Centre. Walk to the southern tip and follow a track past a saline pond to a second, more remote beach.

Bathway Grenada (page 194). A dramatic, picturesque and very long beach on Grenada's northeast coast, Bathway has a number of small bars and snackettes in the vicinity of the visitor centre, but Aggie's restaurant and bar, just over the road from the beach, is my hot tip.

Paradise Carriacou (page 218). Carriacou's most popular beach, though you will hardly ever see a crowd, Paradise has a number of beachside bars and eateries including Hardwood Restaurant & Bar, Sunset Beach Bar & Restaurant, Off The Hook and Banana Joe's. Paradise is also an excellent beach for families with small children.

REMOTE BEACHES

Hope Grenada (page 172). A very long, crescent-shaped beach on Great Bacolet Bay, Hope is accessed via a short walk or drive along a paved road and then a vehicle track. It is shallow and usually calm.

Belle Isle Grenada (page 173). Although Belle Isle Beach can definitely be considered off the beaten path, it is used by local people who live on the southeast coast. Like Hope Beach, Belle Isle is accessed via a combination of paved road and vehicle track. Belle Isle is also shallow and usually very calm.

Cabier Grenada (page 173). On a horse-shoe-shaped bay, Cabier Beach and the neighbouring

Crochu Harbour are occasionally used by local people and holidaymakers staying at the nearby Cabier Ocean Lodge but, more often than not, you will find no-one else there. Access is via paved road and vehicle tracks from the village of Crochu.

Levera Grenada (page 194). Rounding the very northeastern tip of Grenada, with Sugar Load Island, Green Island and Sandy Island just offshore, Levera's expansive beach is an idyllic setting. From March to July it is also a turtle nesting and hatching site. Access to the beach is usually via the Bathway Beach road to the south though you can also get there from Fortune, on the eastern side of Sauteurs.

Anse La Roche Carriacou (page 225). Enjoy a pleasant hike, or a hike and drive, along the High North Nature Trail and then follow the turtle signs down to what many 'Kayaks' believe to be Carriacou's loveliest beach.

Petite Carenage Carriacou (page 226). This is my favourite Carriacou beach. North of Windward, through the L'Apelle Mangrove Forest, with views of Petite Martinique, Petite St Vincent, Palm Island, Union, Mayreau and the Tobago Cays, this is a remarkable spot. The wreck of the grounded *Asylum* at the eastern tip adds individuality, not to mention a great photo opportunity.

BIRDWATCHING

Birdwatching is rather undeveloped in Grenada with relatively few operators offering speciality outings. If you are travelling independently and are interested in knowing where to go then the following places should be on your list: Mt Hartman National Park (see page 125), La Sagesse Nature Centre (see page 169), Levera Mangrove Wetland (see page 183), Lake Antoine (see page 196), High North National Park (see page 222), Grand Etang Lake and National Park (see page 148), and Palmiste Lake (see page 153).

Anthony 'Jerry' Jeremiah ☏473 440 0393 & 473 416 0191; e tonydove200@yahoo.com. Forestry professional who offers private birdwatching tours on weekends. Transportation provided & included in a negotiable fee.

Caribbean Horizons ☏473 444 1555; e info@caribbeanhorizons.com; www. caribbeanhorizons.com. Birdwatching excursions to Mt Hartman National Park, Morne Gazo, Grand Etang & Levera.

BUS TOURS

If driving on Grenada's roads presents too much of a challenge then bus and jeep tours are very good alternatives. In addition to the operators listed below, you should check with your hotel to see if they run tours themselves or whether they recommend anyone. Please note that during the peak season (November–April) many of these operators may be busy with cruise ship tours. If you are coming to Grenada at this time then it is really worth contacting these operators ahead of your visit and then confirming any booking you have made shortly before you arrive.

Bus and jeep tours usually include most of the accessible and popular attractions rather than those that are a little more off the beaten path. In Carriacou taxi drivers offer a fairly standard island tour for around EC$200. You can find them between the Hillsborough jetty and Tourist Information office on Main Street. Check the websites of Grenada operators for details. Here is a selection:

A&E Tours ☏473 435 1444; e aandetours@ spiceisle.com; www.grenadaguide.com/aetours. A&E offers full & half-day bus tours around the island.

Adventure Jeep Tours ☏473 444 5337;

e adventure@spiceisle.com; www. adventuregrenada.com. This operator offers full & half-day open-top jeep tours through Grenada's interior & along the west coast.

Caribbean Horizons ☏473 444 1555;

Here are some of the bird species you may observe in Grenada, Carriacou and Petite Martinique:

Antillean-crested hummingbird (*Orthorhyncus cristatus*)
Bananaquit (*Coereba flaveola*)
Bare-eyed thrush (*Turdus nudigenis*)
Barn owl (*Tyto alba*)
Barn swallow (*Hirundo rustica*)
Blue-faced grassquit/black-faced grassquit (*Tiaris bicolor*)
Broad-winged hawk/chicken-hawk (*Buteo platypterus*)
Carib grackle/blackbird (*Quiscalus lugubris*)
Cattle egret (*Bubulcus ibis*)
Emerald-throated hummingbird/ green-throated carib (*Eulampis holosericeus*)
Glossy cowbird/corn bird (*Molothrus bonariensis*)
Grenada dove (*Leptotila wellsi*)
Grenada flycatcher (*Myiarchus nugator*)

Ground dove (*Columbina passerina*)
Grey kingbird (*Tyrannus dominicensis*)
House wren/rock bird (*Troglodytes aedon*)
Hook-billed kite (*Chondrohierax uncinatus*)
Lesser Antillean bullfinch (*Loxigilla noctis*)
Magnificent frigatebird (*Fregata magnificens*)
Mangrove cuckoo (*Coccyzus minor grenadensis*)
Osprey (*Pandion haliaetus*)
Rufous-breasted hermit hummingbird (*Glaucis hirsuta*)
Smooth-billed ani (*Crotophaga ani*)
Southern mockingbird (*Mimus gilvus antillarum*)
Yellow-bellied elaenia (*Elaenia flavogaster*)
Zenaida dove (*Zenaida aurita*)

e info@caribbeanhorizons.com; www.caribbeanhorizons.com. This long-established & very popular company offers a number of standard half- & full-day island tours incorporating many of Grenada's natural & cultural sites of interest.
Henry's Safari Tours 473 444 5313; e safari@spiceisle.com; www.henrysafari.com. Seasoned operator offering a very wide selection of half- & full-day tours to many of Grenada's natural & heritage sites.
Kennedy Tours 473 444 1074; e kennedytours@spiceisle.com; www.kennedytours.com. Kennedy is an English- & Spanish-speaking guide who offers a variety of half- & full-day AC bus tours around Grenada.

Mandoo Tours 473 440 1428; e mandoo@grenadatours.com; www.grenadatours.com. Mandoo is a very popular private tour operator who offers a wide selection of half- & full-day tours around Grenada.
Pete's Mystique Tours 473 440 1671. Experienced guide Pete offers a range of tours around Grenada that incorporate a little hiking, lots of sightseeing & plenty of local culture. Half - & full-day tours.
Sunsation Tours 473 444 1594 or 473 439 4447; e qkspice@spiceisle.com; www.grenadasunsation.com. Established operator offering a wide selection of half- & full-day tours that incorporate many of Grenada's main attractions.

CYCLING AND MOUNTAIN BIKING

A nice way to explore some of Grenada's villages and country tracks is to hire a bike or take a guided cycling tour. Bike rentals are usually around US$20 per day with

Travellers interested in culture and heritage should try to include the following activities and sites in their schedule.

CULTURAL ACTIVITIES

Boatbuilding Carriacou and Petite Martinique are noted for their traditions of boatbuilding that go back to the islands' 19th-century Scottish settlers. At Windward (Carriacou) and Sanchez (Petite Martinique) you can see these skills being applied by their descendants. For more information see page 204.

Big Drum Dance and Maroon Festivals Also on Carriacou, Big Drum Dance and Maroon festivals find their heritage in both Europe and Africa. Village maroons and *saracas* often take place around harvest time, and the annual Carriacou Maroon & String Band Music Festival is usually at the end of April. See pages 206–7 for more information.

Spice Basket Cultural Village (*Beaulieu; www.spicebasketgrenada.com*) Although a modern development, the Spice Basket Cultural Village is a laudable initiative to put many aspects of Grenada's cultural heritage under one roof. Located in the village of Beaulieu, to the northeast of St George's, the Spice Basket hosts regular music and theatrical events, cultural performances, a cricket heritage centre, and traditional craft and food stalls. For more information see page 145.

HERITAGE SITES

Belmont Estate and Grenada Chocolate Company (*Belmont, Grenada; www.belmontestate.net*) From tree to bar, see how the Belmont Estate grows, harvests and dries organic cocoa in a traditional manner, and then try some of the Grenada Chocolate Company's famous chocolate. See page 188 for more information.

discounts available for weekly hire. Grenada's roads are good and exploring some of the vehicle tracks and coastal pathways make for a fun and interesting few hours. Carriacou is a great place for road cycling and mountain biking. It is always worth checking with your hotel to see if they can recommend anyone who rents bicycles.

Adventure Trailblazer Tours 473 444 5337; e adventure@spiceisle.com; www.adventuregrenada.com. Adventure Trailblazer Tours offers independent bike hire & guided tours. Rentals come with a complimentary route sheet that includes several on- & off-road options. All mountain bikes have front suspension shocks & hire includes safety helmets & security locks. Guided bike tours include a personal guide to help you explore.

Lambi Queen 473 8162 & 406 4122. Head for the Lambi Queen Bar & Restaurant on Tyrrel Bay in Carriacou & ask about mountain bike rental.

FISHING

Fishing enthusiasts travelling to Grenada can choose between a sedate coastal trip with a little fishing followed by a beach barbecue, or a full- or half-day charter excursion for some serious sport fishing. If the former is your preference, check with the charter-boat operators listed on page 81 or ask your hotel if they can recommend water taxis or fishermen. For sport-fishing charters, see page 74. Half-

River Antoine Rum Distillery Near La Poterie and Tivoli, Grenada. Producing pure cane rum from sugarcane grown and harvested on its estate lands and using the same production methods and machinery it did when it started in the 1700s, River Antoine is a fascinating heritage site. See page 188 for more information.

Dougaldston Estate Near Gouyave, Grenada. Although Dougaldston is rather a sad imitation of its former self these days, that should not put you off visiting this historic estate on the southern outskirts of Gouyave. The traditional *boucan*, the cocoa drying shed, was remarkable in its time and is still interesting to see today. For more information go to page 146.

Nutmeg Pools at Gouyave and Grenville Hurricane Ivan devastated Grenada's nutmeg crop in 2004 but the sector is gradually recovering. In Grenville the nutmeg processing station, or 'pool', is still restricted to simply receiving nutmegs from farmers and then transporting them to Gouyave where they are processed for export. Both pools offer tours. Most people go to the Gouyave pool these days as there is more going on, but I actually prefer the tour at Grenville. It is a little less rehearsed, more relaxed and personal. Both are worth a visit, however, and you will also be doing your part to support those who still depend on the nutmeg for their livelihoods. For more information see pages 147 and 166.

Amerindian Petroglyphs The first people to settle on Grenada and Carriacou were Amerindian tribes who migrated north from the South American mainland. Carriacou has some fascinating archaeological sites, with some interesting ceramics on display at the Carriacou Museum in Hillsborough (see page 218). On the main island there are two notable petroglyph (rock carving) sites at Duquesne and Mt Rich (see page 191).

day sport fishing usually costs between US$400 and US$500 with full-day charters around US$700–800.

Grenada's west coast waters deepen to around 1,000m after a short 20–30-minute boat ride. Charter operators tend to fish along this contour and then deeper at the 2,000m mark, which is around one hour from the dock. Anglers can expect to catch an assortment of large pelagics including yellowfin tuna, blue marlin, white marlin, sailfish, dorado and wahoo.

Sport-fishing operators employ the **tag-and-release** policy advocated by the Billfish Foundation when catching billfish during their fishing trips. Billfish include Atlantic blue marlin, sailfish, white marlin and short- and long-bill spearfish. Tag and release means that when caught, the fish are not brought into the boat, nor are they brought back to shore. Instead, once alongside the boat, the billfish are tagged and an estimate of the weight of the fish is made by the crew based on its size and length. The fish is then fully revived, ensuring oxygenated water is flushed through its gills and it is strong enough to be released. While it is being resuscitated, all hooks are carefully removed.

The Billfish Foundation's tag-and-release programme provides scientists and fishery managers worldwide with data on billfish migration patterns, age and growth rates, feeding and spawning grounds, stock structure and numbers. Sport-fishing operators around the world are encouraged to participate in tag-and-release

The Spice Island Billfish Tournament has been running since 1964 and attracts sport fishermen from all around the region. It takes place in January at the height of the billfish season and is a modified tag-and-release tournament. This means that the participants are encouraged to tag and release the majority of billfish they catch, and only land the ones they believe are large enough to win the tournament. The three-day event is hosted by the Grenada Yacht Club. Entry fee is around US$200 per angler and there is considerable prize money on offer. The prize for the angler breaking the current blue marlin record is EC$30,000. For more information go to www.sibtgrenada.com.

sport fishing by joining the Billfish Foundation and stocking their fishing boats with official tagging supplies. As part of a conservation effort started by fishermen themselves, the Billfish Foundation has succeeded in bringing about successful regulations and petitions regarding endangered species and long-line fishing. For more information go to www.billfish.org.

Grenada Sportfishing ✆473 418 5508 or 473 443 4343; e molliedalby@hotmail.com; www.grenadasportfishing.com. Prize-winning & experienced skipper Badger offers half- & full-day fishing trips aboard his 2006 Luhrs 38 Convertible, comfortably accommodating up to 6 anglers. Fully equipped with top-brand tackle, fighting chair & galley. All year round marlin fishing. Billfish tag-&-release policy employed. Prices include transport to & from your accommodation & onboard refreshments.
Reel Affair ✆473 435 4521. Sport fishing aboard *Reel Affair II*, a Bertram 38 Convertible, skippered by Howard A Otway. Fully equipped with top-brand tackle, this charter operates billfish tag & release. Half- & full-day fishing trips available for up to 6 anglers. Call for more information & prices.
Spice Kayaking & Eco Tours ✆473 537 5713; www.spicekayaking.com. Based at the

Allamanda Beach Resort, this operator offers kayak fishing tours from Grand Anse Beach & around the bays of the southwest. Tours last around 3 hours & include refreshments, fishing tackle & bait.
True Blue Sportfishing ✆473 444 2048 or 473 407 4688; e grclifford@spiceisle.com; www.yesaye.com. Skipper Gary Clifford offers full- & half-day fishing trips aboard his 1988 Innovator *Yes Aye*. Fully equipped with top-brand tackle & fighting chair. Billfish tag-&-release policy employed. Max 5 people. Refreshments included.
Wayward Wind ✆473 439 7929 or 473 538 9821; e stewart@grenadafishing.com; www.grenadafishing.com. Captain Stewart offers full- & half-day sport fishing on his fully equipped Bertram 31 with top-quality fishing tackle & fighting chair. A billfish tag-&-release policy is in operation. Up to 4 people.

GARDEN TOURS

Grenada's climate and volcanic soil provide the perfect growing environment for a wide variety of vegetables, tropical plants, flowers and flowering trees. The island is also home to beautiful private gardens and accomplished gardening enthusiasts, some of whom have won awards at London's prestigious Chelsea Flower Show, where Grenada always does very well. In 2011 the team won its ninth gold for its exhibit 'Castaway'. For more information see www.grenada-at-chelsea.org.uk. Although some enthusiasts have opened up their private gardens to the public, many have not. Please respect this and do not turn up at private homes unannounced. Two companies, Sunsation and Caribbean Horizons, have established working relationships with some of these very talented people and their tours incorporate a number of Grenada's beautiful private gardens. You may also be interested in looking up the Horticultural Society of Grenada (*www.hortigrenada.com*).

Bay Gardens St Paul's, St George's; ⟍473 435 4544 or 473 404 6266. Located near the village of St Paul's this long established, beautiful & varied tropical garden is certainly worth a visit. Entrance fee EC$10pp, includes an informative guided tour of around 45 mins. (See page 167 for more information on visiting the Bay Gardens.)
Caribbean Horizons ⟍473 444 1555; e info@caribbeanhorizons.com; www.caribbeanhorizons.com. The Floral Delight Garden Tour is designed by a member of Grenada's winning Chelsea team & takes enthusiasts to both private & commercial gardens such as the Hyde Park Gardens, the Bay Gardens, Smithy's Garden, Balthazar Estate, Tower House Garden, St Rose Nurseries, Gemma's Garden, & Sunny Side Garden. This tour can be combined with a rather unique Bee Keepers Tour. Contact for prices.
De La Grenade St Paul's ⟍473 440 3241 or 473 435 4819; e dlgignd@spiceisle.com; www.delagrenade.com. Located on the main road in the village of St Paul's, De La Grenade Industries is an extremely successful, award-winning company that produces high quality & extremely delicious nutmeg products. In addition to a factory tour (see page 168), the company also offers a guided 30-minute tour of its tropical gardens. The cost is US$5 per person. The gardens are home to a wide variety of tropical plants, flowers, herbs & trees – including nutmeg, of course.
Hyde Park Tropical Garden Hyde Park, St George's; ⟍473 440 8395; www.hydepark.gd. Originally a small estate & transformed into a tropical garden that is noted for its collection of orchids, this 1.5 acre private garden also contains a variety of palms, bougainvilleas, heliconias & more. Bookings can be made directly or via Caribbean Horizons & Sunsations tour companies.
Laura Herb & Spice Garden Laura, St David's; ⟍473 443 2604. Located near the elevated village of Perdmontemps, & with expansive panoramas of the southeast coast, enjoy a guided walk around the gardens of this spice-production business, learning about Grenada's natural spices, what they look like, how they smell & what they are used for. Tours cost EC$5pp & last around 30mins. For more information see page 167.
Sunsation Tours ⟍473 444 1594 or 473 439 4447; e qkspice@caribsurf.com; www.grenadasunsation.com. Enjoy a leisurely visit to 2 private gardens, Sunny Side & Hyde Park, accompanied by the owners. Tour price US$60.

GOLF

At the time of writing, Grenada has just one golf course, though there have been rumours of a second being planned. The **Grenada Golf Course & Country Club** (⟍ *473 444 4128*) is located to the northeast of Grand Anse Beach (look for the sign on the main coastal road between Grand Anse and St George's). It is a nine-hole course with good views of both the Caribbean Sea and the Atlantic Ocean. Club hire, instruction and caddy service are available. The clubhouse has a restaurant and bar. A number of resort hotels at Grand Anse offer complimentary golf club membership as part of their hotel rates. Please contact the club for green fees and note proper golf attire is required when playing.

HASHING

Hashing originates from the game *paper chase*, also known as *hare and hounds*, that was described by Thomas Hughes in his 1857 novel *Tom Brown's Schooldays*. At the start of the game someone is designated the hare, and everyone else forms a group of hounds. Torn-up paper was used to represent the scent of the hare and when the chasing hounds found it they would know they were on the right track. The hounds had to catch the hare before it reached the ending point of the race.

The idea was picked up by a group of British colonial officers and expatriates in Kuala Lumpur in 1938 when they all gathered on Mondays to play hare and hounds in order to help clear weekend hangovers. One of the members suggested they name the group Hash House Harriers after the 'hash house' where they were billeted and which was notorious for its poor food. At the end of the race the members rewarded themselves with cigarettes and alcohol. After World War II, the game was resurrected by most of its surviving original members. Today there are hundreds of 'Hash House' chapters around the world – groups that gather regularly and set a hash to run or walk, and at the end enjoy some food and drink.

The Grenada Hash House Harriers meets every two weeks, at 16.00 on Saturday afternoons, and often attract hundreds of participants of all ages and levels of fitness. Although it is still very much an expatriate event, many Grenadians have also been drawn to the activity.

The trail is set in advance by one or two hares with a duration of around one hour in mind and with both start and finish line at the same rum shop or bar. The trail is marked, true to tradition, with small piles of shredded paper – usually obtained from a bank or an office – and can include 'false trails' just to spice things up a little and help the backmarkers to catch up. Many regulars have 'hash names' and there is a specific terminology and set of phrases that are used. Often described as 'a drinking club with a running problem' hashing is a fun way to see the island and meet new friends. For information about the Grenada Hash House Harriers and to find out about the next scheduled hash, go to www.grenadahash.com.

HIKING

The three islands of Grenada are scenic and alluring, and the very best way to appreciate and get close to them is to take a walk. There are walks and hikes for everyone, whatever their ability, time constraints or interests. For the adventurous there are mountain and river hikes, and for the more sedate ramblers there are coastal, lakeside and village walks. Grenada's interior has a network of trails running between the Grand Etang Lake, Mt Qua Qua, Fédon's Camp and the three waterfalls that make up the Concord Falls. These hikes were always for the more adventurous, but since Hurricane Ivan they have become even more difficult. Fallen trees and landslides have seriously affected some routes and you really should hire a guide. This is particularly the case with Fédon's Camp and the trails from Fédon's Camp and Mt Qua Qua to Concord, though there have been efforts by local hiking enthusiasts to open them up. The trail from Grand Etang Lake to the summit of Mt Qua Qua is clear but very exposed and not without its share of risk due to high-elevation deforestation and soil erosion. Hikes to the summit of Mt St Catherine, the Paraclete Falls, and the Tufton Hall Waterfall are rather obscure and physically challenging. Again, I recommend a guide.

Very few trails currently have blazes or signs along the route or even at the trailhead itself. Where there is a clear path this is not a problem but when paths fork, cross rivers or pass through open clearings, it is easy to get lost. And things change. A bamboo thicket that marks a trailhead or a turning today may well be scaffolding tomorrow.

THE BENEFIT OF HIRING A GUIDE Good trail guides know which way to go when routes are not clear, they have often received specialised training, and they can provide interesting information about the history of the trail, the area, and the flora and fauna that you may encounter along the way. Hiring a guide also provides a valuable source of income to local people and, by extension, their villages. In the rural communities of Grenada where farming has suffered following hurricanes, this kind of income is very welcome, and needed. By increasing the demand for guides, visitors are also potentially creating career and employment opportunities for young Grenadians. And no matter how detailed the guidebook, there is absolutely no substitute for local knowledge, anecdotes, and the reassurance a good guide can provide when a trail is new, daunting or difficult.

For those 'extreme hikers' who are interested in exploring some of the lesser-known trails of 'hidden' Grenada, you may find it quite difficult to find guides or operators who have sufficient knowledge of these routes. Many registered guides and tour operators specialise in mainstream hiking trails only, such as St Margaret's Falls. In this case some hotels or tour operators may be able to put you in contact with local people. Grenada's most famous hiker, Telfor Bedeau, may be able to help you (see page 79). Try to avoid just turning up in a remote location and asking for a guide if you can, though in some cases it may be the only way. Try to hire someone with a good reputation or who has been recommended, and always let someone else know where you are going.

SETTING OUT The degree of preparedness required for your hiking trip will naturally depend on the difficulty and duration of the trail itself. It is essential to make sure your departure time is early enough to get back before nightfall. Always plan to return to the trailhead by 17.00 at the latest, and inform someone of your plans and when you expect to return.

Take plenty of water with you; at least one or two litres each. It is very easy to dehydrate in the humidity of the rainforest and the heat of the tropical sun. Rivers and streams may provide handy refills if supplies run low, but only when you are sure there are no farmlands or houses upstream. If you are not sure, ask your guide. Wear sensible footwear such as walking shoes, trainers or strong sandals (see *Hiking Gear* box page 78). Flip-flops are really not a very good idea, and neither is walking barefoot.

Walking in Grenada's interior, especially at high elevations, can often mean getting wet and dirty. A towel and a change of clothes either to take along or to leave in your car at the trailhead is a good plan. If you take a change of clothes on the hike with you, be sure to put them in a waterproof or plastic bag. It is also a nice idea to have drinks and food waiting in a cooler on your return. As trails can become muddy and slippery and some of them require climbing through tree roots, you should take along a small first aid kit for any cuts, knocks or scratches you may pick up as souvenirs along the way.

It is not sensible to go to waterfalls or cross rivers if there has been heavy rain, or if heavy rain is expected. Flash flooding is not theoretical, it does happen, and people have been caught out by it, even at spots such as St Margaret's Falls. Use common sense and a degree of caution when deciding where to go in bad weather. If local people advise against a hike due to heavy rainfall or swollen rivers, do not go.

HIKING-TOUR OPERATORS

A & E Tours ↘473 435 1444; e aandetours@ spiceisle.com; www.grenadaguide.com/aetours. Bus tours & guided hiking to Concord Falls, Seven Sisters Falls, Grand Etang National Park.

Caribbean Horizons ↘473 444 1555; e info@caribbeanhorizons.com; www. caribbeanhorizons.com. Wide variety of generic & special-interest tours offered, including regular & advanced hiking.

Here are some tips about the kind of hiking gear that is good for Grenada.

FOOTWEAR Footwear has to be rugged, able to stand up to tough terrain, get muddy and wet, keep you upright, and then be able to do it all over again the next day, without fail, and without falling apart. If you plan on doing a lot of hiking and getting off the beaten path then footwear should be an important part of your preparation. Try to avoid heavy boots, and especially hard plastic soles. Heavy footwear will weigh you down and hard plastic soles are treacherous on wet rocks and wooden steps. Something with a little give is better, or look for shoes with Vibram soles which are designed to maximise grip. Closed toes are also important. Hiking sandals are fine but avoid anything with an open toe design. You need to protect your feet. I like to wear Merrell all-terrain hiking shoes and occasionally Keen hiking sandals, depending on where I am going. A pair of sneakers can work well, but be prepared to dispose of them at the end of your trip. They may be a little soggy and have a rather unpleasant smell!

CLOTHING Clothing should be lightweight. T-shirts are just fine, though don't wear your best ones, and purpose-made hiking shirts with UV and mosquito protection are great, though expensive, options. Lightweight shorts that you can swim in and which dry out quickly are good. If you plan on climbing some of Grenada's peaks then you should also bring long hiking pants to protect you from areas of razor grass. Long-sleeved shirts are also good for this and afford you more protection from mosquitoes, chiggers and so on (see page 42). A hat to protect you from both rain and sun is advisable, as is a pair of sunglasses. And bring a rain jacket for high elevations.

ACCESSORIES A waterproof rucksack is a good idea but failing that bring along a waterproof bag that you can carry inside a regular rucksack to protect valuables and sensitive items such as cameras, phones and other hand-held devices. Your rucksack should be comfortable to wear, have padded straps and some degree of protection for your back. Keep the size small but functional. Outer webbing to carry water bottles and clips for walking poles are very useful.

A water bottle or a wearable hydration system is a must-have. Some products have built-in filters that enable you to use tap water (which is usually safe to drink in Grenada) rather than buy bottled spring water each time you go out. If you are trying to minimise your environmental impact, and keep your costs down, then a reusable solution such as this is ideal. CamelBak has a number of good products.

Walking poles do help. Telescopic poles also allow you to stash them when they are not needed. They are a great aid to your legs on long forest trails, they provide support and stabilisation on steep descents, and they are also really useful on river crossings, especially if you are not quite sure how deep the water is! I take my Leki walking pole everywhere.

You should take a small medical kit with you that includes antiseptic solution or swabs, gauze, bandage, tape, and painkillers. Bring mosquito repellent that contains DEET and also sunscreen. A combination knife may also come in handy. A situation that requires a GPS unit or a compass is also one where you probably ought to forget about the gadgets and just hire local guide.

Grenada Eco Dive & Trek Coyaba Beach Resort; ✆473 444 7777; e dive@ecodiveandtrek.com; www.ecodiveandtrek.com. Dive & hiking operator based at the Coyaba Beach Resort on Grand Anse Beach offering a range of hiking from easy to more advanced trails.

Henry's Safari Tours ✆473 444 5313; e safari@spiceisle.com; www.henrysafari.com. Offers a variety of generic & speciality tours with a range of hiking options, from the easy to the more difficult trails.

K & J Tours ✆473 440 4227; e kjtours@grenadaexplorer.com; www. grenadaguide.com/kjtours. Half- & full-day bus-tour operator offering a selection of hikes. Contact for more details.

Kennedy Tours ✆473 444 1074; e kennedytours@spiceisle.com; www. kennedytours.com. Offering a selection of AC island bus tours as well as hiking. Options include the easy to the more advanced hiking trails.

Mandoo Tour & Taxi Service ✆473 440 1428; e mandoo@grenadatours.com; www. grenadatours.com. Specialising in AC bus tours to major attractions as well as a range of hikes, mostly along the more accessible routes, but also Mt Qua Qua.

Pete's Mystique Tours ✆473 440 1671; e pmistictors@spiceisle.com; www. mystiquetours.com. Island-wide bus tours to major attractions plus guided hiking on some of the easier trails.

Sunsation Tours ✆473 444 1594; e qkspice@ spiceisle.com; www.grenadasunsation.com. English-, German- & French-speaking operator with a range of tours including hiking.

Telfor Hiking Tours ✆473 442 6200. Telfor Bedeau is a national treasure when it comes to hiking. Much written about & at over 70 years of age Telfor has been hiking Grenada for most of his life & few could claim to know the mountains, waterfalls & trails better than him.

KAYAKING

Kayak hire and guided kayak tours are available both in Carriacou and on Grenada's southwest peninsula. You can kayak from the beach at Grand Anse or in sheltered bays and around coastal mangroves.

In addition to the following operators, you could also check with the dive shops on Grand Anse Beach, at True Blue, L'Anse Aux Epines and in Carriacou (see Grenada Scuba-Diving and Snorkelling Operators on page 86 for more details). Your hotel may also offer kayak rental or free kayaking.

First Impressions ✆473 440 3678; e starwindsailing@spiceisle.com; www. catamaranchartering.com. Sea safari tours around the west & southeast coasts include kayaking, fishing, snorkelling, BBQ on the beach & more.

Spice Kayaking & Eco Tours ✆473 439 4942; e info@spicekayaking.com; www.spicekayaking.

com. Guided mangrove & eco tours in kayaks on Grenada's south coast around the mangroves, beaches & reefs of Clarke's Court Bay & Hog Island. Tours of 4 and 6 hours can include lunch, fishing & snorkelling. Fully rigged fishing kayaks are also available for expeditions off Grand Anse beach. All tours include safety equipment, briefings & light refreshments.

OFF-ROADING AND JEEP TOURS

A nice way to experience some of Grenada's interior without too much exertion is to take a tour in a vehicle that is equipped for either off-roading or taking on some of the island's steeper mountain routes. Some of these tours may involve short forest hikes or bathing in rivers or pools – so come prepared.

Adventure Jeep Tours ✆473 444 5337; e adventure@spiceisle.com; www.

adventuregrenada.com. Operating modified all-terrain jeeps with open sides for views. Full-day tours include forest & plantation ride, waterfall, sulphur spa & lunch. Price includes hotel pick-up & drop-off, lunch & site entrance fees.

RIVER TUBING

Grenada's Great River is the island's longest, finding its source deep within the Grand Etang Forest Reserve and meeting the Atlantic Ocean at the expansive Great River Bay to the north of Grenville. The Great River is a clean, fast-flowing river, and is home to one of Grenada's pastimes: river tubing. Taking place on the Balthazar Estate to the west of Grenville and near the community of Bylands, the journey lasts around 90 minutes and takes you downriver, riding the currents and passing picturesque tropical vegetation. A safety briefing and demonstration is provided along with all the equipment you will need – a buoyancy jacket and an inflatable tube – before you set off, accompanied by guides who are there to provide assistance and security. Popular with day visitors arriving on cruise ships, river tubing is certainly a different way to explore and enjoy Grenada's natural environment. Travellers with back, neck or heart conditions should seek advice before river tubing. You should also note that the Great River is actually quite shallow in places so the ride can be a little bumpy and you may well run aground from time to time. Ask about river conditions in advance. Also check with operators for minimum age restrictions if you are planning on river tubing with your children. Prices are around US$45 per person.

Adventure River Tubing \ 473 444 5337; e adventure@spiceisle.com; www. adventuregrenada.com. Usually offering 3 scheduled departure times of 09.00, 11.30 & 14.00 & requiring reservations, there is a min group size of 10 & a max of 40 per tour.

SAILING BOAT CHARTERS, DAY CRUISING AND WATER TAXIS

The waters around Grenada and the Grenadines offer some of the very best sailing in the Caribbean. Whether you are travelling to Grenada on your own boat or hoping to charter one when you arrive, there are a number of options and services to choose from. Grenada has plenty of beautiful sheltered bays and anchorages, well-appointed marinas, marine servicing and repair facilities, and professional charter operators. World-class marina developments exist at Port Louis in the Lagoon south of St George's, at Le Phare Bleu Marina in Petite Calivigny Bay, and also at Prickly Bay in L'Anse Aux Epines on Grenada's south coast (see page 41 for more marina and haul-out information).

Several operators offer half- and full-day motor or sailing boat excursions around Grenada and Carriacou. These usually cost anywhere between US$50pp and US$150pp depending on the duration and distance of the trip. Check for prices, availability and minimum passenger quotas.

Excursions usually include snorkelling-equipment hire, refreshments and, if sailing all day, a packed lunch or a beach cook-up of some kind. Remember to take sun protection with you – in the form of lotion, a hat, or a long-sleeved shirt. It is extremely easy to get sunburned aboard a boat. Drink lots of water and try to limit your exposure to direct sunlight. When snorkelling, wear a T-shirt to protect your back and shoulders from those harmful rays.

Popular charters around Grenada take in the southwest coast, and the bays and islands of the southern coastline. Some head all the way up to Sandy Island and the Levera Archipelago, others circumnavigate the island completely. From Carriacou

Grenada Sailing Festival (*www.grenadasailingfestival.com*) This is a five-day regatta that takes place towards the end of January each year and attracts yachting enthusiasts from all over the world. Hosted by the Port Louis Marina, this event-filled festival includes yacht racing, live music entertainment, a workboat regatta, a swimming gala, kayak racing, and of course lots of food and drink.

Carriacou Regatta (*www.carriacouregatta.com*) Started in 1965 and held over the Emancipation weekend every year (end of July/beginning of August), this region is hugely popular and has become one of the largest sailing events in the region. It features yacht, sloop, long open boat and traditional work-boat races, the last forming the centrepiece of the festival with 12 classes of work-boat races that feature participants from around the region. Participants and spectators can enjoy both sporting and cultural events as well as competitions and family activities.

South Grenada Regatta (*www.southgrenadaregatta.com*) Hosted by Le Phare Blue, the South Grenada Regatta is a three-day sailing festival that usually takes place towards the end of February. It includes racing around Glover Island, dinghy racing, a 'pirates trail' and many other family oriented events.

you can explore the outlying islands or even journey up to the Tobago Cays in the Southern Grenadines.

Water taxis are an inexpensive and often fun way to get around on the water. On Carriacou good places to find water taxis are on Paradise Beach, Dover and Windward. Prices are negotiable. Enquire at your hotel or with your cottage or villa owners; often they will recommend someone they know, use and trust.

Carib CATS ☎ 473 444 3222; e helvellynhouse@ spiceisle.com; www.travelgrenadagrenadines. com. All-inclusive & very popular sailing excursions aboard a 60ft sailing catamaran that has been custom-built for day charters. A southern full-day cruise lasts around 7hrs & departs from Grand Anse Beach. It sails around the southwest peninsula & includes a BBQ picnic & snorkelling. The 4hr snorkel cruise incorporates the reefs of the west coast. The sunset cruise is a 2hr relaxing meander along the pretty west coast. The 8hr northern cruise heads up to the islands off the Levera Archipelago National Park, near Sauteurs. The trip includes snorkelling & a beach BBQ. Dinner & party cruises also available. Check website for further details.

Catch the Spirit ☎ 473 444 4753; e sanvics@spiceisle.com. A 32ft twin-engine pirogue offering customisable, private half- or full-day trips. Great for snorkelling, fishing, cruising or sunbathing.

First Impressions ☎ 473 440 3678; e starwindsailing@spiceisle.com; www. catamaranchartering.com. Full-day catamaran sailing tours around the island. Sunset tours, dinner cruises, party cruises & other private charter options are also available. Call or email for prices & schedules.

Footloose Caribbean Yacht Charters ☎ 473 405 9531; e footloos@spiceisle.com; www.grenadasailing.com. Day charters for private groups. Sail from St George's to Sandy Island or Île de Ronde or around the southwest peninsula to Calivigny & Hog islands. Prices include drinks, lunch & snorkelling-equipment hire. Both trips require a minimum of 4 persons. See website for further details on charters & pricing.

3

Grenada Seafaris ☎473 405 7800;
e seafarisales@hotmail.com; www.
grenadaseafaris.com. Short, fast & fun rides
along the west coast in a custom-made, high-
speed 'safari boat'. 1 or 2hr tours take you to the
Carenage & the beaches & coves of the west
coast. Exhilarating. Pick-up & drop-off on Grand
Anse Beach. Private charters also available. A
Seafari trip may not be for those with back
problems, disabilities or who are pregnant. Call
for advice.

Horizon Yacht Charters ☎473 439 1000;
e info@horizongrenada.com; www.
horizonyachtcharters.com. Bareboat (no crew or
provisions) or crewed, fully equipped yacht
charters from Grenada & around the Grenadines.
Yacht handling & chartering briefings, advice on
provisioning & land-based accommodation &
excursions. See website for details & pricing.

Mostly Harmless Carriacou; ☎473 443 7984;
e goldhill@spiceisle.com; www.
carriacoucottages.com. Snorkel trips, half- & full-
day cruises on the *Mostly Harmless*, a 28ft
modified motor launch. Call or email for prices.

Sea Fun Adventure Port Louis Marina;
☎473 419 000. Worth seeking out when you
arrive on Grenada is Sea Fun Adventure at Port
Louis Marina. Rent & pilot your own outboard

motor-powered dinghy or take a guided tour.

Shadowfax Banana Boat Tours
☎473 437 3737; e shadowfax@spiceisle.com;
www.bananaboattoursgrenada.com. Half- & full-
day sailing in the catamaran *Shadowfax*. The 4hr
Snorkelling Cruise takes you from St George's
Harbour along the west coast to snorkel the reefs
of the Molinère Protected Seascape. The 6hr
Champagne & Lobster Cruise takes you around
the southwest peninsula where you will snorkel
& have a champagne & lobster lunch on the
beach of Hog Island; fish broth, chicken &
vegetarian dishes also available if requested in
advance. An 8hr sailing trip takes you on a
complete circumnavigation of Grenada with a
stop-off at Sandy Island for swimming,
sunbathing & snorkelling; lunch is included or
how about a 2hr Sunset Cruise with champagne?

Tachyon Yachting ☎473 458 6529;
e info@tachyonyachting.com; www.
tachyonsailing.com. Full- or half-day private
charters aboard a 47-foot Robertson & Caine
luxury blue-water sailing catamaran with
enough space for 6 guests & 2 crew. Sail around
the southwest peninsula or up to Sandy Island in
the northeast. See website for rates, trip details &
availability.

SCUBA-DIVING

Grenada is the self-proclaimed 'wreck-diving capital of the Caribbean'. There
are indeed numerous sites within recreational dive limits, including the largest
shipwreck in the Caribbean, the *Bianca C* (see box on page 84). Conditions along
the many inshore reefs of both Grenada and Carriacou are usually quite easy.
There are lots of marine creatures, colourful reef fish, and hard and soft corals, as
well as interesting underwater topography including drop-offs and flat reefs. On
some sites, usually those in more exposed waters, you can also expect to see larger
creatures such as eagle rays and reef sharks. Visibility is usually good though it
can vary according to weather conditions and prevailing currents which can create
turbidity by stirring up the sandy seabed. All scuba-diving must be undertaken via
one of Grenada's dive centres and is usually from a boat.

Sea conditions in sheltered waters make Grenada and l good places to learn
to scuba-dive or to do an accompanied try-dive. Most dive centres have in-
house professional instructors offering a range of recreational and speciality dive
courses.

Certified divers must remember to bring their licence card. Unless you plan on
doing some wreck diving, few operators will ask to see log books given the relatively
easy conditions here. If it has been a while since your last dive trip, do the sensible
thing and take a short refresher and local orientation dive with an instructor
before jumping off a boat. It will make your diving both safer and, with renewed

confidence, much more enjoyable. Typically a two-tank boat dive will cost around US$100 and many operators offer discounted dive packages.

GRENADA DIVE SITES So far all the explored and named reefs are located around the southwest peninsula. This area is home to a number of shipwrecks and some interesting reef formations. The southwest is also where all of Grenada's mainland dive centres are currently located, many of which are linked to resort hotels.

Here is a broad selection of the most popular dive sites in the southwest. You will certainly come across others because dive centres have their favourites (they sometimes name new sites themselves or areas of reef they like to dive) and because site names have not been formally standardised.

Flamingo Bay (depth 6–28m) is a frequently visited and highly rated dive site. Located within the Molinère Protected Seascape, it is a reef and wall dive with plenty to see and, because it is fairly shallow, it is also a popular snorkelling spot. Dive encounters include large shoals of small reef fish such as chromis and Creole wrasse, sea fans, whips, sponges and elkhorn coral. Look out for seahorses, lobster, moray, grouper and rays. **Happy Valley** (depth 6–28m) is also a popular reef and wall dive located within the Molinère Protected Seascape, close to the shore. It too has an abundance of marine life, including large shoals of reef fishes, anemone, black coral and sea whips along the wall itself. Look out for the coral-encrusted admiralty anchor. **Dragon Bay** (depth 6–28m) is also located within the Molinère Protected Seascape. It is a reef dive that begins in the shallows and gradually descends before reaching a wall. It has some interesting volcanic topography including deep rock fissures. There are plenty of colourful reef fish, green morays, grouper and angelfish to see. **Molinère Reef** (depth 6–28m) is a broad expanse of reef with hard and soft corals, colourful fish, sea plumes and sea rods. It is located within the Molinère Protected Seascape and is also popular with snorkellers. At its northern edge is the **Underwater Sculpture Gallery** (see page 85). Just beyond Molinère Reef is the wreck of the *Buccaneer* (depth 22m). It is an 54 foot steel schooner with an open hull that experienced wreck divers can explore. Look out for giant grouper, octopus and garden eels. **Grand Mal** (depth 19–25m) is a deep dive along a wall to the north of St George's Harbour. Usually a drift dive, this one is for more experienced divers.

Directly east of St George's Harbour is the shallow wreck of the *Veronica* (depth 6–12m). This is a nice site for those who have little or no experience of wreck diving. A 120 foot cargo vessel, it has a deck with machinery including an anchor windlass and a crane. The hold is open and empty and now home to a wide variety of interesting marine creatures. To the southeast of the *Veronica* is the top of **Boss Reef** (depth 6–24m). This is a long stretch of reef that extends southwards with hard and soft corals, patrolling barracuda and some large green morays. This reef formation includes sites known as **Valleys**, **Japanese Gardens**, **Middle Boss** and **Lower Boss**. Also part of this system is **Northern Exposure** (depth 10–23m), a pretty reef with lots to see including brain corals and the occasional passing hawksbill turtle. *Shakem* (depth 30m) is the wreck of a 150 foot cargo ship that was transporting bags of cement to the port at St George's in 2001. Overloaded and listing from its heavy cargo, the boat sank within sight of the harbour and landed on the bottom completely upright. It is now an interesting site for experienced divers and, though a relatively new artificial reef, it is already home to a variety of marine life. *Unity Courier* (depth 12m) is a dive over three sections of a sunken vessel that went down in the Carenage in 1991. It was cut up into four sections with three of them placed off Quarantine Point (the site is sometimes called 'Three Wrecks'). The

BIANCA C: 'THE TITANIC OF THE CARIBBEAN'

The *Bianca C* began life as the *Marechal Petain* when it was launched in June 1944 at the La Ciotat yard near Marseilles. Two months later and still incomplete, it was being towed to Port Bouc when it was sunk by the Germans who were in the process of retreating from the south of France. It lay on the bottom until 1946 when it was raised and taken back to its original boatyard at La Ciotat where it was renamed *La Marseillaise* and refitted as a cruise ship. Its maiden voyage was in 1949 when it sailed with 736 passengers from Marseilles to Yokohama.

In 1957, it was sold to the Arosa Line of Panama and renamed *Arosa Sky* where it undertook further refitting and made its maiden voyage from Bremerhaven to New York. Two years later it was sold to the Costa family of Genoa who owned a shipping line called the Linea C. Refitted and renamed, this time after the family's daughter, the cruise ship *Bianca C* ran between Italy and Venezuela, pausing at the Caribbean en route. In 1961, while anchored in St George's Harbour, a fire started in its boiler room and quickly spread throughout the ship. With the help of its crew and the small sailing vessels of local Grenadians, all but one of its 673 passengers were evacuated. Unfortunately, passenger Rodizza Napale did not make it out.

Days later, the *Bianca C* was still burning and the British frigate *Londonderry* managed to cut its anchor chain and attach a towline. The aim was to tow it away from the entrance of the harbour and beach it somewhere around Point Salines. East of the harbour, the tow rope broke and, having taken on so much water during towing, the *Bianca C* sank in depths of over 40m, its final resting place. See also *Christ of the Deep* box on page 102.

---

ship's two boilers lie side by side nearby. It is an interesting dive with soft corals, reef fish and the occasional stingray. **Quarter Wreck** (depth 8–20m) is the remaining quarter, in fact the stern section, of the *Unity Courier*. Together with a nearby coral reef, you can explore its propeller, engine room, deck and pilot house.

The *Bianca C* (depth 28–40m) is the Caribbean's largest diveable shipwreck. Nicknamed 'the Titanic of the Caribbean', this wreck is an atmospheric and interesting dive (see box above). At 600 feet long and sitting upright, the ship attracts large pelagics as well as crustaceans, moray eels and rays. Interesting features include the swimming pool, the promenade staircase and the funnel. The *Rhum Runner* (depth 30m) is the wreck of a charter catamaran that was used as a tourist and party vessel. The wreck is usually explored first and then you move to a shallow reef that is teeming with colourful and interesting marine life. **Whibble Reef** (depth 15–30m) is a great reef dive with beautiful hard and soft corals and lots of fish life including shoals of jacks, passing pelagics and large barracuda. There is a good chance of meeting nurse sharks and hawksbill turtles on this dive. **Purple Rain** (depth 6–25m) is so named because of the large shoals of Creole wrasse that divers often encounter over this beautiful reef. Usually a drift dive, this site is one of the prettiest in the southwest, with giant barrel sponges, lots of reef fish, barracuda, rays and turtles. **Kahonee** (depth 6–15m) is a shallow coral garden with a wealth of life and activity. Divers regularly see lobsters, spotted morays and nurse sharks. The deeper edges of this dive site are sometimes also known as **Black Wall**, which descends to around 30m. **Windmill Shallows** (depth 18–40m) is a narrow coral-encrusted ridge and wall that plummets into the abyss on the extremities of Grenada's inshore reef system. It is a stunning reef and, because of the depth, attracts large passing pelagics. Usually there are currents on this drift dive.

On Grenada's exposed south coast dive conditions are usually more challenging. There can be rougher surface chop and there are often fairly strong currents. These sites are suitable for experienced or advanced divers only. They include the *San Juan* (depth 22–31m), the wreck of a 105 foot-long cargo ship lying upright and regularly attracting reef sharks, nurse sharks and eagle rays. The *Hema 1* (depth 30m) is the wreck of a freighter that sank in 2005 in rough Atlantic conditions on its way from Grenada to Trinidad. It is prone to strong currents but advanced divers can enjoy the wreck with lots of nurse sharks, who seem to have made it their home, as well as patrolling reef sharks and eagle rays. *King Mitch* (depth 28–34m) is the wreck of a World War II minesweeper that sank 5km from the southern coast of Grenada. Because of its location it is an advanced dive, often with rough

THE UNDERWATER SCULPTURE GALLERY

Grenada's Underwater Sculpture Gallery was the creation of UK sculptor Jason deCaires Taylor, whose works explore the relationship between art and the environment. Over time we are able to observe the natural ecological processes that take place as his sculptures become artificial reefs, therefore transitioning from pieces of art to become more at one with nature. Jason's sculptures are located in shallow, clear waters enabling them to be viewed by scuba-divers, snorkellers and people on clear-bottomed boats. The visibility around the Molinère reef system is usually good and surface conditions calm.

Since the initial installation of these works sea conditions and storms have caused a certain degree of damage to some pieces. Indeed *Siena* and *La Diablesse* are no longer in situ. There are plans afoot for Jason to revisit Grenada with some new and some replacement works. For updates see his website www.underwatersculpture.com or ask Phil at Dive Grenada on Grand Anse Beach.

Vicissitudes is the most iconic piece, a circle of figures, all holding hands, located at a depth of 5m. The figures are life-size casts of children from different ethnic backgrounds. *Vicissitudes* is a reflection of how children change as a result of and by adapting to their environment. Each of the sculptures physically changes over time according to sea and weather conditions and through the natural growth of corals. The *Un-Still Life*, at a depth of 8m, is a table with cement objects on top, including a vase, a bowl and some fruit. It is a classic still-life image, yet also 'un-still' because it is constantly changing with its environment, especially coral growth. The *Lost Correspondent* is a man sitting at a desk in front of a typewriter. Scattered over the desk are newspaper clippings of articles and news about the political events of Grenada in the 1970s and 1980s. *Grace Reef* at a depth of 4m comprises 16 figures of a Grenadian woman, all scattered over a wide area of sand. Each of the figures is positioned facing a different direction, and from time to time some of them become partially, or even completely, covered depending on the strength and direction of tide and current. Other artworks within the sculpture park include *TamCC Project* in 2m, *The Fall from Grace* in 7m and *Arawak Head* in 5m. In 2011, to commemorate the anniversary of the *Bianca C* fire and rescue, a replica of the *Christ of the Deep* statue (see page 102) was sunk and has become a new addition to the sculpture park.

surface conditions and strong currents. Shark sightings are virtually guaranteed. **Shark Reef** (depth 10–20m) is located off Glover Island on the south coast. Atlantic surface swells and strong currents make it a site for experienced divers only. The large rocks, hard corals, overhangs and deep water conditions attract nurse sharks, eagle rays, lobster, crabs and the occasional grouper.

GRENADA SCUBA-DIVING AND SNORKELLING OPERATORS

Aquanauts Grenada True Blue Bay Resort, L'Anse Aux Epines & Spice Island Beach Resort, Grand Anse Beach; True Blue ✎473 444 1126; Spice Island Beach Resort ✎473 439 2500; e aquanauts@spiceisle.com; www.aquanautsgrenada.com. PADI Gold Palm resort. Operates 3 fully equipped dive boats & offers dive courses, morning & afternoon diving. Equipment hire, retail shop, enriched air (nitrox) & underwater scooters available.

Devotion 2 Ocean Rex Grenadian Resort, Point Salines; ✎473 444 3483; www.devotion2ocean. com. PADI Gold Palm IDC offering a range of recreational- & professional-level scuba courses as well as daily boat diving.

Dive Grenada Flamboyant Hotel, Grand Anse Beach; ✎473 444 1092; e info@divegrenada. com; www.divegrenada.com. PADI 5 Star Dive Centre offering courses, daily boat diving & snorkelling. Equipment hire available. Located on

the beach front at the Flamboyant Hotel.

Eco Dive & Trek Coyaba Beach Resort, Grand Anse; ✎473 444 7777; e dive@ecodiveandtrek. com; www.ecodiveandtrek.com. A PADI 5-star resort offering dive courses, daily boat diving, watersports & hiking. Enriched air (nitrox) & equipment hire are available.

Native Spirit Scuba Grenadian Grand Beach Resort, Grand Anse Beach; ✎473 439 7013; e info@nativespiritscuba.com; www. nativespiritscuba.com. Right off the beach at Grand Anse, Grenadian-owned & operated PADI dive centre offering dive training & daily boat diving. Equipment hire available.

Scubatech Calabash Hotel, L'Anse Aux Epines; ✎473 439 4346; e info@scubatech-grenada.com; www.scubatech-grenada.com. PADI dive centre located on the south coast at Prickly Bay, offering courses & daily boat diving. Equipment hire available.

NORTHERN ISLETS DIVE SITES Advanced divers may be interested in a day excursion to the sites located between the islands of Grenada and Carriacou. There are dive sites at **Île de Ronde**, **Three Sisters**, **Frigate Rock**, **Diamond Rock** and **Bird Rock**. Conditions can be difficult on these sites with surface swell, surge and very strong currents. Reef formations are pristine and sightings of large pelagics are common. There are also some interesting cave formations at the Sisters dive sites. Advanced divers should definitely try to make these sites part of their trip.

CARRIACOU DIVE SITES Fondly known as the 'land of reefs', Carriacou offers excellent scuba-diving and snorkelling. The reef formations are pristine and there is an abundance of hard and soft corals, sponges and colourful marine fishes. Nurse sharks, barracudas and turtles are common sightings. There is no standardisation when it comes to dive-site names and none are marked by moorings. Operators have their own names, favourite sites and ways of diving them. Nevertheless, here is a selection.

Around the diminutive **Mabouya Island** to the west of Carriacou, there are interesting reef formations and wreck sites. Many of the reef sites suit less experienced divers though they can develop a little current from time to time. Sites around this island include **Mabouya North**, a spectacular wall dive to 20m which is suitable for most divers; **World of Dreams** (depth 8–20m), a sloping reef with plenty of giant soft corals and the occasional stingray; and **Sharkey's Hideaway** (depth 8–20m), a reef formation descending steeply to undulating rock formations that hide sleeping nurse sharks. **Mabouya South**, also known as **Twin Tugs**, is a wreck site at a depth of around 25m. The *Westsider* is a 1960s tugboat that worked the waters of the Caribbean before being deliberately sunk off Mabouya Island as an artificial reef. *Boris*, another tug, was also sunk as an artificial reef near to the *Westsider* in September 2007. Though they are young as dive sites, many interesting marine creatures are moving in, making them fun and interesting dives for the more experienced.

Sandy Island, also to the west of Carriacou, has a long reef starting at around 7m that plummets into deeper water at 20m, making for a nice wall dive suitable for both inexperienced as well as more advanced divers. This reef is usually explored as two dives and site names include **Sandy Island North, Sandy Island South** and **Western Adventure**. The other site often visited off this island is **Sandy Island Lighthouse** (depth 7–22m), which is a steeply sloping reef also suitable for all levels of diving ability. Look out for crabs, lobsters and moray eels as well as an abundance of reef fish including snapper and angelfish.

To the north of Sandy Island there is a small island called **Jack A. Dan**. This easy reef dive (depth 7–20m), also known as **Millennium 2000**, is popular with beginners as it has little current. It starts in the sandy shallows, follows a nice reef with coral formations, and always has lots of creatures to see including shrimps, lobster, moray eels, stingray and even the occasional passing eagle ray.

At **Sister Rocks** to the west of Mabouya Island and Carriacou there are a number of sites that suit the more adventurous scuba-diver. Reef and wall dives tend to have strong currents but are inhabited by a wide variety of marine creatures, colourful reef fish, hard and soft corals, tube and barrel sponges, patrolling barracuda, and nurse and reef sharks. **Barracuda Point** (depth 9–23m) is one such wall dive and **Sister Rocks** (depth 9–35m), sometimes also called **Deep Blue**, is usually a drift dive because of the strong current, where you may encounter large schools of jacks as well as barracuda and sharks.

To the south of Carriacou is **Frigate Island** where there is a challenging dive called **Chinatown** (depth 8–23m), sometimes also called **Chinese Pagodas**. Strong currents in the convergence of the Caribbean Sea and the Atlantic Ocean mean this dive is definitely one for advanced scuba-divers only. Usually explored as a drift dive, this sloping reef has some dramatic hard coral formations as well as barracuda, sharks and the occasional eagle ray.

CARRIACOU SCUBA-DIVING AND SNORKELLING OPERATORS

Arawak Divers ✆473 443 6906; e arawakdivers@spiceisle.com; www.arawak.de. Located at Tyrrel Bay, this English- & German-speaking PADI dive centre offers training & daily boat diving. Equipment hire available. **Carriacou Silver Diving** ✆473 443 7882; e scubamax@spiceisle.com; www.scubamax. com. English- & German-speaking PADI Gold

Palm IDC centre offering recreational & professional dive training & daily boat diving. Equipment hire available. **Lumbadive** ✆473 443 8566; e lumbadive@ lumbadive.com; www.lumbadive.com. English- & French-speaking Beuchat dive centre located in Tyrrel Bay offering PADI training courses & daily boat diving. Equipment hire available.

SNORKELLING

Most dive operators also offer snorkelling trips to inshore reefs. A popular destination on the main island is the Molinère Protected Seascape which is home to the **Underwater Sculpture Gallery** (see page 85), **Flamingo Bay** and **Molinère Reef** itself. Longer excursions on charter-boat cruises from mainland Grenada usually also include snorkelling and can take you to **Hog Island** in the south or **Sandy Island** in the north. Snorkelling trips are great fun for all the family and a nice way to enjoy the sights of underwater Grenada. Visibility in the shallows

3

is usually good and surface conditions calm. Snorkellers can expect to see a wide variety of colourful marine fish as well as corals and sponges. On Carriacou dive operators and water taxis offer snorkelling trips to **White Island** and Sandy Island. If conditions are favourable, accomplished snorkellers may also wish to take a look at the reef system just off **Anse La Roche Beach**.

TURTLE-WATCHING

From March each year giant leatherback turtles (*Dermochelys coriacea*), the largest of all living sea turtles, return to the beaches of Grenada and Carriacou to lay and bury clusters of eggs in the sand, which usually hatch in June and July. Some of Grenada's tour operators, plus specialist conservation and research groups, offer evening expeditions to observe these wonderful creatures. Tours usually start at around 20.00 and last until midnight or beyond, depending on activity. There are no guarantees of turtle sightings but the chances are very high. Operators usually expect you to observe a strict code of conduct on these tours and will provide briefings. No flash photography or flashlights may be used as they can disturb, distress and disorientate turtles. Nor can there be any physical interactions with these creatures. Dress for cool night-time conditions, prepare for rain and sitting in the sand, and protect yourself from mosquitoes and sand flies (see 41). Please be aware that the Grenada government permits the hunting of sea turtles at certain times of the year. Disturbing or collecting sea turtle eggs is illegal at all times.

Caribbean Horizons ✎473 444 1555; e info@caribbeanhorizons.com; www. caribbeanhorizons.com. Night-time trips to the Levera Archipelago National Park.
KIDO Ecological Research Station Carriacou; ✎473 443 7936; e kido-marina.fastigi@gmail. com; www.kido-projects.com. NGO that aims to preserve natural resources & ecosystems. Turtle-watching trips offered. Contact for details.
Ocean Spirits e info@oceanspirits.org; www. oceanspirits.org. NGO focused primarily on the protection of Grenada's marine turtles. Helps to coordinate turtle-watching trips with guides. Contact for details.

WHALE- AND DOLPHIN-WATCHING

The first thing you should know about a whale-and-dolphin trip (or 'safari') is that it never guarantees sightings. It could simply turn into a pleasant boat ride. Nevertheless, the chances are good, with success rates claimed to be above 90%. And if you do encounter whales, it will be an experience you are unlikely to forget. Certain times of the year are better than others. Usually sightings are more common between December and April though some species are observed all year round. A good tip is to ask about recent sightings before you book. You may be lucky enough to see humpback whales (*Megaptera novaeangliae*), sperm whales (*Physeter macrocephalus*), Bryde's whales (*Balaenoptera brydei*) and pilot whales (*Globicephala melaena*). Usually if whales are scarce, or if they have been spooked by predators, the boat captain is able to locate pods of dolphin somewhere along the coast. Dolphin sightings include spinner dolphins (*Stenella longirostris*), bottlenose dolphins (*Tursiops truncatus*), Fraser's dolphins (*Lagenodelphis hosei*) and common dolphins (*Delphinus delphis*).

First Impressions ✎473 440 3678; e starwindsailing@spiceisle.com; www. catamaranchartering.com. Offering a 4hr whale & dolphin excursion aboard a purpose-built whale catamaran for up to 35 passengers along the northwest coast of Grenada. Though sightings are never guaranteed, First Impressions boasts a 97% success rate. Contact for prices.

Part Two

GRENADA

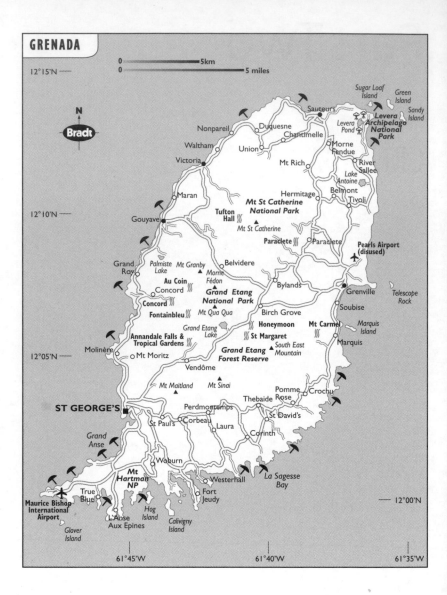

GRENADA

12°15'N

0   5km
0   5 miles

Bradt

N

Sugar Loaf
Island
Green
Island
Sandy
Island

Sauteurs
Levera
Pond
Levera
Archipelago
National
Park

Nonpareil
Duquesne
Chantimelle
Morne
Fendue

Waltham
Union
Mt Rich
River
Sallee

Victoria
Lake
Antoine

12°10'N

Maran
Hermitage
Belmont
Tivoli

Mt St Catherine
National Park

Tufton
Hall
Mt St Catherine

Gouyave
Paraclete
Paraclete
Pearls Airport
(disused)

Grand
Roy
Palmiste
Lake
Mt Granby
Belvidere

Au Coin
Morne
Fédon
Bylands

Concord
Grand Etang
National Park

Concord
Birch Grove

Fontainbleu
Mt Qua Qua
Honeymoon
Mt Carmel
Marquis
Island

Grand Etang
Lake
St Margaret

Annandale Falls &
Tropical Gardens
Marquis

Molinère
Mt Moritz
Grand Etang
Forest Reserve
South East
Mountain

12°05'N

Vendôme

Mt Maitland
Mt Sinai
Pomme
Rose
Crochu

Thebaide

ST GEORGE'S
Perdmontemps
St David's

St Paul's
Corbeau
Laura
Corinth

Grand
Anse
Woburn

Mt
Hartman
NP
Westerhall
La Sagesse
Bay

Maurice Bishop
International
Airport
True
Blue
Fort
Jeudy

12°00'N

L'Anse
Aux Epines
Hog
Island
Calivigny
Island

Glover
Island

61°45'W
61°40'W
61°35'W

Telescope
Rock

Grenville

Soubise

Birch Grove

St George's

Most travel guides, magazines and directories tend to describe Grenada's capital, St George's, as one of the prettiest towns in the Caribbean. Whether travellers agree with this sentiment or not, few would dispute that it is certainly very pleasing on the eye. Built around a large natural harbour, the town's white- and pastel-coloured houses, stone churches, terracotta tiles and galvanised roofs fill the hillsides with an exuberance of colour as they rise up from the water's edge. Add to this the surrounding blue sea, luxury sailing boats at anchor, cruise ships and a verdant backdrop of mountains and lush tropical forest and it is easy to see why most people reach for their cameras when they see this capital for the first time.

Located in the southwest of mainland Grenada at 12°02'N and 61°48'W, St George's is the administrative centre and major seaport of this tri-island state. The town is constructed around St George's Harbour, a natural haven that is said to have been carved by a particularly fortuitous burst of volcanic energy. There are two significant areas of the harbour: the Carenage on the northeast side and close to the main town; and the Lagoon, on the southeast side and home of the island's main port, a large marina development and an anchorage. To the north of the capital is St George's Bay and several residential areas including Sans Souci and Tempe. To the east of the capital are the high hillside areas of Mt Helicon and Richmond Hill. To the south of St George's there are the residential settlements of Paddock, Springs and Belmont. To the south of Belmont is Grand Anse and the southwest peninsula.

The capital still bears some of the scars of Hurricane Ivan, though most are healing. Sadly one or two buildings stand in ruin or disrepair, either abandoned or in the process of attempting to raise enough funds for renovation, restoration or, in some cases, a complete rebuild. Despite this, St George's is a lively place, full of interest, beauty and history. Visitors should be prepared for the hills of the town, some of which are very steep, but which add character and always offer captivating views and scenes of vibrancy and life. Visitors to St George's are regular and numerous, thanks to the proximity of the international airport and the cruise-

St George's

4

DON'T MISS

If your visit to St George's is brief, think about taking the self-guided walking tour (see page 105), otherwise try to make it to the following places:

Young Street Art galleries and local craft shops (page 98)
Grenada National Museum (page 101)
Fort George – offers a great view of St George's and the Carenage (page 101)

ship berth on the northwest side of town, so Grenadians are very used to seeing their capital even further crowded by an influx of international travellers. They are friendly, welcoming and more than happy to help you out with directions or offer you the chance to purchase their wares. Be sure to engage with the people of this pretty island capital, take your time to walk around and explore, and you will find your visit to St George's both pleasurable and memorable.

A BRIEF HISTORY

Though Columbus sighted and claimed Grenada in 1498 it was not until the mid 17th century that the first Europeans settled on the island. The Governor of Martinique, Du Parquet, purchased Grenada, Martinique and St Lucia from the Company of the Islands of America in 1650 for 1,660 livres. Of course, all of this was unknown and quite inconsequential to the Kalinago who had been living on Grenada for at least the previous 300 years. Upon landing on what is today known as the Ballast Ground to the west of the Lagoon (where the Port Louis Marina now stands), Du Parquet and his comrades were greeted by Kalinago chief Kaierouanne. Historians disagree on what happened next. Du Parquet offered the chief gifts – either as an appeasement according to some, or a land purchase according to others. Some also believe the gifts were in exchange for assistance in warding off the British. Regardless of which of these versions is the truth, all agree that Du Parquet spent the next year erecting housing, a church, and fortifications.

There was once a sandbar running across the mouth of today's Lagoon (the Lagoon was known by the French as Etang d'Eau Salée, meaning 'saltwater lake'), joining the Ballast Ground with the area known today as 'The Spout' to the south of the port in the vicinity of Tanteen. The French crossed the sandbar and began clearing the Tanteen area of its trees to start work on a large tobacco plantation. The settlement was named St Louis after the reigning French monarch, Louis XIV. It was also referred to as Port St Louis and, more commonly, **Port Louis**. Realising their visitors were here to stay, the Kalinago mounted a series of isolated attacks but were eventually either killed or driven off the island by French soldiers (see page 180).

Unfortunately the location of the settlement of Port Louis had one or two problems. The first was malaria. The settlers soon discovered that the brackish, stagnant waters of the Etang d'Eau Salée, then shallow and landlocked by the sandbar, was a perfect breeding ground for mosquitoes. The second problem was flooding. Tidal surges and storms meant that the relatively low and flat ground upon which Port Louis was built was frequently vulnerable to an unwelcome deluge. As the Kalinago had been routed, it seemed an opportune time for the settlers to pack up and move to a more comfortable place. This was to be the higher ground to the north of today's Carenage (then called simply 'Le Port'). By 1710 Port Louis was left to the whims of nature and the new settlement was named **Ville du Fort Royal**. Fort Royal was the name given to a fortification that had been constructed earlier, in around 1667, on the western end of today's Carenage. The fort was enlarged in the 1700s after the abandonment of Port Louis.

On 10 February 1763, the island was ceded to the British under the Treaty of Paris. The British renamed Ville du Fort Royal **St George's Town** (later shortened to St George's) after the country's monarch, King George III, and the fort was also renamed Fort George. In 1776, war broke out between England and France again and in 1779, under the command of the Count d'Estang from Martinique, French

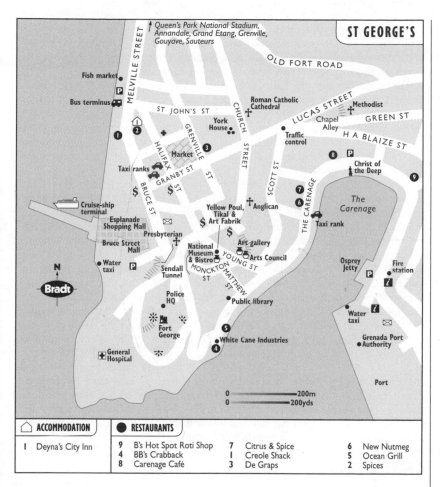

Queen's Park National Stadium,
Annandale, Grand Etang, Grenville,
Gouyave, Sauteurs

OLD FORT ROAD

MELVILLE STREET

Fish market

Bus terminus

ST JOHN'S ST

Roman Catholic
Cathedral

LUCAS STREET

Methodist

GREEN ST

York
House

CHURCH STREET

GRENVILLE ST

Chapel
Alley

H A BLAIZE ST

HALIFAX ST

Market

Traffic
control

GRANBY ST

BRUCE ST

Taxi ranks

SCOTT ST

Christ of
the Deep

Cruise-ship
terminal

Yellow Poui,
Tikal &
Art Fabrik

Anglican

THE CARENAGE

The
Carenage

Esplanade
Shopping Mall

Presbyterian

Taxi rank

Bruce Street
Mall

National
Museum
& Bistro

Art gallery

Arts Council

YOUNG ST

Osprey
Jetty

Fire
station

Water
taxi

Sendall
Tunnel

MONCKTON ST

MATTHEW ST

Police
HQ

Public library

N

Bradt

Water
taxi

Fort
George

White Cane Industries

Grenada Port
Authority

General
Hospital

Port

0 ————— 200m
0 ————— 200yds

⌂ ACCOMMODATION	● RESTAURANTS						
1 Deyna's City Inn	9 B's Hot Spot Roti Shop	7	Citrus & Spice	6	New Nutmeg		
	4 BB's Crabback	1	Creole Shack	5	Ocean Grill		
	8 Carenage Café	3	De Graps	2	Spices		

forces recaptured Grenada. The French seizure of the island had been relatively easy and it was with this in mind that their first task was to improve its military fortifications. Unfortunately for the French, their occupation only lasted until 1783 when Grenada was once again ceded to Britain, this time under the Treaty of Versailles. The British continued what the French had started and soon St George's was a very fortified capital indeed. In addition to Fort George and the redoubts at Hospital Hill, the approaches to the north and the east of town were overseen by the four forts of Richmond Hill. Ironically all the forts became quite redundant immediately upon their completion. The Treaty of Versailles marked the final defeat of the French and the beginning of a period of British rule that lasted for around the next 200 years.

The town of St George's began to grow as the island's capital. The mangroves and swamps around the Tanteen area were cleared and drained. Mosquitoes were driven out firstly through the introduction of guppies (*Lebistes reticulatus*), small fish that are native to South America and which feed on mosquito larvae; the second method was the less environmentally friendly use of the chemical DDT in the 1950s. The Tanteen area was ultimately reclaimed by burning and burying the capital's refuse there. In the 1960s the sandbar across the Lagoon was cut and the

1980s saw dredging efforts aimed at widening the entrance and deepening the water for use as an anchorage. Residential houses and businesses expanded northwards to the Queen's Park area along St George's Bay, eastwards into the hills, down to the Carenage and around and beyond the Lagoon to the south.

The Spout, between the Lagoon and the Carenage, where French settlers first moored their sailing vessels, became the island's main port. Following a huge regeneration project in 2000 costing some US$11million, the port was extended and updated to accommodate large container ships. In the same year, the Esplanade on the western shore of the main town was also levelled and redevelopment began to create a large jetty and terminal facility that would accommodate cruise ships. This work was completed in 2004.

From the floods and disease of the first settlement of Port Louis, the capital has witnessed its fair share of setbacks and disasters. In 1771, a fire that began in a French bakery burned all through the night. Because the town's houses and buildings were constructed almost entirely of wood, by the next day virtually everything had been reduced to ashes. In 1774, another fire, this time one that was suspected of being started deliberately, destroyed much of the town once again. In May 1792, despite the imposition of building standards and regulations that required materials to include stone, brick and tile, a fire that began aboard a ship laden with rum destroyed much of the Carenage. In 1885, the Bonfire Act prohibited the lighting of bonfires in the town during the traditional 5 November Guy Fawkes Day celebrations. When 100 citizens were given the status of special constables to help enforce this law, opponents began rioting which, somewhat ironically, resulted in small fires breaking out around the town. Further fires in 1920, 1925, 1952, 1975, 1979, 2000 and 2002 all threatened to cause more damage to the town than eventually transpired. In 1955, Hurricane Janet caused widespread devastation to the island which included severe damage to St George's and the sinking of the wooden harbour buildings. In 2004, Hurricane Ivan, the worst storm in Grenada's history, either damaged or totally destroyed the majority of buildings in the capital. Some of this damage is still evident today.

GETTING THERE

BY TAXI From Maurice Bishop International Airport it costs EC$50 to St George's and the journey takes around 15 minutes.

BY BUS Public buses are the most common mode of transportation in and out of the capital. All buses to and from St George's start and finish their journeys at the bus terminal on Melville Street near the cruise-ship terminal and the Esplanade Mall. Here are the buses that travel to and from the capital. (See *Getting around* in *Chapter 2*, page 53, for more about Grenada's bus system.) Please note, no public buses run to or from Maurice Bishop International Airport.

Zone 1 Lagoon Road–Grand Anse–Calliste	**Zone 4** St Paul's–La Borie
Zone 1 Belmont–Grand Anse–Calliste	**Zone 5** Grand Roy–Gouyave–Victoria
Zone 2 Springs–Woodlands–Woburn	**Zone 5** Gouyave–Victoria–Sauteurs
Zone 2 Calivigny–Westerhall–Grenville	**Zone 5** Concord–Grand Roy–Gouyave
Zone 3 Richmond Hill–Morne Jaloux–Marian	**Zone 6** Grand Etang–Birch Grove–Grenville
Zone 4 St Paul's–Perdmontemps–Vincennes	**Zone 7** Annandale–New Hampshire–Willis
Zone 4 Beaton–La Tante–Pomme Rose	**Zone 7** Beaulieu–Boca–Vendôme
Zone 4 St Paul's–Mardigras	**Zone 7** River Road–Tempe–Mt Parnassus

Zone 8 Cherry Hill–Fontenoy–Happy Hill
Zone 8 Cherry Hill–Fontenoy–Mt Moritz
Zone 8 Happy Hill–Beauséjour–Brizan

BY FERRY Osprey Lines (*www.ospreylines.com*) operates a high-speed ferry service between St George's, Carriacou and Petite Martinique. In St George's, the ferry arrives and departs from the jetty opposite the fire station on the Carenage. The journey between Carriacou and St George's takes about 90 minutes. The ferry departs from St George's at 09.00 Monday–Saturday and 08.00 Sunday, and at 17.30 Monday–Friday and Sunday. From Carriacou the ferry leaves for St George's at 06.00 Monday–Saturday, and 15.30 daily. The prices are EC$160 or US$62 for an adult return and EC$80 or US$31 for an adult one-way ticket. For children aged between five and 12, the price is EC$1( ) or US$38 for a return, and EC$50 or US$19 for a one-way ticket. For children under five years the prices are EC$20 or US$8 for a return and EC$10 or US$4 for a one-way ticket. The ferry does not usually operate on Christmas Day, Boxing Day, New Year's Day or Good Friday. Please check the Osprey Lines website or call 473 440 8126 for updates on timetables and fares before you travel.

BY HIRE CAR

From south to north If you are driving from Grand Anse and heading into town or up the west coast towards the north then here is how to do it. Assuming you are on Lagoon Road driving north around the Lagoon, stick to the left at the roundabout near the Botanical Gardens and follow the road past the port. After the Tanteen recreation ground stay left at the next roundabout and follow the water. You should find yourself curving to the right and then on to the Carenage.

Follow the Carenage right around to the other side. Look out for the public library because the road that runs to the right of it, Matthew Street, is the one you need to take. When you reach a fork at the top on Monckton Street, go left and you should find yourself at the entrance to the Sendall Tunnel. Drive through the tunnel and just follow the road as it emerges on to Bruce Street, past the Esplanade Mall, the bus terminal and the fish market, keeping the sea to your left. Soon you will find yourself arriving at the junction with the national stadium. The road to the right goes to the east and the Annandale Falls, the road straight ahead follows the west coast to Gouyave and eventually Sauteurs.

From north to south Assuming you are driving south from Gouyave and heading towards Grand Anse or the airport, or are just planning on a trip to St George's, here's how. At the junction with the national stadium, take the road on the right (left goes east). Follow the road until you reach the outskirts of the capital. You will see the fish market and the bus terminal on your right, and the Sendall Tunnel ahead of you. If you want to park in town then there is a car park above the bus terminal (alternatively, you can park for free around the far side of the Carenage near the fire station). If you are heading south, carry on, and before you reach the Esplanade Mall you must look out for a left turn up Granby Street towards Market Square. At the first junction on Granby Street you will see you are on the southwestern corner of the market. Turn right along Halifax Street and follow the road uphill. At the top of the hill you will be at a four-way junction. Go straight ahead, over the brow and down Young Street. Be careful on the brow as you are momentarily blind to what is ahead of you. You will see the Carenage in front of you but do not drive all the way down as part of it is one-way only. The last street on the left just before the Carenage is Scott Street. Take a left up there and follow it

St George's   GETTING THERE

4

all the way to a traffic light junction. The road to the right is H A Blaize Street and is the one you should take. A short distance along H A Blaize Street you will see a road on the right called Hughes Street. Go down it towards the Carenage again and then turn left. Follow the road around the Carenage and then around towards the port. At the roundabout take the road to the right past the port and the Tanteen recreation ground until you reach the Lagoon. Keep to the left around the Lagoon and you will be south of St George's on the road to Grand Anse and Maurice Bishop International Airport. Just follow the signs.

GETTING AROUND

Driving in St George's will be a challenge the first couple of times but after that you should find it is actually quite straightforward. The things that will throw curveballs at you as you sit wide-eyed and white-knuckled on your first attempt will be the rather poorly signposted one-way system, some very narrow and steep streets, lots of pedestrians who seem hell-bent on throwing themselves in front of your vehicle, somewhat small and hard-to-see traffic lights, and, if you are not accustomed to it, driving on the left.

Without doubt the best and most practical way to explore today's St George's is **on foot**. It is a fairly compact town and nothing is really very far, though please be warned, there are some very steep hills! Most roads have properly paved footpaths, though not all, and around the market you may be forced to walk on the road itself so please be careful and aware of traffic. Finding your way around is fairly straightforward. St George's is built on a hill that climbs up and inland away from the sea. The hill has a ridge that essentially splits the main part of town into two halves: on one side of the slope is the main shopping and market area (known as Bay Town); on the other side of the slope is the Carenage, a much quieter area. South of the Carenage, the road runs through Tanteen, past the port and around the Lagoon.

TOURIST INFORMATION

Grenada Board of Tourism Burns Point, at the southern tip of the Carenage between the port authority buildings & customs house; ☏ 473 440 2279 & 473 440 2001; e gbt@spiceisle.com; www.grenadagrenadines.com; ☉ 08.00–16.00 Mon–Fri. This is a useful place to pick up brochures, leaflets, maps & other resources. The staff can also help to organise tours for you. There is a second office opposite the Osprey Ferry Terminal, also on the Carenage.

⌂ WHERE TO STAY

See page 57 for accommodation price codes.

MID-RANGE AND BUDGET HOTELS AND GUESTHOUSES

⌂ **Deyna's City Inn** (12 rooms) Melville St; ☏ 473 435 7007; e cityinn@spiceisle.com. Located in the bustling Bay Town sector of St George's, Deyna's rooms are nicely decorated & have en-suite bathroom, AC, TV, phone. Continental b/fast inc. Long-term rentals also available. **$$**

⌂ **Tropicana Inn** (20 rooms) Lagoon Rd; ☏ 473 440 1586; f 473 440 9797; e tropicanainn@flowgrenada.com; www.tropicanainn.com. Motel-style accommodation located opposite the Lagoon to the south of St George's. Each room has double bed, en-suite bathroom, AC, TV, phone. Internet access available. Popular restaurant & bar serves a range of good value Caribbean & international

dishes. Take-away service also available. **$**
🏠 **St Ann's Guest House** Paddock; ☎473 440
2717; e info@stannsguesthouse.com. Long
established, family run guesthouse located in
Paddock, to the east of the Lagoon & within easy
walking distance of the capital. **$**

VEGAN RETREAT
🏠 **The Lodge** (2 rooms) Richmond Hill;
☎/f 473 440 2330; e thelodge@spiceisle.com;
www.thelodgegrenada.com. Luxury vegan
escape, located high on the ridge of Richmond
Hill with views of the interior & the coast. Each
room has a 4-poster bed, en-suite bathroom &
private veranda. Bedrooms & laundry are cleaned
with vegan products. To offset carbon footprints,
a tree is planted for every guest who stays at the
lodge. Fruits & vegetables are grown on site. The
vegan restaurant serves b/fast, lunch & dinner.
Price inc b/fast & airport transfers. **$$$**

SELF-CATERING APARTMENTS AND COTTAGES
🏠 **Pelican Apartments** (4 apts) Belmont;

☎473 440 1121; e augumar@spiceisle.com;
www.grenadaexplorer.com/pelican. Located
close to the Lagoon & within easy walking
distance of the Carenage & the capital. Each self-
catering apt has 2 bedrooms, bathroom, living
area, kitchen, ceiling fans, TV & phone. Verandas
have great views of the Lagoon & St George's
beyond. Weekly **$$**
🏠 **Lexus Inn** (18 apts) Belmont; ☎473 444
4780; e lexus@spiceisle.com. Pleasant, clean
budget accommodation with ocean views, Lexus
Inn is located on the main highway in Belmont,
halfway between St George's & the beaches of
Grand Anse. 1- & 2-bedroom fully furnished &
equipped self-catering apts with AC bedrooms,
Wi-Fi, & private balconies. **$**
🏠 **Lazy Lagoon** (10 cabins) St George's;
☎473 443 5209; e lazylagoon@caribsurf.com;
www.grenadaexplorer.com/lazylagoon. Simple
garden cottages & wooden cabins with
kitchenette, private bathroom & balcony
overlooking St George's Lagoon. Horni Baboon
bar & restaurant located nearby. **$**

✗ WHERE TO EAT AND DRINK

CARIBBEAN AND INTERNATIONAL
✗ **Victory Bar & Grill** Port Louis, Lagoon Rd;
☎473 435 7263; ⊕ daily. Excellent local &
international dining in the new Port Louis Marina
development. **$$**
✗ **BB's Crabback Caribbean
Restaurant** Carenage; ☎473 435 7058.
Waterfront eatery on the Carenage serving
Grenadian & international dishes. Very popular with
visitors & locals. Good value & recommended. **$$**
✗ **New Nutmeg** Carenage; ☎473 435 9525;
local & international dishes, bar & nice views of
the Carenage. Popular with locals & visitors.
Steaks, chicken, seafood, burgers, local juices &
more. **$$**
✗ **Ocean Grill Restaurant & Bar** Carenage;
☎473 440 9747. Waterfront restaurant located on
the Carenage. Local & international lunches &
dinners. **$$**
✗ **Museum Bistro** Young St. Located at the
back of the Grenada National Museum, serving
fresh daily bistro-style lunches & juices. **$$**
✗ **Citrus & Spice Restaurant & Bar** Carenage;
☎473 435 9741. An appetising selection of

international dishes with a local flavour. Wi-Fi
available. **$–$$**
✗ **Spices Restaurant & Bar** Deyna's City Inn,
Melville St; ☎473 435 7007. Wide selection of
delicious Creole & international dishes at this
popular downtown restaurant & bar. **$–$$**
✗ **Tropicana Inn Restaurant & Bar** Lagoon
Rd; ☎473 440 1586; Good selection of very
reasonably priced Caribbean & international
dishes. Take-away also available. **$–$$**
✗ **Creole Shack Restaurant** Melville St;
☎435 9376. Very popular & affordable eatery
serving good Creole & international food. Located
above the United Grocers Supermarket (entrance
just inside & up the stairs). Good value & very
popular. **$–$$**
✗ **B's Hot Spot Roti Shop** Carenage;
☎473 440 6438. Great rotis. **$**
✗ **Carenage Café** Carenage; ☎473 435 7691.
Local food, snacks, sandwiches, coffee & fruit
juices. **$**
✗ **De Graps** Grenville St. Located above the
bustling marketplace serving a good selection of
reasonably priced local food & drinks. **$**

FAST FOOD
✖ **Jamaican Patty Shack** Melville St. $

✖ **KFC** Granby St & Melville St. $
✖ **Subway** Esplanade Mall, Melville St. $

SHOPPING

St George's has lots of small shops and boutiques selling everything from household items to clothes, food and drink. Larger supermarkets tend to be located outside the capital closer to Grand Anse, though there is one on the Carenage and another near the bus terminal. The Esplanade Mall and Bruce Street Mall, also located near the bus and cruise-ship terminals, have a selection of souvenir and duty-free shops. Outside the Esplanade Mall there is a small vendors' market with stalls also selling crafts and souvenirs. This market tends to be busier and have more variety during the cruise-ship season. St George's market tends to be fuller and busier on Fridays and Saturdays though there will usually be stalls open on other weekdays too. Unfortunately the market has become quite a tourist trap with stalls in the covered section selling almost exactly the same selection of souvenirs. Most shops in Grenada close on Sundays.

In terms of payment, shops will almost always accept US dollars and some may also accept British pounds and euros. Boutiques and souvenir shops will usually accept major credit cards.

SUPERMARKETS
The Food Fair Carenage. Wide selection of local & imported foods, beverages & household items.
United Grocers Bruce St. Large supermarket in a busy part of town that carries a wide selection of products. Upstairs, the Creole Shack Restaurant is a handy place for an inexpensive bite to eat.

CRAFT, DUTY-FREE AND SOUVENIR SHOPS
Art Fabrik Young St. Hand-painted clothing, batiks, jewellery & gifts.
Art & Tings Esplanade Shopping Mall, Bruce St. Various artworks, carvings & prints.
Classique Grenada Craft Centre, south of the Carenage. Ceramics & pottery.
Colombian Emeralds International Esplanade Mall, Bruce St. Jewellery.
Duty Free Caribbean Esplanade Mall, Bruce St. Fragrances, cosmetics, alcohol, tobacco.
Ganzee Esplanade Mall, Bruce St. T-shirts, spices, chocolate, general souvenirs.
Liz Art & Craft Grenada Craft Centre. Ornaments, wood carvings & clothes.
New Dimension Esplanade Mall, Bruce St. Souvenirs, gifts & spices.
Spice Isle Plantations Grenada Craft Centre, south of the Carenage. Handmade soaps & bath products.
The Gift Shop Off Wharf Rd on the southeastern corner of the Carenage near the Grenada Port Authority building, selling a selection of gifts and souvenirs.
Tikal Young St. Local & international arts & crafts shop.
White Cane Industries Carenage. Handmade crafts created by the visually impaired, disabled and other people in need of support. Located between the Ocean Grill Restaurant & BB's Crabback Caribbean Restaurant.
Yellow Poui Young St. Art gallery with original paintings & sculptures by over 80 local & international artists.

OTHER PRACTICALITIES

BANKS AND MONEY TRANSFERS Banks are open 08.00–14.00 Monday to Thursday and 08.00–16.00 Friday. They are closed on Saturdays, Sundays and public holidays. Most banks have ATMs.

$ First Caribbean International Bank Church St   **$ Republic Bank Ltd** Bruce St
$ Grenada Co-operative Bank Ltd Church St   **$ Scotiabank** Halifax St

There are Moneygram and Western Union offices located on the Carenage.

SECURITY AND HEALTH Grenada is a safe place, the vast majority of its people are kind and friendly, and really the only precautions you need to take are the same ones you would back home. St George's, especially around the Esplanade Mall and the Carenage, will attract people trying to make a living selling souvenir items, or offering guide and tour services, because those places are where the majority of tourists are to be found. As you walk around the capital you will attract the attention of numerous taxi and bus drivers who are also on the lookout for business. There is no malice in any of it – people are just trying to earn a living. For some inexplicable reason many people will speak to you in an American rather than their own, very beautiful Grenadian accent – but try not to let it put you off.

Begging From time to time you may be approached by people asking you for money, but it is quite rare. If it does happen, it is usually in the form of a very polite request asking for a dollar or two for food and drink. The most common place for this seems to be around the Carenage, and in particular near to the jetty where the Osprey ferry arrives and departs. Whether you decide to give or not is up to you, but always be polite, regardless of how persistent people might be.

Police You will see plenty of police officers walking the beat and directing traffic in and around St George's, especially during the cruise-ship season. They will be happy to help you with directions if you find yourself a little lost. The emergency telephone number for police assistance is ☏ 911, and the police headquarters is located at Fort George.

Hospitals and pharmacies There are quite a few pharmacies in St George's, including a large one on the northwest corner of the market. The General Hospital is located on the south side of Fort George.

St George's General Hospital ☏ 473 440 2051

See also the *Health* and *Safety* sections in *Chapter 2*, pages 41 and 48.

COMMUNICATIONS
Post office Grenada's postal service is called the **Grenada Postal Corporation**. The main office is located at Burns Point, on the southern tip of the Carenage in St George's, near to the port. There is also a small post office located on Bruce Street, opposite the Esplanade Mall. A stamp for a postcard to either the UK or the US costs around EC$1.

Internet With Wi-Fi hot spots and mobile devices so readily available, internet cafes seem to have become a thing of the past and there are very few options in and around the capital. Almost all hotels offer wireless internet access and, if you are arriving under sail, you should get on to the web at the Grenada Yacht Club and Port Louis Marina.

Innovative Computer Café H A Blaize St, St George's. Internet café & other computer services.

WHAT TO SEE AND DO

THE CARENAGE The Carenage is probably the most recognised and photographed part of St George's. Acknowledged for its outstanding natural beauty as well as its classic Caribbean Georgian architecture, a slow meander around the Carenage is a pleasant activity for any visitor.

Said to be a partially filled submerged volcanic crater, the Carenage takes its name from the French *carénage* meaning careenage, a place where ships are repaired and cleaned. This name reflects the history of this natural harbour, once known simply as 'the port', where French and subsequently British ships, sloops and schooners put in for supplies and repairs. Though the port has now moved to the Tanteen area, the Carenage is still used by vessels of all kinds including long-liners, water taxis and boats transporting both people and supplies to and from the islands of Carriacou and Petite Martinique.

At the southern tip of the Carenage towards Tanteen, in an area known as Burns Point, there are the port authority buildings and customs house. Between these buildings you will find the offices of the **Grenada Board of Tourism** (see page 37), and from here there is a footpath that goes all the way around the Carenage. Opposite the capital's fire station is the departure and arrival jetty for the Osprey Line's **Grenada ferry service** between the main island, Carriacou and Petite Martinique (see page 39).

Looking across the still waters of the Carenage you can see Fort George on the far left together with St George's General Hospital and the renovated Caribbean Georgian buildings of the financial district further to the right. The hill of 'Carenage Town' or 'Over Town' is plain to see with its brightly painted houses, warehouses and offices. On the top of the ridge is the ruined Anglican cathedral and the recently restored Roman Catholic cathedral. Beyond them, down the other side of the hill, are the bustling shops and market stalls of the Bay Town district.

Continuing around the Carenage the road passes a number of businesses and some small local eateries. On the northern shore of the Carenage, facing out to the open waters of St George's Harbour, you will see some traditional English telephone boxes, some in good repair, some less so. Around this area of the Carenage you will occasionally see brightly painted fishing boats tied up and selling fresh fish to passers-by. Also along this shoreline, near a set of covered benches called Pedestrian Plaza, is the **Statue of Christ of the Deep**, presented by the people of Genoa, Italy, to the residents of St George's for their assistance in saving the passengers of the *Bianca C* when it caught fire in the harbour in 1961 (see box on page 84).

Continuing around the Carenage there are a number of eateries serving good local food such as **B's Hot Spot Roti Shop** and the **Citrus & Spice**. Also along the western side of the Carenage is **The New Nutmeg** restaurant which is popular with visitors and locals alike. Opposite The New Nutmeg is a taxi stand. From this side of the Carenage it is possible to see all the way across St George's Harbour and beyond to Grand Anse Beach. The last stretch of the Carenage passes the renovated buildings of the financial district to two further restaurants, the very popular, and definitely worth a visit, **BB's Crabback Caribbean Restaurant** and the ideally situated **Ocean Grill Restaurant & Bar**. If you are in this area please be sure to visit **White Cane Industries** where crafts are handmade and sold by disabled and visually impaired people, plus folk in need (see box opposite).

Between the Georgian buildings along the western edge of the Carenage is the **Grenada Public Library**. The original library was founded in 1846 and was located in a building shared by the Supreme Court registry and the General Post Office. Following reorganisation and expansion it was moved to its current site in 1892. The library also houses the national archives. (*Note: at the time of writing the Grenada Public Library was closed for urgent building renovations and it may be some time before the library is re-opened.*)

To the right of the library is the junction of the Carenage with Matthew Street. At the top of Matthew Street, on the corner of Monckton Street and Young Street, is the **Grenada National Museum** (*473 440 3725*; e *grenadamuseum@caribsurf. com*; ⊕ *09.00–16.30 Mon–Fri, 10.00–13.00 Sat, closed Sun; adults EC$5pp, children EC$2.50pp*). The museum was established in 1976 in an attempt by a group of private citizens to preserve and promote the island's cultural heritage. This group of individuals went on to form the Grenada Historical Society. The museum is located in one of the oldest buildings in Grenada, a former French army barracks constructed in 1704 as part of the original settlement of Fort Royal. The building was home to the town's jail between 1763 and 1904 and later became used as a warehouse and hotel. The museum has a number of permanent collections as well as alternating displays and exhibitions by local schoolchildren. A visit starts with an introduction to the island's indigenous people, the Amerindians and specifically the Kalinago. There are fine examples of ceramics and also Yoruba artefacts. The European occupancy of Grenada is represented by a collection of plantation machinery and tools as well as examples of firearms and cannons. There are also interesting displays of the history of conflict on the island from the battles between the French and the British to the Fédon Rebellion and the more recent revolution and US intervention. Whether you find yourself exploring St George's for just a day or for longer, the Grenada National Museum is well worth a visit. Afterwards treat yourself to some lunch and a fresh fruit juice at the **Museum Bistro**.

Next to Monckton Street is Young Street, which also has a number of arts and crafts stores including Art Fabrik, Tikal and Yellow Poui, all of them worth a visit. And if you are looking for a bottle of cold water and a good value snack, check out D Roti Shop, also on Young Street.

FORT GEORGE Fort George is located on Fort George Point at the northern entrance to St George's Harbour. Its initial construction was started by the French in 1667 when they first settled on the island. It was then called Fort Royal. When the French moved from their original settlement at Port Louis up to the new town of Ville du Fort Royal in the early 1700s, the fort was redesigned, enlarged and

The statue of *Christ of the Deep* that stands on the side of the Carenage in St George's is a replica of the original which lies underwater off San Fruttuoso Bay, Genoa, Italy. The original 1954 work, *Il Cristo Degli Abissi*, by Guido Galletti was recast and presented as a gift from the people of Genoa, via the Costa Shipping Line, to the people of Grenada. The statue is made of bronze and is around 2.8m in height. It is a figure of Jesus Christ with arms outstretched in a gesture of blessing to mariners leaving port. The inscription on the statue reads:

> To the people of Grenada in grateful remembrance of the fraternal Christian hospitality shown to passengers and crew of the Italian liner Bianca C, destroyed by fire in this harbour on October 22 1961. Dedicated by the Costa Line of Genoa, Italy.

Just before it was about to set sail for Europe, the Italian luxury liner *Bianca C* caught fire in St George's Harbour. With over 300 passengers and 200 crew members on board, the ship was evacuated with only one death and eight casualties. The surviving passengers were housed by the people of St George's until they managed to leave the island several days later. The ship did not sink, but its burned-out hulk was obstructing the entrance to the harbour, so a decision was taken to move it. While it was being moved it sank 2.4km off Quarantine Point (see box on page 84).

The original idea was to have the statue facing out to sea, overlooking the wreck of the *Bianca C*. After much wrangling and disagreement, it was originally placed on the eastern entrance to the Carenage. In 1989, it was moved to its current position, though no longer in sight of the *Bianca C*'s final resting place.

strengthened. In 1763, when Grenada was ceded to the British under the Treaty of Paris, the garrison was expanded further to include military barracks and was renamed Fort George. Following the Treaty of Versailles in 1783, the need for fortification became less and less. Between 1854 and 1979 Fort George was used as the headquarters of the Grenada Police Force.

In 1979, Fort George became the headquarters of the People's Revolutionary Army and was renamed Fort Rupert in honour of the father of then prime minister Maurice Bishop. On 19 October 1983, Maurice Bishop, together with 24 supporters, was executed by the People's Revolutionary Army, leading to the US military intervention in Grenada just six days later (see Revolution and Intervention, page 18).

Today Fort George is once again home to the headquarters of the Grenada Police Force and the site of some of the original military barracks is now the location of the Grenada General Hospital. Some of the administrative buildings within the fort have suffered the effects of both time and hurricane, and paint rather a sad picture. Though it is the police headquarters, the fort is open to the public and is accessed from the west side, near the entrance to the General Hospital, up a narrow paved road and then some rather steep steps to a ticket booth. The entrance fee is US$2.

You will find yourself on the top of the compound on the west wall where cannons point out to sea. Along the south wall, from a small grassy area, you can enjoy great views of St George's Harbour, Port Louis Marina, and Grand Anse. If you make your way down the steps to the internal compound you will find yourself in the very place where Maurice Bishop and his supporters were executed in 1983 (see page 18).

On the wall you will see a plaque erected in 1993 in memory of those who were killed. You can either exit the fort the way you came or through the small archway in the courtyard. Follow the steps out to the car park. Opposite the police headquarters buildings, you should see a fenced walkway and viewing platform. From here there are really good views of the capital and the Carenage.

BAY TOWN Bay Town, in reference to St George's Bay, is the name given to the northwestern half of St George's. To get from the Carenage to Bay Town, or vice versa, there are two options: climb and then descend the steep ridge that runs along the centre of town, or pass through the **Sendall Tunnel**. Named after a former governor, this 100m-long tunnel was constructed in 1895 to provide more direct and easier access to each of the two sides of St George's. It is located between Bruce Street near the Esplanade in Bay Town, and Monckton Street near the Carenage. It is a narrow tunnel, just 4m high, and is a one-way street for vehicles travelling from south to north, in other words from the Carenage to Bay Town. People also walk through this tunnel, usually hugging one side in single file. Take care when doing this and be sure to pass your fellow pedestrians when no vehicles are approaching.

On the northwestern end of the Sendall Tunnel is Bruce Street and the bustling Melville Street. Here you will find the **Esplanade Shopping Mall** and the **Bruce Street Mall**. Outside the Esplanade Shopping Mall, especially on cruise-ship days, you may come across entertainment, street vendors and a number of guides offering tours. Inside the malls you will find a selection of fast food eateries, boutiques, and lots of duty free, souvenir and gift shops. Also within the Esplanade Mall, at the very far end, is the entrance and exit for the **cruise-ship terminal**.

Melville Street has a number of small snackettes and local eateries such as the very popular **Spices Restaurant & Bar** and **Creole Shack Restaurant**, both of which are inexpensive and worth trying. Melville Street is also where you will find the **St George's Bus Terminus** which is the hub of the island's bus system. Naturally this is a very busy and noisy place. Despite the crowds, the apparent confusion and the hubbub, the bus system is actually very straightforward and well organised. Once you know the number of the zone you are travelling to, just find the next bus in line with that number. All of the buses about to depart line up in number order. Conductors usually stand outside the bus trying to get it filled so the driver can depart. You can always double-check with the driver about the bus route, fare and destination. (For more information on Grenada's buses see pages 52–3.) Above the bus terminal is a car park; the entrance is on the north side.

Further along Melville Street is the **fish market** where you can buy a wide variety of locally caught fish and seafood. Opposite the fish market you will see a number of small barber shops, bars and vendors selling fruits and vegetables. Melville Street continues northwards to Queen's Park where it becomes the main road along the west coast to Gouyave and to Sauteurs in the north.

From opposite the Esplanade Mall on Melville Street, there are two roads that head into the heart of Bay Town. They are Granby Street and Hillsborough Street. These two streets contain a number of general stores and boutiques. At the intersection with Halifax Street, at the very centre of the Bay Town district, is **Market Square**. When the French settlers moved from Port Louis to the new town of Ville du Fort Royal in the early 1700s, they set out this square as a parade ground and assembly point for their military. During the British occupation of the island it was used as a public square where political meetings and public executions would take place. This is where the captured insurgents of the Fédon Rebellion (see page 142) were executed and also where a cage and gibbet were erected for the incarceration, punishment and torture of escaped slaves. In the late 1700s the square was also used for Sunday markets where slaves would gather and meet on their rest day to socialise and enjoy the food they had grown and cooked.

Today Market Square is a very noisy and busy place, particularly on Friday and Saturday mornings which are the capital's main market days. It is surrounded on all four sides by roads, and visitors have to compete for space with each other, with street vendors, with stallholders and with vehicles to enjoy the lively atmosphere, the produce and the general vibes of the market. The colourful stalls are crammed very close together and sometimes it seems there can be no way through. It is almost as if they were just dropped haphazardly from the skies, with no order and little organisation. Nevertheless, with a great deal of patience, an open mind and a sense of fun and adventure, visitors should throw themselves wholeheartedly into the hullabaloo and enjoy the market to its fullest. The vendors are friendly and happy to explain their produce, show you their spices and even tell you how to cook an oil-down if you ask nicely enough. Look out for fresh fruits and vegetables as well as a wide selection of seasonings and spices. You will also see people selling clothes, accessories, music CDs, DVDs and natural oils. If you get there early enough you may also see fishermen selling bundles of live blue crabs. You should be aware that the market has become quite a tourist trap and you may find yourself constantly asked if you would like to buy spices and souvenirs. It can become a little tedious and the wares, though interesting enough, appear to be almost exactly the same on every stall, especially in the covered market area. Even though they are now very accustomed to tourists, if you would like to take photographs of market vendors, it is both prudent and polite to ask for permission first.

If you can find it, you may come across a **cenotaph** in the market square. There have been a number of odd location choices for a memorial to honour Grenada's fighting men, starting with the Esplanade in the 1960s. Prime Minister Gairy had it removed from this spot in 1968 and placed it where the Wallace Fountain used to stand in Market Square. The market and the monument became a bit of a mess, however, and it became less and less practical to have a cenotaph in a location that was more and more infrequently used for public gatherings. In 1994, a new cenotaph was placed in the Botanical Gardens near the ministerial offices between the Tanteen and Paddock areas of town. This is now the place where wreaths are laid each year on Armistice Day.

Surrounding the market, Granby Street, Halifax Street, Hillsborough Street and Grenville Street are crammed with a variety of stores, boutiques, roadside snackettes and local eateries. The whole area, especially the northern end of Halifax Street, has the feeling of a bazaar. It is fascinating and infectious, though perhaps a somewhat intimidating place for visitors who are not accustomed to this kind of brouhaha.

St John's Street runs from Melville Street, opposite the bus terminal, across the ends of Halifax and Grenville streets and then steeply uphill where it meets Church Street. Granby Street becomes Market Hill which heads steeply upwards to also join up with Church Street. Along the top of Church Street is **York House**, once the home of the Houses of Parliament, now sadly a rather neglected ruin. Built in the late 18th century, York House was originally a residential home. From the early 1800s, following the death of its original French owner, the building, one of the largest in the town at that time, was used as a home for both Parliament and Supreme Court. It also hosted state functions, banquets, exhibitions and concerts. Unfortunately York House suffered a great deal of damage during Hurricane Ivan, including the complete loss of its roof, forcing it to be abandoned until funds can be allocated to its reparation. Hopefully this fine building will not stand abandoned and broken for too much longer. It is one of very few pre-colonial British buildings left (almost) standing in Grenada and is therefore very much part of the island's cultural heritage.

CHURCHES At the top of Church Street, very close to York House, is the **Roman Catholic Cathedral of the Immaculate Conception**. A small church known as St James's Chapel stood on this site in around 1804 when a decision was taken to replace it with something larger. As was common across the Caribbean at this time, the emancipation of slaves meant that they were allowed to worship freely in church. As the churches had only ever been built to house a limited number of worshippers from the white plantocracy, this sudden influx meant that many were too small. Records indicate that churches, particularly the Roman Catholic ones, were either enlarged or reconstructed during the 19th century. Most liberated slaves took to the Roman Catholic rather than the Anglican Church, either through the influence of French masters or in open rejection of the Church of their former British masters. Thus the numbers attending Anglican churches declined and the Roman Catholic churches began to thrive.

A confusion of dates upsets the exact story of the development of the capital's Roman Catholic cathedral. As with most cathedral constructions it is fair to assume that bits were added to the original over time. Parts of the tower are said to be the oldest surviving components of the church, dating as far back as 1818 and the life-size crucifix is believed to have been added in 1876. The cathedral was completed sometime around 1884. Unfortunately much of the cathedral was destroyed during Hurricane Ivan in 2004. For a long time only the tower, the walls and the frames of the arched windows stood somewhat precariously in this spot, a very sad reflection of its former glory. There was no roof, the windows on the windward side had all gone and the interior was succumbing to the elements. But a campaign finally succeeded in raising enough funds for its restoration and the cathedral rises above the skyline of the capital once more.

Further down Church Street in the direction of the Carenage there is **St George's Anglican Church**. Located next to St George's Anglican School, this church too suffered the trauma of Hurricane Ivan and, rather sadly, further destruction by treasure-seekers. Reduced to a shell, there is no roof, many windows have gone and the interior is exposed to rain. The bell tower remains however, and still chimes the hour.

In 1690, French settlers erected the town's first church on this site – St James's Roman Catholic Church. During British occupancy in 1784 it was confiscated and transformed into an Anglican church. An earthquake in 1825 destroyed it and it had to be rebuilt. Inside the church, along its walls were a number of marble plaques, some of which remain, but some of which appear to have been wrenched rather ruthlessly away. One plaque, which was there when I wrote the first edition of this guide, but had disappeared when I returned to write this one, was a fascinating snapshot of history, commemorating those who were held captive and later executed on the orders of Julien Fédon during the insurrection of 1795–96 (see page 142). The plaque stated that it was sacred to the memory of Ninian Home, former governor and one of 47 people who were executed by the rebel leader. In case the plaque is never recovered, here is what it said:

St George's is best enjoyed on foot, though its hilly topography means you also have to be fairly fit. If you are here for a short time and would like to explore the 'best bits' then give this self-guided walk a try. It should take between two and three hours depending on your pace. Take a bottle of water and be prepared for plenty of steps and some very steep hills!

Start in front of the Esplanade Mall on Bruce Street near the Sendall Tunnel. With your back to the mall, walk towards the tunnel. On the right-hand side of the tunnel entrance you will see steps climbing up the side of the hill. Walk all the way to the top where you will meet a tarmac road. If you wish to take time to explore Fort George, the entrance is round to the right and the entrance fee is US$2. For more about it see page 101. Alternatively you could choose to look down over the town from the viewing platform which you will find up the steps opposite the police headquarters to the left.

From Fort George walk towards the town down the narrow Grand Etang Road, past St Andrew's Presbyterian Kirk (see below) and traffic lights to the four-way junction at the top of the ridge. Be careful of traffic on Grand Etang Road as well as at the junction itself. Turn right here and walk down Young Street. Stick to the left. Along this street you will pass several craft shops and art galleries such as Tikal, Art Fabrik and Yellow Poui, all of which are worth investigating.

Continue all the way down Young Street to the end. You should now be at the Carenage. Before heading to the left for a walk around the Carenage, take a short diversion to the right to see the public library building. Stroll around the Carenage at your leisure, past a couple of very nice local bars and eateries. When you reach the cargo and tour boats in the corner of the Carenage, continue around the water's edge until you reach the *Christ of the Deep* statue (see page 102) and the traditional red telephone boxes. Now look across the road for a street running off the Carenage, called Hughes Street. It is opposite the telephone boxes. Walk up Hughes Street to the top where you should turn left. You are now on H A Blaize Street. Be careful of oncoming traffic here. It is a little tricky. Stick to the right if

Proprietors and inhabitants of this colony, all of whom were taken prisoners on 3rd March 1795, by an execrable banditti, composed principally of white new-adopted subjects of this island, and their free colour'd defendants, who stimulated by the insidious arts of French Republicans, lost all sense of duty to their sovereign, and mindful of the advantages they had long enjoy'd by participating in the blessings of the British Constitution, open'd on that day those destructive scenes which nearly desolated the whole country; And on 8th April following, completed the measure of their iniquity, by barbarously murdering (in the Rebel Camp at Mount Quaqua) the above innocent victims to their diabolical and unprovoked cruelty.

Located close to Fort George is **St Andrew's Presbyterian Kirk**, which is known locally as the 'Scots' Kirk'. Now sadly in a state of ruin following Hurricane Ivan, this church is testament to the relatively high population of Scots who arrived in Grenada, Carriacou and Petite Martinique among the first British settlers. The influence of these people is still very evident throughout all three islands in the form of place names, family names and the traditions of boatbuilding in Carriacou and Petite Martinique. The beautiful Gothic church with its prominent bell tower was constructed in 1831 with the assistance of Freemasons. Today it is unfortunately too dangerous to enter.

you can. Walk along this street until you reach Green Street on your right. Walk up it a short distance until you come to St George's Methodist Church. Now look for some steps going up Chapel Alley to the left of the church. Climb up these steps and then turn left on Lucas Street. You should find yourself opposite the Swedish Consulate. A little further down the road is the Consulate of the Netherlands.

Continue along the right-hand side of Lucas Street past some stone arches on your left and a box from where police officers direct traffic during rush-hour periods. You will come to a junction with Church Street where you should turn right. You will pass the ruins of York House (see page 104) on your left, before arriving at the restored Roman Catholic cathedral. Take a look inside though please respect any service that may be taking place.

From the cathedral walk back along Church Street past York House and straight over the junction with Lucas Street. On your left you will see a very pretty, privately owned period house, then the Anglican school followed by the ruins of St George's Anglican Church. Take a look around.

From the ruined church, follow the road as it curves to the left in front of the Grenada Co-operative Bank on Simmons Street, and look out for cobbled steps going downhill on the right-hand side of this short road. Walk down these steps until you emerge at the bottom. You are back on Young Street. A little to the right is Monckton Street and the Grenada National Museum (see page 101). The museum is really worth visiting and the bistro at the back is a handy place for a bite to eat and well-earned refreshments.

Turn right out of the museum and walk to the end of Monckton Street. On your right you should see the entrance to the Sendall Tunnel. With care and due attention to traffic, which will be travelling in the same direction as you, walk through the tunnel in single file on the left-hand side. You will emerge at Bruce Street and the Esplanade Mall where you began your walk. If it is a Friday or a Saturday, and you still have the time and the energy, consider a walk up Granby St (opposite the Republic Bank) to explore the market.

ST GEORGE'S ENVIRONS If you continue along Melville Street and follow the coastal road beyond the bus terminal and the fish market you will eventually arrive at the St John's River and the Queen's Park **National Stadium** (number 5 or 7 bus from town). Queen's Park was designated a 'place of recreation' by the Grenada government in 1887 and it became the home of cricket and then horse racing. The space was also used for parades, various other sports events, festivals, music concerts, political rallies and carnival celebrations. In 1997, the original pavilion was demolished to make way for a national sports facility. The project was completed in the year 2000 at an estimated cost of over US$20million. In 2004, Hurricane Ivan destroyed everything. A year later, in 2005, the People's Republic of China began work on a US$30million reconstruction project with the aim of completing a cricket stadium that would host matches for the 2007 Cricket World Cup. The new National Stadium was completed in time and has a seating capacity of around 15,000.

To the south of the National Stadium is the cemetery and up above it, **Hospital Hill**. The name comes from the French *Morne L'Hôpital*, where the settlement's first hospital was located in the 1730s. The British constructed a set of three gun batteries in this position in the 1760s and it proved to be their main, though

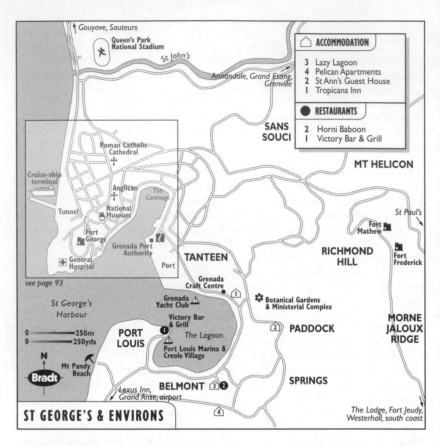

see page 93

ST GEORGE'S & ENVIRONS

ultimately losing, defensive line during the successful French invasion of 1779. This conflict wrought considerable damage to the original fortifications and, once the Richmond Hill forts had been built, the batteries of Hospital Hill were abandoned. Today these sites remain neglected and are overgrown with weeds.

South of the Carenage is the port and an area called Tanteen. Tucked into a corner, very close to the port and almost at the back of the customs house and the Grenada Board of Tourism office, is the **St George's Postal Corporation**. Opposite the busy entrance to the port is the Tanteen Recreational Ground used for local sports events. Behind the playing field is the Marryshow Community College and a short distance to the south of it, the **Botanical Gardens**. The gardens began life as a botanical station, constructed in 1887 as a facility to aid in the development of the islands' agriculture. They provided the islands' farmers and agriculturalists with research, experimentation and education facilities, as well as a nursery for plant propagation. After many years, interest in and use of the station declined and the area became a garden showcasing some of the islands' tropical flowers, plants and trees. In 1968, a small zoo was opened at the rear of the gardens. In the 1980s both the zoo and the gardens entered a period of neglect. The zoo was closed and in its place new government ministry offices were constructed. Unfortunately this building work encroached upon much of the flora, thereby reducing the gardens to a small park. The gardens also house the new cenotaph (see page 104) and a small bandstand.

A short distance from the Botanical Gardens and the playing field is the **Lagoon**. Once landlocked and full of rather stagnant, brackish water that, together with the mangroves of Tanteen, served as an ideal breeding ground for mosquitoes, the Lagoon was dredged and opened up in the 1980s and 90s to create a quite beautiful anchorage. The Lagoon is home to the **Grenada Yacht Club**, which was founded in 1954, and **Port Louis Marina.**

PORT LOUIS Located on the site of the first French settlement (the malaria has long since departed), Port Louis is an ongoing development project that will eventually include boutique hotels and luxury homes, tropical gardens, tennis courts and more. At the time of writing, the marina and Creole Village were up and running. Managed by Camper & Nicholson, the marina offers berths for vessels up to 180 feet as well as all the technical services required by yachts and motor cruisers. The Creole Village is home to the Victory Bar & Grill, a number of boutiques, a charter yacht company and tour operator services. For boat lovers, whether you own one or not, this is a really nice place to come for a short stroll and a bite to eat. On the western shoreline of Port Louis is a rather secluded beach that will also be integrated into the final product.

The Port Louis development has plans to include the renovation of a former luxury hotel, the **Islander** (once also known as the Santa Maria and location of the 1957 Hollywood film *Island in the Sun*). For more information about this project go to www.portlouisgrenada.com and www.cnmarinas.com/marinas/port-louis. There is ample parking here and access is free.

RICHMOND HILL AND FORT FREDERICK To the east of St George's, high above the town, are the two remaining forts of **Richmond Hill**. Originally there were four of them: Fort Frederick, Fort Mathew, Fort Lucas and Fort Adolphus. Only Frederick and Mathew are recognisable and accessible today, with Fort Frederick, the main fort, an interesting visitor attraction. The fortifications along the ridge of Richmond Hill go back to 1778 when the British built defences there. With the aim of defending St George's from an attack from the east, the forts face inland and look out across the interior towards Mt Parnassus, Mt Maitland and beyond. During the French invasion of 1779, these defences were easily overrun and it was for this reason that, once in power, the French set about strengthening them. But it was not until the British returned that the forts were finally completed. By then the Anglo-French wars were over.

Fort Frederick is definitely worth visiting (*top of Richmond Hill, to the east of St George's; US$2; number 3 bus from town*); it is an impressive fortification and has been well preserved and maintained. From the highest points of the fort there are super views for miles around. You can see St George's, the southwest peninsula and Grand Anse, the south coast and Fort Jeudy, and, to the north and east, the Grand Etang Forest Reserve and the mountains of the interior.

LANCE AUX EPINES COTTAGES

GRENADA WEST INDIES

5

The Southwest Peninsula

Grenada's southwest peninsula is very different to the rest of the tri-island state. It is home to the majority of Grenada's hotels, resorts, holiday apartments and villas, restaurants, tour operations, marinas and anchorages, luxury residential homes and even gated communities. Its proximity to the capital, St George's [112 C1], and to the Maurice Bishop International Airport [112 B3], together with its spectacular beaches, turquoise seas and beautifully natural and tranquil bays, all combine to provide Grenada with an attractive and almost entirely self-contained tourist industry.

This region is for travellers who are looking to relax on a beach, take in some sun, enjoy the sea, unwind, and live and dine in more than a little luxury. Indeed, Grand Anse Beach [112 C2], one of the Caribbean' s most famous stretches of sand, is perhaps all that some visitors to Grenada may ever actually see. Thanks to a number of well-equipped, state-of the-art marinas and very picturesque natural anchorages, the south is also very popular with the international sailing community. Yachts lie at anchor in many of the peninsula's secluded bays and you will often bump into 'yachties' in supermarkets, hotels, restaurants and bars, rediscovering their land legs, catching up on creature comforts, and provisioning for their onward voyage.

GETTING THERE

If you are arriving at Maurice Bishop International Airport [112 B3], check to see if your hotel or resort will meet you with a free shuttle service. Many do. If you are travelling by taxi then expect to pay in the region of EC$40 to Grand Anse and L'Anse Aux Epines, and EC$35 to True Blue. If you are driving a hire car from the airport, simply follow the main highway for around five minutes until you reach the first roundabout. True Blue is to your right. Continue straight ahead for Grand Anse and L'Anse Aux Epines. After a long stretch of road past an industrial estate

The Southwest Peninsula   GETTING THERE

5

DON'T MISS

If your time in Grenada is limited, here's a don't-miss list.

Grand Anse, **Morne Rouge** and **Magazine beaches** (page 122)
Scuba-diving (page 127)
Roger's Bar on Hog Island (page 129)

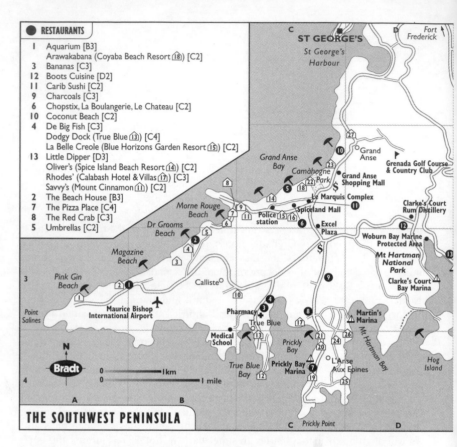

RESTAURANTS

1	Aquarium [B3]
	Arawakabana (Coyaba Beach Resort ⑱) [C2]
3	Bananas [C3]
12	Boots Cuisine [D2]
11	Carib Sushi [C2]
9	Charcoals [C3]
6	Chopstix, La Boulangerie, Le Chateau [C2]
10	Coconut Beach [C2]
4	De Big Fish [C3]
	Dodgy Dock (True Blue ⑬) [C4]
	La Belle Creole (Blue Horizons Garden Resort ⑮) [C2]
13	Little Dipper [D3]
	Oliver's (Spice Island Beach Resort ⑭) [C2]
	Rhodes' (Calabash Hotel & Villas ⑰) [C3]
	Savvy's (Mount Cinnamon ⑪) [C2]
2	The Beach House [B3]
7	The Pizza Place [C4]
8	The Red Crab [C3]
5	Umbrellas [C2]

THE SOUTHWEST PENINSULA

you come to a second roundabout. L'Anse Aux Epines is the road to the right, and then right again at the very next junction. Grand Anse is left at the roundabout and then left again at the next. Grand Anse, True Blue and L'Anse Aux Epines are all signposted so you will not have too much difficulty.

If you are staying at La Source or Maca Bana Villas [112 A3], instead of heading towards St George's and Grand Anse, follow the airport road in the opposite direction, past the staff car park and around a couple of sharp bends to a narrow road that runs towards the very end of the southwest peninsula. Your accommodation is located along this road on the right-hand side.

GETTING AROUND

If you have a hire car you should have little trouble finding your way around the southwest peninsula as Grand Anse, L'Anse Aux Epines and Maurice Bishop International Airport are all very well signposted. A number 1 bus from St George's will get you to Grand Anse and as far south as Calliste. A number 2 bus will get you to Grand Anse from the southeast. Once in Grand Anse there is an 'off-route' system that takes in the beaches, hotels and bays of the southwest peninsula. The bus fares here are a little more expensive than elsewhere on the island (see page 52 for more on Grenada's bus system).

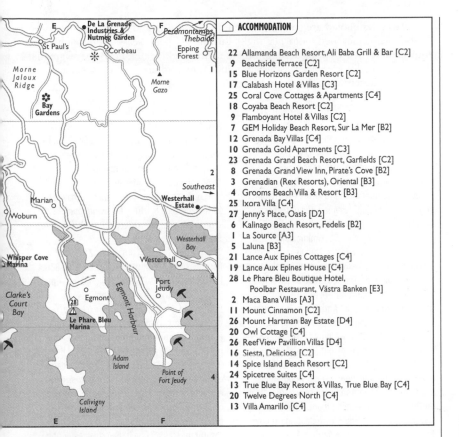

ACCOMMODATION

22 Allamanda Beach Resort, Ali Baba Grill & Bar [C2]
9 Beachside Terrace [C2]
15 Blue Horizons Garden Resort [C2]
17 Calabash Hotel & Villas [C3]
25 Coral Cove Cottages & Apartments [C4]
18 Coyaba Beach Resort [C2]
9 Flamboyant Hotel & Villas [C2]
7 GEM Holiday Beach Resort, Sur La Mer [B2]
12 Grenada Bay Villas [C4]
10 Grenada Gold Apartments [C3]
23 Grenada Grand Beach Resort, Garfields [C2]
8 Grenada Grand View Inn, Pirate's Cove [B2]
3 Grenadian (Rex Resorts), Oriental [B3]
4 Grooms Beach Villa & Resort [B3]
25 Ixora Villa [C4]
27 Jenny's Place, Oasis [D2]
6 Kalinago Beach Resort, Fedelis [B2]
1 La Source [A3]
5 Laluna [B3]
21 Lance Aux Epines Cottages [C4]
19 Lance Aux Epines House [C4]
28 Le Phare Bleu Boutique Hotel,
   Poolbar Restaurant, Västra Banken [E3]
2 Maca Bana Villas [A3]
11 Mount Cinnamon [C2]
26 Mount Hartman Bay Estate [D4]
20 Owl Cottage [C4]
26 Reef View Pavillion Villas [D4]
16 Siesta, Deliciosa [C2]
14 Spice Island Beach Resort [C2]
24 Spicetree Suites [C4]
13 True Blue Bay Resort & Villas, True Blue Bay [C4]
20 Twelve Degrees North [C4]
13 Villa Amarillo [C4]

FILLING UP You will find petrol stations along the main road between Grand Anse and St George's and another on the junction of the Maurice Bishop Highway (the road to the airport) and L'Anse Aux Epines.

🏠 WHERE TO STAY

The southwest peninsula has the largest selection of hotels, resorts, apartments and villas anywhere in Grenada. Most places accept major credit cards and many offer a wide variety of packages that may include meals, tours, use of watersports equipment, and even golf course membership. Before you finalise any booking, check whether the price quoted to you includes taxes and service charges, and if you are likely to want to use internet and Wi-Fi services be aware that some hotels charge extra for this. Travel agents in the US and the UK are likely to offer better deals than the hotels' rack rates so check with them after researching your favourites. Prices are often negotiable, especially if you plan on staying for several nights in the low season (July–September).

The accommodation listed below is deliberately selective and by no means comprehensive – there is lots to choose from in the southwest, including a wide selection of private holiday homes, apartments, cottages and villas to rent. For more extensive listings of the latter you could check www.spiceislevillas.com.

Price codes quoted are current at the time of writing and are loosely based on double occupancy per room per night during the peak season, or roughly the equivalent for self-catering accommodation with weekly rates. Please be aware that these price codes are meant as broad guides only and are subject to change. See page 57 for accommodation price codes.

HIGH-END BOUTIQUE HOTELS AND LUXURY RESORTS

🏠 **Spice Island Beach Resort** [112 C2] (67 rooms) Grand Anse; ☎473 444 4258; e reservations@spicebeachresort.com; www. spicebeachresort.com. Award-winning luxury hotel located right on Grand Anse Beach. Light, airy & immaculately designed, the hotel has a selection of suites, all of which have balcony or patio, AC, flat-screen TV, DVD, minibar, phone & en-suite bathroom facilities. The Oleander, Ocean & Garden suites have living rooms & are situated in tropical gardens. The Sea Grape Beach suites are right on the beach & have private patio garden & hammock. The Anthurium Pool suites have a private entrance, garden & personal plunge pool. The Luxury Almond Pool suites have a private swimming pool, outdoor dining terrace & sea views. The Royal Collection Pool suites have a private swimming pool & cedar wood sauna. The Cinnamon & Saffron Beach suites are located on the beach & have living room, dining room, wet bar, master bedroom with floating canopy bed, 2 bathrooms, private gardens & hammocks. The hotel is home to Oliver's restaurant for fine Creole & international dining, & the Sea & Surf Terrace & Bar. Spa treatment & recreational activities available. All inclusive pricing: b/fast, lunch, afternoon tea, dinner, beverages, golf club membership, tennis court use, non-powered watersports facilities (kayaks, Hobie Cats, etc). **$$$$$**

🏠 **Calabash Hotel & Villas** [112 C3] (30 suites, 5 luxury villas) L'Anse Aux Epines; ☎473 444 4334; f 473 444 5050; e calabash@ calabashhotel.com; www.calabashhotel.com. Beautiful & luxurious hotel comprising 30 elegantly furnished suites located in 3ha of tropical gardens with pool, secluded beach & bay frontage. Rhodes' Restaurant offers fine dining & the beachside deck bar serves refreshing drinks. Each suite has en-suite bathroom with shower & whirlpool bath, AC, TV, DVD, minibar, Wi-Fi, iPod dock, private patio or balcony. A maid serves b/ fast for you each morning. The Thornycroft Suite

has a private pool. Facilities include watersports (scuba-diving centre located on site), tennis & swimming pool. Luxury villas, the Swallow, Tree Frog, Pool House, Caribali & Hummingbird, are located on the exclusive Amber Belair development, a secluded peninsula to the west of the Calabash & L'Anse Aux Epines. All have en-suite bedrooms, kitchen, AC, living room, TV, swimming pool, housekeeper & cook. B/fast inc. **$$$$$**

🏠 **Laluna** [112 B3] (16 suites, 7 villas) Morne Rouge; ☎473 439 0001, US toll free ☎+1 866 4 LALUNA; f 473 439 0600; e info@laluna.com; www.laluna.com. A fusion of Italian & Indonesian design, Laluna is an exclusive, luxury boutique hotel comprising 16 suites & 7 villas (available for purchase) perched on a wooded hillside overlooking the secluded Portici Beach. Privately located within mature tropical gardens, each suite has 4-poster Balinese king-size bed, en-suite bathroom, AC, TV, CD player, day bed, ceiling fan, phone, wireless internet access, private deck & plunge pool. Swimming pool, restaurant serving fine Italian cuisine, lounge & cocktail bar. Massage, yoga & spa treatments are also available. Intimate & chic, Laluna will appeal to those seeking solitude, luxury & wellness. **$$$$$**

🏠 **La Source** [112 A3] (100 rooms) Pink Gin Beach; ☎473 444 2556; ☎(US) +1 866 830 1531 ☎(UK) 44 1245 459906 f 473 444 2561; e lasource@theamazingholiday.com; www. theamazingholiday.com. Extremely private, high-class resort located on the powder-white sands of Pink Gin Beach. All-inclusive packages focus on relaxation, rejuvenation & luxury. Gourmet food, yoga, tai-chi, meditation & massage treatments, aerobics, 9-hole golf course, tennis, archery, a range of watersports & scuba-diving all feature in a complete experience for those who wish to get away from it all. All rooms have AC, ceiling fan, king-size or twin beds, en-suite bathroom, balcony or terrace. La Source has 3 restaurants, 3 bars & a café-deli. Very private all-inclusive option that is ideal for travellers who want to relax & have access to everything they need without having to go far. Prices inc all food, drinks, services & activities. **$$$$$**

🏠 **Mount Cinnamon** [112 C2] (21 suites & villas) Grand Anse; ☏473 439 9900; f 473 439 8800; e reservations@mountcinnamongrenada. com; www.mountcinnamongrenada.com. Peter de Savary luxury resort located at the southern tip of Grand Anse Beach. Contemporary & colourful, the hotel's daring design successfully fuses European & Mediterranean chic with the essence of Grenada to produce vibrant & comfortable accommodation. Suites & villas are furnished with sitting rooms, kitchen & b/fast bars, TV, balcony with sea views. Mount Cinnamon is also home to Savvy's Mediterranean & Creole restaurant. Wedding packages available.**$$$$$**

🏠 **Coyaba Beach Resort** [112 C2] (80 rooms) Grand Anse; ☏473 444 4129; f 473 444 4808; e reservations@coyaba.com; www.coyaba.com. Luxury resort hotel with a distinctively ethnic feel, paying homage to the island's first settlers in name, thoughtful design & furnishings. Beautifully airy with tropical gardens, the resort is located right on Grand Anse Beach. Rooms overlook pool or gardens & have en-suite bathroom, AC, TV, Wi-Fi, ceiling fan, mini-fridge, safe & phone. The Arawakabana restaurant serves fine local & international cuisine. Carbet restaurant serves up poolside grills & 3 bars should keep you well watered. Massage & beauty services, tennis, swim-up bar, gym & watersports – inc PADI 5-Star Centre also available. Wedding packages offered.**$$$$**

MID-RANGE HOTELS AND RESORTS

🏠 **Grenadian (Rex Resorts)** [112 B3] (212 rooms) Magazine Beach; USA & Canada ☏+1 305 471 6170; UK & Europe ☏44 20 8741 5333; www. rexcaribbean.com. Large resort located on the very beautiful Magazine Beach. A wide selection of room options include hillside, beachfront, ocean view & deluxe suites. All rooms have AC, TV, en-suite bathroom, fridge, balcony or patio. The resort has 3 restaurants (Cinammon, Oriental & Spicers), 2 bars & a lounge. Regular evening entertainments. Activities include watersports, scuba-diving, tennis, fishing & windsurfing. Children's club, children's pool & children's restaurant menus. Prices are not published

though are available on request. Check website for links to booking accommodation or contact your local travel agent (package deals will be considerably cheaper than rack rates). Good all-inclusive option, especially for families.

🏠 **True Blue Bay Resort & Villas** [112 C4] (38 rooms, villas & suites) True Blue; ☏473 443 8783, US toll free ☏+1 888 883 2482; f 473 444 5929; e mail@truebluebay.com; www.truebluebay. com. Imaginatively designed resort hotel with a selection of very tastefully decorated en-suite rooms, suites & villas. True Blue Restaurant & the popular Dodgy Dock Restaurant & Lounge Bar offer both formal & casual waterfront dining with regular live entertainment. Rooms have AC, TV, ceiling fan, kitchenette, patio or balcony. Villas have fully equipped kitchen & private plunge pool. Resort facilities also include boutique, car rental, marina, dock & berths, scuba-diving, yacht charters, ocean kayaks, sport fishing charters, Hobie Cats & 2 swimming pools. You could even indulge in cooking & cocktail-making classes. Very nice accommodation with great on-site facilities. Kid-friendly. B/fast inc. **$$$–$$$$**

🏠 **Grenada Grand Beach Resort** [112 C2] (250 rooms) Grand Anse; ☏473 444 4371; f 473 444 4800; e paradise@grenadagrand.com; www.grenadagrand.com. Enormous resort hotel located on 20 acres along Grand Anse Beach. Rooms & suites have en-suite bathrooms, private balcony or patio with either beach or garden view, AC, TV, phone & internet access. The resort's impressive facilities include tropical gardens, the 100m fantasy pool with waterfalls, jacuzzis & sunken bar, & the 20m sunset pool. The Fantasy Bar & Grill, the Sunset Bar & the Waterfront Restaurant offer drinks & dining. Tennis, watersports & scuba-diving all available. Babysitting service offered. A great option for families. Packages available. **$$$–$$$$**

🏠 **Flamboyant Hotel & Villas** [112 C2] (67 hotel & villa rooms) Grand Anse; ☏473 444 4247; f 473 444 1234; e flambo@spiceisle.com; www.flamboyant.com. Large hotel with room, suite, self-catering studio & villa accommodation located on the southern tip of Grand Anse Beach. All accommodation has en-suite bathroom, AC, TV, phone, laptop data port, private balcony or patio with sea views. Some rooms have kitchenettes & villas have fully equipped kitchens. Facilities include swimming pool, sun terrace, large restaurant, beachside cabana, & The Owl sports & entertainments bar. The hotel is home to Dive Grenada, offering a full range of PADI courses as well as regular boat & snorkelling excursions to nearby sites. Wedding packages available. **$$$–$$$$**

⌂ **Allamanda Beach Resort** [112 C2] (50 rooms) Grand Anse; ☎ 473 444 0095; f 473 444 0126; e stay@allamandaresort.com; www.allamandaresort.com. Located right on Grand Anse Beach, the Allamanda is an established resort hotel with 50 1- & 2-bedroom ground- & upper-floor rooms that are equipped with en-suite bathroom, AC, ceiling fan, TV, phone & safe, fridge, & private balconies. Some suites also have a whirlpool bath. Wi-Fi is also available. In the centre of the resort is the swimming pool, sun terrace & Ali Baba Grill & Bar serving various BBQ & kebab dishes. Amenities & activities include massage, tennis & watersports. Dive packages also available. **$$$**

⌂ **Kalinago Beach Resort** [112 B2] (29 rooms) Morne Rouge Bay; ☎ 473 444 5254; f 473 444 1189; e kalinagobeach@spiceisle.com; www.kalinagobeachresort.com. New & modern resort located alongside the white-sand beach of the beautiful Morne Rouge Bay. Traditional decor & furnishings with modern facilities such as AC, Wi-Fi, iPod dock & cable TV. Private verandas with sea views, swimming pool & sun terrace. Fedelis Restaurant offers local & international dishes. Wedding packages offered. **$$$**

⌂ **Grenada Grand View Inn** [112 B2] (77 rooms & apts) Grand Anse; ☎ 473 444 4984; f 473 444 1512; e gvinn@spiceisle.com; www. grenadagrandview.com. Located close to both Grand Anse & Morne Rouge beaches with great sea views. All rooms have AC, ceiling fans, fridge, en-suite bathroom, balconies. Apts have kitchenette. Facilities include Pirates Cove Restaurant Terrace & Bar, serving local & international cuisine. Dinner theatre offers a 'spicy musical revue'. Swimming pool & conference room. **$$**

⌂ **Siesta Hotel** [112 C2] (37 rooms/apts) Grand Anse; ☎ 473 444 4646; f 473 444 4647; e stay@siestahotel.com; www.siestahotel.com. In pleasant gardens & within walking distance of Grand Anse Beach, the family run Siesta Hotel has 37 rooms, suites & apts that all face the sea.

Each room has en-suite bathroom, AC, TV, phone, refrigerator & private veranda or terrace. Swimming pool & Deliciosa Restaurant, serving Creole & international cuisine, enhance the hotel's amenities & pleasant, friendly ambience. **$$**

HIGH-END SELF-CATERING APARTMENTS, COTTAGES AND VILLAS

⌂ **Lance Aux Epines House** [112 C4] (8 rooms) L'Anse Aux Epines; ☎ 473 415 1770; f 473 444 3321; e info@lanceauxepineshouse.com; www.lanceauxepineshouse.com. Luxury accommodation in renovated English colonial-style estate house. Tropical gardens, beach, waterfront, dock, yacht moorings, sailing boat, 65ft infinity swimming pool, jacuzzi, billiards room. Rooms have en-suite bathrooms, AC, TV, internet, 4-poster beds. Converted Sugar Mill Tower House is located separately & has 2 en-suite bedrooms. Price inc housekeeping staff. **$$$$$**

⌂ **Maca Bana Villas** [112 A3] (7 villas) Magazine Beach; ☎/f 473 439 5355; e macabana@spiceisle.com; www.macabana.com. Located above Magazine Beach, Maca Bana's eco-friendly villas are thoughtfully designed around tropical fruits & plant themes. They are spacious, private & luxuriously furnished. All have AC, flat-screen cable TV, iPod docks, lounge, bedrooms, en-suite bathrooms, fully equipped modern kitchen, utility room, screened private sun deck with hot tub. Mobile phones loaned to guests. Private cooking classes offered & art lessons with resident fine artist Rebecca Thompson. Beauty spa, yoga and Pilates. Perched above one of Grenada's loveliest beaches and with the fabulous Aquarium restaurant right next door, Maca Bana is a great place to stay. **$$$$$**

⌂ **Ixora Villa** [112 C4] (3 dbl bedrooms) L'Anse Aux Epines; ☎ (UK) 44 121 246 6066; f (UK) 44 121 246 7077; e info@ixoravillagrenada.com; www.ixoravillagrenada.com. Stylishly designed & furnished villa located in Coral Cove. 3 bedrooms, bathrooms, living area, sun terrace, kitchen, swimming pool, gazebo, whirlpool bath, utility room, internet connection, library, private jetty & kayak. **$$$$$**

⌂ **Mount Hartman Bay Estate** [112 D4] (8 suites) L'Anse Aux Epines; UK ☎ 44 843 357 5561; f 843 357 5562; e enquiries@mounthartmanbay.

com; www.mounthartmanbay.com. Located on a private peninsula on the south coast, with private beach, helipad & jetty, this stunning accommodation consists of 8 sumptuous Gaudiesque 'cave' suites with AC, flat-screen TV, DVD, 4-poster or king beds, private verandas. Facilities include 27m infinity swimming pool, jacuzzi spa, library & home cinema, gym, sun terrace, private speedboat with captain for cruising & waterskiing, in-house gourmet chef, waiting staff & maid service. **$$$$$**

🏠 **Villa Amarillo** [112 C4] (4 suites) True Blue; \/f 473 439 0858; e annaglean@spiceisle.com; www.grenadaexplorer.com/amarillo. Villa accommodation comprising 4 2-bedroom suites, pool, gazebo & tropical gardens. The villa has AC, TV, Wi-Fi, ceiling fans, living room, kitchen, laundry room, terrace & verandas. Minimum stay 1 week. **$$$$$**

🏠 **Le Phare Bleu Marina & Boutique Hotel** [113 E3] (9 villas) Petite Calivigny Bay; \473 444 2400; e hotel@lepharebleu.com; www. lepharebleu.com. Chic beach villas (6 of them 2 bed, 3 others 1 bed), all with fully equipped kitchens, TV, DVD, AC in the bedrooms, private outdoor patios. Garden Villa has private plunge pool. Le Phare Bleu is a full-service marina (see page 125), with unique lightship restaurant, poolside bar & restaurant, minimarket (try the freshly baked bread) & laundry service. Located on Petite Calivigny Bay at the southern tip of the lovely Egmont peninsula, Le Phare Bleu is a great option for boat lovers & dreamers. **$$$$**

🏠 **Owl Cottage** [112 C4] (2 bedrooms) L'Anse Aux Epines; e smith@owl-cottage.com; www. beachside-properties.com. Secluded villa accommodation a short distance from the beach. 2 bedrooms, living area, kitchen, AC, TV, ceiling fans, large balcony, swimming pool, terrace garden. Minimum stay 1 week. **$$$$**

🏠 **Reef View Pavilion Villas** [112 D4] (2 villas) L'Anse Aux Epines; \473 439 5979; e reefview@spiceisle.com; www. reefviewgrenada.com. Luxury villas located on a hillside, with sea views & private swimming pools. Tradewind pavilion has 3 bedrooms, bathrooms, AC, TV, living area, kitchen, verandas, internet, swimming pool & rooftop with bar, BBQ & views. Turtleback pavilion is a 1-bedroom suite with similar facilities & also has private swimming pool & rooftop area. **$$$$**

🏠 **Grenada Bay Villas** [112 C4] (2 bed villa, 1 cottage) True Blue; www.grenadabayvillas.com. Not yet open at the time of writing. Private & fully equipped SC accommodation located on the True Blue peninsula with infinity pool, large terrace, gardens & sea views. Check website for more details & prices.

MID-RANGE SELF-CATERING APARTMENTS, COTTAGES AND VILLAS

🏠 **Blue Horizons Garden Resort** [112 C2] (26 1-bedroom suites, 6 studios); Grand Anse; \473 444 4316; f 473 444 2815; e blue@grenadabluehorizons.com; www.grenadabluehorizons.com. This pleasant resort is located within 2.5ha of tropical gardens with colourful flowers & many species of local birds. A short walking distance from Grand Anse Beach, Blue Horizon's 26 1-bedroom deluxe suites have AC, TV, fully equipped kitchen, CD player, phone, Wi-Fi, safe & terrace. The slightly smaller superior studios have king-size bed, kitchen & terrace. La Belle Creole, a popular fine-dining restaurant serving Creole & international cuisine, is situated on site. Good SC accommodation choice for families & those who want to be within walking distance of the beach without being right on it. **$$$**

🏠 **Twelve Degrees North** [112 C4] (8 apts) L'Anse Aux Epines; \/f 473 444 4580; e 12degrsn@spiceisle.com; www. twelvedegreesnorth.com. Located by the beach at L'Anse Aux Epines. Each suite is furnished with en-suite bathroom & private balcony facing the sea. Maid & housekeeping service providing b/ fast & lunch on your balcony. Pool, sun terrace, pavilion bar, tennis court, laundry service & watersports. No children. **$$$**

🏠 **Lance Aux Epines Cottages** [112 C4] (7 cottages, 4 apts) L'Anse Aux Epines; \473 444 4565; US & Canada toll free \1 877 444 565; f 473 444 2802; e reservations@laecottages.com; www.laecottages.com. Relaxed & friendly family run SC resort beside a pretty beach at L'Anse Aux Epines. The 1-, 2- & 3-bedroom cottages & apts are located in beautiful garden surroundings with hammocks, picnic tables, lovely beach & sea views. Each very well-maintained cottage & apt has living room, fully equipped kitchen, AC, phone & internet connectivity. Shared big-screen TV & games room also includes billiards, table tennis. Look out for traditional oil-down on the beach on Sundays. Great option for independent travellers, especially those with children. **$$$**

⌂ **Grooms Beach Villas & Resort** [112 B3] (22 rooms & SC villas) Point Salines; ☏ 473 439 7666; f 473 439 7555; e info@ groomsbeachresort.com & reservations@ groomsbeachresort.com; www.groomsbeachresort.com. Modern resort located close to Dr Groom's Beach offering regular hotel rooms & SC villa accommodation. Villas have fully equipped kitchens, Cable TV, Wi-Fi, private verandas & sea views. Swimming pool & restaurant serving local & international dishes. **$$–$$$**

⌂ **Jenny's Place** [112 D2] (4 suites, 2 apts, 1 room) Grand Anse; ☏/f 473 439 5186; e info@jennysplacegrenada.com; www.jennysplacegrenada.com. Located on the northern end of Grand Anse Beach. Suites & apts face the ocean & have bedroom, private bathroom, TV, AC, Wi-Fi, ceiling fans, private veranda. Apts also have fully equipped kitchen. Oasis Restaurant & Bar serves b/fast, lunch & dinner daily. Disabled friendly. B/fast inc. **$$**

⌂ **Spicetree Suites** [112 C4] (2 2-bedroom suites) L'Anse Aux Epines; ☏ 473 439 5979; e reefview@spiceisle.com; www. reefviewgrenada.com/spicetree. Bayleaf & Cinnamon holiday suites with bedrooms, bathroom, living area, fully equipped kitchen, AC, TV & veranda. Outdoor garden & BBQ. **$$**

⌂ **Coral Cove Cottages & Apartments** [112 C4] (11 cottages & apts) L'Anse Aux Epines; ☏ 473 444 4422; f 473 444 4718; e coralcv@spiceisle.com; www.coralcovecottages. com. Owner-managed 1- & 2-bedroom cottage apts located in large, pleasant gardens on the beach with swimming pool, tennis courts & boat jetty with gazebo. All apts have private bathroom, living area, TV, ceiling fans, kitchen & veranda. **$$**

⌂ **GEM Holiday Beach Resort** [112 B2] (20 apt suites) Morne Rouge; ☏ 473 444 4224; f 473 444 1189; e gem@spiceisle.com; www. gembeachresort.com. SC apt suites located on the beautiful Morne Rouge Beach, a short distance to the southwest of Grand Anse. Each suite has bedroom with en-suite bathroom, fully equipped kitchen, living area, AC, TV, phone & internet access, private veranda. Sur La Mer Restaurant, Fantazia Bar & Nightclub, Kalinago Beach Resort & Fedelis Restaurant are located nearby. Wedding packages available. **$$**

⌂ **Grenada Gold Apartments** [112 C3] (18 apts) Maurice Bishop Highway, nr Grand Anse; ☏ 473 420 4653; www.grenadagoldapartments. com. Unfinished at the time of writing, Grenada Gold plans a high standard of contemporary SC accommodation & services packages at affordable prices for independent travellers. 1- & 2-bed suites have fully equipped kitchen, lounge, bathroom, AC, TV, DVD, Wi-Fi & veranda. Maid service, airport & beach shuttle, spa, tours, & car rental packages available. **$–$$**

✖ WHERE TO EAT AND DRINK

The southwest peninsula is crammed full of great places to eat and drink. From haute cuisine to casual beachside barbecue and beer, the range of dining experiences should have something that matches both your palate and your wallet. Calling ahead, especially for dinner, is always recommended, particularly if you are looking for something seasonal, like lobster or lambie. Sunday lunchtime is usually very busy, especially at the more popular beachside restaurants, so arrive early to get seated. Many restaurants will take a day off on either Sunday or Monday, though hotel restaurants are open every day. Most restaurants and certainly all hotel restaurants will accept credit cards. Check menu prices to see if tax and service charge have been included or not. See page 59 for restaurant price codes.

CARIBBEAN AND INTERNATIONAL – FINE DINING

✖ **Rhodes' Calabash Hotel L'Anse** [112 C3], L'Anse Aux Epines; ☏ 473 444 4334; ⊕ daily. Haute cuisine restaurant by UK chef Gary Rhodes.

Recipes are a delicious fusion of Creole influences & Rhodes's unique style of cooking. Lovely waterside setting at the Calabash Hotel. Dinner reservations required. **$$$**

✕ **Laluna** [112 B3] Morne Rouge; ☎ 473 439 0001; ⏰ daily. Award-winning restaurant at the exclusive Laluna boutique hotel. Noted for fine Italian & Creole fusions. Dinner by reservation. **$$$**

✕ **Oliver's** [112 C2] Spice Island Beach Resort, Grand Anse; ☎ 473 444 4258; ⏰ daily. Gourmet international & Creole dining in very beautiful setting. Reservations recommended. **$$$**

✕ **Västra Banken** [113 E3] Le Phare Bleu Marina, Petite Calivigny Bay; ☎ 473 444 2400. Fine dining aboard a converted lighthouse ship in the Le Phare Bleu Marina & Resort. Take pre-dinner drinks on the top deck before enjoying some fine contemporary Caribbean cuisine. Dinner reservations recommended. **$$$**

✕ **Savvy's** [112 C2] Mount Cinnamon, Grand Anse; ☎ 473 439 9900; Closed Sun & Mon. Fine Mediterranean dining with a hint of the Caribbean. Located in the colourful setting of Mount Cinnamon with pool & poolside bar. Dinner reservations recommended. **$$$**

✕ **Aquarium** [112 B3] Magazine Beach; ☎ 473 444 1410; Closed Mon. Very popular & unique restaurant built into the cliffside with wooden decking & direct access to the beach. Highly recommended. The more casual beach bar is a great place for lunch & a drink when taking a swim or soaking up the sun. Live music & BBQ on Sun. Don't miss it. **$$$**

✕ **The Arawakabana** [112 C2] Coyaba Beach Resort, Grand Anse; ☎ 473 444 4129; ⏰ daily. Haute Caribbean & international cuisine in a beautiful setting. Dinner by reservation. The Carbet Restaurant & Pool Bar, also part of the Coyaba Beach Resort, has à la carte poolside dining & drinks. **$$$**

✕ **True Blue Bay Restaurant** [112 C4] True Blue Bay Resort, True Blue; ☎ 473 443 8873; ⏰ daily. Specialising in a combination of Caribbean & international dishes, served along the waterside. Dinner by reservation. **$$$**

✕ **The Beach House Restaurant & Bar** [112 B3] Located off the airport road next to the Rex Grenadian Resort; ☎ 473 444 4455; Closed Sun. Excellent food & service in a beautiful setting alongside Dr Groom's Beach. Highly recommended. Dinner reservations advised especially in the peak season. **$$$**

✕ **La Belle Creole** [112 C2] Blue Horizons Garden Resort, Grand Anse; ☎ 473 444 4316; ⏰ daily. Fine international cuisine with a Creole influence in beautiful tropical garden surroundings. Dinner reservations recommended. **$$$**

CARIBBEAN AND INTERNATIONAL – CASUAL

✕ **Poolbar Restaurant** [113 E3] Le Phare Bleu, Petite Calivigny Bay; ☎ 473 444 2400. Sea & poolside restaurant offering good casual dining (b/fast, lunch & dinner). Regular themed food nights & occasional live music. **$$**

✕ **Fedelis Restaurant & Bar** [112 C2] Kalinago Beach Resort, Morne Rouge; ☎ 473 444 5254. Located on the tranquil crescent beach of Morne Rouge, Fedelis offers good local & international dining against a gorgeous backdrop. **$$**

✕ **Ali Baba Grill & Bar** [112 C2] Allamanda Beach Resort, Grand Anse; ☎ 473 438 2222. Casual poolside restaurant on Grand Anse Beach specialises in Middle Eastern & Mediterranean cuisine. Great kebabs. **$$**

✕ **Dodgy Dock** [112 C4] True Blue Bay Resort, True Blue; ☎ 473 443 8783; ⏰ daily. Very popular deck & terrace bar beside the water. Casual & relaxed atmosphere with good Grenadian & international dining. Regular live music. Open all day every day. **$$**

✕ **Beachside Terrace Restaurant & The Owl Sports Bar** [112 C2] Flamboyant Hotel, Grand Anse; ☎ 473 444 4247; ⏰ daily. Wide selection of local & international cuisine with great views of Grand Anse Beach. The Owl has regular evening entertainment & serves bar snacks. **$$**

✕ **De Big Fish** [112 C3] True Blue; ☎ 473 439 4401; ⏰ daily. Chicken, ribs, fish, fajitas, shrimp & vegetarian dishes. Located on a deck by the waterside in True Blue Bay, near the coastguard station. Regular live music. **$$**

✕ **Deliciosa** [112 C2] Siesta Hotel, Grand Anse; ☎ 473 439 1700; ⏰ daily. Mexican, Creole & international dishes. Seafood, meat, chicken & vegetarian options also available. **$$**

✕ **Boots Cuisine Restaurant & Bar** Woodlands [112 D2] ☎ 473 444 2151. Unassuming & easy-to-miss restaurant located along the main south coast road near Clarke's Court. Tasty local cooking by Boots. Good value & worth trying. Dinner strictly by reservation. **$$**

✕ **Pirate's Cove Terrace Restaurant & Bar** [112 B2] Grenada Grand View Inn, Morne Rouge; ☎473 444 2342; ⊕ daily. Local & international cuisine, overlooking the beautiful Morne Rouge Beach. Dinner theatre entertainment. Call for details. $$

✕ **Umbrellas** [112 C2] Grand Anse Beach; ☎473 439 9149. ⊕ daily. Located near the Coyaba Beach Resort serving a good selection of tasty & affordable bar food. Upstairs sun deck & downstairs bar with sports on TV. Don't miss it. $$

✕ **Coconut Beach** [112 C2] Grand Anse Beach; ☎473 444 4644; ⊕ Creole & international dishes served both on & beside the beach. Seafood, steaks, chicken & more. ⊕ Wed–Mon; closed Tue. $$

✕ **The Red Crab** [112 C3] L'Anse Aux Epines; ☎473 444 4424; closed Sun. Relaxed restaurant with a good selection of international & local dishes. $$

✕ **Sur La Mer** [112 B2] Gem Holiday Beach Resort, Morne Rouge; ☎473 444 4224; ⊕ daily for b/fast, lunch & dinner. Beachside cabana restaurant serving Creole, seafood & international dishes. Located alongside the picturesque Morne Rouge Bay. BBQ & live music at weekends. $$

✕ **Little Dipper Restaurant & Bar** [112 D2] Lower Woburn; ☎473 444 5136; closed Mon. Genuine hidden treasure along the Woburn highway. Cosy, friendly, great local food & wonderful sea views. Recommended. $$

✕ **Bananas** [112 C3] True Blue, St George's; ☎473 444 4662; ⊕ daily. Lively restaurant, sports bar & nightclub with casual dining including tapas, BBQ, wings, burgers & wood-fired pizza. $$

✕ **Charcoals Caribbean Grill** [112 C3] L'Anse Aux Epines (main road); ☎473 440 4745. Casual & relaxed restaurant serving tasty BBQ food & drinks. $$

✕ **The Pizza Place & Tiki Bar & Restaurant** [112 C4] Prickly Bay Marina; ☎473 439 5265; ⊕ daily. Very casual waterside dining includes fabulous pizzas, burgers, sandwiches & seafood. Very popular with expats, yachties & visitors, especially on Friday nights for happy hour & live music. $$

✕ **Oasis Bar & Restaurant** [112 D2] Jenny's Place, Grand Anse Beach; ☎473 439 5186. Located at the northern tip of Grand Anse Beach, offering a good selection of local & international dishes. $$

✕ **Le Chateau Restaurant & Bar** [112 C2] Le Marquis Complex, Grand Anse; ☎473 444 2552; ⊕ daily. Relaxed restaurant serving a wide selection of Creole & international dishes including seafood, steak & chicken dishes. Open daily. $–$$

✕ **Native Food & Fruits** [112 C2] Spiceland Mall, Grand Anse. Fresh fruits & delicious juices. $

ITALIAN

✕ **La Boulangerie** [112 C2] Le Marquis Mall, Grand Anse; ☎473 444 1131; ⊕ daily. Covered terrace setting for great Italian pizza & pasta dishes. Also open for b/fasts, serving fresh juices, croissants & pastries. Try the homemade Italian ice cream. $$

✕ **Di Vino** [112 C2] Le Marquis Mall, Grand Anse; ☎473 439 7227; ⊕ Mon–Sat. Italian wine bar serving a selection of cold cuts such as prosciutto, salami, bresaola & more. $$

CHINESE

✕ **Oriental Restaurant** [112 B3] Rex Grenadian Resort, Magazine Beach; ☎473 444 3333; ⊕ dinner only on selected days. Located within the Rex Grenadian Resort on the road to the airport, serving a selection of dishes from the east. Call first. $$

✕ **Chopstix** [112 C2] Spiceland Mall, Grand Anse; ☎473 444 7849; ⊕ Mon–Sat. Take-away or sit-down Chinese food in the Spiceland Mall. $–$$

SUSHI

✕ **Carib Sushi** [112 C2] Le Marquis Mall, Grand Anse; ☎473 439 5640; ⊕ Mon–Fri, lunchtimes only. Fresh local fish, Japanese style. Sushi, sashimi, uramaki, hosomaki & more. $$

FAST FOOD

✕ **KFC** [112 C2] Grand Anse. Southern fried chicken located next to the Spiceland Mall. $

✕ **Grillmaster** [112 C2] Spiceland Mall, Grand Anse. Burgers, chicken, fish & fries. $

Check out a little stall near the traffic island at Grand Anse. If it is still there, you can occasionally buy great boneless chicken roti.

BEACH BARS

♀ **Garfield's Beach Bar** [112 C2] Grand Anse

Beach. Located near the Grenada Grand Beach Resort. Small & cosy but a great place for a snack, a cold beer & some relief from the sun.

♀ **The Owl** [112 C4] Flamboyant Hotel & Villas, Grand Anse; ☎473 444 4247; ⊕ daily until late. Late bar, music, games & karaoke.

SHOPPING

The shopping malls of the southwest peninsula have well-stocked supermarkets, fast-food restaurants, clothes boutiques, craft and souvenir shops, banks and ATMs. The Excel Plaza also has a small cinema.

SHOPPING MALLS
Excel Plaza [112 C2] Grand Anse. On the road between Grand Anse & the junction for L'Anse Aux Epines & the airport.
Grand Anse Shopping Centre [112 C2] Grand Anse. On the main road between St George's & Grand Anse, near the Grenada Grand Beach Resort.
Le Marquis Mall [112 C2] (The 'Roundhouses') Grand Anse. Alongside the roundabout junction in Grand Anse, near the beach.
Spiceland Mall [112 C2] Grand Anse. Alongside the beach in Grand Anse, opposite the Coyaba & Allamanda resorts.

SUPERMARKETS
The Food Fair [112 C2] Grand Anse Shopping Mall; ⊕ Mon–Sat
IGA Real Value Supermarket [112 C2] Spiceland Mall; ⊕ daily (Sun from 10.00)

ART, CRAFT, SOUVENIR AND BOOKSHOPS
Art & Soul [112 C2] Spiceland Mall, Grand Anse. Original paintings and prints by Susan Mains. Recommended.
Art & Soul Books [112 C2] Spiceland Mall, Grand Anse. Well-stocked bookshop with a good selection on Grenada (including this book!).
Imagine [112 C3] Calabash Hotel, L'Anse Aux Epines & Grand Anse Shopping Mall. Original handicrafts, gifts & souvenirs using natural materials.
Presents Too [112 C2] Excel Plaza, Grand Anse. A selection of gifts & books.
Grand Anse Craft & Spice Market [112 C2] Grand Anse Beach. Spices, souvenirs, beach gear, crafts & refreshments.

OTHER PRACTICALITIES

MONEY AND BANKS You will find banks with ATMs at the Spiceland Mall [112 C2] (Grenada Co-operative Bank), on the main Grand Anse junction (RBTT Bank), opposite the Grand Anse Shopping Mall [112 C2] (Scotiabank), and on the junction for L'Anse Aux Epines and Point Salines (Republic Bank). You will also find an ATM at Maurice Bishop International Airport [112 B3].

MEDICAL You will find fairly well-stocked pharmacies in the Spiceland Mall and in True Blue next door to Bananas restaurant [112 C2].

SAFETY The southwest has a lot of tourists yet it does not really attract very much crime. Generally speaking it is a safe place and, although you will certainly be subject to the attention of beach vendors, taxi and tour drivers, and other 'entrepreneurs' seeking to do business with you, there is nothing here that should concern you. Many hotels and resorts employ security guards, as do some of the malls, but you should view them being there as a deterrent and not because of a high level of crime.

If you do find yourself in difficulty you will find a police station in Grand Anse near the Spice Island Beach Resort.

WHAT TO SEE AND DO

BEACHES The southwest peninsula has a number of beautiful beaches, the majority of which are very accessible. Most are located in the north, on the Caribbean side of the peninsula.

Grand Anse Beach [112 C2] Grand Anse is Grenada's signature beach. Over 3km in length and located some 5km to the south of St George's, it is where you will find a number of the island's premier resorts and luxury hotels. As it consists of fine, white powdery sand with the gentle rollers of an azure Caribbean, it is easy to understand why many of Grenada's visitors are drawn to this spot and then very rarely move away from it again.

Despite its enormous popularity, it never appears to be too crowded. Towards the northern end, off the Grenada Grand Beach Resort [112 C2], it is probably at its busiest as the hotel is huge and has a very long beach frontage. Sunloungers and parasols can appear to crowd this small section at times, but there is more than enough room on the beach for everyone. Students from St George's University tend to hang out at Garfield's and Umbrellas is always a popular spot. Looking out from Grand Anse across St George's Harbour, you can clearly see the capital, Fort George, the Carenage, and sailing boats and motor cruisers at anchor.

From Jenny's Place [112 D2] at the northern tip to the Flamboyant Hotel [112 C2] at the very southern end, you will find a number of beachside bars and restaurants serving a variety of cold drinks, breakfasts, lunches and even fine dining. Also, if you are looking for watersports, most dive shops have a presence here. They offer a range of services including scuba-diving lessons, boat diving, boat trips, snorkel hire, ocean kayak and Hobie Cat hire. Vendors trudge up and down the beach in the high season, especially near the hotel frontages, in the hope of selling trinkets and souvenirs, snacks, clothing and even a massage.

If you are not staying at one of Grand Anse's large resort hotels, you must find a public access point. You can get on to the beach in a number of different places including the path next to the Coconut Beach Restaurant, another one near Eco Dive and Umbrellas, a track between Mount Cinnamon and the Spice Island Beach Resort, and at the end of Camàhogne Park, opposite the Spiceland Mall.

Morne Rouge Beach [112 B2] Morne Rouge is a really beautiful horseshoe-shaped beach and bay located to the southwest of Grand Anse Beach. It has fine white sand and is very sheltered, so the sea is usually completely calm and perfectly clear. Small almond trees are scattered along the rear of the beach providing welcome shade. Never really busy, Morne Rouge is a great escape and perfect for families with small children. Look out for the *Rhum Runner II* party boat excursions that arrive in the afternoons of the high season, however, bringing cruise-ship tourists ashore for an hour or so. As with Grand Anse, vendors also ply this beach.

To get to Morne Rouge Beach, follow the main Grand Anse Beach road past the resort hotels and then around the corner and up the hill along the perimeter of the Flamboyant Hotel. Head over the ridge and then straight down the next hill, ignoring the road on the left. Follow the road down to the bottom and around to the left until you reach the entrance of the Gem Holiday Beach Resort. To the right of the gates are some steps leading down to the beach. Sur La Mer is a handy though rather pricey restaurant and bar. It serves decent lunches and is a nice place to enjoy the shade with a fresh juice, a cold beer or perhaps a rum punch.

right When word spreads about a boat-launching, makeshift bars and cooking pots materialise as local residents gather to watch (PC) page 205

below left The *Spice Mas* carnival is a mix of the traditional and the modern, as booming amplifiers meet vivacious costumes (GBT) page 29

below right Grenada's national dish — oil-down — is traditionally cooked in a single pot over an open fire (PC) page 57

bottom left Established after Hurricane Ivan in 2004, Gouyave's Fish Friday showcases some of Grenada's finest seafood (SGU/JY) page 146

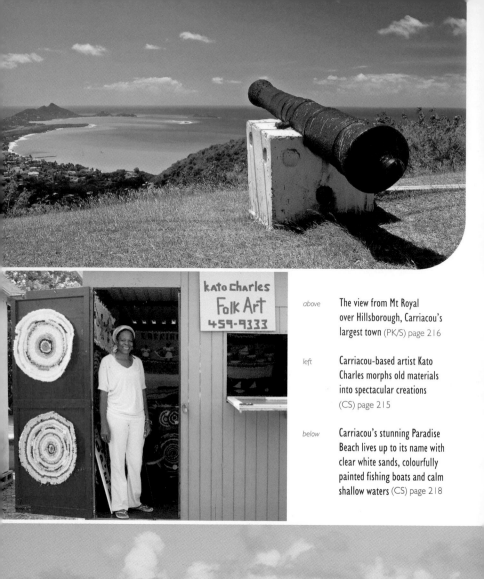

above   The view from Mt Royal over Hillsborough, Carriacou's largest town (PK/S) page 216

left   Carriacou-based artist Kato Charles morphs old materials into spectacular creations (CS) page 215

below   Carriacou's stunning Paradise Beach lives up to its name with clear white sands, colourfully painted fishing boats and calm shallow waters (CS) page 218

kato charles
Folk Art
459-9333

above left The impressive stone windmill tower of the old Belair Estate, once used for crushing sugarcane (CS) page 221

above right A boatbuilder hard at work in the village of Windward, with Petite Martinique beyond (RJL/S) page 204

above left The elusive and rare Grenada dove (*Leptotila wellsi*) is Grenada's national bird (AJ) page 6

above right The bananaquit (*Coereba flaveola*) is very common to the Caribbean and may be found during hikes in the forest or visits to tropical gardens (BH) page 7

left Cattle egrets (*Bubulcus ibis*) in Hillsborough's botanical gardens (CS) page 217

below The Levera Archipelago is home to a beautiful coastline, offshore islands and reefs, and a giant leatherback turtle nesting site (CS) page 182 *right*   Common in dry forest areas, this green iguana (*Iguana iguana*) was spotted in Carriacou's High North National Park (CS) page 202

below left   Don't get too close to the giant toad (*Bufo marinus*), which uses a milky secretion called bufotalin as a defence measure (CS) page 8

below right   The mona monkey (*Cercopithecus mona*) was probably brought to Grenada by slave traders (CS) page 7

bottom   The red-legged tortoise (*Geochelone carbonaria*), or *morocoy*, is rarely sighted, though you may see them in the wild on Carriacou or Frigate Island (CS) page 8

above, above left & left

From pod to delicious organic Grenada Chocolate, 'dancing the cocoa' at Belmont Estate is the traditional and fun way of polishing the beans (all CS) page 188

bottom left & below

Before Hurricane Ivan, Grenada was the world's second largest nutmeg producer. Surrounding the nutmeg is mace which, when dried, is used as a natural meat preservative (bottom left, CS & below, SS) page 22

right   Grenada's banana industry has struggled in recent years due to large-scale food production (CS) page 23

below   Take your pick: lobster is a speciality at Aggie's Restaurant & Bar on Bathway Beach (PC) page 183

bottom   The colourful fruit market in St George's (BB/A) page 91

above *Vicissitudes*, and other pieces in Jason deCaires Taylor's striking Underwater Sculpture Gallery, are slowly becoming artificial reefs (RG/S) page 85

left Hawksbill turtles are often seen around Grenada's wrecks and reefs (BS/DK/DG) page 10

below left The self-proclaimed 'wreck-diving capital of the Caribbean', Grenada is also home to an array of interesting underwater topography (EG) page 82

below Within the nooks and crannies of Grenada's reef systems live green and spotted varieties of moray eel (EG) page 9

Portici Beach This beach is quite tricky to reach. It is located below the Laluna luxury boutique hotel [112 B3] to the south of Morne Rouge Bay and Petit Cabrits Point. To get there from Morne Rouge, you must walk around the rear perimeter fencing of Laluna and then follow a path down and alongside the resort until you reach the beach. From the main airport road, follow the signs to the Beach House Restaurant [112 B3], and at a fork in the road, bear right. This road becomes a dead end near some residential houses. A path to the right of a house at the end of the paved road eventually joins up with the track that follows the Laluna perimeter fencing. It is quite an effort to reach this one and, unless you are beach-bagging, you may want to skip it in favour of one of the others.

Dr Grooms Beach [112 B3] This is a really nice white-sand beach located to the south of the hard-to-reach Portici Beach and north of Magazine Beach. From the main airport road simply follow the signs to the Beach House Restaurant and Grooms Beach Villa & Resort. At the fork, take the left down to the Beach House. You will see a sign on the right pointing to a wide track around the perimeter of the restaurant. This is the way to the beach. The Beach House is ideally placed to make this a great place to soak up the sun and the surf and to follow up your day with some really excellent dining (see page 119 for details).

Magazine Beach [112 B3] My favourite beach on the main island, and quite often deserted, Magazine Beach is a little further towards the peninsula's southwestern tip, between the Rex Grenadian Resort and the Aquarium Restaurant at Maca Bana. To get there you must head for the airport and follow the road past the terminal building. It will curve to the right, past staff car-parking areas before turning back around again to the left on a road that goes to the La Source resort, Maca Bana and the Aquarium. Before you reach any of these, however, at the apex of the hairpin bend that curves around to the left, there is a wooded area on the right-hand side with a vehicle track next to it. Next to a large house you should spot a paved road heading steeply downhill. This will take you to the beach. It is beautiful and there is a very welcome area of shade beneath a small beachside copse of manchineel (see page 43) and almond trees. The water is clear but deepens very quickly so it may not be ideal for youngsters. At the southern end of Magazine Beach you will find the fabulous Aquarium Restaurant which, on Sundays, has a barbecue and live music.

Pink Gin Beach [112 A3] Pink Gin Beach is to the south of Magazine Beach and is very beautiful. Alongside it is the exclusive La Source resort and the beach is very difficult to access unless you swim or are in a boat.

L'Anse Aux Epines Beach [112 C4] This beach is located on the western side of the L'Anse Aux Epines peninsula, a little to the north of the Prickly Bay Marina. It is a narrow stretch of white-sand beach and its waters are very calm, making it great for families with small children as well as for all the sailing boats that anchor in the bay. On the western end of the beach is the Calabash Hotel, in the middle is L'Anse Aux Epines Cottages, and at the eastern end is a small park where you will find public access. From the traffic junction in Grand Anse, head south to L'Anse Aux Epines and look for the entrance to L'Anse Aux Epines Cottages. Access to the beach is just a little further along the main road, on the right-hand side.

Just after passing the Clarke's Court distillery, in the very corner of Woburn Bay, you will see a sign for the Woburn Bay Marine Protected Area. One of several marine protected areas in Grenada and Carriacou, this one aims to restore and preserve a healthy mangrove habitat that is essential to the wildlife, in particular birds, in this area. A wooden viewing platform has been constructed along the shoreline which should be of great interest to birdwatching enthusiasts. Implemented by the Grenada Fund for Conservation, this project also aims to raise conservation awareness and gain the help and co-operation of the local community.

EXPLORING THE REGION
Along the south coast from Point Salines to Fort Jeudy
The southwest coast of Grenada comes to an end at **Point Salines** [112 A3], which is also the location of the Maurice Bishop International Airport [112 B3]. The road to the airport continues a little way beyond it, before coming to the end of the peninsula. It passes several hotels and restaurants along the way, including the very popular Aquarium Restaurant, Maca Bana Villas and the La Source resort. Along the south coast, to the east of the airport, is **True Blue** [112 C3]. This is where you will find St George's University of Medicine. To the east of True Blue is **Prickly Bay** [112 C4] which is a very popular natural anchorage with marina facilities. Prickly Bay is located to the west of the **L'Anse Aux Epines** peninsula [112 C4], where there are a number of resort hotels, luxury villas and self-catering holiday accommodation, as well as some very epicurean private homes. L'Anse Aux Epines, meaning 'thorny or prickly bay', was so named in reference to the acacia trees, and the different varieties of cacti, that grow in abundance within the dry coastal woodland of this region. You may notice that there are several different ways of spelling L'Anse Aux Epines, and very often you will see it written 'Lance aux Epines'. *L'Anse* was the original French spelling and meant 'bay' and over time it has simply become anglicised, hence the variations you see today. Just to make it even more complicated, most people drop the 'aux' when pronouncing the name, so when spoken it simply becomes 'Lance Epines'.

The tiki bar and pizza restaurant at Prickly Bay Marina [112 C4] is very popular with expat residents, visitors, watersports operators and the sailing community, especially on Friday nights when happy hour lasts for much longer than the usual 60 minutes. The marina is located a little beyond the L'Anse Aux Epines public beach access (see opposite), down a rather steep and narrow road. The Calabash Hotel [112 C3], a little before you reach Prickly Bay Marina, is where you will find Rhodes', the signature restaurant of the acclaimed British chef. A walk to the end of L'Anse Aux Epines is pleasant, especially after a large lunch. You can saunter past and admire the luxurious houses and the equally salubrious sailing boats of the marina, before reaching the rugged headland of Prickly Point. There are nice views along the coastline and also out to Glover, Hog and Calivigny islands (see page 129 for details of this leisurely stroll).

Glover Island [112 B4] is located to the west of the peninsula and was once the site of a whaling station. As early as the mid-19th century, whaling boats were plying the waters of the Caribbean and in the 1920s a station was constructed on Glover Island by Norwegian whalers. The station processed whale oil for export and meat for local consumption. During the second half of the 1920s, the life of Glover Island's whaling station came to a premature end. Through a combination of

LE PHARE BLEU AND THE VÄSTRA BANKEN LIGHTSHIP

Le Phare Bleu [113 E3] is a modern marina and boutique hotel complex at Petite Calivigny on Grenada's southwest coast. One of its most interesting features is the *Västra Banken*, a gourmet restaurant aboard a former lightship.

Between the 1850s and the 1930s Sweden built 33 lightships to be positioned in places where permanent lighthouses could not be sited; near sandbanks, submerged reefs, or places where there were strong currents. Their job, of course was to warn ships of the danger.

Lightship number 23 was built between 1900 and 1901 and was called *Fyrskepp nr 23*. One of the more modern lightship designs, she had a tubular mast and a lantern house. During her period of service she was positioned in three different stations, each of which would have been painted in large white letters over a bright red hull. The last position was a place called Västra Banken which is to the north of Stockholm. In 1970 a permanent lighthouse was built there and the lightship was decommissioned.

The town of Öregund bought her and gave her a home in the harbour but she fell into disrepair and her superstructure was removed and installed in the harbour as a museum. The remainder of the ship was sold to a scrapyard where a private enthusiast bought her and installed a new deck and mast. Some 15 years later her new owner used her as a houseboat and installed the lantern house from *Fyrskepp nr 21*. The present owner had her brought to Grenada in 2005.

The age of the Swedish lightship came to an end in 1972 and a handful, such as *Fyrskepp nr 23*, the *Västra Banken*, have been restored and maintained.

a decline in whale numbers and new factory boats that could handle the processing themselves, the need for Glover simply disappeared. In 1929, the station was dismantled though some ruins remain.

To the east of L'Anse Aux Epines is the **Mt Hartman National Park** [112 D3]. It is an area of dry coastal woodland on a wide peninsula between Mt Hartman Bay and Clarke's Court Bay. It is also often referred to as the 'Dove Sanctuary' because it is thought to be home to around 20% of the global population of the Grenada dove (*Leptotila wellsi*) and has been designated an Important Bird Area (IBA) by Birdlife International. Though usually very dry, the national park is a very pretty place, one of quiet solitude and natural beauty. In 2007, Grenada's government of the day stated that in fact only 30% of the Mt Hartman Estate had been designated a restricted area, paving the way for a large resort development project. This project has caused some alarm among environmentalists though so far the diggers have not arrived in earnest. Instead, **Hog Island** [112 D4], located at the mouth of Clarke's Court Bay, was purchased by a large hotel and resorts company who constructed a causeway linking the island to the mainland. Then the recession hit and further development of Hog Island was put on hold.

Hog Island has been and currently still is a popular sailing and day-trip anchorage and home to **Roger's Bar**, which has reached almost legendary status within the yachting community (see page 128). The island's small beaches are popular places to relax with drinks and a barbecue. A number of tour operators run half- or full-day trips that touch down at Hog Island. Some trips include snorkelling, beach barbecues and fishing for your own lunch. All are fun ways to spend a day in the area (see page 80 for more information). Enjoy it while it lasts.

The Southwest Peninsula   WHAT TO SEE AND DO

5

Scuba-diving certainly offers an extra dimension to your holiday and, if you are comfortable in water and have a spirit of adventure, then I recommend you spend a morning or two 'getting wet'. If you are already a certified diver and your holiday is the only time you ever go, then consider taking a quick refresher with an instructor before diving properly. It will give you the confidence you need to feel relaxed on your dives.

If you are travelling with equipment please be aware that it is likely to count as excess luggage when it comes to check-in. This can be expensive. I travel with my mask, regulator and dive computer in my hand luggage, I always pack my wetsuit but fins and buoyancy compensator device (BCD) are left to the mercy of the weighing scales. They can always be rented. Consider taking your dive booties to wear with rented fins.

At first, scuba-diving looks and sounds all very complicated, so many people find walking into a dive shop a little daunting. There is no need to worry about any of that. Scuba-diving is actually quite straightforward and dive-shop staff will be happy to explain it to you without any pressure or making you feel silly. It is, after all, in their interest for more people in the world to take up diving.

If you do not dive and you are thinking about giving it a go on holiday, consider the 'referral' option. This means that you do two-thirds of your course at your local dive shop and in a swimming pool environment, and the final third when you are on holiday. All the theory, the skills and the exams are out of the way before you come. All you have to do is repeat them in the sea for your instructor. After that you are certified and can dive as often as time and budget allow. By doing it this way you spend less of your valuable holiday time reading manuals, swotting and generally annoying your partner, and more of it enjoying yourself; which is what your holiday is all about.

Woburn [113 E2] (both Upper and Lower) is located to the east of the Mt Hartman Estate. Separating Woburn from Mt Hartman is the pretty Woburn Bay (also known as Clarke's Court Bay) where you will see sailing boats at anchor or alongside the jetties of the Clarke's Court Bay Marina.

The **Egmont and Petit Calivigny** peninsula [113 E3] is naturally beautiful with secluded bays and mangroves. Numerous luxurious residences have been constructed here, and there is a steady stream of work in progress. For those of us without such resources, it is a lovely place to sit and dream. From the coastal road to the east of Woburn you will see a sign to **Le Phare Bleu** [113 E3]. Follow this road and at the bottom of the hill go right, over the bridge. The expanse of water you can see, with its margin of dense mangroves, is Egmont Harbour [113 F3] (sometimes also referred to as Petit Calivigny Harbour) and it is very tranquil and quite beautiful. Once over the bridge, follow the road to the left and then straight up and over the hill. Below you is Le Phare Bleu, a complex that includes state-of-the-art marina facilities, boutique hotel accommodation and two restaurants, one of which is located on the refurbished lighthouse boat at the end of the jetty (see box on page 125). It is a very pleasant place to relax and you are made to feel very welcome, whether you are part of the boating fraternity or just someone with a tendency to spend countless hours gazing longingly and bleary-eyed at sailing boats you may be fortunate enough to own in another lifetime.

Calivigny Island [113 E4] is located off Petit Calivigny Point and can be very clearly seen from the coastal road in Lower Woburn or from Le Phare Bleu. It is a privately owned island and, though beaches are part of the public domain in Grenada, in the past visitors have consistently reported harassment from security personal and made very unwelcome there. This situation is said to have improved but to avoid any unpleasantness it is, regrettably, probably best avoided.

Fort Jeudy [113 F3] is an established and very upmarket residential community. It is a long peninsula to the east of Egmont Harbour and has a very pretty coastline with great views. You can get right to the Point of Fort Jeudy by following the paved road and then a track to the rugged coastline (see page 131). There are fine views along the coast to Calivigny Island, Egmont and Adam Island as well as a number of rocky outcrops to the east in the parish of St David.

ACTIVITIES AND SPECIAL INTERESTS If you can tear yourself away from the great food, the cocktails and the beaches, there are some fun activities on offer in the southwest.

Scuba-diving Grenada is developing a reputation for its scuba-diving and, off the southwest peninsula, there are some very nice reefs and a selection of interesting shipwrecks that are definitely worth exploring. If you cannot scuba-dive, why not give it a go? All of Grenada's dive operators offer instructor-accompanied try-dives as well as full certification courses. For those of you who are already certified, all scuba-diving here is from a boat and you are guided by a divemaster who usually drifts with a surface marker buoy above reef formations. Wrecks are usually for experienced divers as they are often deep and have current. Some operators offer pre-blended enriched air (nitrox) to those who are certified to use it. For information on Grenada's dive sites, see page 83.

For a complete list of scuba-diving operators, go to Chapter 3, page 86. Most scuba-diving operators offer three or four boat dives per day – two in the morning and one or two in the afternoon. They often schedule their dives in advance and post them on noticeboards in the dive shop so you can see the sites they plan to visit each day. Remember that operators will require proof of certification before they take you. PADI, SSI, NAUI and BSAC are recognised everywhere. If you are wreck diving you should also bring along your logbook in case proof of experience is requested. Rental equipment is always available and scuba cylinders are aluminium rather than steel.

Boat trips A boat trip could either be a sedate sailing cruise or a wild and exciting speedboat ride. Some excursions include lunch, barbecue and snorkelling. Usually operators will pick you up from the most convenient place for you, often right off Grand Anse Beach [112 C2].

For a list of operators see page 80. It is also worth checking with your hotel to ascertain whether they recommend or have working relationships with tour operators or water taxis. Some of the best days out can be had with local water-taxi operators or fishermen who will take you around the coast on their small boats, try to catch some fish with you, and then prepare a makeshift barbecue on a beach somewhere. Give it a try.

Ocean kayaking and Hobie Cat sailing Several of the dive shops along Grand Anse Beach [112 C2] offer ocean kayak hire as do many of the resort hotels. You can also hire Hobie Cats and do a little sailing. Usually sea conditions are calm as most of the inshore waters are sheltered. Take care on Grand Anse Beach when entering and exiting the water, however, as the surf can kick up from time to time. The bays and mangrove coastlines of the south coast are especially interesting places to explore by kayak. Be sure to wear a buoyancy jacket and protect yourself from the sun with a combination of T-shirt, hat and sunscreen. It is extremely easy to get sunburned when you are out on the water. For a list of operators, see page 79.

Whale- and dolphin-watching Grenada's waters have whales and dolphins all year round though the best months for spotting them are between December and April. You are never guaranteed sightings on your trip but success rates are high and it is an unforgettable experience to see these magnificent creatures up close. Look out for humpback whales (*Megaptera novaeangliae*), sperm whales (*Physeter macrocephalus*), Bryde's whales (*Balaenoptera brydei*), pilot whales (*Globicephala melaena*) or pods of dolphins including spinner dolphins (*Stenella longirostris*), bottlenose dolphins (*Tursiops truncatus*), Fraser's dolphins (*Lagenodelphis hosei*) and common dolphins (*Delphinus delphis*). **First Impressions** [112 C2] (✆ 473 440 3678) offers a four-hour whale and dolphin trip aboard a purpose-built power catamaran. Their office is located at the Allamanda Beach Resort where you can check on prices and to see when trips are scheduled. See page 88 for additional contact information.

Golf
The Grenada Golf Course & Country Club [112 D2] is located to the east of Grand Anse, up in the heights of the Belmont area. It is a well-maintained, challenging nine-hole golf course with pleasant views of both the Caribbean Sea and the Atlantic Ocean. Club rental, instruction and caddy service are all available. Green fees are about US$20 for nine holes. (*For more information* ✆ 473 444 4128.) If you are staying at one of the resort hotels at Grand Anse you may find they offer complimentary golf club membership and transportation to the course.

Roger's Bar on Hog Island [113 D4] A treat with a sell-by date, sadly, as private development on Hog Island threatens to end a long-running Grenada institution. So go there while you still can!

Roger sets up his make-shift bar (there's no electricity; all the lights, amps and so on run off batteries) and on Sundays there is a sort of pilgrimage across the water to chill out, kick back and enjoy the vibes. Roger's is popular with locals, expatriats, and the yachting community and the atmosphere is relaxed and friendly. Plenty of local fishermen in the Woburn Bay area offer return rides for around EC$10–20. You could also check with marinas such as Le Phare Bleu (see page 40) and tour operators such as Shadowfax (see page 80).

Clarke's Court Rum – Grenada Distillers [112 D2] One of three noted Grenada rum distillers, Clarke's Court offers a 20-minute tour of its plant for EC$5 per person. It is fascinating and, naturally, you get a chance to buy at the end.

Located in the Woodlands area, just north of Woburn Bay, the distillery began production in the 1930s and your guide will show you some of the machinery that was used to move, cut and ultimately squeeze sugarcane brought here from large plantations such as Beauséjour on Grenada's west coast. The machinery was steam-driven using the waste product of the squeezed cane, called *bagasse*, and inside the factory there is a steam turbine and large gear arrangement that would have driven the three-stage cane crusher. Today, sadly, cane is no longer harvested and crushed. Instead the raw materials for rum-making and sugar processing are imported from countries such as Guyana.

Molasses are heat-treated to extract sugar crystals – the main product of the factory – and then mixed with water and yeast and allowed to ferment for several days. The potent mixture is then distilled to produce alcohol, which is used for the rum-blending process, and ethanol, which is used for products such as rubbing alcohol. The alcohol is mixed and infused with a combination of secret ingredients by the master blender to produce different brands of Clarke's Court rum.

The tour ends in Nick's Barrel House where you are invited to sample rums and buy some to take home. Independent travellers should note that this tour is very busy during the height of the cruise-ship season.

For more information go to www.clarkescourtrum.com or call ☎767 473 5363.

WALKS, HIKES & SCENIC OFF-ROAD DRIVES Here are a few suggestions for those interested in adventuring beyond the short journey from sunlounger to tiki bar.

Grand Anse Beach [112 C2] At 3km in length, a leisurely stroll along Grand Anse Beach is not only a pleasant way to pass an hour or so, it is also a good workout. Dawn and dusk are the best times to walk it, when the temperature is cooler and there is less chance of sun damage. With the **Coconut Beach Restaurant**, the very hip **Umbrellas Beach Bar**, and the Flamboyant Hotel's **Beachside Terrace Restaurant** all located en route, refreshments are never too far away and are always a great incentive to keep going. From one end to the other takes around an hour or so, depending on how many times you can resist jumping into the sea for a bathe, or stopping for liquid refreshments along the way. Remember, beer and rum punch are no substitutes for water and, though the reverse may also be true, do be sure to hydrate your body properly.

L'Anse Aux Epines to Prickly Point [112 C4] This is a pleasant, leisurely walk through the well-to-do residential area of L'Anse Aux Epines to the wild and rugged headland of Prickly Point. It should take no more than two hours there and back. You will pass some very fanciful private residences and a marina. Places to eat and drink include Gary Rhodes's restaurant at the Calabash Hotel and the pizza restaurant and tiki bar at Prickly Bay.

Start your walk at the small playing field near the entrance to the Calabash Hotel in L'Anse Aux Epines. After you pass the L'Anse Aux Epines Cottages resort (a great place to stay), you will see a small park with beach access. Take a short diversion down to the shore for a view across the bay and perhaps a dip in the water. It is a really pleasant place to bathe; it is calm, sheltered and also great for kids. Follow the road as it snakes slowly up the hill past large residential houses and holiday villas. After around 15 minutes you will see a sign and a road down to the Prickly Bay Marina and Prickly Bay Waterside development. The design of the luxurious waterside apartments is meant to reflect the shape of superyachts, complementing the maritime theme of this area. The bar and restaurant here is a great place for pizza and a beer and is quite lively on Friday afternoons and evenings. So maybe on the way back …

Just keep following the road all the way to the end. Depending on your pace, this will take anywhere from 45 minutes to a little over an hour. Pass the lighthouse residence and walk to the end of the point. You will see a dramatic coastline of volcanic rocks and cliffs with a wild sea smashing against them. It is quite beautiful. You will also have good views across Prickly Bay to the True Blue peninsula.

Mt Hartman National Park and Hog Island [112 D3/4] The Mt Hartman National Park is an environment of dry scrub forest and small hills. It is fringed on its western and southern shoreline by Mt Hartman Bay, and on its eastern shoreline by the lovely Woburn Bay and Clarke's Court Bay. It is also the primary habitat of the endangered Grenada dove.

Hog Island is located just a short distance off the southeastern coast of the park. It was purchased by a large hotel and resorts company who constructed a causeway linking the island to the mainland. Then the recession hit and further development of Hog Island was put on hold. This was good news for the iconic Roger's Bar which, to the joy of locals and the yachting community, was granted a temporary reprieve. For some reason, unexplained, the causeway is gated and locked; perhaps it is unfinished, not commissioned, or there are liability issues. Who knows. But it is a shame. I did hear a rumour that occasionally, on Sundays (which is when everyone boats over to Roger's Bar), the gate is unlocked and people can cross over. But it is only a rumour ... And all this may soon change, of course.

In the first edition of this guide I described a loop hike through Mt Hartman National Park but sadly this is no longer possible. The park is, however, a lovely place for a hike, a stroll, or a drive in an off-road vehicle, and the possibility of being able to cross to Hog Island makes it even more appealing. There is lots of bird life here, including the all-elusive one ...

It can be very dry in this region with little shade, so please ensure you have plenty of water, sunscreen and a hat. Aside from the sun, the route is not too demanding. There are one or two slopes, some rather large cows and sometimes horses to negotiate along the way, but for the most part it is easy-going.

To get there take the road towards Woburn from Grand Anse and look for a sign on the right indicating the Mt Hartman National Park. If you are travelling by bus, take a number 2 from the terminus in St George's and get off by the sign. Next to the sign there is a small road that quickly becomes a rough dirt track as it passes some local residences. This is where the trail begins.

Follow the vehicle track downhill as it passes the houses and then leaves them behind in favour of dry woodland. After just a few minutes you will reach some farm buildings and a large iron gate. Pass through the gate and continue along the wide track. It runs reasonably straight and flat for quite a distance before curving around to the east. Remember to keep your eyes and ears open for the elusive Grenada dove! Moving onwards you should be able to see the rocky peak of Mt Hartman.

Continue straight along the main track, ignoring any spurs, and follow it as it curves back to the south and begins a gradual climb uphill. At the top of the hill the track goes sharply back around to the east. Soon you will have good views of Woburn Bay and Hog Island. These views improve as you continue down the hill towards the sea.

At the bottom of the hill the track bends around to the south and then forks. Here you have an option. The track to the right is a little diversion. If you follow it on foot for around 10 minutes you will reach a T-junction as the track meets the mangroves of the shore. A little walk to the right will bring you to a small beach. There are three wrecks grounded near the shore but also good views across the bay. This is quite a nice spot for a dip in the water or a picnic. A little further to the right are two more beaches, though somewhat smaller. The track continues into overgrown scrubland so don't take it any further.

Back at the fork in the trail, take the left-hand track to a small clearing. You have reached the gated causeway bridge. There are views of Clarke's Court Bay, Hog Island and lots of sailing boats at anchor.

If you are lucky, or perhaps the situation has changed since the time of writing, you may be able to cross over the causeway to Hog Island. There are a couple of good beaches, and Roger's Bar, of course, connected by some very rough scrubland tracks.

The Point of Fort Jeudy [113 F4] As with many places of beauty in Grenada, especially in the south, Fort Jeudy has become a somewhat exclusive area; a gated community of opulent residential homes, neighbourhood watches, and 'beware of the dog' signs. At the very end of this lovely peninsula, there is the point itself, an area of natural beauty with marvellous views along Grenada's rugged coastline, as well as to the more sheltered sanctuaries of Egmont and Calivigny. Hopefully, this area will remain accessible to all.

This short drive passes through the residential community of Fort Jeudy until you reach the point itself. You will pass some extremely luxurious residences. When you come to Fort Jeudy you will meet a wild, rugged and very beautiful volcanic rock coastline. There are also great views along the coast.

On the east coast road, south of Marian, before you reach Westerhall, there is a sign welcoming you to Fort Jeudy and New Westerhall (another community on the peninsula). This is the start of the drive. If you are on foot and would like to walk it instead (it will take about three hours there and back), take a number 2 from St George's.

Follow the paved road past the checkpoint (it is usually open and unmanned) until you reach a junction. Take the 'Sunset' option. The road is a rough track and pleasant driving. On your right you should catch glimpses of the lovely Egmont Harbour. When you come to a junction with Seaside Circle, stick to the right and follow the road all the way to its conclusion – a small roundabout by the very last power pole. Now get out and walk, following the wide trail to the left. Before heading to the end, take a look at the coastline on your right (if you are facing the point) for a fine view of Egmont Harbour and Calivigny Island. The narrow track heading down is used by fishermen to reach the rocks below. No, don't do it.

Pass instead over the grassy headland to the end of the bluff where you will reach volcanic cliffs. The semi-submerged rocks out to sea are constantly battered by the waves, as are the cliffs below you. Don't walk too close to the edge – it is slippery and the rock crumbles. Along the cliff edge you should see a narrow trail that runs to the right. Follow it a short distance until you see a cave in the cliffside where the waves roll in. It's a pleasant, remote spot. Take a seat on the grass and enjoy.

On the walk back, follow the trail along the eastern side of the bluff back to the roundabout. If you fancy an alternative route on the way back to the main east coast road, take a right at Seaside Circle and follow it all the way around to Sunrise Drive and then take the main road out.

6

Gouyave, Grand Etang and the West

It would be wrong to state that by heading north from the elegant resorts and marinas of the southwest peninsula you are heading into the 'real' Grenada. All of Grenada is real; it is simply becoming a more diverse and interesting place. But the differences are immediately apparent. As you head into the interior, you begin to climb, your surroundings are lush and green, and buildings smaller and fewer. Forest takes over, steep ridges offer breathtaking and often toe-curling views, traffic noise abates and nature moves in around you. Along the west coast, the road twists and turns alongside black-sand beaches, up and around tall cliffs, and through small villages where life is played out along the roadside, in snackettes and rum shops, in the fields, and from colourful wooden fishing boats. Welcome to an unpolished, very natural, and quintessentially candid Grenada.

GETTING THERE

If you are driving up to Gouyave from the southwest peninsula you must head for St George's, drive around the Carenage and pass through the Sendall Tunnel (see page 95 for details). Continue past the bus terminus on Melville Street until you reach the Queen's Park National Stadium. Just before the stadium there is a tiny roundabout with one road heading north along the coast and a second heading east along the river. Gouyave and the west coast are straight on. If you are travelling by bus to Gouyave from St George's, take a number 5.

To get to Annandale and the Grand Etang National Park and visitor centre by car from the south, you need to follow the same road north from St George's until

DON'T MISS

If your time is limited, here is the don't-miss list for this part of Grenada:

Fish Friday (page 146)
Concord Falls (page 152)
Grand Etang Visitor Centre (page 137)
Gouyave Nutmeg Processing Station (page 147)
The Spice Basket Cultural Village (page 145)

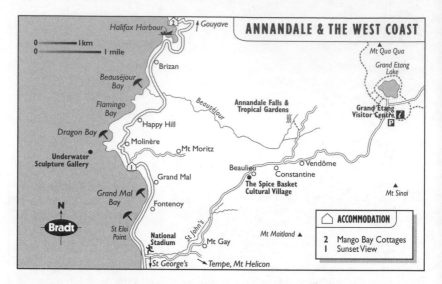

you arrive at the small roundabout junction before the National Stadium. This time turn right along the river. When you reach the next junction, simply follow the signs. It takes about 30 minutes to get to the Grand Etang National Park from St George's. If you are travelling by bus take a number 6 from the terminus on Melville Street. For Annandale, take a number 7.

It is possible to get to the Grand Etang National Park by car from Gouyave. This road is a challenge, however, because of quite poor signage.

GETTING AROUND

Buses are a good way to get around this region. They run very frequently along the west coast road as well as through the interior from St George's to the Grand Etang National Park. A hire car will give you that extra flexibility, of course, and if you do not fancy walking from the main road up to the Concord waterfalls, for example (although it is a lovely stroll), then a hire car is a must as no public buses make this trip. Public buses also do not usually take the route inland from Gouyave via Belvidere to the Grand Etang National Park.

FILLING UP There are petrol stations along Grand Mal Bay, in Gouyave and Victoria, and on the inland route from the National Stadium in the Queens Park area.

WHERE TO STAY

Once you leave the southwest peninsula, accommodation options are much fewer. Nevertheless there are still some nice places to stay.

See page 57 for accommodation price codes.

HOTELS AND GUESTHOUSES

🏠 **Rumboat Retreat** (4 rooms) Mt Nesbit, Gouyave; ☎ 473 437 1726; www.rumboatretreat. com. Set in a forest & garden location with sea

views, Rum Boat Retreat is tastefully designed & furnished with 4 rooms each with en-suite bathrooms, two of which face the sea. There is a large open veranda, communal lounge area &

kitchen where the in-house chef will prepare meals for you. Surrounding gardens contain a wide variety of tropical flowers, fruits & vegetables. Enjoy some rum tasting & local cooking with attentive & friendly owner Lisette or take off on the Rum Boat's small motor launch that is available for inshore sea trips, fishing, island & beach BBQs. Friendly, good value, & plenty of Grenadian spirit. **$–$$**

🏠 **Sunset View Restaurant & Beach House** (4 rooms) Grand Mal; ☎473 440 5758; e tropicanainn@spiceisle.com; www. tropicanainn/sunsetview.htm. Partner guesthouse to the Tropicana Inn on the Lagoon in St George's. Rooms have en-suite bathroom, AC, TV & private patio with sea views. Popular bar & restaurant serves local & international cuisine either outside on the deck or in the dining room. Friendly service. **$**

SELF-CATERING
🏠 **Mango Bay Cottages** (4 cottages)

Woodford Estate, nr Concord; ☎/f 473 444 3829; e info@mangobaygrenada.com; www. mangobaygrenada.com. Located near to Black Bay & Concord, very attractive, nicely furnished SC cottages enjoying tropical gardens & sea views. Cottages have private bathroom, kitchen, ceiling fans & veranda. **$$**

🏠 **Mango Palma** (3 apts) Mt Nesbit, Gouyave; UK☎020 8248 4798; Grenada ☎473 416 9447; e mangopalma@yahoo.co.uk; www. mangopalma.co.uk. Garden apt has 1 bed, fully equipped kitchen, bathroom & sea views. Plum Tree apt has 2 beds, fully equipped kitchen, bathroom & veranda. Ocean View apt has 3 beds, fully equipped kitchen, lounge, bathroom, private veranda with sea view. **$– $ $**

🏠 **Willie's Court Apartments** St Benoit St, Gouyave; ☎473 437 0235. Budget SC accommodation in the heart of Gouyave. Studio apts have 1 bedroom, private bathroom, living area, AC, fans, fully equipped kitchen. **$**

✖ WHERE TO EAT AND DRINK

Dining options in this region are limited. I have listed a few local eateries that are fine for a quick bite to eat or a lunchtime snack but if you want international restaurant dining then you will have to make your way down to St George's and the southwest.

Fish Friday in Gouyave is definitely worth a try, however. It starts at about 18.00 and you can sample a wide selection of seafood dishes (see page 146).

✖ **Sunset View Restaurant & Beach House** Grand Mal; ☎473 440 5758. Pleasant waterside restaurant & bar serving a range of Grenadian, international & BBQ dishes. **$–$$**

✖ **Kelly's Hot Spot** Lower Depradine St, Gouyave; ☎473 444 8322. Popular local eatery with bar. Good for roti, chicken & fries, that kind of thing. **$**

✖ **Mo's Delight Restaurant & Mini Bar** Upper Depradine St, L'Anse, Gouyave. Colourfully

decorated eatery serving a selection of local food & drink. **$**

✖ **Paul's Catering & Mini Restaurant** Upper Depradine St, L'Anse, Gouyave; ☎473 444 9204. Local dishes, fish, chicken & fries. **$**

✖ **Spiceisle Restaurant & Bar** Lower Depradine St, Gouyave. Good selection of local food & drink. The seaside deck is popular on Friday nights. **$**

SHOPPING

Shopping is fairly limited in this region. In Gouyave you will find the essentials only. There is a fairly well-stocked supermarket on Lower Depradine Street, opposite the junction with St Peter's Street, as well as a few smaller convenience stores. There is also a fresh produce market on Lower Depradine Street that is at its liveliest on Fridays and Saturdays. The fish market is on Upper Depradine Street (the L'Anse).

LOCAL CRAFTS AND SOUVENIRS You will find craft and souvenir stalls at popular attractions such as Concord Falls, Annandale Falls and the Grand Etang visitor centre. The Spice Basket Cultural Village has a number of craft shops and, if you are looking for nutmeg jams, syrups and so on then you should also check out the shop at the Gouyave Nutmeg Station. Veronica's Vision (see box on page 140) has original screen-printed clothing and accessories and is also an outlet for other local products.

OTHER PRACTICALITIES

MONEY AND BANKS There is an RBTT Bank with Blue Machine ATM on Central Depradine Street in Gouyave.

MEDICAL There are two well-stocked pharmacies on Lower Depradine Street in Gouyave. If you take regular prescription medication, you should be sure you bring enough with you and not rely on these pharmacies having what you need.

SAFETY Should you need them, there are police stations on the main streets in Gouyave and Grand Roy. As with the majority of Grenada this area is very safe and you should not have any trouble. Common sense is always your guidance. You may encounter one or two beggars on the streets of Gouyave. Consider helping them out with a few coins if you can.

WHAT TO SEE AND DO

THE GRAND ETANG NATIONAL PARK The Grand Etang National Park was established in 1992. It is a 1,000ha swathe of mountainous forest located in the centre of the island to the northwest of the 1,540ha Grand Etang Forest Reserve that was created as far back as 1906. The name 'Grand Etang' is derived from the French meaning 'large lake', in reference to the 12ha crater lake which sits at an elevation of 530m at the southeastern boundary of the national park. Also located within the Grand Etang National Park are the summits of Mt Qua Qua, Mt Granby and Morne Fédon (also commonly known as Fédon's Camp or simply Fédon). Waterfalls found within the park include the three that comprise the Concord Falls – Concord, Au Coin and Fontainbleu. Located on the southwestern perimeter of the park is the frequently visited Annandale Falls.

The mountainous ridges of the national park are steep and narrow. They are home to a variety of trees including gommier (*Dacryodes excelsa*), a tall gum tree that Amerindians used for making their canoes; mahogany (*Swietenia mahagoni*); teak (*Tectona grandis*); balata (*Manilkara bidentata*); and maruba (*Simarouba amara*), to name just a few. Prior to Hurricane Ivan in 2004, the tall trees of the Grand Etang National Park and the Grand Etang Forest Reserve provided a high forest canopy that in turn created a wet rainforest habitat on these elevated slopes and ridges. Unfortunately the high winds of the hurricane had a devastating effect upon the rainforest, particularly on the windward-facing slopes that were exposed to the full force of the storm. The taller trees were either uprooted or cropped by the wind and the result is that there is no longer a high canopy creating wet rainforest conditions. This in turn means that many of the plants, flowers and creatures which you would normally expect to find in Grenada's rainforest habitat are no longer as prevalent as they once were; in fact some are now quite scarce. Despite the storm, the forest is growing and recovering though it will clearly take many more years to re-establish habitats.

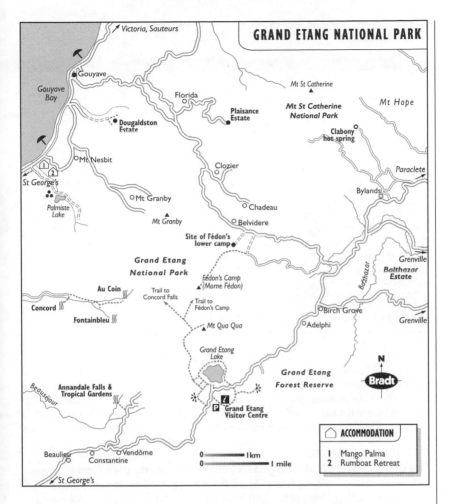

The forests of Grand Etang are also home to the **mona monkey** (*Cercopithecus mona*) which was probably introduced to the island from Africa during the years of the slave trade. The monkeys used to be a popular visitor attraction though sightings have become fewer in the wake of two hurricanes. Of particular concern is the destruction of the monkeys' habitat and the fact that there appears to be little enforcement of the law ensuring their protection from hunters within the national park's boundaries. Hopefully something will be done about this before the mona monkey goes the way of the agouti (*Dasyprocta leporina*) and is hunted out of existence in Grenada altogether.

Yet, despite natural disaster and conservation issues, the Grand Etang National Park is still very beautiful and the high mountain ridges offer unsurpassed panoramic views of the island. At the Grand Etang Lake, there is a **visitor centre** with a collection of interesting and informative presentations about the geological formation of Grenada's mountainous interior, and about the types of vegetation, habitats and species of wildlife visitors may encounter here. Entry to the Grand Etang National Park at the time of writing is US$2 per person and is paid at a booth near the visitor centre and at entrance to the lake itself. There are a number of hikes

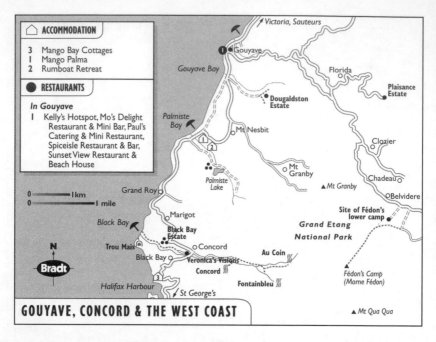

ACCOMMODATION

3 Mango Bay Cottages
1 Mango Palma
2 Rumboat Retreat

RESTAURANTS

In Gouyave
1 Kelly's Hotspot, Mo's Delight
Restaurant & Mini Bar, Paul's
Catering & Mini Restaurant,
Spiceisle Restaurant & Bar,
Sunset View Restaurant &
Beach House

▲ Mt Qua Qua

throughout the park though some of the more inaccessible and challenging ones have yet to be properly cleared and repaired following the storms. Some of these trails require local knowledge as well as sharp cutting tools to clear the route. More accessible trails include those to the Concord waterfalls, around the Grand Etang Lake and up to the summit of Mt Qua Qua. Some of the island's tour operators offer excursions and guided hikes to these sites.

EXPLORING THE REGION

The west coast from St George's to Gouyave

Along the coast from St George's to Molinère is the sweeping Grand Mal Bay with its petroleum storage tanks and oil depot. The area has a very urban and industrial feel, particularly with the outskirts of St George's just a short hop away around St Eloi Point.

Mt Moritz is a village located on a hill to the east of Molinère. Today it is an ordinary Grenadian village but it started out as a community of poor white farm labourers who came from Barbados in the latter half of the 19th century. Having very little need for business or social interaction with anyone outside the area, it essentially became a closed community and stayed that way for almost 100 years. It was not until the 1970s and 80s that things really changed in Mt Moritz with many of its residents migrating overseas and people from surrounding villages beginning to move into the area. The few descendants of those original settlers still living there are affectionately known as Mt Moritz Bajans.

Beauséjour Bay is located between **Brizan** and **Happy Hill**. It is a large sandy bay and an outlet for the Beauséjour River that finds its source in the mountainous interior of the Grand Etang National Park, and runs to the sea via the Annandale Falls. The area was settled by the French in the mid 17th century and, due to its location at the mouth of one of the island's largest rivers, became a 'beautiful place' for people to live outside of Port Louis (St George's). Inland from the bay is the former Beauséjour Estate, once a 280ha sugar estate that was also home to an ice

MOLINÈRE PROTECTED SEASCAPE

Commonly referred to as the Molinère Marine Park or sometimes the Grenada Marine Park or Marine Reserve, this area of protected seascape is located on the west coast between Molinère Point and Flamingo Bay, just 5km north of St George's, or just 15–20 minutes by boat from Grand Anse Beach. This protected area of underwater habitat is home to a variety of hard and soft corals, sea fans and sponges. There is an abundance of colourful schooling reef fish as well as seahorses, grouper, moray eels, turtles and occasional manta and eagle rays. Dive sites that fall within this protected area include Flamingo Bay (6–27m), Happy Valley (6–27m), Dragon Bay (8–28m) and Molinère Reef (18–40m). The Underwater Sculpture Gallery is located on the northern edge of Molinère Reef (see page 85). The best way to explore the Marine Reserve is by boat with a dive operator (see page 86) though there is a steep access road on the apex of a bend on the main coastal route in Molinère. Look for the sign, and be careful. If you are not a scuba diver, why not try snorkelling instead? The waters are usually clear and there is a lot to see. Dive operators offer snorkelling tours and instruction.

factory in the mid 1900s. Beauséjour was the site of military conflict during the US intervention in 1983.

Just before you reach Beauséjour Bay you pass **Flamingo Bay**, **Dragon Bay** and **Molinère Point**. This area forms part of the **Molinère Protected Seascape** and is very popular with scuba divers and snorkellers (see box above). The very interesting **Underwater Sculpture Gallery** is located just off Molinère Point.

Halifax Harbour is a pretty bay spoiled by the encroachment of a large and very pungent landfill site on the nearby Perseverance Estate. A tranquil anchorage surrounded by greenery and a narrow stretch of sand, Halifax Harbour is picturesque, especially with its very own shipwreck grounded on the southern bank. The location of the landfill site has been the subject of controversy as not only does it threaten this natural haven, it is also positioned near to one of the island's endangered Grenada dove habitats. A little to the north of Halifax Harbour are the ruins of the former Woodford Estate, once an Amerindian settlement and then later a thriving sugar estate. In 1778, a coastal battery was constructed here to protect the entrance of Halifax Harbour (then known as Petit Havre). The coastal road climbs high above the northern side of the bay and there are good views down to it.

Black Bay is perched on the hillside of the 37ha Black Bay Estate, an agricultural area that was once the site of a sugar plantation and mill. The estate was purchased in 2006 and the owners were planning to build an organic farm and resort there. At the time of writing nothing has happened. The area still contains the ruins of a waterwheel, machine works and former estate buildings though they are now on the private land of the Black Bay Estate. The bay is quite sheltered and the beach is rich black sand. On Black Bay Point, a small rocky outcrop to the south of the beach, is a natural cave known locally as **Trou Mais**. It is believed Amerindian settlers may once have stored corn and other agricultural produce here. (See page 155 for details of how to get there.)

The road inland from Black Bay runs through the village of **Concord** and along a river valley directly to the first of three waterfalls, where it comes to an end. The valley is beautiful, lush and green. Small farms (or 'gardens' as they are referred to locally) mingle with occasional cocoa and nutmeg trees that grow on the hillsides above the sparkling river below.

Grand Roy is one of the largest villages between St George's and Gouyave. It sits along each side of the Grand Roy River and is a colourful place with a lively atmosphere and friendly people. Beside the road is an old cannon on the site of a former gun battery.

South of **Mt Nesbit**, a small residential community that was once a fortification during the Fédon Rebellion (see page 142), the coastal road passes alongside **Palmiste Bay** where there is a narrow sandy beach suitable for picnics and bathing. Running inland from the coast is a rough, narrow road that climbs up the hillside towards **Palmiste Lake**, also known locally as Palmiste Dig. Originally a manmade lake that was created by damming the Great Palmiste River to provide water power to the former Palmiste Estate, it is now a natural and peaceful sanctuary for wildfowl. (See page 153.)

Located to the north of Mt Nesbit is the community of **Mt Granby**. This village sits at the top end of a valley that leads to the summit of a 680m mountain ridge bearing the same name. While the village itself is a fairly ordinary residential community of board and block houses and the road up to it simply ends at small hillside farms, the valley in which it sits is really very beautiful indeed. Ascending the long narrow road up to the village, you pass through extraordinarily lush greenery covering the steep slopes and ridges of the surrounding hillside. The villagers who have lived here for most of their lives talk of an old track that runs up and over the ridge across to the settlement of Belvidere, in the shadows of Fédon's Camp.

Just before you arrive in Gouyave you will come to the **Dougaldston Estate** which was established in the mid 18th century and is one of Grenada's oldest working estates. Though originally it was around 300ha in size, over the years it has gradually been getting smaller and smaller as lots are sold off for the construction of new homes. It started out as a sugar estate, and the ruins of the original waterwheel and machine works can still be seen below the Great House which stands at the top of the hill behind. Copper pots lie on the ground all around and the place has a distinct feel of abandonment and decline. Following sugar production, the estate moved into spices, and in particular nutmeg and cocoa. Today the *boucan* (a drying house) still operates, though in very limited fashion, processing cocoa beans and drying them in retractable wooden trays. You may also see local women removing mace from nutmeg crops, ready for processing at the 'Pool' in Gouyave.

Gouyave The small fishing town of Gouyave (pronounced *gwav*) is located on the northwest coast of Grenada in the parish of St John, some 20km from the island's capital, St George's. Though the area was no doubt inhabited by early Amerindians, the settlement is thought to have been established in the 1730s by the French who named it Bourg de L'Anse Gouyave. In 1763, when Grenada was under British rule, the village was renamed Charlotte Town after the wife of reigning monarch King George III. Though both names became interchangeable for many years afterwards, Grenadians now commonly refer to the town as Gouyave and this is how it appears on maps.

'Anse', or L'Anse, is an old French Creole word meaning 'bay'. Anglicised versions of the word are also written as 'L'Ance' or sometimes simply 'Lance'. The northern half of Gouyave is still referred to by locals as the L'Anse (or Lance).

The people of Gouyave and the surrounding parish of St John have traditionally eked a living from the sea and from the land. This is still the case, though the devastating effects of Hurricane Ivan in 2004 threw the island's agricultural economy into serious decline. One of the island's three major nutmeg-processing stations is located in Gouyave, the other two being in Grenville and Victoria. The station in Gouyave, commonly referred to as the **Gouyave Nutmeg Pool**, or sometimes simply 'the pool', is the only one of the three that still processes nutmeg and mace for domestic and overseas consumption. (See page 147.)

Gouyave's main thoroughfare is named after Jean de Pradines, a French planter of the 1700s. On the southern half of the town the road is called Lower Depradine Street, in the centre of the town it is Central Depradine Street, and in the north of

FISHERMAN'S BIRTHDAY

The Roman Catholic feast of St Peter is celebrated on 29 June each year. This feast day is very significant to the people of Gouyave and is therefore a time of great celebration. St Peter is the Roman Catholic patron saint of fishermen and, of course, Gouyave is one of the largest fishing communities on the island. In addition to this, Gouyave is also the location of the Diocese of St Peter in Grenada.

On Fisherman's Birthday, Gouyave's villagers, especially those directly associated with fishing, attend a morning church service. Afterwards, the congregation assembles by the numerous colourfully painted fishing boats that are drawn up along the shoreline. Once the priest has completed the formalities of blessing the fishermen's boats and fishing nets, the fun begins. There are fishing-boat races, displays of fish, speeches by visiting dignitaries, a variety of entertainment from comedians and singers, and, naturally, lots of dancing, eating and drinking. The celebrations also include award ceremonies for best catch and fisherman of the year. The event is very entertaining and has survived Hurricane Ivan to complement Fish Friday as a heritage event and attraction for visitors. These community events not only promote the village, they help to provide an essential source of income for local people. They are also a great way to let your hair down and just have some fun.

the town, the area known as the L'Anse, the road becomes Upper Depradine Street. It is along this main thoroughfare that the majority of shops, eateries and bars are to be found. Also located on this street is the police station, the fire station, the post office, bank and ATM, and the Gouyave Nutmeg Pool. Shops consist primarily of convenience stores, boutiques, salons and hardware stores. The Gouyave fisheries are located on Upper Depradine Street in the L'Anse area.

The main junction in Gouyave is with St Peter's Street which runs from the town into the interior and all the way across to Grenville. St Peter's Street is where you will find the immaculately renovated St John's Anglican Church (St John the Divine) and the St Rose Modern Secondary School. The church was built in 1846, with some later additions, and was the first permanent Anglican chapel in the parish of St John. Adjoining St Peter's Street is St Dominic Street where you will find both the old and the new Roman Catholic churches. Construction of the original church was started in 1829 on the site of a previous chapel, but was not completed until many years later. Built in the so-called Caribbean Gothic revival style, its octagonal

FEDON'S REBELLION

Julien Fédon was born the son of Pierre Fédon, a French jeweller who travelled from Bordeaux, France, in 1749 to the Caribbean island of Martinique. His mother was a freed black slave residing in Martinique. The family emigrated to Grenada in the 1750s and, in 1780, Julien married Marie Rose Cavelan who was a 'free coloured', or mulatto woman. In 1791, they purchased the 182ha Belvidere Estate in today's parish of St John. The estate had a labour force of around 100 slaves.

When they arrived in Grenada in the 1750s the island was under French rule. In 1763, Grenada was ceded to Britain under the Treaty of Paris, but was recaptured by the French in 1779. In 1783, the island was once again ceded to Britain, this time under the Treaty of Versailles. It was during the next ten years or so that a number of factors influenced the life of Julien Fédon. The first was the repressive regime of British colonial rule following the island's recapture after the Treaty of Versailles. Despite belonging to the island's largest population group, 'free blacks' and 'free coloureds', many of whom, including Fédon, had become wealthy estate owners, the British denied them the rights, privileges and political freedoms enjoyed by white Protestants. A second influence on Julien Fédon was the French Revolution of 1789. It proved to be both his inspiration as well as his downfall.

Fédon was encouraged by the republican Governor of Martinique, Victor Hugues, and appointed commandant-general of the French republican forces in Grenada. During the early hours of 3 March 1795, inspired by the republican cry of 'liberté, égalité, fraternité', Fédon, together with a band of around 100 former slaves and 'free coloureds', led a raid on the settlement of Grenville. They burned and plundered houses, dragged the British inhabitants out into the streets and executed them. At roughly the same time as the attack on Grenville, another detachment of rebels attacked Gouyave. On their return to the mountains, they were joined by large numbers of slaves who had abandoned plantations in the area, as well as a third detachment of insurrectionists who had advanced south from Sauteurs. By the following day, almost every Frenchman and a large number of slaves and 'free coloureds' had joined Julien Fédon at his headquarters in Belvidere. The rebellion had begun.

Over the next year, Julien Fédon led the uprising from his camp fortifications in Belvidere. The fighting was widespread and the rebellion of slaves, the burning

open metal bell tower is unique in Grenada. The church was replaced by a newer, larger one in 1902 and today it stands abandoned and is sadly in a state of ruin. In a side street off St Dominic Street you will find market vendors selling local produce. Together with St Dominic Street, this side street is one of the locations for Gouyave's weekly **Fish Friday** (see page 146). On Friday nights these streets are crammed with stalls selling a wide variety of fresh fish dishes. It is extremely popular with both visitors and locals, who are all out to sample the fare and have a nice time. Also on St Dominic Street you will see the new St Peter's Catholic Parish Church, which is a very pretty stone church with high wooden ceilings and pews, large arched windows and blue stained glass projecting an interesting glow onto the whitewashed walls.

The northern end of St Dominic Street emerges on the main thoroughfare of Central Depradine Street. To the north is a colourfully painted bridge over the Little River and into Upper Depradine Street, or the L'Anse. Beyond the bars and buildings on the western side of the L'Anse is the bay itself. Here you will find a

and plundering of estates and the killing or capture of British planters took place throughout Grenada. Fédon based his camp fortifications high in the mountains above his estate. His lower camp, known as Camp de la Liberté, was at the foot of the Montagne du Vauclin (now known as Morne Fédon) and a series of upper fortifications ran from the summit of this mountain across the ridge to Mt Qua Qua. His upper camp also later became known as Camp de la Mort, due to the bloody fighting and executions that took place there throughout and towards the end of the campaign.

On 8 April 1796, Fédon lost a brother in a failed and bloody attack on his camp by the British. In revenge he ordered the execution of 48 prisoners at his upper camp, including former governor Ninian Home. Despite the fact that his supporters were running the beleaguered British quite ragged the length and breadth of the island, Fédon failed to make a successful full-scale attack on St George's and historians agree that it is primarily this failure that ultimately led to his defeat. Too many times he resisted the opportunity to attack and allowed the British to regroup and re-strengthen. This failing also caused him to lose the faith and support of his republican commanders in Martinique and Guadeloupe.

On 9 June 1796, a full-scale offensive was launched by the British on Fédon's encampments at Belvidere. Fédon's headquarters at Camp de la Liberté were successfully taken, forcing Fédon and his remaining men to retreat to the heights of the mountain. Next came an attack on the high lookout called Vigie. Fédon's men suffered huge losses during this attack, forcing those who survived to cross the mountainous ridge to his last camp. Realising that they had lost, Fédon and some of his men threw themselves down the steep mountainsides. Those who didn't were either captured or killed.

No-one knows what happened to Julien Fédon as his body was never recovered. The most accepted version of events is that somehow he survived his escape from the steep mountain slopes but was drowned in an attempt to sail by small boat to the salvation of his brother in Trinidad. The rebellion lasted 15 months during which time it is estimated that machine works and buildings were destroyed on around 100 estates across the island. Crops for the years 1794 to 1796 were all lost.

beach full of colourful fishing boats, people mending nets and making general preparations for their next outing. You will also see the new fisheries complex that was funded and constructed by the Japanese.

Two routes from the west coast into the interior The road from the National Stadium on the northern outskirts of St George's goes to the Grand Etang National Park. It passes through a number of communities before reaching the village of Beaulieu where you will find The Spice Basket Cultural Village, an innovative new project that brings together Grenadian food, arts and crafts, theatre, music and heritage (see opposite). Beyond Beaulieu you come to a fork (unsignposted and confusing at the time of writing) between the villages of Constantine and Vendôme. The narrow road to the left hugs the side of a very steep cliff before reaching the Annandale Falls. Because of its accessibility and proximity to the southwest peninsula, this short but pretty waterfall is extremely popular with visitors. It has a deep pool and an attractive tropical garden. (See opposite.)

Taking the right-hand fork at the junction leads you up into the heights of the Grand Etang Forest Reserve and Grand Etang National Park. You will notice the temperature becomes a little cooler and the tall banks along the sides of the road are now covered with tropical plants, mosses and ferns. As it nears its highest point, the road is steep with several hairpin bends. If you are driving, take it slowly and use your horn around these corners to let others know you are there. Once at the peak, the road descends slightly as it follows the ridge and shortly arrives at the national park visitor centre. From here there is access to the Grand Etang Lake (see page 148) and the hiking trail to the summit of Mt Qua Qua (see page 149). The road beyond the lake descends steeply through St Margaret (where you will find the St Margaret's Falls – see page 170), Adelphi, and on towards Grenville and the east coast (see *Chapter 7*).

Florida, **Clozier** and **Belvidere** are rural farming hamlets on or near the inland road that runs from St Peter's Street in Gouyave, along the northern edge of the Grand Etang National Park and on to Grenville. They are very scenic and I urge you to take a drive around this area if you have time (see page 154). These estate lands were significant nutmeg producers prior to Hurricane Ivan in 2004 as their high elevation and cool temperatures were ideal for the nutmeg tree to thrive. Nutmegs continue to grow here, along with other crops such as cocoa, peas and beans, but their numbers are much fewer than they used to be and the people of these rural farmlands have to work very hard to make ends meet. From Florida the road climbs to Plaisance Estate (also known as Mt Pleasant), which used to be a major agricultural centre before the storm. The estate continues to operate though sadly it is a faint shadow of its former self. The Florida area is very pretty. It is lush and green, and the narrow and winding country roads are lined with nutmeg trees.

Belvidere is the location of the former Belvidere Estate, once owned by Julien Fédon, leader of the insurrection of 1795 (see box on page 142). The estate produced coffee, cocoa and spice and became very prominent as one of the island's best producers during the late 1800s. During the early 1900s it changed over to nutmeg cultivation and became one of the largest and most successful nutmeg-producing estates in the world. More recently, as with many once thriving agricultural estates in Grenada, Belvidere suffered at the hands of Hurricane Ivan and the majority of the nutmeg crop was lost to the storm. The crops are coming back, the trees are growing again, and local people still cultivate nutmegs, cocoa, vegetables, ground provisions and a variety of fruit crops. Belvidere is remote, unspoilt and very beautiful. With lush greenery as far as you can see, and with high mountain ridges all around (you can see Morne Fédon, Mt Qua Qua and Mt St Catherine from various spots around here), you should try to get up here if you can. It is about as far removed from the beaches, resorts and marinas of the south as you can get.

ACTIVITIES AND SPECIAL INTERESTS
The Annandale Falls and Tropical Gardens
The Annandale Waterfall is probably the most frequently visited of all the islands' falls and cascades. This is because it is one of the most accessible and is located just 16km from the capital, St George's. Named after the surrounding estate, this waterfall is around 10m high with a fairly deep pool. It sits on the Beauséjour River and is set against a backdrop of forest and very colourful tropical gardens.

Because it is so frequently visited, it has lost just a little of its natural charm, though it is still very pretty. Access is via a paved footpath leading to a viewing platform. There are plenty of vendors, a nearby bar for refreshments, and people offering photographs of themselves jumping from the waterfall for a few dollars. Despite a few 'touristy' downsides, the Annandale Waterfall is an accessible site that offers visitors a small taste of the island's natural attractions. It also has a stunning tropical garden, which many seem to either forget or ignore, with a well-defined footpath that takes you to the top of the waterfall and then back down to the exit. It is a really nice walk, especially for those who are interested in flowers and plants. Keep a lookout for the resident mona monkey (see page 7).

En route to the waterfall, just before the entrance, and on the opposite side of the road, is a second waterfall which, in the wet season, is often fuller and higher than the main attraction (but don't tell anyone I said that). There is a rough track to this cascading fall from the bridge on the main road. Also along the main road, just before you reach the entrance to the falls, you will see a number of craft and souvenir vendors as well as a couple of interesting bars. When visiting the Annandale Falls, you should bear in mind that it will be very busy during the cruise-ship season so a good time to go is later in the afternoon when the crowds and tour buses have dispersed.

The road to Annandale is north of the capital, St George's. It can be a little confusing if you are driving as signposts are limited once you reach the outskirts of the capital. From the southwest, pass around the Carenage and the Sendall Tunnel and turn right along River Road just before the National Stadium. Follow the road to a signposted junction. Tempe is to the right, Grand Etang and Annandale to the left. Continue along this road until you reach Beaulieu and Constantine – look out for the Spice Basket Cultural Village (see below) and the Amba Kaila store on your right – and you should come to a fork in the road. Perhaps someone will have thought to put a sign here, but if not: the road to the right goes to Grand Etang, the fork to the left goes down to Annandale. Follow the narrow road along the cliff for around five to ten minutes (use your horn – people drive way too fast along here) until you come to the waterfall trail entrance. If you are travelling by bus from the terminal in St George's, you need to take a number 7 that is marked Annandale and Willis.

The Spice Basket Cultural Village
The Spice Basket Cultural Village is an innovative project located in the Beaulieu Valley on the main road to Grand Etang and Annandale. If you are travelling by bus take a number 7. The village has a bar and restaurant serving Grenadian and Caribbean food, it has shops selling local arts and crafts (including White Cane Industries, see box on page 101), it houses a cricket memorabilia museum, a pavilion for live music, entertainment and even

weddings, and it has a huge theatre and concert hall, something Grenada has really been missing in recent years. The buildings have a very Caribbean feel (some look like the traditional, colourful board houses you still see in Grenada's rural villages, for example), and the staff seem to have big smiles and a sense of urgency and excitement. Perhaps it is because the project is fairly new, but it is indeed quite different and, if you visit, you cannot help hoping that it will be an incredible success for the country, the local communities, and the visionary people behind it.

In the cruise-ship season expect the Spice Basket to be bursting at the seams, of course, but look out for the regular evening entertainment and try to fit it into your schedule if you can. It will need supporting.

For more information you could visit www.spicebasketgrenada.com; e info@spicebasketgrenada.com, or ☏ 473 437 9000 or 473 232 9000.

Fish Friday at Gouyave
Established after Hurricane Ivan in 2004, the Gouyave Fish Friday event is proving to be a huge success. Set up as a local community project with the aim of cementing the identity of Gouyave as a fishing village as well as generating income for the people living in the parish of St John, Fish Friday is now a regular on the Grenada calendar of events. It attracts locals as well as visitors, with many hotels and tour operators running regular Friday night excursions to the town. The atmosphere is lively and extremely friendly, and there is usually live music in the form of steel pan or drumming to accompany your evening out.

Located along a couple of narrow backstreets in the heart of Gouyave, Fish Friday is essentially two lines of stalls cooking and selling a wide variety of tasty and fresh seafood dishes. Here you can sample fried, steamed and sauté fish, grilled lobster, fish cakes, fish kebabs, titiri, shrimp and lambie. The smell of cooking, the sizzling of the frying pans, the smoke from the barbecues, the live music and the banter all combine to generate a fun and interesting evening. Stroll along the stalls and sample a little of everything. There is always plenty of liquid refreshment to accompany your fish dishes, including beers, local juices and, of course, a wide selection of Grenadian rum.

Fish Friday starts at around 19.00 and runs until around midnight. A number of tour operators run bus excursions to Fish Friday (see page 70). Your hotel may also organise trips for its guests.

The Dougaldston Estate
The Dougaldston Estate is one of the oldest functioning estates in the Caribbean. It was established as a sugar estate in the 1700s and continued operating into the 1800s. Though some of the estate has been sold off as residential and agricultural lots, it once ran to around 300ha in total area and produced nutmeg, spices, cocoa and bananas. Today most of the original estate buildings and machine works are neglected and lie in ruins. However, the historic, functioning cocoa-processing station remains, making the estate well worth a visit, despite a very obvious decline in productivity and finance. The station also boasts the introduction of a number of innovations such as a cocoa bean polisher and a nutmeg oil distillery. The estate still claims to have the last remaining, and still working, cocoa steam drier in Grenada.

The Dougaldston Estate is located south of Gouyave along the banks of the Little River. From Gouyave, go south along the coast and turn left over the bridge along the riverbank. At the junction, instead of following the main road to the right, continue straight on along the river beside some banana plants. The road becomes rough and soon reaches the remains of a stone wall marking the entrance to the estate. The path to the left goes to the still functioning cocoa station and the path straight on leads uphill to the ruins of the former estate buildings. These ruins are interesting in terms of their historical context though far too overgrown and run-down to explore safely. They include a stone aqueduct that carried water to the wheel that drove the machinery, the Great House at the summit of the hill, and large copper pots that would have been used as part of the cane-juice filtering process as well as for cooking by the estate's enslaved workforce.

Though hardly functioning much these days, the cocoa station provides a fascinating glimpse into Grenada's past. The main wooden building is the *boucan*. Beneath the boucan there are large drying trays that are pushed out manually along iron rails to enable the cocoa to dry naturally in the sun. When the sun goes in or when it rains, the trays are pushed back under the shelter of the building. When the station is processing more cocoa than the trays can handle, which is rare these days, there is a movable roof operating along a second set of rails to cover cocoa that is drying on the ground. Near to the boucan you can also see the wooden fermentation bins that are used for the first stage of the cocoa process (see page 21 for more information on how cocoa is processed). Inside the boucan there are displays of cocoa and other spices that are produced in Grenada together with some antique machinery.

At the time of writing, access to the estate is free and you can go there every day except Sunday.

The Gouyave Nutmeg Processing Station (⏰ *08.00–16.00 Mon–Fri; 15–20min tours US$1 or EC$2.70pp*) The nutmeg processing station at Gouyave, referred to by local people as 'the pool', is located in the centre of the village on the coastal side of the road, just south of the bridge to L'Anse. Owned by the Grenada Co-operative Nutmeg Association, it is the largest of three nutmeg processing stations in Grenada. It was constructed in 1947 on the site of a former coastal battery that was built by the French in the 1700s to protect this west coast settlement from attack and invasion.

The co-operative was formed in 1952 with the aim of removing the monopoly of nutmeg processing, sales and export from the plantation owners. Farmers who are members of the co-operative agree to sell their produce exclusively through the co-operative. In its heyday Gouyave would process up to 2,700 tonnes of nutmegs per year for export. The impact of Hurricane Ivan devastated the industry, however, and today Gouyave is the only station on the island still processing nutmegs for domestic consumption and export. Despite this serious setback, the Gouyave station is a fascinating place, and a visit there gives you an insight into an important aspect of Grenada's agricultural tradition, its troubled past, its stark economic present, and its uncertain future. Wooden machines and long curing trays, together with men and women engaged in manual sorting, grading and packaging activities, combine to paint a fascinating picture of the island's cultural heritage as well as providing an educational insight into the processing of nutmeg and mace.

The nutmeg station has a gift shop where you can buy nutmegs, spices and a variety of local products and crafts. Several tour operators include a visit to Gouyave Nutmeg pool and it is usually part of a cruise-ship shore excursion. If you are travelling independently, please take the time to visit and support the nutmeg workers of Grenada. The tour is definitely worthwhile.

If you come across a tour guide who speaks so quickly that it sounds like he has memorised a script (I will not mention his name), don't be afraid to ask him to slow down. Because the 'pool' is on the cruise-ship circuit, visitors can be processed through the station as efficiently as the nutmegs themselves. Speak up, interrupt,

6

and be sure to get the most out of your visit. You can take photos here but if you want to take pictures of the workers, please be polite and ask them directly for permission first.

WALKS, HIKES AND SCENIC DRIVES At the time of writing a number of the trickier interior hikes are overgrown and quite impassable, which is a great shame. If you decide to tackle any of the more challenging trails, be sure to take a local guide with you or go with a tour operator. Many of these hikes follow very narrow, precipitous ridges, there are often spur trails, there is little or nothing by way of signs, and access may be blocked by fallen trees or landslides in some places. Always exercise caution and ensure you are properly prepared. (See page 77 for a list of tour operators and guides.)

Grand Etang Lake Shoreline Trail
The Grand Etang is a 12ha crater lake located at an elevation of 530m above sea level at the heart of the Grand Etang National Park. Prior to Hurricane Ivan in 2004, the lake's forest habitat included fine specimens of gommier and mahogany trees, several varieties of ferns, heliconia, gingers and many other plant and flower species. This dense forest habitat was home to a number of birds, frogs, lizards, opossum, armadillo, mongoose and the mona monkey. Unfortunately, because the hurricane destroyed the majority of tall trees, the habitat has changed and is currently in a state of flux, still trying to sort itself out. But it is definitely recovering and, even though many of the tallest gommier and mahogany trees are gone, the mona monkey is more frequently sighted and is thought to be doing well, despite the attention of hunters. The lake is still a natural beauty, the surrounding forest is lush and dense once again, and the circular hike around it is an enjoyable though often quite a soggy one.

Give yourself between 1–1½ hours and expect mud – lots of it. I have walked this trail in both the dry and the wet season and it is always muddy. The far side of the lake especially can be quite swampy. So carry or leave a towel and a spare set of clothes in your car. Take plenty of water with you as it can also be very hot and humid along the trail despite the altitude. A fee of US$2 is payable on entry to the park.

The trail starts near the Grand Etang visitor centre. Buy your pass from the ticket booth and then walk down the steep main road away from the building. You will reach a second booth and a sign pointing to the lake. Simply show your pass and walk down the wide track to the lake. You will see a wooden picnic gazebo and some steps and a wooden handrail running up the hillside. Walk up the steps to a second gazebo and look for a sign indicating the start of the shoreline trail. If you continue up the steps you will come to the Mt Qua Qua trail (see opposite).

This path is easy to follow – you cannot possibly get lost – but the terrain can be a little challenging, especially after heavy rains. The first 20 to 30 minutes is a pleasant woodland trail which is fairly dry and mostly free of obstacles. There are the occasional steps and you must manoeuvre yourself around a narrow stretch of tree roots, but it is for the most part straightforward and uncomplicated. The second 20 to 30 minutes can be a different challenge altogether. The path is rough and usually swampy. In fact there are some stretches that can appear impassable, though there is usually a workaround if you are patient and look for it. To add to the misery of swamp and mud, there are no views of the lake during this stretch. Once you are two-thirds of the way around, however, you do see the lake again and the path becomes much easier and far less muddy. Take time to enjoy the environment, the plants, the birdlife and the peace and quiet of the lake. Listen out for the very unusual and extremely shrill call of a tree dwelling beetle, known locally as the *coq soleil*, as well as tree frogs, cicadas and crickets.

This final 20 minutes is easy going. You will emerge at a concrete dam, which you must cross. From here the track runs up to the main highway. Carefully cross the road and pick up the trail again on the other side. Walk up the steps to the top of the ridge. Once at the top, take a diversion to the left. Follow the trail for five to ten minutes up the hill to a viewing point. There are panoramas across the forest reserve to the east coast. Back along the trail to the junction, take the trail straight on and up the hill to the Grand Etang visitor centre.

There are washrooms and an outside tap at the rear of the visitor centre where you can clean up a bit (though you may prefer to head straight down the mountain to Grand Anse and throw yourself into the sea), and the visitor centre itself is really worth a look.

For information on how to get to the Grand Etang visitor centre see Getting There on page 133.

The Mt Qua Qua Trail
Mt Qua Qua is located within the Grand Etang National Park. It is actually the highest part of a long ridge that runs from the south side of Grand Etang Lake northwards to Fédon's Camp (see page 150). The ridge rises to a peak on the northwestern side of the lake at a height of 720m, the point known as Mt Qua Qua.

The trail to Mt Qua Qua is very easy to follow, it climbs at a steady gradient to the summit and is actually not that physically demanding. The trickiest part of this hike is the height. The trail runs along the very top of the narrow ridge. There is little tree cover on either side and the drops are extremely precipitous. In some areas, landslides and weather have caused the trail to erode and it is slippery with a few short, but steep and hair-raising scrambles. This hike is not for acrophobia sufferers. The sheer drops on either side of the narrow trail and exposure to the elements make it more mentally than physically challenging and if you have a problem with heights, you will find this hike very difficult, if not impossible. The spectacular views on a clear day, however, make this hike well worth the effort.

It should take you around 3 hours there and back. The trail starts near the Grand Etang visitor centre. Buy your US$2 pass from the ticket booth and then walk down the steep main road away from the centre. You will reach another booth and a sign pointing to the Grand Etang Lake. Show your pass and walk along the wide track down to the lake. You will see a wooden picnic gazebo and some steps heading uphill. Walk all the way up to the top of the steps, past the next gazebo and the sign for the shoreline trail (see opposite) until you reach a sign for the Qua Qua trail to the right. This is the start of your mountain hike.

Follow the trail straight on past another sign on your right for the lake walk. The route is narrow and begins a gradual ascent through trees to along the ridge. There are great views down to your left all the way across the Grand Etang National Park to the southwest peninsula and Point Salines. Please do not lean on the wooden railing if it is still there. From this point the trail drops sharply downhill. Take it easy and watch your footing. Again, please do not put your weight on the wooden railings as you climb back uphill. This is a very tricky section – and one of the worst if you are bad with heights – in fact it is so mentally challenging that you will probably have difficulty preventing yourself from turning back. Once you are up this slope, the foliage returns and the trail, though still narrow and steep, is less frightening.

As you ascend the trees become less dense and there are lovely views back across Grand Etang Lake itself. It is interesting to observe the damage to the forest that

In 2008 when I was researching the first edition of this guide I was determined to get to the top of Morne Fédon. Those with knowledge of the area told me the trail was a wreck and impassable. Hurricane Ivan had killed it. But I was determined and I was introduced to a local man in Gouyave by the name of Gurry for whom Julian Fédon was much more than a name, he was a national hero. 'Yes,' said Gurry. 'Of course I can take you there.'

It was 5am and still dark when we set off along a steep farm track in the heart of Belvidere. The countryside was silent, not a cricket stirred, and only the sound of our feet tramping through rough grass and over stone disturbed the absolute serenity of the morning. We walked for around half an hour. A small wooden shack with a red and rusty tin roof emerged from the gloom as the sun began its slow ascent over the horizon to the east. The sorry structure was ramshackle and apparently abandoned, despite a rather hopefully scrawled sign in black paint declaring 'Private. Back soon.'

Beyond the shack lay a field of bananas engaged in what appeared to be a losing battle with ever-persistent creepers and weeds. The farm track came to an end and we began to weave our way through the plantation itself, heading towards the foot of a tall ridge where we would begin our ascent. A dog barked somewhere in the distance and a solitary cock crowed. I sensed a warning against this tomfoolery, but brushed it off with a somewhat unconvincing shrug, following the slight figure of Gurry, my guide, as he arrived at the edge of the field.

The original trailhead had disappeared under a massive landslide in the hurricane of 2004. Our plan was to climb this ridge, hopefully pick up the old trail once we reached the top, and then, with any luck, follow it to the summit of the mountain. Gurry had not been here since before Ivan. There were a lot of unknowns on this journey and plenty to be concerned about, but I had a book to write and that meant getting to the location of Fédon's last stand. Gurry grinned, as if reading my mind, and then set off up the hill.

The ascent of the ridge was steep and muddy, the bush dense and very unforgiving. Forging ahead, we cut narrow strips of brightly coloured cloth and tied them to trees to mark our path, determined our return journey would be a little easier. Both of us carried machetes and we needed them. My arms and legs burned with the exertion of clearing and climbing and when we reached the crest of the ridge I flopped to the ground in a heap. Gurry wandered off and soon returned smiling; he had found the old trail.

Sadly, any hopes of our journey becoming easier were soon dashed by a wall of landslides, fallen trees, razor-grass thickets and tangled undergrowth. Clearly, no-one had been here since Hurricane Ivan and the climb to the summit was now a

still remains following the hurricanes. Notice the dead trees that still protrude from the new growth around them. This face of the ridge experienced the full force of the hurricanes and deforestation was severe. But, as you can see for yourself, it is all growing back again.

Looking ahead, you should be able to see the trail as it follows the ridge around to the right and to the summit of Qua Qua. The closer you get to the peak, the better and clearer the views, but continue to take care as the trail is narrow and tricky in places. If you have a clear day, you should be able to see the west coast and the Concord River Valley, the peak of Fédon's Camp, Grand Etang Lake, the east

nightmarish prospect. Huge gommier trees, torn from the earth by winds stronger than I could imagine, blocked what remained of the path. Sometimes we would clamber over them, nervously hoping our feet would find firm ground on the other side; other times we would crawl in the mud beneath them, not daring to think about how fast they were wedged. In several places the trail and ridge crest had fallen away completely and we found ourselves swinging precariously around the broken bases of trees, desperately grasping at roots and branches, anything that seemed tethered, with nothing below us but air and no-one but a stray dog and a cockerel to ever hear our final cries. Everything was wet; the saturated ground, the tree trunks, the branches, the leaves, and even the air around us as we approached the moist cloud forest environment of moss, ferns and mountain palm. We slipped and fell more times than we could count, pulling ourselves up again with all the strength we could muster, our bodies soaked through and covered in a layer of slime. Razor grass ripped exposed skin from ankle to face, adding blood to the unappetising soup. Beneath our sodden clothes, red ants marauded and chiggers hitched a ride in our most sensitive regions. But we had reached that point when nothing mattered other than getting there. Wearily we trudged on.

It took about five hours to reach the summit; a small circle of grass and rock with a stone memorial to Fédon standing at its centre. Grinning from ear to ear, we shook hands and slumped against the stone, out of breath, hearts beating so fiercely they threatened to jump right out of our chests. After a short time Gurry turned and sat facing the memorial to his hero. I left him in peace for a while before he caught my eye and nodded. And then off we set again.

On my return visit to Grenada, this time to research the second edition, people told me the same as they did back in 2008. However, I have come across Grenadians who have hiked there with local groups – from the settlement of Nianganfoix instead of Belvidere – and some of the tour operators offering hiking (see page 77) may be able to give you some assistance. It seems more people are interested in the trail and are now trying to get there. There has been talk of a government-funded hiking and heritage trail – though cost-cutting and the recession seem to have upset plans. If you are a hiking enthusiast, and you are fit, I recommend you try it if you can find someone to accompany you. The views from the top are fabulous, you really get a feel for the history (see page 142) and it is quite an achievement to make it there.

'Gurry' is the nickname of Justin A Modeste of Gouyave. He knows a lot of places in this area, and if he cannot take you he probably knows someone who can. His number is 473 415 9311.

6

coast and the southwest peninsula. Make your way along the path to the boulders at the summit and enjoy. Hopefully the weather is good and you can enjoy your achievement and being up here.

Further trails from Mt Qua Qua Before Hurricane Ivan it was possible to continue from the Mt Qua Qua trail to Fédon's Camp and also to the Concord waterfalls. Unfortunately, as with many of the more difficult, extreme and exposed hikes, the trails are not properly or regularly cleared and are usually quite overgrown. Passage along these routes requires a knowledgeable local guide with a sharp machete. I do not recommend trying these hikes without a guide. Hopefully this situation will change and something will be done to improve the condition of these once popular, challenging and very beautiful hiking trails. This is a historic as well as a beautiful area and linking Mt Qua Qua properly and safely with Concord and Morne Fédon once again would be fabulous. Should these trails have been cleared by the time this book goes to print, I think you should still take a guide with you.

For details of how to get to the Grand Etang visitor centre and the trailhead for the Mt Qua Qua hike see Getting There on page 133.

The Concord Falls There are three waterfalls (some talk of a fourth) that collectively make up the Concord Falls. The first waterfall is very easy to reach from the west coast. Because of its accessibility it is popular with both locals and visitors and features on many cruise-ship shore excursions and organised bus trips. The two waterfalls beyond the first are known as Au Coin and Fontainbleau. They require a hike (see below). The trailhead for both is at the first waterfall. Before Hurricane Ivan in 2004 the waterfalls could also be reached via a more difficult route from the interior, along a trail from Mt Qua Qua and Fédon's Camp.

The turn-off for the Concord Falls is very well signposted on the west coast road between Black Bay and Grand Roy – so long as you are approaching from the south. If you are coming from the north, the sign is completely obscured! If you are travelling by bus from St George's take a number 5. Buses do not go all the way up to the waterfalls so you either have to walk or hitch a ride from the coastal road junction. Going by bus and walking to the waterfalls from the main road is a really pleasant hike. Simply follow the narrow road up the valley for around an hour until you reach the first waterfall. In a car it will take around 15–20 minutes.

Concord – first waterfall (Concord) The first waterfall is about 15m high and tumbles over a smooth rock face into a large pool that is good for bathing. From the pool the river flows over a second cascade that you can view from the top.

The entrance to the waterfall is near the shop and bar on the side of the road. It is well signposted. Follow the signs and pay an entrance fee of EC$5pp. Stone steps lead down to the pool and the best photographs are taken from here. Although the pool is around 6m deep you should think twice about jumping in, regardless of what you may see local guides doing. There have been fatalities here. If you just cannot resist it, then please jump, rather than dive.

When you leave the waterfall take a look at the craft shops along the road. Elvis Clarke (who can also guide you to the other waterfalls for a negotiable fee), along with others there, make jewellery from black coral washed up on the shores of the west coast.

Concord – second waterfall (Au Coin) The hike to the second waterfall (Au Coin) follows the vehicle track beyond the first waterfall. It usually takes under an hour to get there. Walk along the track to a small river and then cross it. The trail narrows and can be a little muddy though it is fairly flat and easy going as it passes through a small nutmeg plantation. Cross the river again and then climb up over some rocks and a gentle slope. You should be able to see some nice river cascades and small pools. Cross the river again and keep following the clear trail as it widens and an old stone road becomes visible through the grass beneath your feet. On the left you may notice some thick clusters of bamboo plants. From here the path begins another gentle ascent. You will see colourful ginger lilies, nutmeg, cashew and mango trees before the trail levels out and begins a short descent. Cross the river once more and then pass over a concrete bridge.

Just after this bridge there is a fork in the trail. Go left. Follow it as it narrows and gets a little rougher, steeper and muddier. It may be a bit overgrown here but have faith the trail is there. Cross the river again. Follow the trail for a very short stretch and then go back down to the river for a final crossing. Climb up the narrow, muddy path past bamboo and clusters of pretty heliconia. Keep climbing. You are now quite high above the river, which should be running down on your left-hand side.

Take it steady down the muddy track to the river. You may be able to see the waterfall ahead of you. Now follow the river, sticking to the right for a while before reaching some large boulders where you have to cross over to the left in order to reach the foot of the waterfall. Scramble over more large boulders and perhaps some fallen trees to reach the pool where you can take a refreshing bathe. The waterfall is a nice one, around 20m high, cascading in sections down a steep cliff face.

Concord – third waterfall (Fontainbleu) The hike to the third waterfall is the most difficult. About an hour there and the same back, it is predominantly a river hike and should only be attempted by people of reasonable fitness. The rocks along the river can be slippery, you have to scramble over some tricky cascades and you also have to climb over, around and perhaps under fallen trees and bamboo. A local guide with a sharp machete is a good idea. The Fontainbleu waterfall was a popular hike prior to Hurricane Ivan but the trail was damaged and is now very overgrown. Subsequent landslides and fallen trees have made sections of the river near impassable, which is where your machete-wielding guide will earn his fee. The waterfall is a cascade of around 15–20m falling into a deep pool and is surrounded by a circular cavern. This river hike is great fun, though difficult, and the waterfall's pool is a pleasant, remote place to bathe.

The hike follows the first half of the trail to the second waterfall, so follow it all the way to the stone bridge. At the fork on the other side, take the trail to the right. It may be very overgrown. Walk up the ridge and pass to the left of a wooden shack along a somewhat overgrown trail that narrows considerably with steep drops down to the river on your right. Keep going but be careful. The track descends and follows the river for a while before coming to an end.

Once at the river simply follow it upstream (against the flow of water) for around 30 minutes. Your journey will be very tricky in places and you may have to look for routes along the bank if fallen bamboo thickets have blocked your passage up the river. You will come to a number of large, fallen trees and further evidence of landslides that have not been cleared. Just imagine the force of nature that brought these trees down and washed them into this river valley. You have to climb up over them to get to the waterfall. Be very careful as the wood is rotting and some pieces will move. Take your time and test each log or branch before giving it your full weight.

Once over them, rejoin the river and follow it as it snakes around to the left. You should now be in sight of the waterfall. There is also a small cascade to your right though this may not always be evident in the dry season. Approach the pool with caution as the final track is covered with weeds that conceal holes, rocks and rotting branches. Enjoy the waterfall and perhaps a refreshing dip in the pool.

Palmiste Lake (Palmiste Dig) Palmiste Lake, often called Palmiste Dig by locals, is a manmade lake formed by the construction of a dam across the Great

Palmiste River on its course from the hills of Mon Plaisir and Mt Granby down to Palmiste Bay. It is believed the thick stone walls of the dam were built by the French during their occupancy of Grenada during the early 1700s. The water was then channelled a short distance downhill to power a waterwheel, which in turn would drive the cogs and machinery to crush sugarcane. Historical records show that the estate was an 82ha sugar plantation owned by a family called Heritiers Delesnables. During the British occupation of Grenada, the estate increased to 140ha and had a workforce of almost 200 slaves. Today, like many estate buildings, it is in ruins and covered by bush. However, some of it is accessible with care, and it is worth a short diversion.

The lake is pleasant. It is very calm, the area is peaceful, and there is a lot of birdlife. The margins are overgrown and are strewn with large volcanic boulders but there are clear views of the lake and, with great care, you could also walk along the dam wall for a closer look.

On the main west coast road between Grand Roy and Gouyave is Palmiste Bay. (If you are travelling by bus from St George's take the number 5 and get off at Palmiste Bay.) Opposite the bay is a narrow and somewhat obscured paved road that runs past a building marked 'Newlo'. This is the route you must take. The road winds its way uphill past some new houses and then turns into a rough vehicle track as it climbs up through the forest. If you are driving, it is best to find a place to turn and park before the track gets too rough. It is not too far up the hill and the walk is a pleasant one. Though covered in bush you may catch sight of the old estate ruins. From here the lake is around 15 minutes further up the track. When you arrive at the lake you can see the thick stone wall of the dam on its western edge. If you decide to walk along it please take care as it can be moss-covered and slippery. Walk up the track beyond the wall to the boulders for nice views.

Florida, Clozier and Belvidere This is a scenic drive into the elevated countryside and the farmlands above Gouyave. You don't need a 4x4, the road is paved, but it is rather narrow and winding. Depending on your speed and how many times you stop for photographs or a chat with locals, you can easily be back to the beginning in 30 minutes or so.

Start in Gouyave and turn up St Peter's Street. Drive through the village past the Anglican Church and school, and follow the road along the river. Keep going straight, ignoring a sign on your right for Clozier and Grenville. The road will eventually curve sharply to the left and cross over the river. Follow the road past a few houses and through the countryside. After a couple of sharp curves, look out for a sign to Florida on your left. Take this road. It is very narrow so use your horn on bends but enjoy the countryside and the views. By this time you should be expert and be able to identify mango trees, cocoa, bananas, and nutmeg of course. No? Oh dear. Well enjoy it anyway.

Eventually this road ends up at a junction in the village of Florida. Take a right and follow it to another junction. Take the 'Dig Road' to the right (the rough road on the left heads up to Mt Pleasant, once a thriving agricultural estate, sadly now in decline). The outskirts of this village are a bit run-down but soon you leave it behind and are surrounded by lovely countryside once again. At the next junction you have a choice. To the left the road heads inland to Belvidere and eventually Grenville, to the right the road heads back to Gouyave. If you would like to explore a bit further go left and at the next junction follow the road to the right. It is marked Belvidere and Grenville. Drive for as far as you like – a good turning point, if you wish to head back, is somewhere near the private Belvidere Gardens. You will see a sign. Enjoy the peace and tranquillity of this landscape and the fabulous views. To your right you should be able to see the high ridge of Morne Fédon and Mt Qua Qua, and the high mountain to your left is Mt St Catherine, Grenada's tallest peak.

You can continue following this road towards Grenville or you can simply head back and follow it all the way back to Gouyave (just go left when you finally reach the T junction at the river). Look out for a natural spring emerging from the bank on your left (there is a bamboo pipe). Take a drink if you like – the water is fresh and good.

Black Bay The short hike from the village of Black Bay follows the Concord River and passes the overgrown ruins of a sugar estate (now the privately owned Black Bay Estate) as it makes its way to a crescent-shaped bay with black volcanic sand. For the adventurous, there is a climb to a cave known as Trou Mais, meaning 'corn hole', on Black Bay Point, which is said to be a place Amerindians used as a storeroom for their crops. You will need to bring along a flashlight if you wish to explore it. This area was also the site of a coastal battery built by the French during the 1700s. The walk to the bay is easy, though there is a small river crossing, and should only take you about 30 minutes or so each way.

In Black Bay village, just south of Grand Roy and directly opposite the sign for the Concord Falls, there is a narrow paved road running down between some houses towards the shore. If you are in a car try to find a safe place to park on the main road and then walk, rather than getting stuck down this side road. If you are travelling by bus, take a number 5 and get off when you see the sign for Concord.

A short walk of around 15 minutes brings you to the end of the paved road. It is a rough vehicle track for a short stretch and then it simply becomes a narrow, though well-worn, trail. The track passes some small, though often quite overgrown, gardens growing saffron, bananas, pigeon peas, dasheen (calalou) and more. It is also lined with a variety of trees including nutmeg, mango, tamarind and cinnamon. Head gently downhill, following the river, which is on your right.

After around 10–15 minutes the trail reaches the river at a small, broken concrete bridge. If you don't fancy the leap from the large rock over to the other side, simply walk across it in the shallower water upstream. Climb up the bank using the rocks, taking care not to slip. You will see the rather unwelcoming sign of the Black Bay Estate. Please respect the private boundaries. Just stick with the riverside track ahead of you and you will be fine. Of course things may have changed by the time this book goes to print; one thing is for sure – locals will have figured out a workaround so just look out for it.

After a short distance along the trail you will see the ruined stone walls of the Black Bay Estate buildings. They are covered in jungle. Beneath the creeping undergrowth there are not only stone walls but also some of the machinery of this former estate, including the waterwheel and the cane crusher which dates back to 1862.

Continue down the riverside track. Another ruin on your right is a stone wall which was part of a *boucan* for cocoa production. When you come to an old bridge with twisted and contorted ironwork, cross over it and follow the trail to your right. You will emerge onto the bay where river meets black sand and sea.

Fairly sheltered, the beach is suitable for swimming. You may see fishermen hauling in nets from their wooden boats around the river mouth.

If you are interested in seeing the corn hole, walk along the beach to the south side (left, if you are facing the sea) and you should find a track to the left of an old white cedar tree. This track is steep and the climb to the top of the point is a tricky scramble through the bush. If it is too overgrown and rough, or you cannot make out the path, turn back. A guide with local knowledge is a good idea as it is surprisingly easy to get lost here. A challenging 15- to 20-minute scramble will take you to up to Trou Mais. Watch out for cow-itch or *pwa gaté* (*Mucuna pruriens* – see page 43) which seems to thrive around here and can cause severe skin irritation. A little to the right, and above the main entrance, is a pot-hole that drops down into the cave. Be careful not to fall in – it is very dark and rumoured to be some 30m long. Take care on the climb back down to the beach.

7

Grenville, Grand Etang and the Southeast

From Mardigras to Balthazar, a vertiginous mountain ridge skirts the elevated and densely forested interior of the Grand Etang Forest Reserve. Its numerous steep ridges and deep river valleys fan outwards to the south and the east, creating an equally dramatic coastline of volcanic outcrops, tranquil bays and beaches, sheltered natural harbours, coastal woodlands and mangrove swamps full of birdlife. Between mountain and coast there resides a magical cocktail of people who eke a living from the soil, the sea, from handmade crafts, stores and boutiques, from tourism, sailing, and from spices and rum. For you the visitor there is a rich variety here, and this area of Grenada is definitely worth exploring.

GETTING THERE

To get to Grenville and along the east coast by car from the southwest peninsula, head for L'Anse Aux Epines but, instead of turning right at the small tyre roundabout junction, go straight on towards Woburn. From there just keep the sea to your right all the way to Grenville.

For St Paul's and the inland road to St David's, head for St George's and, at the roundabout near the north end of the Lagoon, take the fork to the right and follow the signs for Richmond Hill. Stay right at the next fork and, when you reach the next major road junction, which is located on a sharp bend, turn right. Follow this road to St Paul's and Grenville.

If you are travelling by bus, a number 4 will take you from the capital to Vincennes via St Paul's (make sure you see Vincennes written on the front of the bus) and a

DON'T MISS

If your time is limited, here is the don't-miss list for this part of Grenada:

Grenville Nutmeg Station (page 166)
Westerhall Estate rum distillery (page 168)
St Margaret's Falls (page 170)
Mt Carmel Waterfall (page 169)
Bay Gardens (page 167)

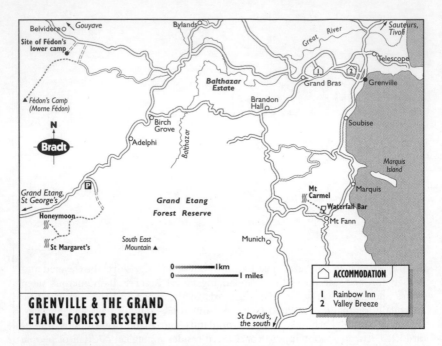

number 2 bus will take you to Grenville along the east coast. From St George's, the number 6 passes through Grand Etang to Grenville.

GETTING AROUND

Buses are a convenient way of travelling between St George's and Grenville and they regularly ply the routes along the east coast as well as via Vincennes and Grand Etang. If you wish to get to the region's bays and anchorages, you must either have a hire car, preferably a 4x4, or be prepared to walk from the main road (see page 169 for details of some of these walks and scenic drives).

The small town of Grenville has a very simple one-way system. There are essentially three streets running in a north–south direction. The street closest to the sea, Victoria Street, is for traffic heading south. The middle street is for traffic heading north, and the third street, the one farthest from the sea, seems to be for traffic heading in both directions. If you get it wrong, don't worry; absolutely everyone will let you know.

FILLING UP You will find petrol stations in Grenville (on both the west and the north side of town), St Paul's, between Pomme Rose and Crochu, and in the Fort Jeudy and Westerhall area.

☖ WHERE TO STAY

Though very limited in number, the southeast coast has some lovely places to stay. See page 57 for accommodation price codes.

HIGH- AND MID-RANGE HOTELS
☖ **La Sagesse Nature Centre** (12 rooms) La

Sagesse Beach; ✆/f 473 444 6458; e lasagesse@ spiceisle.com; www.lasagesse.com. Lovely beachside accommodation in a perfect setting. 5 rooms are in the Old Manor House, which is the former La Sagesse Estate House, 5 more are located within the new resort building, & the final 2 are in a separate cottage. All accommodation is very tastefully furnished & just a short walk from the stunning beach. Room facilities include en-suite bathroom, ceiling fans & verandas. The open-air restaurant has pleasant sea & beach views & serves local & international dishes. La Sagesse also offers nature tours of the surrounding mangrove forest which should appeal to those interested in birdwatching (see page 165 for more on exploring the area). La Sagesse is great for honeymooners & families. The beach & bay are quiet & protected so the water is usually very tranquil. **$$$**

🏠 **Cabier Ocean Lodge** (11 rooms) Crochu; ☏473 444 6013; e info@cabier.com; www.cabier.com. Extremely pleasant & peaceful family run hideaway located on a privately owned peninsula between the tranquil Cabier Beach & Crochu Harbour. Artistically decorated rooms have private bathroom, & veranda with ocean view. Apartment rooms have SC facilities & can be joined up. The fresh sea breeze negates the need for AC or fans. Dining is in the open-air terrace restaurant. Please note, at the time of writing Cabier has a 'petting zoo' plus a small menagerie of caged local animals, a feature that may not appeal to everyone. Remote & tranquil accommodation in a very pretty part of the island. (See also Two Bays Villa & Studio on page 160.) **$$**

🏠 **Epping Forest** (2 dbls & 1 family room, 1 SC cottage) St Paul's; ☏473 440 3333; e eppingforestholidays@hotmail.com; www.grenadaguesthouse.com. Restored plantation house in tropical gardens with swimming pool, forest & mountain views. Peaceful accommodation with a traditional feel; each room has private bathroom, dbl bed, ceiling fan, mosquito net & access to the large shared balcony. The pretty SC 1-bed wooden cottage is built in a traditional style & stands alone in the garden & has fully equipped kitchen, living area, bedroom, bathroom & covered deck. Guests welcome to pick fruits from the garden or simply slumber in a hammock in the shade of a tree. Full English & vegetarian b/fast offered. No credit cards. **$–$$**

BUDGET HOTELS

🏠 **Rainbow Inn** (15 rooms) Grand Bras; ☏473 442 7714. Close to the town of Grenville, family run accommodation with good reputation includes private bathroom, AC, TV & some rooms with private balcony. Good choice for budget travellers. **$**

🏠 **Sam's Inn** (10 rooms, 3 self-contained apts) Dunfermline; ☏/f 473 442 7853; e samsinn@spiceisle.com; www.samsinn.com. Located close to Grenville & Pearls Airport, clean & tidy rooms have private bathroom, AC, TV, ceiling fans, fridge, balcony. Apts have 2 bedrooms, living area, kitchen, TV. Friendly, good value family run accommodation. **$**

HIGH-END APARTMENTS, COTTAGES AND VILLAS

🏠 **Art Gallery Villa** (3 beds) Westerhall; e stay@beyondluxuryvillas.com; www.beyondluxuryvillas.com. Charming, artistic & self-indulgent villa on the exclusive Westerhall Estate. Comfortably sleeping up to 6, the villa has full amenities plus a swimming pool & deck. Fine ocean views & access to nearby beaches. Maid service optional. **$$$$$**

🏠 **Villa Caribella** (3 beds) Westerhall; ☏473 443 5319; f 473 444 2899; e macford@spiceisle.com; www.grenadavilla-caribella.com. Luxury villa accommodation with patio, pool & beautiful sea views. Facilities include bedrooms, bathrooms, living area, fully equipped kitchen, laundry, AC, TV, ceiling fans. Housekeeping service available. **$$$$$**

🏠 **Bel Air Plantation** (5 cottages, 6 villas) St David's Point; ☏473 444 6305, US toll free ☏+1 866 504 3359; f 473 444 6316; e info@belairplantation.com; www.belairplantation.com. Comfortable accommodation located alongside the tranquil St David's Harbour. Cottages have 1 bedroom, villas have 1 or 2. All have private bathrooms, stylishly furnished living areas, fully equipped kitchen, AC, TV, ceiling fans, private verandas. Original artworks decorate each cottage & villa, there is a panoramic lounge, infinity swimming pool, dinghy dock, tropical gardens, spa, gift shop & local & international dining at the Water's Edge Restaurant & Bar. **$$$$**

🏠 **Villa Heron's Flight** (3 beds) Westerhall Point; ☏631 714 4428 & 631 790 5685;

e sales@heronsflight.com; www.heronsflight.com. Luxurious home away from home with swimming pool, gazebo, panoramic ocean views, & tropical garden with secluded beach. 3 bedrooms with en-suite bathrooms, AC, TV, DVD, internet, library, ceiling fans, living area, fully equipped kitchen. **$$$$**

🏠 **Two Bays Villa & Studio** (2 bed villa, 1 bed apt) Cabier, Crochu; ☎473 444 6013; e info@cabier.com; www.cabier.com. Privately owned villa & apartment located close to & managed by the people at Cabier Ocean Lodge. Both villa & apt have fully opening louvre doors to let in light & breeze, they have fully equipped kitchen, DVD & AC if you need it. Well designed, comfortable accommodation in a nice location. There is also a small infinity pool with views over Crochu Harbour. Guests are welcome to dine at Cabier Ocean Lodge. **$$–$$$**

🏠 **Petit Bacaye Villa Hotel & Restaurant** (5 villas) Petit Bacaye; ☎/f 473 443 2902, UK☎44 1794 323227; e hideaways@wellowmead.u-net.com; www.petitbacaye.com. Castaway-style accommodation on the margins of Petit Bacaye Bay. SC villas with private bathroom, inside &

outside shower rooms, kitchen, living area, fans, verandas, decks or private gardens. Narrow sandy beach with tranquil waters suitable for swimming. Restaurant & beach bar serves local & international dishes. **$$**

MID-RANGE AND BUDGET APARTMENTS, COTTAGES AND VILLAS

🏠 **Valley Breeze Guest House** (3 suites) Grenville; ☎473 442 7390; e kelisha83@yahoo.com; www.valleybreezeguesthouse.com. Newly constructed at the time of writing. 1-bed, 2-bed & 3-bed suites all with fully equipped kitchen, lounge, TV, AC & modern furnishings. Located just outside Grenville on the road to Grand Etang. **$–$$**

🏠 **Big Sky Lodge** (2 cottages) Crochu; ☎473 444 7277; e big-sky@grenada-lodge.org; www.grenada-lodge.org. Basic 1-bedroom cottage accommodation with private bathroom & veranda with sea views. Use of shared kitchen & cooking facilities. Wi-Fi, TV & DVD in communal lounge. Restaurant & bar serves local cuisine & fresh juices. **$**

✖ WHERE TO EAT AND DRINK

In addition to the restaurants listed below, look out for some great local cooking in Grenville and the surrounding area. It is always worth giving these places a try. The food is usually good and always very reasonably priced.

✖ **La Sagesse Nature Centre** La Sagesse Beach; ☎473 444 6458. High-quality local & international lunches & dinners in a very peaceful & beautiful setting overlooking La Sagesse Beach & Bay. Dinner reservations recommended. **$$**

✖ **Water's Edge Restaurant & Bar** Bel Air Plantation, St David's Point; ☎473 444 6305. Enjoy local & international cooking as you look out at the sailing boats of the very peaceful St David's Harbour. Dinner reservations recommended. **$$**

✖ **Cabier Ocean Lodge** Cabier Beach, Crochu; ☎473 444 6013. Caribbean dining on the lovely deck of Cabier's alfresco restaurant. Enjoy views

of Crochu Harbour, good food & a cool sea breeze. At the time of writing Cabier has a small menagerie of caged local animals which may not be to everyone's taste. Advance reservations required. **$$**

✖ **Petit Bacaye Villa Hotel & Restaurant** Petit Bacaye; ☎473 443 2902. Caribbean lunches & dinners served in the tropical garden & beach surroundings of Petit Bacaye Bay Villa Hotel. Dinner reservations recommended. **$$**

✖ **Bains Restaurant & Bar** Sandal St, Grenville; ☎473 438 2777. Cosy & good value local eatery at the northern end of Grenville. **$**

SHOPPING

Grenville has numerous small boutiques, market stalls and minimarkets but there is very little in the way of crafts and souvenirs in this area. If you need a pair of cheap trainers or flip-flops, however, this is the place to be. Marquis, just south of Grenville and Soubise, was once known for its screw pine basketwork but this seems to be on the wane. Look out for a craft shop on the road from Grenville to Grand Etang. It is definitely worth a visit.

OTHER PRACTICALITIES

MONEY AND BANKS On Victoria Street, Grenville, you will find the First Caribbean Bank, the RBTT Bank, the Grenada Co-operative Bank, and the Scotiabank. All have ATMs.

MEDICAL There is a fairly large pharmacy on the southern end of Sandal Street (the next one in from Victoria Street) in Grenville. If you take regular prescription medication, you should be sure you bring enough with you and not rely on this pharmacy having what you need.

SAFETY The southeast coast and Grenville is a safe area and its people are generally helpful and friendly. Just take the same common sense precautions you would back home. Should you need police assistance there is a station in Grenville and another in St David's.

WHAT TO SEE AND DO

GRENVILLE The town of Grenville was founded by the British and named after George Grenville who was British prime minister between 1763 and 1765. During the French occupation it was renamed La Baye which, despite changing back to Grenville in 1796, is a name that is still quite commonly used. The town is protected by a long coral reef that stretches the entire length of Grenville Bay and boats must use channel markers for safe passage. Despite these natural hazards there is a thriving fishing community both here and along the length of the coastline southwards through the villages of Soubise and Marquis.

During the Fédon Rebellion of March 1795 to June 1796, Pilot Hill, to the north of the town centre, was a strategic site that changed hands through bloody fighting on a number of occasions. The British routed the rebels in March 1796 after a joint offensive that included Post Royal Hill to the south.

The Grenville of today is a curious town, a place of noise, hustle and bustle, that contrasts starkly with the peace and serenity of the surrounding countryside. There are roadside stalls everywhere it seems, selling fruits, vegetables, spices and cooked food. Clothes boutiques, shoe shops, barber shops, bars and snackettes seem to crowd every space available on the town's narrow bustling streets. Grenville has quite a sizeable East Indian community which is reflected in the features of the people in this area, in some of the food and cooking, and also in the name of a number of the stores and businesses here. Grenada's East Indian community has its ancestry in the indentured labour force that was brought to the island in the mid 19th century as estate owners tried to come to terms with the abolition of slavery and the lack of an inexpensive workforce. Descendants of these immigrants have gone on to become very successful businesspeople and many still live and prosper in this area.

Victoria Street is Grenville's main thoroughfare, running from north to south along Grenville Bay. At the northern end of the street is the **Grenville Anglican Church** and school. Located behind them, on the waterfront, is the new Grenville

fish market, where you can buy all kinds of fresh fish throughout the day. Just follow your nose. Also along Victoria Street you will find the Grenville police station and four banks with ATMs: First Caribbean Bank, RBTT Bank, Grenada Co-operative Bank, and Scotiabank. There are a number of small supermarkets, minimarts, boutiques, pharmacies and a few eateries (such as **Caneye** which sells good Jamaican patties, pizzas, sandwiches and grilled fish – it is a handy place for a quick bite).

The street parallel to Victoria Street where traffic runs in the opposite direction, from south to north, is Sandal Street. It is also lively, noisy and full of interesting eateries, shops and market stalls. Look out for **Well Fed Restaurant & Bar** and **Bains Restaurant & Bar**, which serves very good local food. Also along Sandal Street is the post office, the Grenville Magistrates' Court and, at the southern end, a large and well-stocked pharmacy. More snackettes, roadside stalls and the obligatory pirate DVD stands complete the picture.

There are a couple of short roads bisecting these north–south thoroughfares. This is the location of Grenville's main market area where you can buy fresh local fruits and vegetables and spices.

The **Grenville Nutmeg Station** (or 'pool' as it is known locally) can be found on the innermost thoroughfare. It is one of the three main nutmeg processing stations in Grenada and the short guided tour is well worth it (see page 166).

EXPLORING THE REGION
From the Grand Etang National Park to Grenville The interior road from the Grand Etang visitor centre winds tightly downhill through a wet rainforest environment and then farmlands as it descends and curves around to the east. It is a pretty stretch of road though lacking signposts so you may have to stop and ask the way – alternatively just follow the blur of number 7 buses as they hurtle down the hillside in search of fares, lunch or simply the end of a long day. Along the route there are great views of the forest, mountain ridges and the Atlantic Ocean. From the depths of the forest you emerge in the village of Adelphi and pass colourful board houses, local snackettes and bars such as the First & Last Stop Bar, and a number of small banana plantations that line the road and seem to fill all the gaps between the area's simple residences. The road follows the Great River as it winds its way down to the sprawling rural settlement of Birch Grove. Through Birch Grove the road passes a redundant nutmeg receiving station, concrete and board houses and colourful gardens with ginger lilies and crotons on either side, adding a sharp vibrancy to the lush greenery all around. When you arrive at the Balthazar Estate, a little beyond Birch Grove, you will cross the river. It is a lovely spot and where Grenada's river-tubing activities take place (see page 80 for details). If you are hot and bothered, there is nothing better than a river bath to cool you down so take time out for a splash around. Refreshments and local snacks can be had at the River's Edge Bar on the eastern side of the river. Over the river the road passes through a cocoa plantation and then comes to the village of St James. In this small village there are yet more colourful board houses, another redundant nutmeg receiving station and a couple of snackettes and bars such as the House of Commons Bar, where you can be sure lively political debates take place throughout the day and probably well into the evening. From St James the road continues downhill towards the coast and arrives at the east coast's largest population centre, the small town of Grenville.

Along the southeast coast from Westerhall to Grenville The southeast coast of Grenada juxtaposes pretty rural villages with luxury modern residences. Its terrain is a stimulating combination of wild rocky peninsulas, beautiful bays,

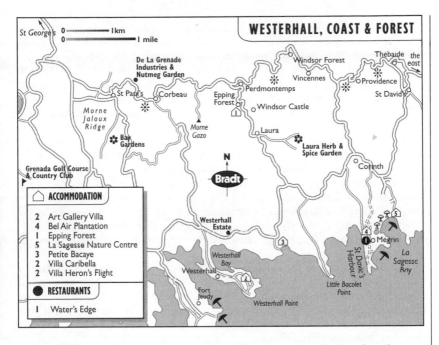

St George's

0 ————— 1 km
0 ————— 1 mile

De La Grenade
Industries &
Nutmeg Garden

St Paul's Corbeau

Morne
Jaloux
Ridge

Bay
Gardens

Grenada Golf Course
& Country Club

Epping
Forest

Perdmontemps

Windsor Castle

Morne
Gazo

Laura

Windsor Forest

Vincennes

Thebaide the
east

Providence

St David's

Laura Herb &
Spice Garden

Corinth

N

Bradt

ACCOMMODATION

2	Art Gallery Villa
4	Bel Air Plantation
1	Epping Forest
5	La Sagesse Nature Centre
3	Petite Bacaye
2	Villa Caribella
2	Villa Heron's Flight

RESTAURANTS

| 1 | Water's Edge |

Westerhall
Estate

Westerhall
Bay

Westerhall

Fort
Jeudy

Westerhall Point

Little Bacolet
Point

St David's
Harbour

Megrin

La
Sagesse
Bay

sandy beaches and mangrove swamps. Modern marinas and natural anchorages offer sheltered havens for both recreational mariners and traditional fishermen. It is a fun place for scenic drives and easy walks, as well as for sailing and a little sun-worshipping. As you travel along the coast from south to north you will clearly see the transition from the luxurious and the modern, with a distinctly overseas feel, to the far less affluent, far more rural, archetypal Grenada.

The Westerhall Peninsula is an exotic tropical sanctuary that has been designed and constructed exclusively for those who can afford to live there – the very wealthy. It is a gated community of luxurious residences, manicured gardens and private boat jetties. The point itself is very scenic and is worth a trip if you have time. On the western side is Chemin Bay and the tranquil waters of Calivigny Harbour, and to the east is Westerhall Bay, a beautiful haven for sailing boats and dreamers.

To the north of Westerhall Point is the **Westerhall Estate** where you will find ruins of the former sugar, cocoa and lime estate and rum distillery, together with its contemporary counterpart. Guided tours of the estate and distillery are offered for a small fee and are very interesting (see page 168 for more information).

Heading east from Westerhall you will pass Petit Bacaye and you may notice signs for a Bacolet Bay development project which, at the time of writing, appears to have come unstuck as a result of the global recession. It was one of several large investment projects that were in progress just a few years ago. Sadly the short-term construction jobs have also gone, impacting the already empty pockets of local people. Perhaps the diggers will be out in force again by the time you pass by.

Before reaching the village of **Corinth**, look out for **Wayne's 100% Pure Cane Juice & Molasses**, a roadside enterprise selling bottled cane juice, cane vinegar, and molasses. It is all homemade and local so why not give it a try. The bottles cost EC$5–20. Further along the road there is a turn-off to St David's Point. The road can be identified by a sign indicating **Megrin**, the site of the first European settlement in Grenada (see page 174). Just to the east of Corinth is the picturesque

La Sagesse Estate. On your left-hand side (if you are travelling east) you will see the ruins of the sugar mill, and on the coastal side of the road is a sign for La Sagesse Nature Centre. This road takes you to the scenic La Sagesse Bay (see page 169).

From La Sagesse, the coastal road begins to climb up towards the village of **St David's**. Set against a lush tropical forest backdrop, St David's Roman Catholic Church is usually the first thing that catches your eye. Standing high above the village and dominating the skyline, it is a captivating picture. Its full title is the Church of the Immaculate Conception and St Joseph, and it was constructed in the second half of the 19th century. Located at a slightly lower elevation and closer to the main road is St David's Anglican Church. Constructed in the first half of the 19th century, this church also holds a very prominent position, looking out over the parish's simple dwelling houses, farmlands, sharp mountain ridges and the coastal forests and bays that ultimately meet the Atlantic Ocean. Across the road from the Anglican church is a large building housing St David's post office, police station and magistrates' court. Although it is the administrative centre of the parish, St David's is actually a small village and it seems that the very minute you arrive is also the moment you leave.

Heading northwards, the twisting coastal road passes through **Pomme Rose**, a pretty village of colourful board and block houses, bars and shops that are perched high up along the hillside above the coast and the sea. In the middle of Pomme Rose there is a road junction on a sharp bend with a narrow secondary road that runs directly down towards the coast and **La Tante Bay**. It is an expansive bay, often very deserted, with a dark-sand beach.

From Pomme Rose the road continues along the coast until it reaches the village of **Crochu**. At the centre of this village is an area called Café Junction. From here a secondary road passes through the small settlement of Mahot, along a narrow ridge and down to Crochu Point, with the very pretty **Cabier Beach** and bay to the north of the coastal headland (see page 173) and **Crochu Harbour** to the south. Both bays are usually very tranquil and quiet save for an occasional fishing boat either putting out or returning through the light surf. Cabier Beach has white sand, shallow waters and a wooded and grassy fringe that is the perfect location for a picnic. Crochu Point itself is occupied by Cabier Ocean Lodge. Just up the road from Crochu is Rastafari Dynesty (✆ 473 444 7358; e *rasdynesty@spiceisle.com*), a nice shop selling authentic African wares including colourful materials, soaps and oils, plus a quaint garden bar where you can enjoy fresh juices and herbal teas. Drop in and say hello to Ogondola Izack if he is around.

From Crochu the road heads north towards Hope Estate and **Great Bacolet Bay**. Hope Estate is a residential development and so new houses are slowly appearing along this steep grassy headland. Great Bacolet Bay has a very accessible crescent-shaped beach with rough, yet motorable vehicle tracks running to its northern and southern ends. Look out for the rocky Bacolet Island (sometimes called Hope Island) located a little offshore at the centre of the bay. The beach is very pleasant, clean and a popular bathing spot with locals. For details on how to walk or drive to Hope Beach at Great Bacolet Bay see page 172.

North of Hope Estate is the village of Mt Fann. Just as you enter this village from the south, on the apex of a bend, you will see a signposted road for **Mt Carmel Waterfall**. In actual fact, the start of the short waterfall trail is very close to this road junction, hidden between the houses near to the very appropriately named **Waterfall Bar** (see page 169 for hiking details).

Continuing north along the coast from Mt Fann, you arrive at the village of **Marquis**. Designated a 'cultural landmark' by the government of Grenada, Marquis is one of the island's oldest European settlements. It was established by the French in the latter half of the 17th century and its full name was Grand Marquis until the British renamed it Grenville when they took over governance of Grenada in 1763. In the early hours of 3 March 1795, Julien Fédon and his followers attacked the town, completely sacking it and killing 11 British settlers. Noted as the start of the Fédon Rebellion, this act began a period of uprising against the British that lasted until June 1796 and brought mayhem to the country (see page 142). The result of this initial attack was that Grand Marquis, or Grenville, was abandoned. A little further up the coast, the village of La Baye was itself renamed Grenville at the end of the rebellion. That village became the main settlement on the east coast and still bears the same name today. Marquis is now a rather spartan village of fishermen and a declining number of craftspeople. Using the boiled and dried leaves of the screw pine (*Pandanus utilis*), these artisans fashion small spice baskets, mats and hats that are sold around the island. Look out for a craft shop on the interior road out of Grenville where you may be able to buy some.

To the north of Marquis is **Battle Hill**. The shrine of Our Lady of Fatima is a draw for Catholic pilgrims who make their way from the St Andrew's Roman Catholic Church in Grenville to this spot each year. For an area of peace and worship, it has a somewhat inappropriate name. This is because, together with Pilot Hill to the north, it was considered a strategic position during the Fédon Rebellion and several fierce battles were fought here.

Before reaching the town of Grenville, you will pass through the village of **Soubise**, a small fishing village where, all along the narrow shoreline, small wooden

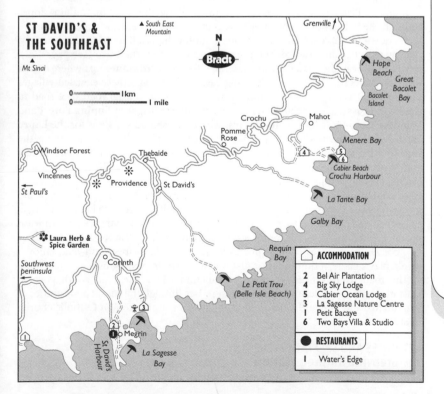

houses sit precariously perched upon cinder blocks for when unpredictable, rough Atlantic seas cause flooding, and where fishing boats are hauled out manually after a hard day's work at sea.

A pretty inland route from St Paul's to St David's Between the villages of St Paul's and St David's there is a narrow, winding road that hugs the steep cliffs and slopes of the mountainous ridge that borders the southeastern edge of the Grand Etang Forest Reserve. It is a picturesque route, often vertiginous, with views of both forest and coast.

The village of **St Paul's** lies a little to the east of Richmond Hill and its forts. It is a simple village of block and wooden houses, a church and police station. It is also the home of **De La Grenade Industries**, producers of nutmeg jams, jellies, syrups and liqueurs (see page 168). Look out for the rather stately and curious building known as 'The Tower'. Built in the 1800s by a British barrister named Renwick and subsequently, it is told, gambled away in a game of cards, it consists of a large family home and a five-storey tower built of granite and brick. It has risen to prominence for its gardens which have been acclaimed by the Royal Horticultural Society for their wide and interesting variety of tropical flowers, trees and shrubs. Now owned by the Slinger family, The Tower's gardens are occasionally included in some of Grenada's organised horticultural tours (see page 74). As it is a private dwelling, please do not simply turn up at The Tower and expect to look around. To the right of the police station in St Paul's there is a small road that goes to the **Bay Gardens**. Here it is possible to simply turn up and take a tour, and if you are interested in tropical flora then the Bay Gardens is definitely worth visiting (see opposite).

From St Paul's the road twists and turns along the steep mountain slopes through the villages of Corbeau, Mt Pleasant and Mt Rose, where there are more views down to the coast. In Corbeau look out for the Wildlife Bar and next to it a narrow road heading towards the pointed summit of Morne Gazo (see page 172). Beyond Corbeau the road continues to the village of **Perdmontemps** where a road junction offers the choice of continuing eastwards through these elevated villages towards St David's, or heading down towards the main coastal road. The road to the south coast passes through the curiously named villages of **Epping Forest** and **Windsor Castle** before reaching **Laura**, where you should see signs for the **Laura Herb & Spice Garden** (see opposite). The road to the east continues along the high forested foothills of Mt Sinai, passing through the villages of **Windsor Forest** and **Vincennes**. The views along this stretch of road are excellent and you also catch a fleeting glimpse into the everyday lives of the people who live in Grenada's rural communities. You will see small farm holdings where subsistence crops are grown on steep slopes and terraces, and the road itself is lined with banana, mango, breadfruit and cinnamon trees. Occasionally a pick-up truck will pass by with fresh produce, building materials, nutmegs, manure or perhaps fish for sale. Snackettes and convenience stores offer opportunities for people to meet and talk, enjoy a drink, play a game of dominoes or just watch the world passing by.

The road from Vincennes meets a junction where the road south goes to Corinth and La Sagesse, and the road east passes through the rural communities of **Providence** and **Thebaide**, before finally emerging at the Roman Catholic church in St David's.

ACTIVITIES AND SPECIAL INTERESTS
The Grenville Nutmeg Station (*15–20-min tour US$1 or EC$2.70pp*) Grenville Nutmeg Station was one of three major stations on the island that used to process

nutmegs. The other two were at Victoria and Gouyave on the west coast. All of this changed with the arrival of consecutive hurricanes in 2004 and 2005. Before the hurricanes, Grenada produced approximately 2,700 tonnes of nutmegs per year and the Grenville Nutmeg Station employed around 160 people to receive and process them. Today there are only around ten and the island still produces less than 50% of pre-hurricane volumes. This means that the Grenville station, or 'the pool', has had to downshift to a regional receiving station. Instead of receiving and processing the nutmegs ready for export, the pool simply receives crops from local farmers and prepares them for transportation to Gouyave where all the processing takes place.

The impact of these hurricanes on the nutmeg industry and upon the lives of ordinary Grenadians has been a silent tragedy, and for some of them it has become too much to bear. Given that it can take up to ten years to grow a productive nutmeg tree, and that young trees produce a much lower yield than mature ones, many in the industry have had to figure out alternative ways of earning a living. Local people have been remarkably resolute in the face of disaster and a visit to the nutmeg stations at either Gouyave or Grenville should be on the agenda of everyone visiting Grenada. By taking a short tour, by learning, by listening and by paying the tour fee, you are making a very positive contribution, regardless of how small it may seem to you. It is also very interesting and enjoyable.

A tour takes around 15 to 20 minutes and takes you through the nutmeg station. You pay the nominal tour fee at the window by the entrance but it would be nice to give your tour guide a little tip at the end. You will see trays of nutmegs and the original wooden machinery that was used to process them. It is fascinating, but when your guide vividly describes how animated, noisy and busy it was before 2004, compared with how quiet and relatively empty you see it today, it is also a little sad. Please travel positively and visit Grenada's nutmeg stations.

The Laura Herb & Spice Garden *(20-min tour EC$5pp. Closed Sat & Sun)* A little off the beaten track but quite accessible via a newly constructed road, the Laura Herb & Spice Garden offers visitors an educational tour of the spice factory gardens. If you don't know what cinnamon, nutmeg, ginger, saffron, turmeric and allspice (pimento) look like before they end up seasoning your food, then this is for you. A guide will help you to recognise a variety of spices, plants, fruits and herbs as well as explain their medicinal properties and how they are used as natural remedies for sickness. The tour is easy-paced and relaxed.

The easiest way to get there is from the main coastal road. A little to the west of Bacolet Bay is a small roundabout with a road running inland and a sign to St George's. Take this road and after a drive of around five to ten minutes you will see a sign to Laura Herb & Spice Garden on the right. Follow a narrow road that curves around the hillside, keeping to the left until you see the factory building. If you are coming from St Paul's, simply follow the winding road through the villages until you reach Perdmontemps. Here you should take a right down a concrete road. From this road you will see a sign on your left.

If you are travelling by bus from St George's, you should take a number 4 and get off at Perdmontemps. You can either walk or hitch a lift from here.

The Bay Gardens *(30–45min tour EC$10pp)* If you are interested in gardening and in particular learning about some of the tropical flora you can see in Grenada and the wider Caribbean, then the Bay Gardens are most definitely worth a visit. It is a charming place with a quaint reception and refreshments building, a very natural garden and friendly and knowledgeable staff to show you around. The

gardens are in two halves, on either side of a narrow road running south from the village of St Paul's. They contain a wide variety of plants, trees and flowers including ginger lilies, heliconias, palms, orchids, bromeliads and bamboo. The flowers attract hummingbirds and butterflies to add that extra air of tranquillity and colour. You could easily spend a couple of hours here. Not to be missed.

The Bay Gardens are located very close to the village of St Paul's. From St George's simply follow the signs to St Paul's or Fort Frederick and Richmond Hill. Instead of turning right to Fort Frederick, follow the road as it winds around the steep hillside ridges until you reach St Paul's. Continue along the main road through the village until you come to St Paul's Police Station. There is a narrow road running downhill right next to the station building. If you follow it for a little way, you will see a sign on the right for the Bay Gardens. Follow this road up and then downhill for a short distance until you come to the reception building for the Bay Gardens which will be on your left. By bus, take the number 4 from St George's to St Paul's and get off by the police station. You then have a short walk of around 15 minutes to the Bay Gardens following the directions described above.

De La Grenade Industries and Nutmeg Garden (*factory tour free, garden tour US$5pp*) The delicious nutmeg jam or jelly that you spread on your toast, or the moreish nutmeg syrup you pour over your pancakes in the mornings, were probably made by De La Grenade Industries in the heights of St Paul's. Starting life as a cottage industry in 1966, De La Grenade is now an extremely successful, award-winning company that produces high quality and extremely delicious nutmeg products. Its range also includes a liqueur with a 200 year-old secret recipe that won Gold at the Monde Selection in Luxembourg, a rum punch, sea moss (a drink made from seaweed), mauby (see page 60), pepper sauce and pepper jelly.

The factory tour is curious but intriguing. You peer down on the production line through gallery windows as your guide explains what is taking place below on the factory floor – hopefully it is not too steamy or you may end up seeing nothing but clouds and for this reason it is better to call ahead. You also have the chance to buy products from the shop.

The garden tour takes around 30 minutes or so. You will see and learn about a wide variety of tropical plants, flowers, herbs and trees – including nutmeg, of course. The two-acre garden is full of colour and peaceful.

De La Grenade is located on the main road in St Paul's. From St George's pass through the village and look to your left; there is a big sign. Definitely worth a visit. For more information and enquiries ⟍ 473 440 3241 or 473 435 4819; e dlgignd@spiceisle.com; www.delagrenade.com.

The Westerhall Rum Distillery (*20-min tour US$3/EC$7pp*) The Westerhall Estate and rum distillery is located on the main coastal road near Westerhall Point. It is well signposted and easy to find. If you are travelling to Westerhall by bus, take the number 2 from St George's.

Sir William Johnstone of Dumfriesshire, Scotland, purchased the Grand Bacaye Estate in the late 1700s and named it after his ancestral home of Westerhall. The estate changed hands a number of times over the coming years. In the 1860s, sugarcane processing began using two waterwheels, two cane mills and two boilers. A manmade canal channelled water from the St Louis River to the wheels which in turn drove the machinery to crush the sugarcane and extract the juice. This juice was then fermented, distilled and turned into rum.

The waterwheels were decommissioned as late as the 1970s and were replaced by a more modern diesel-powered mill. In the 1980s, Morne Delice Sugar Mill was used to crush and boil the cane juice and Westerhall simply carried out the fermentation, distilling and blending processes. Today Westerhall Estate produces a selection of different rums including: Westerhall Plantation Rum, Westerhall Superb Light, Westerhall Vintage Rum, White Jack, and Jack Iron.

In addition to learning about modern blending processes, you will be taken on a tour of the former estate ruins on the hillside behind. For me this is the highlight. The ruins are fascinating and, if you are a photographer, extremely photogenic. The two waterwheels plus a varied assortment of machine works are on display all around the well-tended estate grounds.

La Sagesse beaches and mangrove swamps On the coastal road between the villages of Corinth and St David's you will see the ruins of the La Sagesse Estate buildings. Opposite them is a sign for the La Sagesse Nature Centre. Follow the narrow paved road all the way. There is a path along the right-hand side of the hotel and restaurant that goes to the bay. If you are walking, it will take around 30 minutes from the main coastal road. A number 2 bus will take you to the junction for La Sagesse.

At La Sagesse there is a pretty crescent-shaped beach and bay. The waters are clear and shallow making it an ideal place for families to have fun and relax. Located at the eastern end of the bay is the La Sagesse Nature Centre, with its high-class accommodation and excellent restaurant and bar. At the western end of the beach, just before you reach the rocks, you should be able to see a narrow track. Follow it alongside the mangrove swamps, brackish pool and salt ponds for about five minutes and you will emerge on the other side of the point to a second, more secluded beach.

If you are interested in birdwatching, then the mangrove swamp, inland pond and coastal forest in this area are home to several varieties of waterfowl as well as birds of prey. A network of tracks and trails criss-cross their way through the mangroves and coastal woodland, many of which are overgrown, so please take care not to get lost. For guidance on trails and the varieties of birdlife you may be lucky enough to encounter here, check with the La Sagesse Nature Centre for further details as well as organised nature tours.

River tubing Take a 90-minute river-tubing ride through the tropical vegetation of Balthazar Estate along Grenada's Great River. You receive a safety briefing and demonstration before you set off, and you are accompanied by guides all the way. River tubing is popular with day visitors arriving on cruise ships, so it may be busy at the height of the season. Travellers with back, neck or heart conditions should seek advice before river tubing. Often the river is quite shallow and it can get a little bumpy. Also check minimum age requirements. (See River-Tubing Operators page 80.)

WALKS, HIKES AND SCENIC OFF-ROAD DRIVES
Mt Carmel (Marquis) Waterfall Mt Carmel Waterfall is located on the Marquis River, close to the hamlet of Mt Carmel, which is on the road between Mt Fann and Munich. It is therefore also known as the Marquis Waterfall. The hiking trail to it is short and easy to follow and should take you no longer than 20 minutes or so each way. There is one river crossing, but only if you wish to get up close to the waterfall and another if you wish to see a second, much smaller waterfall, along the same river.

Grenville, Grand Etang and the Southeast **WHAT TO SEE AND DO**

7

To get there from St George's, follow the coastal road along the southeast coast up towards Grenville. After passing through the village of Crochu the road winds its way up the coast in a northerly direction until it reaches a junction on a tight bend. To the right is the village of Mt Fann and the road to Grenville, to the left is the trailhead to the Mt Carmel Waterfall. Look for both a sign and the Waterfalls Bar close to the junction. If you are travelling by bus from St George's you should take a number 2 and get off at this point.

Look out for Thelma who runs the bar and the neighbouring shop. She is lovely and, if there are young men trying to convince you they should guide you there, she is very likely to see them off. You may be asked for a 'tip' for clearing the trail. This is fair enough as the trail is maintained by local people. A contribution of EC$5 should be enough. You don't really need a guide – the trail is very short – but if you do decide to hire one be sure to agree a price before you set off. Do not accept any rather vague 'just give me what you think' or 'we can talk about that later'. And pay when you return, not before you start. I have heard of guides pocketing the money and then only walking part way and simply pointing visitors in the right direction.

The trail is obvious but the trailhead is not. Rather bizarrely, it is through a garden gate to the left of the bar and shop buildings and it passes through the backyard of the neighbouring house. Once at the rear of the house, the path becomes a trail through the woodland, running alongside the Marquis River, though you may not see it at the beginning if the bush is high. Look out for wild gingers if they are in bloom. The trail meanders through woods and grassland and climbs steeply up a low hillock of deep red volcanic soil. Once down the other side – be careful if it is wet – you may notice two consecutive spurs running off to the right. The first spur is a short track that leads down to a bathing pool. (This is actually the nicest pool on the walk.) The second trail, a little further on, goes down to the river and crosses it to the other side. It is a very shallow crossing over rock, but take care as it can be extremely slippery. You must get your feet wet here. On the other side a short track leads to a second, very small cascading waterfall. Once you have finished with these diversions, head back to the main trail.

Continue along the clear track until you reach the Mt Carmel Waterfall itself. To get close to it, you must cross over the river and clamber over a few small boulders. The waterfall is a large cascade caused by the Marquis River tumbling over a huge, flat rock face. Water splashes down onto more rocks and there is a small, though somewhat unappealing, pool to the left.

St Margaret's/Seven Sisters Falls This is a moderately easy hike across private estate land to a series of pretty waterfalls with nice, deep and refreshing bathing pools. The trail follows a steep dirt track and can be quite muddy and slippery in places. You also have to hop across rocks to get over a small river to reach the falls right at the end of the trail. The hike takes about 30 to 45 minutes each way. It is mostly downhill there and uphill on the way back.

Though the trail is, for the most part, very obvious and clear (it is frequently walked by cruise-ship visitors in the high season), it may be worth taking a guide along to help you out over some of the trickier stretches if you are not a regular hiker. Your guide can also tell you about some of the vegetation you will see. Depending on your group size, a guide's services for an individual or a couple should be around EC$20. Official guides are trained and should be able to show you their licence. If you have not already employed a guide via one of the tour operators who run hiking trips here (see *Chapter 3*, page 77), then one will almost certainly make himself known to you when you arrive. Whether you decide to hire a guide or not, you must pay EC$5 per person entrance fee at the shop.

To reach the starting point of this hike from St George's, follow the interior road to Annandale and then Grand Etang. Keep heading towards Grand Etang, which is clearly signposted in and around town but less so once you are out in the country. The road is very steep as you approach the heights of the forest reserve and it has some sharp hairpin bends, so take care and get full value out of your car horn. Pass the Grand Etang Forest Reserve visitor centre and continue along the main road, which now runs downhill for a short distance. You will see a sign for St Margaret's on the right-hand side. Take this narrow road uphill and you will come to the shop and parking area for the St Margaret's Falls on the right-hand side. If you are travelling to St Margaret's Falls by bus from St George's, you will need to take a number 6.

Once you are ready, walk out of the parking area and turn right, following the paved path for a short distance. You will see the path curves down to the right and into the valley below. Follow it as it passes alongside the farmlands of the estate. Along the route you should be able to identify bananas, plantain, nutmeg, cocoa and cinnamon. After a fairly easy walk for around 10–15 minutes, you will reach a wooden house. The wide track curves around to the right but the narrow trail to the waterfalls runs along the left-hand side of the hut as you face it. Follow this trail up and over a ridge, past a makeshift wooden bar (there may be someone offering cold drinks or even guide services at this point).

Follow the path sharply down the other side of the ridge. You should have nice views on your left across the forest. The path levels out for a short distance as it passes through groves of bamboo before heading downhill once again. Make your way down this quite muddy, rocky and, in some places, steep trail for around 20–30 minutes until the waterfalls come into view. Carefully cross the narrow river to get a closer look and to access the pools.

The waterfalls form part of a series known locally as the Seven Sisters. The lower falls are number six, the taller ones above it number five. The four above it are in actual fact rather small cascades that can be accessed via the trail to your right. It takes about 20 minutes to get up to the top and a popular way of descending is simply to jump down each waterfall into the pool below. The seventh waterfall is close by but on a different river. It is called the Honeymoon Falls (see below). The route back to the car park is the same way you came; unfortunately the slippery downhill slopes are now replaced by steep uphill ones.

The Honeymoon Falls This hike runs from St Margaret's Falls up a narrow and steep track to the Honeymoon Waterfall. The trail is tricky. It is uphill, over rocks and mud and has a couple of narrow river crossings. In order to see the waterfall, you must also climb up a fast-flowing cascade right at the very end of the trail. This part is quite tough. It takes about 15 minutes to reach the waterfall from the St Margaret's Falls trail. If you have hired a guide to take you to St Margaret's Falls just ask him to take you up to Honeymoon and pay a few extra dollars at the end. If you are without a guide, please be careful as the trail is rough and the cascade climb is tricky.

Just as you reach the St Margaret's Falls you have to cross over a small river. Before you do, look to your right and you should see a narrow trail heading up into the bush. The trail is wet even in the dry season and there are a number of places you must walk over slippery rocks, clamber over fallen trees, and wade through areas of shallow water. These stretches can be a little treacherous so take care with your footing. Follow this rocky, muddy and wet trail for around 15 minutes until you reach a large set of rocks on the main river. You should be at a small pool with water cascading into it. Now you must cross the pool and climb up the small rock face of the cascade. Look for footholds as you walk very carefully up it through the rather fast-flowing water. Assuming you make it in one piece, follow the rocky riverbed for a short distance to some more boulders. Climb up on top of them and along some fallen trees (careful, they are slippery) to see the waterfall, which is just around the corner.

It is a pretty waterfall and has a pleasant bathing pool, which, they say, is heart-shaped and how the waterfall got its name. See the yellowish streaks on the walls around the waterfall? They are volcanic sulphur discharges. Take care on the rocks if accessing it. On the way back, take your time going down the cascade as this is not the place for a twisted ankle or worse. Make your way along the same route to rejoin the St Margaret's Falls trail.

Morne Gazo Morne Gazo is located to the east of St Paul's and is a conical peak that has great views of the south and west coasts from its summit. You can actually drive halfway up the peak and then walk the rest of the way. If you are travelling by bus, take a bright green number 4 and get off just after St Paul's. Between the villages of Corbeau and Perdmontemps look for a petrol station opposite the **Wildlife Bar** (which is a good place for refreshments on the way back).

There is a narrow road that runs sharply downhill right next to the bar. Follow it past some houses towards the radio mast, which you should be able to see right ahead of you. The road curves around to the left and turns into a rough vehicle track for a short distance. You will reach a sign for Morne Gazo and see a concrete road on the right-hand side that heads up to the mast. Head up the very steep road. If you are in a car, this is as far as you can drive. Even if you just stay here at the mast, you will be able to enjoy great views down to the south coast.

To the right, alongside the bush, you should see a narrow trail. Follow it as it winds its way very sharply uphill. Notice how the volcanic soil begins to change colour to a darkish red, because of its high iron content. The climb up this slope takes about 15–20 minutes and the last stretch is steep and slippery with little to hold on to. Once you make it to the top you will see a wooden viewing platform that has been erected around a tree. Check the platform and its steps to ensure they will hold your weight before attempting to climb up. If it is derelict, don't risk it. The views are panoramic all around. Especially good are the views down to St George's, Grand Anse and the southwest peninsula.

At the bottom of the road up to the mast you may have noticed a sign for the Morne Gazo Forest Reserve. Though it is a rather ambitious description, the area around this peak is indeed a protected area and is described by some operators as a good area for birdwatching. It is also quite a pleasant walk.

Hope Beach on Great Bacolet Bay This is a short walk or drive along a paved road and then vehicle track to a long crescent beach on the shoreline of Great Bacolet Bay. The waters are calm and shallow, making it really good for bathing.

On the road midway between Crochu and the Mt Fann/Mt Carmel junction there is the small community of Hope. If you are travelling by bus, take a number 2 from St George's and ask the driver to let you off at Hope Estate. Just to the south of Hope there is a sign and some stone gateposts on the coastal side of the road pointing to the Hope Development, which is a grand housing project on the former lands of the Hope Estate. Head through the gates of Hope (!) and follow the paved road for no more than 15 minutes if you are on foot, or less than five minutes by car. On a bend you will see a fork with a rough vehicle track heading downhill to the right. Follow this track through the forest to the beach itself. The track is easy, a little muddy in places, but not particularly troublesome. If you are in a car, you may need a 4x4 if the ground is sodden and muddy. If you don't fancy it, just park at the top and walk down. It isn't very far. A little further up the road from this junction is a small clearing on the right with really nice views of Bacolet Bay and the beach.

It is pleasant to walk along the beach. Towards the southern end you will come across benches and a picnic area. There is also a vehicle track from here going back up to the main road that takes about 15 minutes on foot.

Belle Isle Beach on Le Petit Trou Bay
This drive takes you along a narrow ridge and then down a vehicle track to the very pretty Le Petit Trou Bay and then the equally lovely Belle Isle Beach. The beach is popular with locals, though as it is located close to a large housing project this may change in the years to come.

A very short distance to the south of St David's is a sign on the coastal side of the road pointing the way to the Belle Isle & Batou Casse Housing Development. It is not that easy to see, so just stop and ask someone if you can't find it. If you are travelling here by bus, take a number 2 from St George's and get off at the village of St David's.

Follow the clear road along the ridge and through the settlement of Belle Isle. There are good views across the valley to the north and the community of Requin. You will end up at some stone gateposts with a sign saying 'private road'. To the right of the gateposts you should see a vehicle track. This runs all the way down to the beach.

The track is rough, grassy and muddy with one or two large rocks. If you decide to drive down, and many locals do, you will need to engage four-wheel drive. If you are breaking into a cold sweat at the thought of it, just park up out of the way at the top and walk down. It isn't far – just 30 minutes at most, and it is a pleasant stroll through the forest. The tranquil waters of this bay are great for bathing. Waves are almost non-existent and it is shallow, making it a good place for families.

Cabier Beach and Crochu Harbour
Crochu Harbour and Cabier Beach are picturesque and definitely worth the short off-road diversion. There are two beaches and bays separated by Crochu Point, a small rocky outcrop that is the location of the Cabier Ocean Lodge. The small beach on the northern side of the point is Cabier Beach and is perhaps the prettier of the two small bays. It is a peaceful place to relax with a picnic and bathe. There are two routes to it; one fairly easy, the other more of a challenge with a high chance of taking a wrong turn and getting a bit lost. But that's what makes it fun.

If you are approaching the village of Crochu from the south, you will see a sign for Cabier pointing to a narrow paved side road. This is the easy route. It passes Big Sky Lodge and reaches a clearly signposted junction for Cabier Lodge. Just follow the signs. Just before you reach Cabier you will come to a junction. Take the second vehicle track on the left, not the one that goes straight ahead to Cabier, and not the one immediately to the left. Follow this track downhill and around a bend and you should see the sea and beach ahead of you. If you miss it, head towards Cabier and look for a hand-painted sign for the beach on the left.

If you would like to try the trickier, more adventurous route, pass the first sign for Cabier on the main road and continue a little further into Crochu village. On a bend called, and signposted, Café Junction, you should see *Cabier* painted on a low wall. Take this road and follow it through the settlement of Mahot. The road is paved and winds its way downhill along a narrow ridge with board and block houses on either side. There is a turn-off to the left, but ignore it and keep going straight down until you round a bend and come to a T-junction. Turn right, following the sign to Cabier, if there is one.

From here on the paved road gives way to a vehicle track. Pass by some more houses and then take care as the track becomes rough and broken as it runs downhill. At the next junction, turn left and head to the next fork, this time ignoring the left-hand spur and continuing straight on. The road is paved for a stretch from here.

At the next fork you will see a concrete road heading sharply uphill on the left and a grassy vehicle track straight ahead. Take the grassy track to the next fork and turn left, again following the sign to Cabier. On your right-hand side, on private land, you should notice stone ruins of the former Crochu Estate. Ignore the spur to the right at this point and continue straight on until you reach the brow of a hill. You should arrive at a junction. Take the second vehicle track on the left, not the one that goes straight ahead to Cabier, and not the one immediately to the left. Follow this track downhill and around a bend to the beach.

Both Cabier and Big Sky Lodge offer dining, as well as accommodation, but it would be a good idea to call ahead. See page 160.

St David's Point and the Megrin Standing Stone

Megrin is the location of the first European settlement on the island of Grenada. It was a relatively short-lived stay as the settlers found themselves subjected to constant attack and harassment by the Kalinago (see page 12). Four Englishmen named Geoffrey, Hail, Lull and Robinson and 199 fellow companions arrived on three ships destined for South America: the *Diana*, the *Penelope* and the *Endeavour*. The sporadic attacks by the island's indigenous Amerindian people made life intolerable for the new arrivals and with great relief they packed up and left the island one year later when a passing ship stopped to see how they were getting along.

Today the location of the settlement is marked by a large standing rock midway along the peninsula running from the village of Corinth (if you are travelling by bus from St George's, take a number 2 and get off at Corinth) to St David's Point. Unfortunately, like many places of historic or natural interest in Grenada, this one is fast becoming overtaken by the value of the real estate upon which it stands. There are several resplendent mansions on this peninsula, one of them a huge chateau, and lots of markings for others can be seen. At the time of writing, it is possible to get all the way to the tip of St David's Point without any problem and hopefully it will stay that way. This is a nice off-road drive. The point is absolutely lovely; remote, windswept and peaceful. I love coming here.

To the south of the La Sagesse Nature Centre, and a little to the north of the village of Corinth, there is a sign on the coastal side of the road pointing to the Megrin Town Project. The rough road runs uphill and then down along the ridge. There are great views of the very pretty St David's Harbour and yachts at anchor on the right. Pass alongside some large residences and keep following the rather rough and sometimes muddy track down along the edge of the peninsula, past some more houses, until you reach the large standing rock marking the site of the original Megrin settlement. From the rock, continue downhill until the road meets a rocky roundabout. It is best to park up here, or drive down the left-hand track and park at the bottom somewhere out of the way. At the bottom of this left-hand spur, take a right and follow the track until it becomes a grassy trail heading towards the point.

The headland stretches for quite a long way. You may see a number of little trails as well as the main one. You'll figure it out. Just keep heading towards the end! And look out for all the different types of cactus, including the low-growing prickly pear. Also on the ground you may see the sensitive plant (*Mimosa pudica*). It folds away its small leaves if you touch them. Enjoy the views and the wildness of this rugged coastline and be sure to look back at the steep ridges and forest-covered hills of the interior of Grenada. If you make it to the very end of the point, be careful. Coastal erosion means that nothing is very strong or stable so don't go too close to the edge or take any unnecessary risks.

On the way back you could check out the **Waterside Bar** at the Bel Air Plantation Resort. It is off the main road, a little to the south. Look for the signs to Grenada Marine and just follow the road.

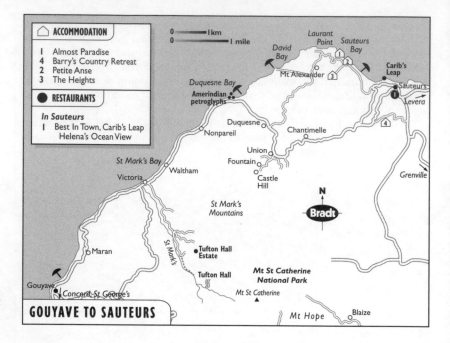

8

Sauteurs, Mt St Catherine and the North

Grenada's north combines natural beauty and cultural heritage. It is very peaceful, its people seem especially friendly, and it is about as far from the resort-like south as you can get – both physically and metaphorically. You can find yourself deep in the rainforest searching for hidden waterfalls, climbing Grenada's highest mountain or walking on long stretches of beach hoping for a sighting of giant leatherback turtles coming ashore. History reveals itself in the form of Amerindian petroglyphs, 'Leaper's Hill', and in fascinating and educational plantation estates such as Belmont and the impressive River Antoine where sugarcane is converted to rum in the same way it was over 200 years ago.

GETTING THERE

There are three ways to get from south to north; either up the west coast via Gouyave, up the east coast via Grenville, or right through the middle via the Grand Etang Forest Reserve. The interior road is arguably the quickest, but perhaps also the most challenging if you are driving. By bus, a number 5 will get you to Sauteurs via the west coast. A number 6 will take you via the interior to Grenville where you can then catch a number 9 up to Sauteurs.

GETTING AROUND

The most flexible way of getting around the north is by hire car. The number 9 bus takes two routes between Sauteurs and Grenville; one via River Sallee, the other via Hermitage and Tivoli. You will often see people in the parish of St Patrick

> **DON'T MISS**
>
> If your time is limited, here is the don't-miss list for this part of Grenada:
>
> **Belmont Estate** (page 188)
> **River Antoine Rum Distillery** (page 188)
> **Bathway Beach** (page 194)
> **Levera Archipelago and Beach** (page 194)

standing by the roadside hoping to hitch a ride, which is a good indicator of how infrequently buses run between some of the villages up here. And if you want to get to the elevated communities of Paraclete and Mt Horne you will either have to hitch a ride or walk, as buses rarely venture along these narrow and somewhat labyrinthine interior roads.

FUEL You will find petrol stations in Victoria, Sauteurs and Tivoli.

🏠 WHERE TO STAY

HOTELS AND GUESTHOUSES

🏠 **Petite Anse** (9 cottages & 2 rooms) Petite Anse, Sauteurs; 📞 473 442 5252; f 473 442 4848; e info@petiteanse.com; www.petiteanse.com. Stunning location, laid-back, friendly & welcoming owners & staff. All rooms have 4-poster bed, en-suite bathroom, AC & ceiling fans, Wi-Fi, mini fridge, private deck or terrace, beach & sea views. Swimming pool, sun terrace, restaurant & bar serving fine dining & local options. Fresh produce for the restaurant grown in the owners' Old Plantation House fruit & vegetable gardens. Wedding & honeymoon packages, hiking & boat tours arranged. Prices seasonal & include b/fast. Meal plans also available. **$$–$$$**

🏠 **Barry's Country Retreat** (10 rooms) La Fortune, Sauteurs; 📞 473 442 0330; f 473 442 0800; e barrysretreat@spiceisle.com; www. barrysretreat.com. Functional rooms with private bathroom, AC, TV. Use of swimming pool & tennis court. Restaurant serves local cuisine. Nice views of the surrounding area. **$$**

🏠 **Morne Fendue Plantation House** (13 rooms) Morne Fendue; 📞/f 473 442 9294; e mornefendueplantation@spiceisle.com. Modern & historic accommodation available in both the main building & a modern annexe of an 18th-century plantation house. Private bathroom, fans & excellent mountain views. Annexe has SC rooms with kitchenettes. Restaurant & bar within the grounds & Betty Mascoll Museum located in main house (for more information see page 192). **$**

SELF-CATERING

🏠 **Moonfish Villas** (2 villas) Bathway Beach; 📞 473 442 2884; e kjp@moonfishvillas.com; www.moonfishvillas.com. Two very comfortable & spacious villas located right on the beautiful Bathway Beach. Each 2-storey villa has 2 bedrooms with en-suite wet room, fully equipped kitchen, lounge, TV, DVD, Wi-Fi & large veranda with ocean & beach views. Shared swimming pool & sun deck. Very friendly owners can arrange meals & tours for you. Min 3-night stay. **$$$–$$$$**

🏠 **Almost Paradise** (8 cottages) Mt Alexander, Sauteurs; 📞/f 473 442 0608; e almostparadise@ spiceisle.com; www.almost-paradise-grenada. com. Pleasant cottage accommodation located on the north coast near Sauteurs. Facilities include private bathroom, outdoor shower, living area, fans, kitchenette, balcony with hammock, & great views of the southern Grenadines. Restaurant serves Mediterranean-style food. Vegetarian & other dietary requirements catered for. English & German spoken. **$$–$$$**

🏠 **The Heights** (1 cottage) Mt Rodney, Sauteurs; 📞 473 442 0842 & 473 414 9147; e grenadaheights@aol.com; www. grenadaheights.co.uk. Delightful 1-bed SC cottage with kitchen, lounge area, bathroom & private terrace. Fabulous views of the southern Grenadines, cooling breezes, peace & quiet. Owner-manager DJ is a warm & welcoming host as well as a first-class chef. Great option for budget, independent travellers exploring the north. **$$**

✖ WHERE TO EAT AND DRINK

✖ **Petite Anse Restaurant & Bar** Petite Anse, Sauteurs; 📞 473 442 5252; 🕐 daily. Fine dining with fresh local produce from the owners' farm. Traditional Grenadian food also available. Open for lunch & dinner. All-day sandwiches & snacks. Great views of beach & sea. **$$–$$$**

✗ Almost Paradise Mt Alexander, Sauteurs; ☎473 442 0608; local & international lunches & dinners with a Mediterranean flair served in open-air restaurant near Sauteurs with superb views of the Grenadines. Dinners by reservation only. $$

✗ Belmont Estate Restaurant Belmont; ☎473 442 9524; closed Sat. Large open-sided restaurant serving excellent local & international dishes, often with products grown on the estate's own farmlands. Try anything with the homemade goat's cheese – it's fabulous. Friendly staff & highly recommended. Alcohol-free. $$

✗ Rivers Restaurant & Bar River Antoine Estate; ☎473 442 7109. Located on the fascinating heritage estate, serving a good selection of local & international cuisine daily. $$

✗ Carib's Leap Restaurant & Wine Bar Sauteurs; ☎473 442 1453. Bar & restaurant with terrace-dining overlooking Sauteurs main street. Very pleasant with good local cooking. Open all day but dinner reservations preferred. $$

✗ Plantation Bar & Kitchen Plantation Hse, Morne Fendue; ☎473 442 9294; ⊙ by reservation. Traditional Grenadian cooking with

marvellous mountain views from the dining terrace. $$

✗ Aggie's Restaurant & Bar Bathway Beach; ☎473 442 2336; closed Mon. The lovely Aggie cooks all sorts of great lunches & dinners but seafood, fish & lobster are a speciality. Ask for her lobster & plantain balls, or the breadfruit & cheese option. Quaint restaurant, fabulous location & great food. Don't miss it. $$

✗ The Heights Café Bar Mt Alexander, Sauteurs; ☎473 442 0843. Excellent local cooking with an international twist from owner, chef & all-round great host, DJ. Relaxed, cosy dining with unbeatable views of the southern Grenadines. Fish dishes a speciality but DJ also cooks a great 'boneless' chicken roti. $$

✗ Helena's Ocean View Restaurant & Bar Sauteurs; ☎473 442 0950; located on the western edge of Sauteurs, Helena's is a pleasant local eatery. Good value lunches, snacks & very nice sea views. Great roti. $–$$

✗ Best In Town Restaurant Sauteurs; ☎473 442 9790. Good local eating option on the eastern end of Sauteurs. Cheap, cheerful & tasty. $

SHOPPING

Shopping in this region is limited to the essentials. There are small supermarkets and convenience stores along the main streets of Victoria and Sauteurs. If you are prepared to look hard enough you can usually find what you want, or something close to it, and don't forget local markets on Saturday mornings for fruit and vegetables.

OTHER PRACTICALITIES

MONEY AND BANKS There are two banks in Sauteurs, the Grenada Co-operative Bank and the Republic Bank. Both have ATMs.

MEDICAL Both Victoria and Sauteurs have pharmacies on their main streets. They are generally well stocked for essentials, emergencies and for babies. However, if you are taking prescription medication you should not rely on these pharmacies.

SAFETY The people of St Patrick are very friendly and you are sure to make new friends on your travels. There have been incidents in the past of people having possessions stolen on Levera Beach though it is a very rare occurrence. Just try to avoid taking valuables out with you. I also suggest you give the Clabony hot spring a miss if you are alone. Although it has been developed and may appear on tourism literature, the spring itself is a rather unappealing place and its isolated location means that it has attracted the occasional opportunist thief. I should stress that incidents of theft are infrequent and Grenada is in the main a very safe place. Should you ever need them, there are police stations on the main streets of Victoria and Sauteurs.

WHAT TO SEE AND DO

EXPLORING THE REGION

Sauteurs Sauteurs is mainland Grenada's northernmost community. Its name is derived from the French 'Morne des Sauteurs' meaning 'Leapers' Hill', the title given to the area following the infamous routing and subsequent suicide of fleeing Kalinago. Rather than surrender to their French pursuers, it is said that around 40 of the embattled Kalinago chose to take their own lives by leaping from a hill to the sea and rocks below. Leapers' Hill (also called Carib's Leap) is still remembered in this small town, and a memorial and visitor centre have been erected on the site (see page 191).

Sauteurs is a very compact place, consisting of a single main street thoroughfare with residential houses located on the hillside behind. To the west is **Sauteurs Bay**, a beautiful and expansive bay with a white-sand beach lined with coconut palms. The beach stretches all the way to Laurant Point and it is usually deserted. To the east of Sauteurs are Irvins Bay, the hamlets of Helvellyn and Levera, and then the Levera Archipelago National Park.

Though somewhat diminutive, Sauteurs is quite a pretty coastal town with a vibrant main street where you will find convenience stores, two banks with ATMs (Grenada Co-operative Bank and Republic Bank), fine local eateries such as Carib's Leap Restaurant & Wine Bar and Helena's Ocean View Restaurant & Bar, the Sauteurs post office and police station, and also bus stops for transportation south along both west and east coasts. The striking **St Patrick Roman Catholic Church** with its bright red brick stands high above the main street near Leapers' Hill on the west side of the town. The church was built in 1851 on the site of the first Roman Catholic chapel, erected in the late 17th century by French Capuchin monks. Accessed via steep stone steps from the main road, the church is bright and airy with a very traditional feel. It is constructed in the Caribbean Gothic revival style, which is typified by the tall, pointed-arch windows and the squat, octagonal bell tower. The voices of children from the school yard next door drift in through the large, open arched windows. From the small courtyard in front of the church there are nice views of the town, the hills beyond and of Sauteurs Bay to the west.

Leapers' Hill is well signposted from the main street. Follow a crescent road that loops back to the main thoroughfare on the east of the town and you will pass a residential community of small wood and brick houses as well as a few welcoming local bars and snackettes. Follow the signs to the gated entrance to Leapers' Hill and the visitor centre (see page 191 for more details).

Towards the eastern end of the Sauteurs main street you will find the **St Patrick Anglican Church** with its tall brick bell tower, and next to it the Anglican school. Renovation and paintwork disguise the true age of this church. It was actually built in the 1830s and is the oldest surviving church in the parish of St Patrick. If you are travelling on a budget, try Best in Town Restaurant. It has good value local lunches.

Sauteurs Bay is fringed by a long and rather lovely beach. Look out for the ruins of a lime kiln on the western end. This was once used to make white lime from coral and other marine organisms, which was then used as a mortar in buildings as well as a fining to remove impurities during rum production.

The road from Gouyave to Sauteurs From Gouyave the road north hugs a scenic coastline, passing through Maran and around to **Victoria**. Once known as Grand Pauvre by the French who established the settlement in 1741, Victoria is the main village of the parish of St Mark. Like its near neighbour Gouyave, Victoria has a tradition of fishing and nutmeg processing, though both have been experiencing a period of decline in recent times. On the approach from the south you will often see crowds of people hauling in seine nets and then walking off with bags and buckets of jacks and rainbow runners. The village is located on the picturesque shores of St Mark's Bay, a sweeping coastline of black-sand beach, rocks and, of course, Caribbean Sea.

Victoria is usually a quiet village with a main street and residential area behind. It has a pretty backdrop of the tall mountain ridges on the western boundary of the Mt St Catherine National Park. Along the main thoroughfare, Queen Street, there are a number of small bars and convenience stores. Also on Queen Street is the **Victoria Nutmeg Station**. Prior to Hurricane Ivan the Victoria station, together with Gouyave and Grenville, was one of the three main nutmeg processing plants in Grenada. Like the Grenville station, the Victoria nutmeg station, or 'pool', is now just used as a receiving station. Growers will bring their nutmegs here from their farms where they are weighed and sometimes dried in racks, but they will then be taken to the Gouyave pool for processing, grading and bagging for export.

Queen Street is also home to the Catholic church and the police station. North of the police station is the Anglican church, the post office and the Victoria fish market. In the centre of town, beside the nutmeg station, is a road that heads inland from Queen Street towards the forests and mountains. This road passes the residential part of the village before winding its way inland along the St Mark's River and up towards the **Tufton Hall Estate**. Tufton Hall is the site of a development project to restore the original plantation house and convert it into an 'eco-spa'. Tufton Hall is also the name given to a waterfall that is higher up the St Mark's River. The waterfall is a tall, narrow, split cascade that also has a lukewarm water stream. The trail was yet another victim of Hurricane Ivan and subsequent neglect. There has been talk of clearing it but at the time of writing access to the waterfall still required a long, tricky, but fun river hike (see page 193).

On the last Saturday of every month, from about 18.00 onwards, the streets of Victoria host the **Sunset City Food Fest**. It is a small but thriving event, on a par with Gouyave's Fish Friday, where people cook up and sell all kinds of great local food. It is definitely worth patronising and if you are looking for something traditional, or a little different – some seasonal *tatou* or *manikou* perhaps (see page 59) – then you may well find it here.

From Victoria the road runs north along the west coast through the settlements of **Waltham** and **Nonpareil**, a hamlet of colourful board houses and fishing boats, nestled against the captivating Crayfish Bay. The road between Nonpareil and Duquesne to the north follows a very scenic coastline. **Duquesne Bay** is a broad crescent-shaped bay of white sand and brightly painted fishing boats. It is also the location for one of Grenada's **Amerindian petroglyph** sites (see page 191). The name Duquesne comes from a Kalinago village chief known as 'Captain' Duquesne who lived in this area in the mid 1700s and who was active during the conflicts between the indigenous people and the newly arrived French settlers. Duquesne, together with Waltham and Victoria, was the site of a military fortification constructed by the French during their occupation of the island in the early 1700s. From Duquesne Bay the road turns inland towards the communities of **Union** and **Chantimelle** before arriving at Sauteurs. The road is a pretty one, winding through

Visitors to the more rural, less commercial and tourist-oriented areas of Grenada will encounter small settlements and villages where people live in concrete, block, stone or board houses (sometimes a combination of these). The simplest and most traditional is the board house, also known as the frame house. This style of dwelling stems back to the 1800s when the peasant class and liberated slaves began to replace their cob houses (walls made from mud and straw) and their thatched roofs with something a little sturdier. Constructed from local woods these board houses were very simple, with a single door, wooden louvre windows, hurricane shutters and a tall pitched roof to provide a degree of protection against wind and rain. Sometimes these little houses were raised on short stilts, depending on their location, to help prevent flooding. The thatched roof was replaced by wooden shingle and some would also have an open veranda. A small garden would surround the house, which was usually a place for growing vegetables, cooking over an open fire, rearing animals, going to the toilet and washing. Although times have changed and hurricanes have wreaked havoc among rural communities and peasant families, the board house remains, though it has evolved a little. These days the shingle roof has usually been replaced by galvanised steel and the louvre windows by glass or a combination of glass and louvre. Many are very brightly painted and decorated with picturesque gardens of crotons, bougainvillea and flowering fruit trees. Simple, rustic and sometimes quite stylish, board houses are a traditional characteristic of Grenada's rural villages and suburban settlements.

forest and along the banks of the Duquesne River, with vibrant flora and colourfully painted board houses on either side.

From the schoolhouse in Union there is a road that runs uphill towards the settlement of **Castle Hill** on the northern slopes of St Mark's Mountains. Just below Castle Hill is the rural hamlet of **Fountain**, where two natural springs emerge from the mountainside and have been tapped by residents. A bamboo pipe channels the water into a small enclosed rock pool where, in times of shortage, local people can come to collect water for bathing. From Fountain there are great views across the forest towards Sauteurs on the north coast. The road from Union passes the village of **Chantimelle** before heading downhill towards the coast and Sauteurs. You will pass forested areas as well as residential housing, convenience stores and bars. Before arriving at Sauteurs there is a road junction. A sign for Leapers' Hill points straight ahead. This is the way to Sauteurs. The road to the right bypasses Sauteurs and runs to Morne Fendue where it joins with the roads heading south to Grenville. Just before you enter Sauteurs you come to an area known as **Marli**. This is the location for one of Grenada's nutmeg receiving stations and also the only one remaining on the island where nutmeg oil processing still takes place.

The Levera Archipelago National Park and the northeast coast The
Levera Archipelago National Park is located at the northeasterly tip of mainland Grenada. Its 182ha encompass marine environment, beach, mangrove forest and swamp, and the 9ha freshwater **Levera Pond**. The park was established in 1992, though not officially opened until 1994 when construction of trails, access roads and a visitor centre, funded by the European Union, had been completed. For some

time there was a great deal of speculation about an eco-resort development here. This project has been the subject of some controversy and seems to have stalled but there is rumour of it reappearing in a slightly different guise. For now, however, the only noise comes from the Caribbean coots, egrets and herons that make their homes around the margins of this pretty lake.

On the northern shores of the national park is **Levera Beach**. This is a most beautifully natural white-sand beach with rolling waves and surf. It is also a protected turtle-hatching site where visitors may be fortunate enough to catch a glimpse of giant leatherbacks (*Dermochelys coriacea*), the largest of all living sea turtles, returning to lay their clusters of eggs. The best time for observing this truly amazing sight is during the months from March (laying) to July (hatching). Levera Beach borders the mangroves and wetlands surrounding the Levera Pond and stretches around to Bedford Point, a rugged volcanic headland that was once the location of a gun battery and small fortification. The ruins are still there. Offshore, across the protected marine environment of coral reefs and sea grass beds, are three small islands. From west to east, they are Sugar Loaf Island (sometimes called Levera Island), Green Island and Sandy Island. Lots of boat trips head for Sandy Island. It is a popular spot for snorkelling and a picnic. Ask your hotel to recommend a fisherman, they usually know one who takes people there.

Beyond Bedford Point and south along the eastern edge of the national park is **Bathway Beach**. Of comparable length to the far more commercial and popular Grand Anse Beach on the southwest peninsula, Bathway is peaceful and lovely, a beautiful contrast to the south. Popular with locals, you will often see people enjoying picnics and oil-downs on the sand by the tables opposite the visitor centre. This is also where you can bathe safely, protected by an in-shore reef. Look out for the nearby Aggie's Restaurant & Bar for good food and a cold beer. The visitor centre contains an informative display describing the volcanic origins of this area, the wildlife and conservation efforts. Staff are helpful and happy to talk you through it.

Inland is the park's centrepiece, the **Levera Pond**. Hardly visible from its perimeter, the 9ha freshwater pond is surrounded by one of Grenada's largest areas of mangrove forest. The pond attracts a wide variety of migratory and resident waterbirds including the rare and alluring scarlet ibis (*Eudocimus ruber*). Naturalists, and in particular birdwatchers, should make tracks for the **Levera Mangrove Wetland** where a short, clearly marked trail leads to a two-storey wooden viewing platform from where you can see most of the lake. The trail can be found by following the road and vehicle track between Bathway Beach and Levera Beach. Look for a large sign on the left.

Following the main road out of Sauteurs on the eastern side of the town, the road turns towards the south, splitting into two routes towards both Grenville and the capital, St George's. Immediately to the south of Sauteurs is the community of **La Fortune** and from here there is a coastal road that runs northeast through Helvellyn and Levera towards the Levera Archipelago National Park. South of La Fortune is **Morne Fendue** where the road forks. The more westerly route skirts the edges of Mt St Catherine National Park and is quite hilly and forested (see page 185), the easterly route is along relatively flatter lands near to the coast. Both roads pass through enchanting villages and have sites of interest to visitors.

Morne Fendue is located alongside the St Patrick River. It is a residential village with a mixture of modern and traditional board houses. Very near to where the main road forks, there is the **Anglican rectory**, a stone building in a picturesque

Yoruba is thought to be one of the world's largest Africa-born religions. Practised by the people of Nigeria, Sierra Leone and Benin, it came to the Americas during the slave trade. As Christianity was forced upon these captive people, a synergy of beliefs was born that manifests itself in many formats throughout the Caribbean region. These belief systems include Santería, Anago, Oyotunji and Candomblé. All of these entail worship of Orishas, spirits that reflect the many manifestations of one almighty god, Olorun or Olodumare. One popular Orisha is the god of thunder and lightning, Shango. Shango's sacred colours are red and white, his symbol is a double-headed axe and he is the owner of three double-headed drums. He is associated with music, dance and drumming. Ritual ceremonies would usually take place around water and feature drumming, dance, animal sacrifice and spirit possession. Though these beliefs and rituals have been discouraged by the Christian church they nevertheless survive in small pockets of many countries throughout the modern world, including Grenada.

setting of well-tended lawn, colourful gardens, trees and river. The main road passes the **Morne Fendue Plantation House**, a guesthouse, museum and restaurant with superb views of the surrounding countryside (see page 192).

Continuing south along the main road you will come to a traffic island where the road forks. The road south of the traffic island is the main bus route between Sauteurs and Grenville. It passes through the village of **Mt Rose**, which has a quaint church and very traditional board houses.

Taking the road east from the traffic island leads to the village of **River Sallee** where there are roads to both **Bathway Beach** and **Lake Antoine**. River Sallee was once a large estate where a waterwheel drove machinery to crush sugarcane. You can still see mill ruins on the western side of town. Following emancipation and the subsequent decline of the estates through lack of a labour force, freed slaves began working the land and eventually created a large rural community that is the River Sallee of today. The name of the village is probably derived from the French, meaning 'salty river', in reference to the highly saline, mineral-rich sulphur springs found in the area. Between the traffic island on the main road south and the village of River Sallee itself, there are a number of small residential houses, some banana fields and then a sign indicating **sulphur springs**. This is one of several areas of residual subterranean volcanic activity in Grenada. Most sites are in the north, and this region around the Chambord Estate near River Sallee is considered the most scientifically interesting. Until fairly recently the springs were also considered the most spiritual by Shango worshippers and Spiritual Baptists who, believing the waters to be sacred or having supernatural powers, would come here on pilgrimages and to perform rituals. The springs are interesting but rather unattractive. Spread over a very small area, the highest concentrations are to be found just a short walk from the road. Follow the sign along a track for around five minutes. You will come to an open area of flat rock with the trademark yellow stains of sulphur deposits and sulphur-rich water. The rock contains a number of small, very gloomy-looking pools. In some of them you will see bubbles rising to the surface. All of the pools you find in this area are cold.

In the village of River Sallee there is a signposted road junction with routes to Sauteurs, Levera and Lake Antoine. The road to Levera passes residential houses, a church and cemetery, and the River Sallee Credit Union. The road continues through dry coastal scrub and grassland before reaching Bathway Beach and then Levera Beach

The road south from River Sallee runs to the villages of La Poterie and Tivoli via Lake Antoine. It is a very rural area with a smattering of board houses, small snackettes and bars. The road hugs Antoine Bay and the road to Lake Antoine itself is very clearly signposted. This 6.5ha crater lake is scenic and wonderfully serene. There is plenty of birdlife, particularly around the vegetation of the littoral margins. The area around the lake is privately owned and farmed for bananas, pawpaw, and other vegetable and fruit crops. See page 196 for details of a walk around the lake. To the east of the lake is Antoine Bay, a wild and rugged shoreline that takes the full brunt of the rolling Atlantic Ocean waves.

South of Lake Antoine is the **River Antoine Rum Distillery** where you can experience the rum-making process almost exactly how it was performed over 200 years ago (see page 188). From River Antoine, the road curves inland at La Poterie and rejoins the main highway at the village of **Tivoli**, which is famous for the Tivoli Drummers who perform at Big Drum festivals on the main island (see page 206). If you are lucky you may hear them practising.

South of Tivoli the road runs toward Grenville through the rural hamlets of **Conference** and **Pearls**. To the east of Conference there is a large coconut plantation before the land reaches marshlands and the narrow beach at Conference Bay, where the waves of the Atlantic Ocean crash relentlessly onto this very exposed stretch of coastline.

A little to the north of Grenville is **Pearls Airport**. Abandoned since 1984, it is a little surreal, but worth a visit. It was built in 1943 when the 153ha Pearls Estate was purchased in preference over Point Salines as the location for the island's first airport. During its construction, Amerindian artefacts were discovered on the site indicating the location of an indigenous settlement. Unfortunately the runway took precedence and the Amerindian site was largely destroyed. The constraints of a small airport and its proximity to high ridges and mountains ultimately resulted in the construction of an alternative facility at Point Salines (the Maurice Bishop International Airport), and Pearls was closed. Today, it is rather an eerie place consisting of skeleton buildings and aircraft wreckage. You will see a Russian Antonov AN-26 and an Antonov 2R. Both were gifts from Russia via Cuba in 1983 during the revolution (see page 17). The AN-26 arrived in Grenada on the day before Operation Urgent Fury began (see page 18). The runway is used as a road connecting Upper Pearls with Lower Pearls, a place to learn how to drive, and occasionally a car-racing venue. From Pearls it is a very short distance to Grenville.

Mt St Catherine National Park and the interior

The Mt St Catherine National Park is located in Grenada's northern interior, south of Sauteurs and east of Gouyave. This mountainous and forested park covers an area of 580ha and is possibly the least accessible place in the whole of Grenada. The park's terrain is rugged and its hills and mountain ridges are very steep and narrow. Vegetation is montane forest with cloud forest at the highest elevations. Most of the windward-facing ridges were damaged by Hurricane Ivan and the loss of many mature trees has caused considerable disruption to what was formerly a wet rainforest environment. Trees are growing back well but the loss of a high canopy that would once have trapped moisture has created a habitat that is in a state of transition and regeneration, and will be for many years to come. At the centre of the park is Mt St Catherine which, at 840m, is the tallest peak in Grenada.

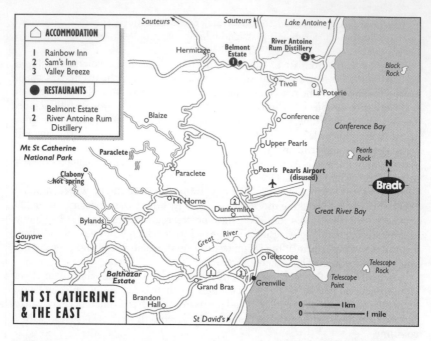

ACCOMMODATION
1 Rainbow Inn
2 Sam's Inn
3 Valley Breeze

RESTAURANTS
1 Belmont Estate
2 River Antoine Rum Distillery

Mt St Catherine National Park

MT ST CATHERINE & THE EAST

There are a number of secondary roads running inland towards the interior of the park though some are in quite poor condition. Hiking trails are rarely maintained and have become overgrown. The ascent of Mt St Catherine itself should not be attempted without a guide who has local knowledge. This particular hiking challenge is not offered by the majority of tour operators, but it is possible up a very steep and muddy track. The best time to attempt it is in the dry season as the mountain's steep ridges are unforgiving and extremely slippery in the wet. **Paraclete, Bylands** and **Mt Horne** are good villages to ask at for local assistance (see box on page 194). Famous Grenadian hiker **Telfor Bedeau**, who was celebrating his 70th birthday with an ascent of Diamond Rock while I was writing this edition, lives in the village of Soubise, south of Grenville. He has climbed Mt St Catherine hundreds of times and still takes people up there. Much has been written about this remarkable man. Give him a call on 473 442 6200 if you would like to engage him to come with you. For anyone just wanting to see the summit from a distance, a 4x4 vehicle can make it to the Cable & Wireless communication masts near the settlement of Blaize, to the northwest of Paraclete. The road is paved but incredibly steep (make sure your brakes work well and your tyres are not worn). The views from the station are spectacular and you can see across the neighbouring peaks to the summit of Mt St Catherine itself.

Immediately to the south of Sauteurs near to the Morne Fendue Plantation House, a less frequently used road cuts a winding path through several pretty villages and picturesque countryside. It follows the St Patrick River southwards, high above its western bank as it passes through the settlements of **Snell Hall** and **Ellie Hall** towards **Mt Rich**. At a road junction on the edge of Mt Rich, look out for a rather derelict and empty building on the river side of the road – it has the appearance of a graffiti-covered bus stop. It is below this sad structure on the far bank of the river that you can see the huge boulder that hosts the **Mt Rich Amerindian Petroglyphs** (see page 191).

The road south of Mt Rich passes through a dramatic cut in the rock and runs alongside small banana, coconut and nutmeg plantations. The village of **Hermitage** is home to a number of attractions. On the north side of the village before reaching the junction for Peggy's Whim and the village church, you will see a sign for the **slave pen**. The sign asks that you call in advance to visit and it is only polite to do so (℡ 473 442 9277). You may be granted permission by the owners of the site to pass onto their land and take a look at the ruins of the former **Hermitage Estate Great House** which, though in very poor shape these days, stands proud on a small hill above the village. Walk up the track next to the sign and follow it as it curves around to the left. At the large iron gates, simply follow the single track around and into the grounds. Continue along the track to the house but do not enter. It is private and, at the time of writing, the building is very unsafe. The 'slave pen' relates to the cellar of the great house where slaves were once brought to be broken and then distributed as workers to the surrounding estates.

A little south of the great house is a sign saying 'Welcome to Hermitage Natural Spring'. A muddy and steep track close to the roadside leads to natural freshwater springs emerging from the hills. Below the road, on the opposite side to the sign itself, you can see this spring water emerging from pipes that channel it from its source for use by the village. Close to the centre of Hermitage there is a junction with a steep road running up to the settlement of Peggy's Whim. A short distance up this road is the **Grenada Chocolate Company** (see box, page 190).

The road between the villages of Hermitage and Tivoli passes the very interesting **Belmont Estate** where you can enjoy a tour of the estate grounds, and gardens, and learn all about organic cocoa processing (see page 188).

Between Hermitage and Grenville, the road passes through the high hillside villages of Paraclete and Mt Horne. The road is narrow and broken in places. It is very steep with some rather unnerving hairpin bends. The views are quite stunning and the journey equally dramatic as the route snakes its way across the vertiginous ridges and slopes of the foothills of the central mountain range and the Mt St Catherine National Park. From Paraclete and Mt Horne there are steep secondary roads and vehicle tracks that climb sharply up the mountain into the regions of **Blaize** and **Mt Hope**. These routes also offer access to a 'Hidden Grenada' (see box on page 194) where the island's least accessible sites may be explored by the more adventurous.

From Paraclete and Mt Horne the road swings back down the mountainside towards Dunfermline and Grenville. An alternative route extends the hillside journey to the settlement of Bylands where there are further routes into the interior. **Clabony**, located on these high forested slopes, is where Grenada's best-known hot spring is found. The network of secondary roads and tracks is very confusing in this area and, although there's a sign and steps once you actually get there, it is best to ask for directions from local people in either Bylands or Clabony. In actual fact the hot spring is very disappointing, especially if you either come from or have visited other countries that are known for their hot springs. Up the new steps is a pool with rather lukewarm, somewhat unappealing water, surrounded by overgrown bush. Of far more interest in this area are the villages, the farms, the rural life and the people themselves who, despite what must be incredibly hard times after the hurricanes, always seem to be resolute, upbeat and very ready to make new friends.

ACTIVITIES AND SPECIAL INTERESTS

The River Antoine Rum Distillery *(St Patrick, 2.5km south of Lake Antoine, near La Poterie & Tivoli; 20-min guided tour EC$5pp inc a rum-tasting session)* A visit to the River Antoine Rum Distillery is a must-do for visitors to Grenada. It is an absolutely fascinating glimpse into the past and is certain to enthral anyone interested in the cultural heritage of the region. If you have been hiking and have come across ruins of sugar estates, machine works, waterwheels and cane presses covered in bush and weeds, this experience will bring those discoveries to life.

'Captain' Antoine was a Kalinago chief with whom the French settlers sought peace following the series of conflicts leading to the tragic events at Leapers' Hill in present-day Sauteurs. Chief Antoine's village was located in the northeast and so a number of places still carry that name today, including River Antoine, Antoine Bay and Lake Antoine. Black Rock, a small islet located in the Atlantic directly east of the mouth of the River Antoine, is also recorded as being originally named Islet d'Antoine by the French.

Constructed in 1785, the distillery claims to have been continuously running since that time, making it unique in the Caribbean. The machinery and the processes of rum production employed by the estate go back to the 18th century, to a period of colonial rule and of course to a time of slavery. The huge waterwheel, some 8m high, is powered by water channelled from the river along an aqueduct and over large wooden paddles. The wheel in turn drives the machinery, which includes a huge crusher used to extract cane juice. The sugarcane harvested from the 180ha estate is cut and then loaded onto a rickety wooden conveyor that transports it up to the crusher. Workers manhandle the cane, pushing it into the crusher and then reloading it for a second run to ensure all the natural juices have been thoroughly extracted. The residue cane, now pulped and dry, is called *bagasse* and is used as a fertiliser and mulch for the cane field.

The cane juice is filtered through wicker mats and then ladled by hand along a succession of enormous copper bowls which are heated by a fire below. The juice develops its sugar concentration before being ladled into cooling tanks where it is given time to allow fermentation to begin. Once this has happened, the cane juice is channelled into large tanks where it ferments for about a week before being superheated and distilled. Bottling is a very manual process. The rum is decanted into large plastic drinks coolers and then hand-poured into bottles.

After your tour you will be invited to try some Rivers Rum, either in its neat form or as a blended rum punch. Go steady if you are driving!

The Belmont Estate *(Located between Hermitage & Tivoli; closed Sat; 30-45-min guided tour of the cocoa process EC$10 pp, 'Tree to Bar' chocolate factory tour with lunch also available on request; large restaurant serves excellent local cuisine; www. belmontestate.net)*. Belmont is a historic estate that dates back to the late 1600s when the first French settlers arrived on the island. The estate was a large coffee and sugar producer before changing over to nutmegs and cocoa in the 1800s.

The estate was first owned by a French family by the name of Bernego before being transferred to John Aitcheson of Airdrie, Scotland, when Grenada came under British rule following the Treaty of Paris in 1763. In 1770, the estate was leased to Alexander Campbell, a high-standing colonialist and colleague of Ninian Home, then Governor of Grenada. Both men were executed during the Fédon Rebellion (1795–96). Despite Grenada falling into the hands of the French between 1779 and 1783, the estate stayed in the Aitcheson family before being sold to the Houston family and then in 1944 to the Nyacks, a local family from the village of Hermitage. The Nyack family was the first of Indian heritage to own an estate in Grenada and it still belongs to them today.

Described as an 'agri-tourism product', the 400 acre Belmont Estate successfully fuses agriculture, history and culture to produce a business and heritage site that should be on every visitor's agenda. Don't miss it. In addition to tours of the cocoa process (see page 21), there is a picturesque tropical garden, a museum, a plant nursery, a gift shop, an organic farm, animals (including morocoy, mona monkeys and macaws), a goat dairy, café and fruits stall, restaurant and occasional cultural events such as 'dancing the cocoa' and drumming. 'Dancing the cocoa' is an interesting spectacle where two estate workers, a man and a woman, dance together in a large copper pot of cocoa beans. After cocoa has been dried, the beans sometimes have a white residue on them – a natural result of the fermentation process, but one that makes them less visually appealing to discerning international customers. Before the advent of special polishing machines, dried cocoa was placed in large copper pots and a couple would 'dance' on them to the beat of a drum. The outcome is a couple of exhausted dancers and some very shiny cocoa.

It is indeed the cocoa and the chocolate that really capture the eye, the nose, and the imagination at Belmont Estate. Now entirely organic, the estate grows and supplies much of its cocoa to the **Grenada Chocolate Company** which is located in the nearby community of Hermitage (see box on page 190). The chocolate factory also has part of its production unit on the Belmont Estate where it makes and sells a variety of delicious bonbons. A solar oven outside the bonbon shop also bakes great chocolate cake. The aroma of cocoa, chocolate-making and cake baking is completely irresistible.

If you are there on the right day you may be lucky enough to see 'wet cocoa' arriving from Belmont's organic cocoa farms. These are buckets of cocoa seeds that have been harvested from ripe cocoa pods. When removed from the pods, the seeds are covered in a thick white pulp. Each bucket is strained for excess liquid and then the contents, pulp and all, are poured into deep wooden fermentation bins where they 'sweat' and the pulp begins to liquefy. The sweating process is important for the taste and quality of the cocoa. It helps to rid the cocoa seeds of too much bitterness and it will usually last for up to seven days. The next stage is drying. The seeds are drained of any remaining liquid pulp and then laid out on large trays to dry naturally in the sun. These trays sit in between rails so that wooden covers can be rolled over to protect them during inclement weather.

'Walking the cocoa' is the traditional way of turning the beans, allowing them to be dried evenly. The beans dry for around seven days in the sun before they are either polished for export or used for organic chocolate-making by the Grenada Chocolate Company.

Belmont Estate's other attractions include a goat dairy and farm. Over 100 thoroughbred goats roam the estate's upper paddock and their milk is used to produce a delicious, light organic cheese. Other animals cared for here, and frequently visited by local schoolchildren, include tortoises (known locally as *morocoy* – see page 8),

8

THE GRENADA CHOCOLATE COMPANY

The Grenada Chocolate Company Ltd was founded in 1999 by an American named Mott Green. It is located in the small community of Hermitage and is collectively owned and managed by an organic cocoa-farmers and chocolate-makers' co-operative. The factory produces organic dark chocolate from local, organically grown cocoa using refurbished antique machines. Production is in relatively small batches and uses purely organic ingredients. The chocolate bars come in distinctive colourful wrappers and are available in four varieties: 60% cocoa, 71% cocoa, 82% cocoa and 'nib-a-licious', which is 60% cocoa with cocoa nibs. The company also produces cocoa tea and a variety of bonbons at its Belmont Estate outlet.

The Organic Cocoa Farmers' Co-operative aims to ensure that both cocoa farmers and chocolate producers share their income evenly as well as promoting organic cocoa production in Grenada and abroad. It has received considerable acclaim worldwide for its approach and its products, and has been lauded in the international press, as well as receiving recognition at the World Chocolate Awards.

Chocolate bars can be purchased in shops throughout Grenada as well as from the Belmont Estate. They can also be purchased via the company's website (*www.grenadachocolate.com*).

At the time of writing, Mott described a new 'Tree to Bar' tour that he hoped to establish at the Belmont Estate. This tour will explain and demonstrate the chocolate-making process, from harvesting the organic cocoa all the way through to a tour of the chocolate factory itself. It will also include lunch at the Belmont Estate. Do enquire about the tour at the estate when you visit.

Mott told me of a venture he was due to undertake in early 2012. In his ambition to produce a purely organic chocolate he planned to put his chocolate aboard the *Tres Hombres*, a sail-powered container ship operating out of the Netherlands, and sail with it from Grenada to New York and then on across the Atlantic to the UK. It would be the first chocolate ever produced entirely organically and be delivered internationally with zero carbon footprint. By the time you read this, he will hopefully have succeeded in his adventure and become even more famous!

mona monkeys (see page 7), donkeys and macaws (a conversation with 'Rainbow' is an entertaining experience).

The museum contains estate heritage items (the original estate house was destroyed by hurricane) and local crafts – the **Grenada Arts & Crafts Co-operative** has an office here and you will also find a branch of the **Imagine Gift Shop** which sells a wide range of original Grenadian crafts and souvenirs.

The **Hearts & Hands Foundation** is another Belmont Estate initiative. The sales revenue from the charity shop goes towards helping the less fortunate with school books, uniforms, tuition and exam fees, food hampers and so on. Please support it if you can.

A colourful snack shop and café offers a selection of fruits, sandwiches, guava cheese, cocoa balls and other light bites, and the Belmont Estate restaurant is open for lunch (except on Saturdays) and dinner by reservation. It is a large, open-sided restaurant with lovely views of the estate and the surrounding countryside. Food is buffet-style and very tasty, served from pots above a row of coal fires.

To get to the Belmont Estate by car **from Sauteurs,** head south towards Grenville. Just as you are reaching Tivoli, turn right. Belmont Estate is signposted. If you are travelling by bus from Sauteurs take a number 9, marked Hermitage and Tivoli. The bus will pass the Belmont Estate – just ask to be dropped off there. If you are driving **from Grenville,** head north to Tivoli and turn left. Belmont Estate is located on the right-hand side of the road, midway between Tivoli and Hermitage.

Leapers' Hill
In 1652, just two years after settling on the island, the French set about ridding themselves of the indigenous people, the Kalinago. Learning of a planned raid by the Kalinago on the settlement of Fort Louis (see page 13), they launched a fierce counter-attack. Many Kalinago were killed and they were forced into retreat. A few managed to escape over the mountains to the east while others fled to the north. The story goes that around 40 Kalinago reached the northern coast on a high rocky peninsula and, preferring death to enslavement or cruelty at the hands of their pursuers, they threw themselves down the cliff. The French named this place 'Le Morne des Sauteurs' (meaning 'Leapers' Hill'), which lives on in the present-day name of the town of Sauteurs.

To get there simply follow the signs from the main street to Leapers' Hill. It is on the western side of town near the St Patrick Roman Catholic church and school. There is an entrance fee of EC$5. This may also include a guided tour. Before paying, check to ensure the interpretation room is actually open, otherwise you will just be paying for a view of the southern Grenadines (and you can get an even better one of those along with a cold drink and a really nice roti at The Heights restaurant – see Where to Eat and Drink on page 178).

Leapers' Hill was developed as a tourist attraction by the Grenada Tourist Board and features on cruise-ship shore excursions. The interpretation room is very interesting and contains ceramic artefacts, basketwork and military paraphernalia. There is also a diorama depicting Kalinago village life based on European historical records and archaeological findings.

Beyond the exhibition room there is a paved path to a covered deck and viewing platform. If the plants and flowers have been pruned back enough, this is a nice place to relax, enjoy views of some of the islands to the south, and cool off in the refreshing sea breeze. A refreshments building, toilet facilities and souvenir shop are located up the steps. There is another viewpoint, this one with a map of the Grenada Grenadines and rocky dependencies to the south.

A tranquil spot with an inglorious legacy, Leapers' Hill is one of very few places remaining in Grenada where an insight into pre-Columbian history can be experienced.

Amerindian petroglyphs at Mt Rich and Duquesne
Petroglyphs are images that have been etched into rock and are found all around the world, created by many different people from a range of historical eras. Grenada's petroglyphs are believed to have been carved by the island's earliest Amerindian peoples and are found at several sites in the north. The best known are those at Duquesne and Mt Rich. Mt Rich is on the road between Sauteurs and Hermitage. The elaborate carvings appear to depict figures and faces, perhaps even monkeys which appear in ancient myths, though we can only speculate on their meaning. Most scholars believe the images relate to gods or mythical figures, and some speculate that, as many are discovered near water, they may perhaps have some symbolic meaning – perhaps during periods of drought.

The Mt Rich petroglyphs are carved on a large boulder now upturned at the bottom of a steep but narrow valley where the St Patrick River flows. There was once a viewing platform for the stone; actually there still is, but it is derelict and covered in graffiti. In fact it looks like a vandalised urban bus shelter. And it has no sign. It is hard to believe that such an important piece of Grenada's heritage appears to have been abandoned in this way. If you can find this structure, and if bamboo growth is not obscuring it, you may be able to see the boulder and make out some carvings, but it is a strain. Much better is to scramble down to it, but this is tricky and in all likelihood involves crossing private land. I discovered some roughly cut steps and a trail near a house to the left of the platform (the house was incomplete at the time of writing). It is a steep scramble to the bottom where there is a short trail that splits. Take the track to the right and then, as you face the river, step into it and walk right for about five minutes until you come to the boulder. The river is shallow, but you may have to negotiate fallen branches. You can't miss the boulder. The carvings are very impressive and it is awesome to witness something that was created such a long time ago, for reasons we do not understand, by the indigenous people who came to live here from the South American continent.

At the southern end of Duquesne Bay are more accessible examples of Grenada's Amerindian petroglyphs. Duquesne Bay is located on the west coast road to the north of Victoria, at the point where the road turns inland towards Sauteurs. Then simply walk on the beach and head left all the way to the rock face at the end. Again, the petroglyphs are not really well cared for. The basin in front of them is often full of rather smelly, stagnant water and rubbish. Nevertheless, these carvings are also impressive and definitely worth a visit.

Turtle-watching Each year between March and July, it is possible to see giant leatherback turtles (*Dermochelys coriacea*), the largest of all living sea turtles, return to Grenada to lay their clusters of eggs and then to see those eggs hatching. Some of Grenada's tour operators and conservation groups offer evening turtle-watching expeditions. (See page 88.)

Helvellyn Estate Pottery & Learning Centre (↘473 442 9252; e helvellynhouse@ spiceisle.com; ⊕ 09.00–17.00 Mon–Sat) The Helvellyn Estate Pottery & Learning Centre was set up in 2006 with the assistance of Moroccan expertise and training. Many of the pieces produced and sold here have a distinctly Moroccan influence but are also combined with local designs. The clay is a local blend, sourced from a number of places in the north and the east of the island.

Local people, schoolchildren and visitors are all invited to participate and try their hand at this difficult art form. Call or email for more information.

The pottery is located on the coastal road between Sauteurs and Levera. As you exit Sauteurs and come to the community of La Fortune, take a left at the junction. Keeping the sea to your left, follow the road for a short distance and look out for the pottery on the left-hand side.

The Morne Fendue Plantation House (↘ 473 442 9294; ⊕ daily; US$5pp) Originally a wooden chattel-style house, then reconstructed in 1908 by George Kent from cut stone and held together with a mortar made from powdered limestone and molasses, the great house at Morne Fendue has a very Scottish feel and is home to an interesting collection of historical artefacts as well as a restaurant and guesthouse. Never really a plantation house itself, the great house was the more convenient location for the management of five estates in the area. On the ground floor there is a museum collection of antique furniture, period costumes, artwork and a display dedicated to former owner Betty Mascoll, a Grenadian-born lady who

served in World War II and subsequently dedicated much of her life to community work as well as being a lifelong member of the International Red Cross. Betty was awarded an MBE and also the recipient of the Florence Nightingale Award. Upstairs there are five bedrooms and a bathroom, furnished in traditional Victorian style. The well-tended gardens at the rear of the house are very colourful and there are expansive views from the terrace of the restaurant, which serves traditional Caribbean fare by reservation.

To get to the Morne Fendue Plantation House from Sauteurs head south towards Grenville and you will reach it just a short distance out of the town. It is before you get to the junction for Morne Fendue village and will be on the right-hand side of the road. If you are travelling on foot then it is about a 20-minute walk out of Sauteurs. Alternatively take a number 9 bus.

WALKS, HIKES AND SCENIC DRIVES

Tufton Hall Waterfall This is an adventurous and technically challenging hike up the St Mark's River, through a picturesque valley between the coastal village of Victoria and the foothills of Mt St Catherine, to a cascading waterfall of around 25m in height. It takes 3–4 hours there and back and you have to negotiate your way over and around river rapids and fallen trees along the way. This hike is not for the faint-hearted, nor the inexperienced. You must hold your nerve and be bold in your approach as you make your way up the river. I recommend you hire a local guide if you can or contact some of the operators who offer hiking tours to see if they can help (see page 77), but you may find it quite difficult to get hold of people who have been here. It is not a mainstream hike. Whether with or without a guide don't attempt this hike in periods of heavy rain as this river is prone to flash flooding.

The trailhead is inland from the town of Victoria. Travelling by bus you need a number 5 marked Victoria and Sauteurs but be prepared for an hour-long walk from Victoria to the trailhead. Take the road that heads up the valley from the nutmeg receiving station in the centre of the town. Follow it past a school and uphill through the countryside. At the first fork, take the road to the right. Do the same again at the next fork a little higher up. Stop when you reach the water catchment facility.

Follow the wide track around the fence to the right of the facility and then along the river until it narrows. It is usually quite muddy. Although it can be a little overgrown, the route is obvious. Follow this track for around ten minutes or so until it comes to the riverbank. You should see two concrete weirs where steel pipes collect river water. Owing to hurricane damage and very little use, the hiking trail is very bad from this point. Not only is it completely overgrown, it sometimes disappears entirely. So the best trail becomes the river itself.

Take your time, follow the edges where possible and look ahead to plan your route. You must follow the river for somewhere between 60 and 90 minutes, depending on your pace. Don't rush, watch your step, and when you must cross the river or climb boulders, be sure of your footing and never, never jump. A slip here will mean a graze or a sprain at the very least, and this is not the kind of place where you have to be looking for medical attention.

The hike upriver is fabulous fun but it is really only for the fit and the adventurous. You will come across tall river rapids, deep pools and narrow channels, all of which you have to work your way past. Take care when climbing over fallen trees. Test them before giving them your weight as they may be loose or rotten. They will always be slippery. Keep pushing on until you reach a tall cliff face and the waterfall marking the end of your hike. Look up. You are actually quite close to Mt St Catherine.

Though Hurricane Ivan is clearly responsible for the poor condition of some of the island's hiking trails, the lack of investment (in terms of both time and money) in clearing and maintaining them also means that visitors interested in getting to sites that are off the beaten track have to work that bit harder. Two such places can be found in and around the Mt St Catherine National Park. They are Mt St Catherine itself and the Paraclete Falls. Many other interesting places exist in this area – hot springs in the heights above Tufton Hall Waterfall for example – but discovering them requires the assistance of local experts.

A knowledgeable local guide with a sharp machete for cutting back overgrown bush is essential on these hikes. In the village of Paraclete on the road between Hermitage and Grenville, you could ask for help getting to the Paraclete Falls. The best guide for Mt St Catherine is local hiking legend Telfor Bedeau (see page 77). Getting in touch with the Grenada Hash House Harriers (see page 75), or Philip at Petite Anse (see page 178) are also good options for more information, hiking companions, and perhaps some assistance. Both of the hikes to Mt St Catherine and the Paraclete Falls are great fun though challenging because of the condition of the routes. Properly developed trails in this region would certainly attract more hikers, and no doubt create some employment in communities that have suffered so much from the loss of their nutmeg crops. If hiking is your thing then I encourage you to help create that demand and opportunity by taking on some of these more difficult, yet very beautiful, challenges accompanied by good local guides.

THE SUMMIT OF MT ST CATHERINE Mt St Catherine is Grenada's tallest peak at 840m. There are several routes to the top but perhaps the most common trail starts in the hills above Blaize, off the narrow and extremely steep single-vehicle road that runs up to some telecommunications masts. The duration of this hike is about 4–5 hours there and back. The terrain is usually very muddy and steep.

On the northern outskirts of the village of Paraclete on the road between Hermitage and Grenville, there is a road made of two concrete vehicle tracks that runs steeply uphill towards a very appropriately named area called Hope.

Experienced mountaineers and hikers will tell you that most accidents occur on the return leg. So, though filled with exuberance and a sense of achievement, it is important that you maintain your concentration as you return downriver to the concrete weirs, the track and the start of the trail.

Sauteurs to Levera (and on to Bathway Beach)

Levera Beach can be accessed from either Bathway Beach or along the north coast from Sauteurs. The road from Sauteurs to Levera is a pleasant one-hour walk or a short drive. The road is paved for most of the journey but becomes a rough vehicle track as it approaches and descends to Levera Beach. If you are driving, you either need a 4x4 or you should park up and walk when it becomes rough.

Head east from Sauteurs and where the road curves south at La Fortune take a left turn by a stone building towards Helvellyn and Levera. Pass through the residential communities of La Fortune, Helvellyn and Levera (you should see the Helvellyn Estate Pottery on your left – see page 182) and continue all the way along this road until it peters out into a rough track. Pause halfway to look at the very unusual and unquestionably original artwork of Doliver Morain that may take you

Probably the steepest road you have ever driven, it eventually reaches a telecommunications tower. If the cloud ceiling is high enough, you are rewarded with tremendous views of the forest, the coast and Catherine herself.

One route to the top starts a little way down the road from the tower. It runs quite steeply downhill for a stretch and then follows a narrow ridge towards the mountain. From then on it is an uphill scramble all the way, slipping and sliding in the mud, and trying to find a tree or a plant that doesn't uproot in your hand when you grab on to it in hope and perhaps a little desperation. Actually it is not that bad, but it is certainly steep, always very muddy, and it is extremely strenuous. Be sure to take plenty of water and be prepared for bad weather. Pace yourself and cross your fingers for a clear view from the top.

THE PARACLETE FALLS There are two relatively unknown waterfalls hidden in the densely forested foothills of Mt St Catherine. One waterfall is around 20m tall but becomes more of a trickle during the dry season; the other is around 15m and is always full with a small pool beneath. The hike to these waterfalls is tough, along a track which is very steep and always muddy. Your guide will take you uphill from the village junction in Paraclete. You follow a paved road that soon becomes rough and uneven. From the village junction to the trailhead it will take around 30 minutes on foot or around ten minutes by 4x4 vehicle. Where the track splits, take the left-hand route and follow it until it narrows to a single path. The path winds sharply uphill and emerges on a narrow ridge. There are great views of the east coast down to Marquis Island and beyond.

You will pass through a nutmeg plantation that suffered at the hands of Hurricane Ivan. Follow the path down the side of a very steep ravine. It can be really muddy here with very few footholds and little to hang on to. Be careful or you could very easily find yourself careering uncontrollably downhill (like I did!).

The descent to the bottom of the narrow valley takes around 30 minutes (or about three if you lose control). Once there you will find it very wet underfoot. Walk a short distance upstream and you should come to the waterfalls.

a little by surprise along the roadside. His work depicts moments of Grenadian history and makes political and social commentary. Doliver also collects antiques and other curios.

Walk down the rough track which opens up into a small area of grassy pastureland where cows and horses graze. Walk along the grass through the volcanic rocks to the beach.

Enjoy a stroll along the beach, following it around the corner right to the end and the sign stating that the beach is a protected turtle nesting site. From here you can pick up a wide vehicle track that runs south of Bedford Point and the margins of Levera Pond before finally emerging at the northern end of Bathway Beach. It takes about 30 minutes on foot from Levera to Bathway and you pass the Levera Mangrove Wetland (see page 183) en route.

Levera Beach is a great place for a picnic. It is quiet and stunningly beautiful, particularly with the backdrop of **Sugar Loaf**, **Green** and **Sandy islands**. If you decide to bathe, take care as the sea can be choppy, there can be a strong undertow and in some places there are unpredictable cross-currents.

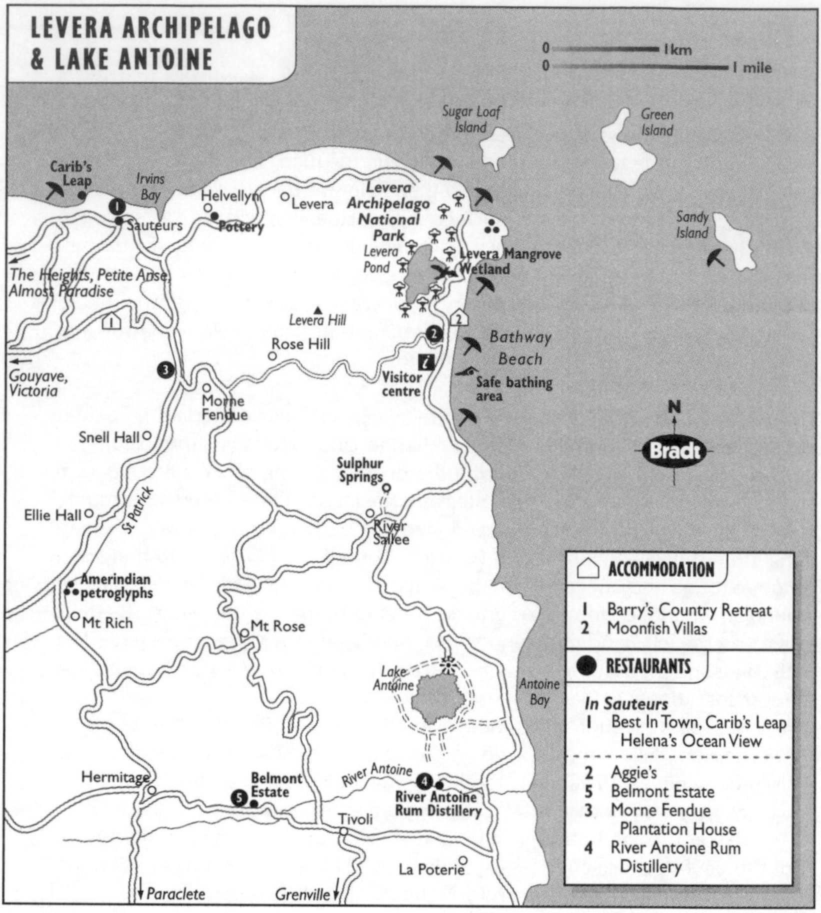
LEVERA ARCHIPELAGO & LAKE ANTOINE
0 1km
0 1 mile
Sugar Loaf Island
Green Island
Sandy Island
Carib's Leap
Irvins Bay
Sauteurs
Helvellyn
Pottery
Levera
Levera Archipelago National Park
Levera Pond
Levera Mangrove Wetland
The Heights, Petite Anse, Almost Paradise
Levera Hill
Rose Hill
Bathway Beach
Safe bathing area
Visitor centre
Gouyave, Victoria
Morne Fendue
Snell Hall
Sulphur Springs
Ellie Hall
St Patrick
River Sallee
Amerindian petroglyphs
Mt Rich
Mt Rose
Lake Antoine
Antoine Bay
Hermitage
Belmont Estate
River Antoine
River Antoine Rum Distillery
Tivoli
La Poterie
Paraclete
Grenville
N
Bradt
ACCOMMODATION
1 Barry's Country Retreat
2 Moonfish Villas
RESTAURANTS
In Sauteurs
1 Best In Town, Carib's Leap
Helena's Ocean View
2 Aggie's
5 Belmont Estate
3 Morne Fendue Plantation House
4 River Antoine Rum Distillery

Lake Antoine Lake Antoine is a 6.5ha crater lake located close to the northeast coast. The land around the lake is privately owned so the path is kept clear for three-quarters of the way thanks to the farmers who plant by the lake. Unfortunately there is a stretch where they do not plant or require access and this small arc has become very overgrown with dry, tall scrubland bush. Nevertheless, with some confidence and persistence it is passable and means you can walk in a complete loop around this pretty crater lake without having to retrace your steps. The lake is beautiful and serene and there is an abundance of wildlife; in particular lots of waterfowl can be seen and heard in and around the arum lilies that crowd the littoral margins. The hike all the way around the lake will take 60–90 minutes.

If you are driving to Lake Antoine, head south from Sauteurs towards Grenville and when you reach the Morne Fendue Plantation House, turn left at the next junction and pass through the village of Morne Fendue. At a roundabout, turn left to River Sallee and from there follow the signs to Lake Antoine. Once you reach the sign, follow it up a short hill where the road ends. There are no bus routes that pass Lake Antoine so if you are heading there under your own steam you will need to get to River Sallee by number 9 bus and either walk or hitch a ride from there.

As you face the lake, you should take the track on the right, walking around the lake in a counter-clockwise direction. The barrier is to prevent unauthorised vehicles from using the track. Follow this wide farm track downhill until you reach a fork. Take the least-used and more overgrown-looking track on the right. The track to the left goes down to farmlands and the lake margins. For a little while your view of the lake is obscured by trees but once you get past them the views are uninterrupted. The geological formation of the crater itself is also clear to see both in the lake and in its surrounding topography. You feel like you are inside a volcanic rim.

At the next trail junction, with a low concrete wall and gutter on your left, go straight on, now hiking uphill around the western margins of the lake. You will also notice that between you and the lake there is an area of dense banana plantation, which skirts the entire western shore. You may come across people working this area of farmland.

When you have been walking for around 30–45 minutes or so you will reach a junction of four paths. One route is a continuation of the vehicle track you are on and comes out onto the coastal road to the north of the River Antoine Estate, another vehicle track heads off to the right, and a narrow path disappears into the bush on the left. Take the bushy path on the left.

Have faith and follow this rather overgrown trail. The lake will be on your left-hand side (though you will not see much of it) and there is dry scrub woodland on your right. The trail is level for a stretch and then begins to climb for quite a distance. It levels out again and then descends. Once it flattens out you have about 10 more minutes to go. The woodland disappears and is replaced by tall grass and a few scattered 'jungle wrecks'. Take care where you tread around here and head for the wide road which will bring you back to the junction where you began your walk. You should have great views of the northeast coast, Green Island, Sandy Island and, off in the distance, the beautiful island of Carriacou.

198

Part Three

CARRIACOU AND PETITE MARTINIQUE

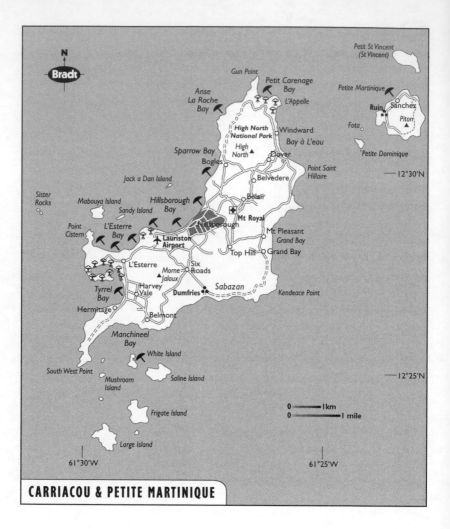

CARRIACOU & PETITE MARTINIQUE

9

Background Information

GEOGRAPHY

CARRIACOU Carriacou is located at 12°29'N, 61°27'W, some 37km north of Grenada. It is the largest of the Grenada Grenadines with an area of 34km². At its extremes it measures 11.3km by 4.8km.

Carriacou's main town is **Hillsborough**, which is on the central west coast on the fringes of a large bay. It is the island's administrative centre and one of two commercial ports. This is also where the high-speed Osprey ferry service between Grenada, Carriacou and Petite Martinique arrives and departs. Carriacou's main yacht anchorage, and second commercial port, is Tyrrel Bay, a natural horseshoe-shaped bay on the west coast.

Carriacou has an undulating coastline with a number of secluded bays, both white- and black-sand beaches, dramatic cliffs, rugged limestone and lava outcrops, mangrove forests, fossil beds and swamps. A broken ridge runs along the spine of the island with its two highest points being in the north and in the south. **High North** is 291m and **Morne Jaloux** (usually referred to as Chapeau Carré) is 290m. The interior is partially forested, and partially farmed. Farms tend to be smallholdings that support the needs of families and local communities rather than anything on a larger scale. This subsistence farming produces crops such as pigeon peas, beans, corn, cabbages and a variety of ground provisions. Common fruits grown in Carriacou include pawpaw (papaya), watermelon, grapefruit and pineapple.

Outside of Hillsborough, most communities are small villages linked by a simple road system, most of which is paved. In one or two areas, notably along the coast between **Mt Pleasant** and **Limlair**, the road is unpaved. At Lauriston Point, between Hillsborough and Tyrrel Bay, there is a small airstrip called Lauriston Airport where daily flights operate to and from Grenada.

PETITE MARTINIQUE Located approximately 5km to the northeast of Carriacou at 12°31'N and 61°23'W, Petite Martinique has an area of just 2km² and consists of a single peak, called **Piton**, which rises to 225m. Residents mainly live around the western and southern shorelines with the remainder of the island inhabited only by goats and cattle.

CLIMATE

Carriacou and Petite Martinique experience a similar climate to Grenada, though here there are no mountains and tropical forests to catch clouds and stimulate rains.

Water shortages can be a problem from time to time, particularly during the dry season (January to June). Most houses have a cistern that uses captured rainfall, which is usually safe to drink, though bottled water from the mainland is also widely available in shops and restaurants on both islands. Be prepared for the full force of the sun here. There is little shade and the dry season's sun can burn your skin very quickly. The wet season is between July and December. During this time the islands are much greener but are vulnerable to storms and heavy rainfall.

NATURAL HISTORY AND CONSERVATION

HABITATS, FLORA AND FAUNA The natural habitats of Carriacou and Petite Martinique are predominantly **coastal** or **dry scrub woodland** environments with semi-deciduous trees such as the white cedar (*Tabebuia heterophylla*), the campeche or dogwood (*Haematoxylum campechianum*), acacia (*Acacia*), black sage (*Cordia curassavica*) and the blackthorn (*Pisonia aculeata*). Along the littoral margins of beaches and bays you may see torchwood (*Jacquinia armillaris*), sea grape (*Coccoloba uvifera*), sea almond (*Terminalia catappa*), and plenty of manchineel (*Hippomane mancinella*) – see page 43. Carriacou has coastal **mangrove forests** and **oyster beds**. Here you will find black mangrove (*Avicennia germinans*), red mangrove (*Rhizophora mangle*), and a variety of crustacean and bird species.

Green iguana (*Iguana iguana*) are commonly seen in the dry forests of Carriacou and you may also come across the opossum, known locally as **manicou** (*Didelphis marsupialis insularis*). Though hunted for its meat on the main island, this interesting marsupial is largely left in peace here. If you are lucky, as I was, when out walking in the countryside, you may come across the very rare **red-legged tortoise** (*Geochelone carbonaria*) which is known locally as the morocoy. This creature was hunted almost to the point of extinction but has been bred in captivity and reintroduced to the wild. It seems to do well on Carriacou and the neighbouring Frigate Island.

The marine environment around Carriacou and its outlying islets is interesting, colourful and diverse. Healthy reef systems, both shallow and deep, attract lots of schooling fish, migratory pelagics, turtles, and other sea creatures, and they are adorned with a wide variety of hard and soft corals, sponges, and crinoids.

CONSERVATION Carriacou has a number of areas that have been designated national parks, protected seascapes or protected cultural landmarks. At the northern tip is the **High North National Park**, which covers the immediate forested area around High North peak as well as the coastline to the west and to the north. To the west of High North, Anse La Roche is one of the island's prettiest and most secluded bays. To the north is the L'Appelle mangrove forest and bird sanctuary, and beyond it Petit Carenage, a quite beautiful isolated bay and beach. In the centre of Carriacou is the **Belair Forest Reserve** (Belair Park). This area has a small, protected teak and mahogany forest and is where a well-preserved stone windmill tower can be found. Windmill ruins like this one are scattered all around Carriacou. They were once used as a means of harnessing wind power to run machinery that would crush sugarcane and squeeze limes. Unlike Grenada where rivers and waterwheels were used by sugar estates, this has never been an option on Carriacou and Petite Martinique.

The **Sandy Island/Oyster Bed Marine Protected Area** runs from the southern tip of Hillsborough Bay, around Lauriston Point and Point Cistern to the northern tip of Tyrrel Bay. It incorporates the mangrove swamps and oyster beds on the northern edge of Tyrrel Bay, the reef systems of Mabouya Island and Sandy Island off the west coast, and the mangrove swamps off Lauriston Point. These coastlines are home to a number of sea and shore birds such as tropicbirds, boobies, pelicans, oystercatchers, terns and frigatebirds.

HISTORY

The name Carriacou is thought to be derived from the original Amerindian name for the island, Cárou-cárou, whose meaning is 'land of reefs'. Archaeological studies and excavations have found lots of evidence to suggest that Carriacou was inhabited by Amerindians. The majority of finds have been along the windward coastlines of Grand Bay and Sabazan, reinforcing the theory that the island's original settlers would have lived primarily off the sea, though may have also undertaken some basic farming. Intricate pottery, tools, body stamps and *zemi* stones (see box, below) have also been unearthed. The Carriacou Museum in Hillsborough (see page 218) has a fine display of local Amerindian artefacts.

It is thought that European settlers did not arrive on Carriacou and Petite Martinique until the early 18th century. Their coming brought the establishment of estate lands and, with that, slave labour. The estates mainly produced cotton, sugar and limes. At the time the islands would have had a great deal of woodland but the need to grow crops resulted in a high level of deforestation, which in turn resulted in the loss of natural water catchments. Once the cotton and sugar industries fell into decline during the latter half of the 19th century following emancipation, estates were abandoned and former slaves who stayed there found themselves with little land, little water and very little opportunity. Many people left the island in search of a livelihood elsewhere.

As there were so many abandoned settlements, the people of Carriacou and Petite Martinique were able to purchase land quite cheaply from the government and so they began to survive on fishing, boatbuilding, smuggling and subsistence farming. The crops grown then reflect those still grown today, with pigeon peas, corn and ground provisions being the most common. Following the decline of the estates, smuggling became integral to the islands' economies – some say it still is – as islanders felt the squeeze of economic hardship setting in. Many islanders left Carriacou and Petite Martinique to seek employment abroad, particularly in the UK, and those who remained complained bitterly that they were being neglected by mainland Grenada. Indeed the perceived lack of interest and investment in both

Background Information HISTORY

ZEMI STONES

Associated with Amerindian spirit worship, *zemis* or zemi stones are sculpted objects or idols that are believed to either symbolise or be inherently endowed with a supernatural power. Sometimes carved from wood or conch shell, though usually from stone, zemis have been unearthed at archaeological sites throughout the Caribbean and there are records of them even being presented to newly arrived Europeans. A common form of zemi is the three-pointed stone version which is believed by some academics to represent the volcanic islands of the Caribbean and their intrinsic nature spirits. You can see examples of these symbolic zemis at the Grenada Museum in St George's (see page 101) as well as at the Carriacou Museum in Hillsborough (see page 218).

9

islands remains a fiercely debated topic even today, though the talk of secession that surfaced in the 1990s appears to have waned.

Lauriston Airport was constructed on Carriacou in 1968 and was upgraded in 1994. It is a small airfield capable of accommodating light aircraft only. In 1997, the government appointed a minister for Carriacou and Petite Martinique Affairs, who is permanently resident on Carriacou.

CARRIACOU AND PETITE MARTINIQUE TODAY

Today the islands are very popular with sailing enthusiasts and travellers looking for an interesting destination that is still somewhat off the beaten path. Though some have returned from overseas to retire, many young Carriacouans who have an opportunity to leave and seek their fortune elsewhere will usually take it. Ironically the woodland that was once cut down to grow crops is now once again returning to bush as farming lots and former estate lands outnumber the people willing and able to work them.

Carriacou and Petite Martinique have a very rural feel and the simple life of boatbuilding, fishing and farming has a beguiling allure to those looking for a lifestyle change. As is the case in Grenada, overseas investors are building properties as homes, holiday lets or a combination of both. Communities such as Harvey Vale and Craigston, as well as those with a heritage of European settlers such as Windward, have developed as hideaways for seekers of alternative lifestyles or for those just looking for a little sun, sea, peace and quiet. Carriacou's beautiful white-sand beaches are a draw for day trippers on holiday in Grenada, and the annual Carriacou Regatta attracts sailing enthusiasts from all over the world.

PEOPLE

Carriacou has a population of around 6,000 and, as in Grenada, English is the official language. The people of Carriacou are officially referred to as Carriacouans but are more commonly known as **Kayacs**. They are a very friendly people with a strong cultural identity that has been shaped in a distinctly different manner from their compatriots on mainland Grenada. They have an important heritage, which is preserved today in the shape of feasts (known locally as *saracas*), music, celebrations, workmanship and folklore. **Petite Martinique** has a population of fewer than 1,000. Most people make a living from fishing, boatbuilding, and subsistence farming.

CULTURE

BOATBUILDING Both Carriacou and Petite Martinique have a strong maritime history of boatbuilding. In Carriacou this activity is very firmly centred on the

---

CROMANTIE CUDJOE

According to legend, Cromantie Cudjoe was a slave who fought against the British during the Fédon Rebellion (see page 142) and then escaped by swimming to Carriacou. He has become a symbol of rebellious spirit whose life story is one of myth and speculation. Whatever the truth, he is considered an ancestral spirit of Carriacou and, as he was also an accomplished drummer, a song is usually sung in his honour during Big Drum Dance (see page 206).

Word spreads very quickly around Carriacou and Petite Martinique about a forthcoming boat-launching. They are very popular events and can draw quite a crowd. In Carriacou, boat-launchings usually take place in the small coastal hamlet of Windward and on launch day it becomes a hive of activity. Ground provisions, meats and traditional *cou-cou* are prepared in big, heavy pots that are heated over several open fires near the boat-launching area. A makeshift bar materialises and drinks are handed out to both spectators and those helping with the launch itself. The boat to be launched stands close to the shoreline, facing the sea. It is held up by wooden props on either side and beneath it are heavy timber poles that will serve as rollers. A line is attached to the keel and tied to a securing post behind the boat, ensuring that when the wooden supports are removed, the boat does not slide out of control down to the sea.

Occasionally prayers are said and a priest blesses the boat with holy water. Usually the owner will splash rum and water on the ground around his boat. Sometimes rice is also scattered about. Music accompanies the event. From time to time this may be in the form of drumming, but more often is in the shape of traditional sea shanties that are sung next to the boat, and accompanied by guitars and fiddles. Next comes 'cutting down', the process by which the boat is carefully laid on its side on the rollers. In a synchronised effort, the supporting poles are cut, with very sharp axes, at their base. By doing so, each pole gets shorter and shorter and the boat begins to lean over to one side. If this is done properly, the boat comes gently to rest on the heavy wooden rollers ready for the next stage. It is an intense, exciting and very atmospheric activity with both spectators and master boatbuilder yelling out instructions at the tops of their voices.

The finale is the launch itself. With a combination of ropes and sheer brute force, the boat is eased down the rollers towards the sea. Hopefully the boat reaches the water and floats upright in all its majesty. Whatever the outcome, food is enjoyed and drinks flow from dawn until dusk when the revellers finally make their way home again.

community of Windward on the island's northeast coast. In Petite Martinique, you will see boats being built along the shore at Sanchez. Scottish shipbuilders were some of the earliest European settlers in this area and they began establishing a boatbuilding industry on the islands in the 1830s. At first these were small wooden sailing boats that were used primarily for fishing, but this soon turned into the construction of larger wooden trading schooners and sloops. Though the tradition of boatbuilding still lives on in Windward and on Petite Martinique, during the height of the boatbuilding industry, between the 1830s and the mid 1900s, boats were being made by master craftsmen all over the island. It is recorded that in 1929 alone a total of 129 trading sloops and schooners were constructed and launched by the boatbuilders of Carriacou. From the mid 1900s it became more and more common for boats to be made from steel and, as a result, the traditional wooden boatbuilding industry of Carriacou and Petite Martinique fell into a period of decline.

Today, many have returned and, thanks to a revival of the craft and the establishment of the annual Carriacou Workboat Regatta, the tradition of boatbuilding is alive and well again. Master boatbuilders and their willing and enthusiastic young apprentices work on the construction of traditional wooden schooners and sloops for all kinds of customers, from both home and abroad. If you are very lucky, your visit to Carriacou and Petite Martinique may coincide with a traditional boat-launching ceremony.

BIG DRUM DANCE Big Drum Dance is a cultural celebration that consists of dancing, singing and drumming. It is thought that the west African slaves who were transported to the islands in the 1700s somehow managed to keep their heritage alive through folktales, stories, music and song. Drumming played a significant role among these African tribal people and was very prominent during weddings, feasts, prayer, harvest, birth and death. The Big Drum Dance is a manifestation of the past and is now not only a key feature of Carriacou's cultural legacy, but also very much an integral part of everyday life on the island. Why drumming survived so well in Carriacou and not in Grenada is a puzzle. Perhaps it is because the drums that were made and played by slaves were also routinely taken away from them, or banned, as part of their owners' efforts to crush their spirit and identity.

The drums, collectively known as *lapeau cabrit*, which is Creole for goatskin, were originally made from carved wood, but were later more commonly made from small rum barrels. Traditionally three drums are used. The centre drum, and the most important of the three, is called the **cot drum** and is traditionally made with the skin of a young ewe goat to produce a higher note. A piece of cotton thread with three or four straight pins is attached to the top of the drum to add a unique sound. Always standing upright in the centre of the group, the cot drum is responsible for leading the rhythm and requires a skilled and experienced player. The two drums to each side of the cot drum are known as the **bula drums** and are tilted and played between the knees. The bula drums are traditionally made from the skins of ram goats and are also sometimes known as *babble* or *fule* drums. The singing style of the Big Drum Dance usually follows a traditional call-and-response pattern with songs that, though often sung in Creole, speak of a home in Africa; they lament families that have been separated, and tell of a longing to be free. The dances that accompany the drumming and the singing also originate in Africa though they too have a strong Creole influence, as do the costumes of the dancers. There are dances and songs performed to heal sickness, to appease gods, to pray for good harvests, to pray for rain during the planting season, to symbolise the union of a man and woman, or to give thanks for good crops.

If you are fortunate enough to see a Big Drum Dance during your visit to Carriacou, you will be immediately struck by how much more African, rather than

Creole or Caribbean, the celebration actually is. The music, the singing, the dance and the drums themselves will transport you into the past, to a dark time, when people were plucked from their homes in Africa and brought to these islands where they were forced to spend generations enslaved. It is a very spiritual experience.

PARANG *Parang* is a form of Latin American music that is thought to have arrived in Grenada from Trinidad. A typical parang music ensemble usually consists of string instruments, drum and percussion which accompany a singer. The song is usually about someone well known, perhaps a politician or a person from the local community, and it tells a funny story, or perhaps a scandal or a rumour about that person. It can be a rather lively and raucous occasion. Grenada's most popular *parang* takes place in Carriacou at Christmas time.

KALENDA *Kalenda* is a stick-fighting dance thought to have its roots in tribal traditions of west Africa. It is a combination of dance and martial art that became popular at carnival time in the West Indies. Though far less common now, in the main because of its innate danger and risk of serious injury, on occasion it is still possible to see it performed by the *paywo* (clown) at the Carriacou Carnival in February. Two contestants square up, each wielding a metre-long stick which they use to try to either knock their opponent to the ground, or draw blood. The dance (or fight, depending on how you view it) is accompanied by drumming and singing. Kalenda is frequently banned because of concerns over its violence and is no longer allowed during the Grenada Carnival in August.

MAROON FESTIVAL The Maroon Festival, though recently revived as a large annual event, is also a festivity held in villages and communities across Carriacou. Traditionally each 'maroon' was held to give thanks for a bountiful harvest or to pray for one, along with rains, in advance of a forthcoming planting season. Villagers prepare food, commonly referred to as *saraca*, which usually consists of smoked meats, *cou-cou*, rice and peas. At around dusk, the eating and drinking starts and is followed by the traditional 'wetting of the ring', when rum and water are splashed on the ground where the dancing is to take place. By the time the sun has set, the singing begins, accompanied by Big Drum music and traditional dancing which includes the Cromantin dance, the Mandingo dance, the Arada, and the Congo. As it is associated with crops, plantings and harvest, it is commonly said that whenever there is a maroon, 'rain will soon fall'.

If you are planning a stay in Carriacou be sure to ask your hotel if there are any forthcoming village maroon festivals. Often maroons will take place as part of annual village feasts in communities such as Bogles, Mt Pleasant, Grand Bay and Harvey Vale. The annual Carriacou Maroon & String Band Music Festival takes place at the village of Mt Pleasant, Paradise Beach, and the Belair Heritage Park. For more information visit www.carriacoumaroon.com.

PARENTS' PLATE

The parents' plate is a food offering to ancestral spirits that is common at many traditional ceremonies. You may see it at a boat-launching, at a maroon, and certainly at a tombstone feast. Food from the feast, or saraca, is placed on a plate that rests on a white tablecloth with a candle. After midnight, the spirits having had their fill, the plate is removed and people eat from it.

TOMBSTONE FEAST Perhaps one of the islands' most haunting ceremonies is the Tombstone Feast, which takes place on the first anniversary of a burial. Up to this point there would have been no headstone placed on the grave or tomb of the deceased. Instead it is prepared one year later by a stonemason and then carried in a ceremony to the house where the death took place. Traditionally, the tombstone is placed on a bed and covered with a white sheet. The relatives of the deceased gather together and 'wet the ground' by sprinkling rum and water around it. They then speak to the deceased who, it is believed, is now visiting with them, and they also offer their prayers. The headstone is then taken to the cemetery where it is fitted to the body of the tomb. Occasionally the stone slides into a special opening on the end of the tomb, rather than standing upright upon it. More rum and water are sprinkled around the tomb and sometimes an egg is broken to symbolise a new beginning of welfare and prosperity for the surviving family. The following day there is a feast, or *saraca*, accompanied by dancing, singing and Big Drum.

10

The Islands

It is sometimes said that the islands that make up the southern Grenadines have far more in common with each other than they do with either St Vincent or Grenada. I sympathise with that sentiment. But whether true or not, there is definitely a sense of independence here, a collective indifference to the affairs of the world beyond their shores, indeed an almost palpable feeling of existing in the only space that really matters. When talking to those who were born here, who live and work here, or who have arrived by sailing boat and, for one reason or another, have found it difficult to leave, you get the distinct impression that if the islands were cut adrift from their respective nations, life would simply carry on as it always has done.

Carriacou is an island of outstanding natural beauty and rich cultural heritage. As well as perfect white-sand beaches, it has a forest reserve, protected mangrove forests and oyster beds, pristine coral reefs and a large natural anchorage. The traditions of Big Drum Dance, Maroon Festival and Tombstone Feast are vivid reflections of an African heritage that not only survives but is still an integral part of life. Carriacou sloops are famous throughout the worldwide sailing community and are part of a boatbuilding tradition that was born in Scotland, handed down through generations, and is still very much alive today. You could stroll around the hillsides of Carriacou in search of estate and windmill ruins, passing by fields of corn and pigeon peas, perhaps taking time to enjoy some great seafood or the taste of a traditional *coucou* along the way. There is a charm and magic to this tranquil island and everyone visiting Grenada should try to make it here for at least a few days.

Petite Martinique is a very small, yet pretty island of rugged coastlines around a single peak, sleepy communities, fishermen, subsistence farmers and boatbuilders. It feels away from it all, a place where life has slowed down and day-to-day living is hard work, but uncomplicated. People seem to just get on with it, plying their hand-crafted wooden boats between the islands of the southern Grenadines, making a living however they can. Visitors to Petite Martinique will discover lovely people and lots of peace and quiet.

GETTING THERE

CARRIACOU BY AIR

SVG Air ☎473 444 3549 & 473 444 1475; e info@svgair.com/cayak@spiceisle.com; www.svgair.com. SVG Air offers a very quick & convenient way to get to & from Carriacou from Grenada. Scheduled flights operate daily & are inexpensive. Check website for schedules & fares. The flight time is about 20 minutes.

CARRIACOU BY FERRY AND MAIL BOAT

Osprey Lines ☎473 440 8126; www.ospreylines. com. Osprey Lines operates a high-speed ferry service between Grenada, Carriacou and Petite Martinique. From St George's the ferry arrives and departs from the jetty opposite the fire station on the Carenage. You can buy your ticket as you board. The journey takes about 90 minutes. Fares are around EC$160 or US$62 for an adult return. Check the website or call for the latest schedule and ticket prices.

Mail boat The mail boat is a cheap way to travel between Grenada and Carriacou. The journey time is somewhere between 3 to 4 hours and the price as low as EC$25pp each way. Catch the mail boat from St George's Carenage on Tue, Wed, Fri & Sat at 10.00 and from Hillsborough jetty on Mon, Wed, Thu & Sun at 14.00.

PETITE MARTINIQUE BY FERRY The Osprey Lines ferry leaves Carriacou from the Hillsborough jetty. The crossing to Petite Martinique takes about 20 minutes – though unloading and loading can be painfully slow and increase journey time. You can buy your ticket either in advance or as you board. From Petite Martinique the ferry leaves from the jetty at Sanchez to Hillsborough. Fares between Carriacou and Petite Martinique are around EC$60 or US$24 for an adult return. Check the website for latest schedule and ticket prices.

The Osprey Lines office in Carriacou is located on Patterson Street next to the Carriacou Museum. It opens from 10.00 Monday to Friday. Just a word of warning; the service between Carriacou and Petite Martinique sometimes runs late, or the service runs smaller boats instead of the larger catamaran. If you are planning on a day trip, you have a short stay even if the ferry runs on time – just three hours or so. A late service will really eat into your time there. Consider either staying overnight on Petite Martinique or just buying your ticket on the day, from the boat itself, rather than in advance. Osprey Lines does not refund tickets.

PETITE MARTINIQUE BY WATER TAXI Negotiate a deal with a fisherman/water taxi operator in Windward, Dover and Sanchez and travel between Carriacou and Petite Martinique at your own convenience. It can be a little wet, occasionally nerve-wracking in choppy seas, but it is one of those episodes you will probably talk about long after your holiday is over. You could ask local boat owners on the coast in Dover, Windward or Sanchez for prices, or check with your hotel.

GETTING AROUND

The most fun and interesting way to explore Carriacou is on foot and by bus. Combining walking with using local transportation will get you into the heart of this pretty island as well as give you plenty of opportunities to meet and chat with its very friendly residents. Car rental is also a possibility and will certainly suit those who are only on the island for a short time.

There is really only one way to get around Petite Martinique, and that is on foot. You will see people using quad bikes and golf carts, however. You could try thumbing a ride!

CARRIACOU BY RENTAL CAR Car rental is available from a number of operators (see page 54). Hotels and guesthouses either have their own small fleet or can arrange car rental for you. In order to rent a car you must purchase a visitor's licence from the police station. It costs EC$30 and you will be asked to present your domestic driving licence. Car rental prices are usually anywhere between EC$100 and EC$140 per day. If hiring a car, you should note that the petrol station on Patterson Street in Hillsborough is currently the only one on the island.

CARRIACOU BY BUS In Carriacou buses follow a similar system to mainland Grenada, with numbers and designated routes starting and finishing from the terminus in Hillsborough. Buses are small minibuses, the same as on mainland Grenada, and

Number 10: Lauriston, L'Esterre, Harvey Vale & Tyrrel Bay, Belmont
Number 11: Bogles, Dover, Windward
Number 12: Top Hill, Mt Pleasant, Grand Bay

usually have the driver's nickname or motto displayed prominently on the windscreen. Registration plates begin with the letter H and each driver carries an official ID.

Bus fares are very affordable. Most journeys from Hillsborough to anywhere on the island cost around EC$3.50–5. So long as you don't mind waiting for one, buses are a great way to experience real island life and you are sure to meet some interesting and friendly people on your journey. To catch a bus, just go to the terminus in Hillsborough, wait at a bus stop, or by the side of the road, preferably in the shade, and flag one down.

CARRIACOU BY TAXI Private taxis can be hired outside the jetty in Hillsborough or at Lauriston Airport. You can usually pick up a recommendation and contact number from the place you are staying. Here are some examples of taxi fares from Hillsborough: Lauriston Airport EC$20; Harvey Vale EC$35; Petite Carenage EC$40; Windward EC$35.

You can also charter a taxi for a Carriacou tour if your time is very limited. Typically a 2½-hour 'full tour' of Carriacou will cost around EC$200.

WHERE TO STAY

Visitors to Carriacou have a number of accommodation options – probably far more than you would expect. Petite Martinique, on the other hand, has a very limited selection of places to stay.

If you are interested in renting a self-catering villa on Carriacou, there are quite a number of private properties in the Craigston area that people have built and rent out as holiday homes. A small selection are described briefly within the listings below, but Down Island Ltd (*www.islandvillas.com*) has many more. See page 57 for price codes.

CARRIACOU HOTELS AND GUESTHOUSES

Green Roof Inn (5 rooms, 1 cottage) Beauséjour; \/f 473 443 6399; e info@greenroofinn.com; www.greenroofinn. com. Very pleasant inn accommodation with sea & garden views. Each room has bathroom, fans, mosquito nets & veranda. The more private cottage is located within the gardens & comes equipped with bathroom, kitchenette, mosquito net, fan & veranda. Open restaurant & bar with great sea views, serving local & international cuisine. Friendly & comfortable inn with a good reputation. B/fast incl. **$–$$**

Hotel Laurena (26 rooms & apts) Hillsborough; \473 443 8759; www. hotellaurena.com. Large, functional hotel located in Hillsborough. A choice of standard guest

rooms, deluxe suites, or self-contained apts, all with private bathroom, veranda, AC, TV & internet. Apts have a kitchenette. Facilities include fitness centre & restaurant Deluxe suites have jacuzzi tub. Prices seasonal. **$–$$**

Carriacou Grand View Hotel (14 rooms & apts) Beauséjour; \473 443 6348; e info@carriacougrandview.com; www. carriacougrandview.com. Apt hotel located in the hillside behind Hillsborough. Rooms have private bathroom, TV, AC or fan, & balcony. Apt rooms also have a kitchenette. The hotel has a swimming pool, restaurant & bar & forest & ocean views. **$**

Millie's Apartments & Guest Rooms (10 rooms) Main St, Hillsborough; \473 443 7310; e millies@spiceisle.com. Budget accommodation located on the edge of town, offers rooms & apts with private bathrooms. Apts have SC facilities. **$**

The Islands   WHERE TO STAY

10

⌂ **John's Unique Resort** (17 rooms & apts) Hillsborough; ✆ 473 443 8346; f 473 443 8345; e junique@caribsurf.com; www. johnsuniqueresort.com. Budget accommodation located close to the main town. Spacious rooms have private bathroom, TV, fans or AC, private verandas. Apts also have kitchenettes. Restaurant & bar serves local & international food. **$**

⌂ **Kim's Plaza Guesthouse** Church St, Hillsborough; ✆ 473 443 7733; www. kimsplazaguesthouse.com. Basic, but clean & comfortable budget accommodation in the heart of Hillsborough. Rooms have private bathroom, AC, TV. Some have balconies. **$**

⌂ **Sunset Beach Hotel** (7 rooms) L'Esterre; ✆ 473 443 8406; f 473 404 3976; email: sunset-beach-hotel@gmail.com; www.sunset-beach-hotel.com. Located right on Paradise Beach offering very affordable rooms with private bathrooms & ceiling fans that would suit groups of friends or families. The beach bar & restaurant serves b/fast, lunch & dinner daily. **$**

PETITE MARTINIQUE HOTELS AND GUEST HOUSES

⌂ **Melodies Guest House** (10 rooms) Paradise, Petite Martinique; ✆ 473 443 9052; e melodies@caribsurf.com; www.spiceisle.com/melodies. Located on the shoreline, just a few mins from the jetty, basic but clean upper-floor rooms with private bathroom, 4 with veranda & sea view. Ground-floor restaurant & bar. **$**

⌂ **Millennium Connection Guest House** (4 rooms) Sanchez, Petite Martinique; ✆ 473 443 9243; e ieshaodinga@yahoo.co.uk; www.petitemartinique.com/millennium_guest_house.htm. Simple family run guesthouse. One room has private bathroom, the others are shared. Communal lounge & dining. **$**

CARRIACOU SELF-CATERING COTTAGES AND VILLAS

⌂ **Las Tortugas** (2 bedrooms) L'Esterre; e info@lastortugasvillas.com; www. lastortugasvillas.com. Attractive & colourful, private & very spacious villa nestled on a hillside with great views of Paradise Beach. 2 bedrooms with en-suite bathrooms & AC, living & dining area, fully equipped kitchen, recreation room with TV, large veranda & sun deck with infinity swimming pool. Good option for families. **$$$$$**

⌂ **Villa Sankofa** (3 bedrooms) Craigston; ✆ 310 472 2343; e villasankofa@gmail.com; www.sankofainternational.com. Secluded 2-storey villa with contemporary design offers luxurious self-contained accommodation with sea views. En-suite bedrooms, mosquito nets, kitchen, ceiling fan, large living area & veranda. Beach access. Romantic, self-indulgent tropical hideaway. **$$$$$**

⌂ **Tamarind Cottage** (1 cottage) Upper Craigston, Carriacou; e bookings@islandtrees. com; www.islandtrees.com. Self-contained 1-bedroom cottage located in peaceful hillside surroundings with ocean views. The cottage has living area, Wi-Fi, fully equipped kitchen, bathroom, fans, outdoor shower & patios. Price inc jeep hire & jetty or airport transfers. **$$$**

⌂ **Goyaba** (3 bedrooms) Craigston; ✆ 473 443 8182; e islander@islandvillas.com; www.islandvillas.com/villas/goyaba.htm. Master bed has private bathroom, other 2 share. Open-plan living area, kitchen, ceiling fans, large veranda & gardens. Easy access to beach. **$$$**

⌂ **Driftwood** (2 bedrooms) Craigston; ✆ 473 443 8182; e islander@islandvillas.com; www.islandvillas.com/villas/drift.htm. 2-bedroom 2-storey villa on with sea views. En-suite bathrooms, mosquito nets, ceiling fans, open-plan living area & kitchen, verandas. **$$$**

⌂ **Yellow Bird** (2 bedrooms) Craigston; ✆ 473 443 8182; e islander@islandvillas.com; www.islandvillas.com/villas/yellow.htm. Compact cottage with sea views includes living area, kitchen, ceiling fans & veranda. **$$$**

⌂ **Seaclusion Suites** (2 suites) L'Esterre; ✆ 473 407 2779: e bob@seaclusionsuites.com; www.seaclusionsuites.com. 2 1-bedroom, fully furnished SC suites with bathroom, kitchen, b/fast bar, & private veranda with great views of L'Esterre Bay & Sandy Island. **$$**

⌂ **Belair Garden Cottage** (1 cottage) Belair; ✆ 473 443 6221; e info@belairgardencottage. com; www.belairgardencottage.com. Located high in Belair near windmill ruins & teak forest, beautifully designed, quaint & very private cottage with fully equipped kitchenette, bathroom, outdoor shower & large wooden deck with hammock & great views of Petite Martinique & the southern Grenadines. Homemade breads, cakes & boxed lunches prepared by the very friendly accommodation owners on request. Complimentary mobile phone & Wi-Fi. Highly recommended. **$$**

🏠 **KIDO Ecological Research Station** Prospect; ☎473 443 7936; e marina.fastigi@gmail.com; www.kido-projects.com. Located alongside the High North National Park, KIDO offers accommodation designed for ecologists, researchers or students. The villa has 2 bedrooms, bathroom, living area, veranda, reading room. The Pagoda sleeps up to 10 & is ideal for student groups. It has 2 bathrooms & a communal kitchenette. The Octopus has a master bedroom & twin-bed anteroom, private bathroom, kitchenette & patio. Meals prepared on request. Ecotours offered. **$$**

🏠 **Honor & Paul's Apartment** (3 beds) Calabash Gardens, Cherry Hill; ☎473 443 8524; e henry.john@spiceisle.com. Comfortable & modern SC accommodation with great sea views. Apartment has 3 beds, bathroom, lounge & dining area, fully equipped kitchen & wrap-around balcony. **$–$$**

🏠 **Bayaleau Point Cottages** (4 cottages) Windward; ☎/f 473 443 7984; e goldhill@spiceisle.com; www.carriacoucottages.com. Very cosy self-contained wooden cottages with private bathroom facilities, kitchenette, mosquito nets, hammocks, verandas & sea views. Seaside deck offers local & international dinners. *Mostly Harmless* motor launch offers cruising, picnic & snorkelling trips. **$–$$**

🏠 **Palm Trees** (1 cottage) Craigston; ☎473 443 8182; e islander@islandvillas.com; www.islandvillas.com/villas/palmtree.htm. 1-bedroom wooden cottage with nice sea views. Accommodation has master bedroom, mosquito nets, bathroom, kitchen & living areas, spacious verandas. Small bedroom with sgl bed also available. **$**

🏠 **Bogles Round House** (3 cottages) Bogles, Carriacou; ☎/f 473 443 7841; e info@boglesroundhouse.com; www.boglesroundhouse.com. Rustic cottages located in the village of Bogles to the north of Hillsborough. Self-contained units have bathroom, kitchenette, mosquito net, fan & veranda. Mango & Plum cottages sleep 2 people, Lime Cottage sleeps 3–4. Garden has access to the secluded beach at Sparrow Bay. The unique Round House Restaurant is noted for its gourmet dining. **$**

🏠 **Ade's Dream Apartment Hotel** (23 rooms) Main St, Hillsborough; ☎473 443 7317; e adesdea@spiceisle.com; www.adesdream.com. Budget accommodation located on Hillsborough's Main St with studio & economy rooms with private bathroom, kitchenette, TV, AC, Wi-Fi & private veranda. Kitchen facilities for economy rooms are shared. Studio rooms face the sea. Supermarket downstairs, car rental also available. **$**

🏠 **Sand X Beach House** (2 apts) Hillsborough Bay; ☎473 443 8382; e sunkeywp@yahoo.com; www.grenadaexplorer.com/sandx. Located on the airport road, just beyond the St Patrick Catholic Church, on the southern outskirts of Hillsborough. Two fully equipped 2-bed apartments with kitchen, lounge, TV & Wi-Fi. Garden backs on to beach. Owner offers inclusive car rental package & long-term rental deals. **$**

🏠 **Scraper's Bayview Cottages** Tyrrel Bay; ☎473 443 7403; e scrapers@spiceisle.com. Simple wooden cottage accommodation with private bathroom & kitchenette. Scraper's Restaurant serves local & international cooking. **$**

🏠 **Hope's Inn** (6 rooms, 1 apt) Paradise Beach, L'Esterre; ☎473 443 7457. Located right on the beach, 6 upper-floor rooms with shared kitchenettes, bathrooms & balcony. **$**

PETITE MARTINIQUE SELF-CATERING APARTMENTS

Palm Beach Guest House (2 apts) Sanchez; ☎473 443 9103; e Emmanuel.palmbeach@gmail.com; www.petitemartinique.com/palmbeachguesthouse.html. Spacious & affordable apts. One has 3 beds, the other has 1 bed. Both apts have private bathrooms & kitchens, TV & terrace. **$**

✕ WHERE TO EAT AND DRINK

There are some really good places to eat in Carriacou with a varied selection of both international and Caribbean cooking styles. Most restaurants are open Monday to Saturday, some prefer you to call in advance for dinner. Needless to say, because of its diminutive size, dining options are quite limited on Petite Martinique.

CARRIACOU
Hillsborough, Beauséjour and Bogles

✘ **Bogles Round House** Bogles; ☏473 443 7841; closed Wed. Much lauded gourmet cuisine by award-winning chef, Roxanne. Lunch by reservation only, dinner reservations advised. Recommended. $$

✘ **Green Roof Inn** Beauséjour; ☏473 443 6399; closed Mon. Noted local & international dining with pleasant ambience & sea views. Dinner reservations advised. $$

✘ **Kayak Kafee** Hillsborough; ☏473 406 2151 & 473 404 6808; ☉ daily. Popular for coffee, b/fast, lunch & dinner. Try one of Gabriel's smoothies. $–$$

✘ **Seawave** Main St, Hillsborough; ☏473 443 7317; ☉ daily. Pleasant waterside bar & restaurant located opposite Ade's Dream, serving a good selection of affordable local & international dishes. $–$$

✘ **La Playa** Hillsborough; closed Thu. Fun, affordable eatery on the beach at the end of the northern seawall. Follow a trail behind the Jam Rock fruit & veg stand for about 50m. Serves burgers, BBQ, fish & lobster. $–$$

✘ **Laurena II Restaurant & Bar** Main St, Hillsborough; ☏473 443 8333; closed Sun. Excellent value local lunches & dinners for budget travellers. $

✘ **Sandy Lane Bar** Hillsborough; ☏473 443 7440; located out of town on the airport road. Serves chicken & fries on picnic tables by the beach. $

Paradise, Tyrrel Bay and Belmont

✘ **Lazy Turtle Pizzeria** Tyrrel Bay; ☏473 443 8322. Popular with visiting 'yachties' & locals. Pizza & pasta dinners served waterside. Occasional live music, always a good ambience. $$

✘ **Slipway Restaurant** Hermitage, Tyrrel Bay;

☏473 443 6500. Closed Sun evening & Mon. Excellent lunches & dinners served waterside in a unique & friendly restaurant. Dinner reservations advised. Recommended. $$

✘ **Lambie Queen Restaurant & Bar** Tyrrel Bay; ☏473 443 8162. Popular bar & eatery along the shore, serving local & international dishes. Lambie is a speciality. $–$$

✘ **Scraper's Restaurant & Bar** Tyrrel Bay; ☏473 443 7403. Popular eatery serving local & international dishes on the shoreline. $–$$

✘ **Hardwood Restaurant & Bar** Paradise Beach; ☏473 443 6839. Right on the beach, bar & restaurant serving local dishes & drinks. Lobster & lambie are specialities. $–$$

✘ **Sunset Beach Bar & Restaurant** Paradise Beach; ☏473 443 8406. Good value local & international food on Paradise Beach. $–$$

✘ **Off The Hook** Paradise Beach. Bar & grill serving drinks, local cooking & BBQ. Good beach vibes. $

✘ **Old Rum Shop** Tyrrel Bay; ☏473 443 7350. Long-established, rustic bar & eatery serving home-cooked local food & BBQ. $

✘ **Banana Joe's** Paradise Beach. Driftwood bar located on the beach serving welcome refreshments. $

✘ **Cow Foot Inn** Belmont; ☏473 443 8766. Located between Belmont & Six Roads, local eatery where Theresa offers roti, rotisserie chicken & traditional lunches. $

PETITE MARTINIQUE

✘ **Palm Beach Restaurant** Paradise; ☏473 443 9103. Bar & restaurant next to the beach serving local & international dishes. A good place to hang out while you are waiting for the Osprey back to Carriacou. $–$$

✘ **Melodies Restaurant** Melodies Guest House, Sanchez; ☏473 443 9052. On the beach near to the jetty, serving local & international dishes. $

SHOPPING

CARRIACOU Hillsborough is Carriacou's main town and where you will find the majority of shops. As stock has to be brought here by boat the selection is naturally quite limited and, in some cases, also quite dated, but with a bit of effort you should find what you need – or something close to it.

On Main Street you will find a few minimarkets, **Ade's Dream** and **Bullens Super Centre**, plus a number of smaller convenience stores, clothes and haberdashery shops. **Kim's Plaza Supermarket** is on Church Street and **John's Unique Plaza** is on 1st Avenue. Both have a fairly economical selection, but they carry the basics. Visiting sailors usually make a beeline for **Patty's Deli** (\ *473 443 6258*) for hams, cheeses, dairy products and other items considered normal fare elsewhere, but a real source of nectar in these parts (treat yourself to a baguette sandwich, a homemade tart or cheesecake – delicious!). The **fish market** is located on Main Street on the opposite side of the road to the First Caribbean National Bank – look for the sign. Next to it is a Marketing Board (MNIB) building which is quite good for fruit and vegetables. The **Vendors' Market** is near the bus terminus and there are quite a few stalls selling fruits, vegetables and souvenirs. On the corner of Main St and Patterson Street there are a few gift shops and boutiques. **Simply Carriacou**, on Main St next to Patty's Deli, has a nice selection of local arts, crafts and clothing.

Outside of Hillsborough, Tyrrel Bay has a couple of minimarkets that specialise in yacht provisioning. They are fairly well stocked and one of them, Alexis Supermarket, opens on Sundays. For crafts, gifts and souvenirs, **Fidel Productions** in L'Esterre by Paradise Beach is authentic and local. You will find an assortment of crafts, T-shirts, hats, *mojo* jewellery, and other interesting items (see box above).

PETITE MARTINIQUE Following the road away from Sanchez you will come to **Mathew's Shopping Centre**, which is a small minimarket, and the **Millennium Connection**, which combines gift store, clothes boutique and rooms to rent. It also has an internet café. **Emma's Supermarket**, near Paradise, is well stocked with the essentials.

OTHER PRACTICALITIES

MONEY AND BANKS Banks open 08.00–14.00 Mondays to Thursdays and 08.00–16.00 on Fridays. Banks are closed Saturdays, Sundays and on public holidays. You will find the following banks on Carriacou. They all have ATMs.

$ First Caribbean National Bank Main St, Hillsborough

$ Grenada Co-operative Bank Main St, Hillsborough

KATO CHARLES FOLK ART

Kato Charles returned to Carriacou from Canada to pursue her interest in art and craft. Kato uses rags, old clothes, even shower curtains, in fact any coloured material she can get hold of, and knots and weaves them into very original mats, wall hangings, and rag baskets. Her hangings may be abstract patterns but often they also depict Carriacou life; sailing boats, Big Drum dancing, and children at play. You will usually find Kato in the Vendors' Market in Hillsborough. She has a Facebook page: www.facebook.com/katocharlesart.

$ **Grenada Co-operative Bank** Tyrrel Bay
$ **Republic Bank** Main St, Hillsborough

MEDICAL In Carriacou the **Princess Royal Hospital** (☏ 473 443 7400) is located at Mt Royal, Belair. **Carriacou Health Services** (☏ 473 443 8247) is at the southern end of Main St, opposite the Roman Catholic church in Hillsborough. **Bullen's Pharmacy** (☏ 473 443 7468) is also on Main St, and **Hill's Valley Pharmacy** (☏ 473 443 8904) is on Church St, Hillsborough.

SAFETY Both Carriacou and Petite Martinique are extremely safe places. The people are very friendly and you should have no trouble. If you are unlucky and you do need help, the Carriacou police station is on the corner of Church St and Main St in Hillsborough. The Petite Martinique police station is on the road between Sanchez and Paradise. Emergency services is ☏ 911.

COMMUNICATIONS Most hotels and many bars offer Wi-Fi, indeed the whole of Tyrrel Bay has free wireless internet access. Should you need an internet café, there is one in the Bullen Travel office building on Main St, Hillsborough, and another at Millennium Connection on Petite Martinique.

TRAVEL AND TOURISM

Carriacou Board of Tourism Main St, Hillsborough; ☏ 473 443 7948; www.grenadagrenadines.com; ⊕ Mon–Fri 08.00–16.00. Help desk, brochures, tours and maps. Taxi and tour operators can usually be found outside the office or in front of the jetty.

Osprey Lines Patterson St, Hillsborough; ☏ 473 443 8126; www.ospreylines.com; ⊕ Mon–Fri 10.00–16.00. This is where you can purchase advance tickets for the Osprey ferry service to Grenada and Petite Martinique.

WHAT TO SEE AND DO

HILLSBOROUGH Carriacou's main town and administrative centre is Hillsborough, which is located on the west coast of the island. It is a small town with one main business street and two quieter roads running in parallel behind.

Main Street is where you will find most shops, banks, the police station, post office, customs house and jetty. The jetty is where the **Osprey** ferry service and mail boat to and from Grenada and Petite Martinique arrives and departs (see page 209 for details of schedules and fares). Outside the jetty gates, to the left as you exit, is the **post office** (⊕ 08.00–15.00 Mon–Fri). Opposite the jetty, on the corner of the junction with Church Street, is the **Grenada Board of Tourism** office (⊕ 08.00–16.00 Mon–Sat), which is located in the Carriacou & Petite Martinique Memorial Centre.

Walking north along Main Street (left as you exit the jetty gates), you will pass a number of local snackettes such as **Steamboat Fast Food & Take-away**, **Ann & Sharon's Snack Bar** and **De Matrix Snack Bar**, all of which are good for inexpensive local bites. Also in this direction is the Republic Bank with a Blue Machine ATM. Opposite the Republic Bank is the Digicel shop where you will find Bullen Tours & Travel, a Western Union money transfer desk and an internet café. A little further down the street is the Grenada Co-operative Bank.

Continuing north along Main Street you reach **Ade's Dream** where there is a supermarket, car-hire office and rooms to rent. The **Sea Wave Restaurant & Bar** and the **Laurena II** are very good value local eateries. At the end of Main Street, as

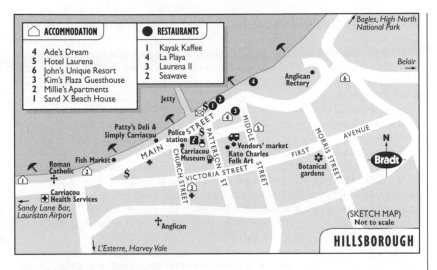

HILLSBOROUGH

it curves inland away from the sea, there are several colourful snackettes and stalls such as **Jam Rock**, where you can get your shoes mended. A little beyond the bend, on the way out of town towards Bogles and Belair, is the Anglican rectory, once the Beauséjour Estate Great House.

Back at the jetty, this time turning south along Main Street, you will see **Bullen's Super Centre**, a supermarket selling basic foodstuffs and household goods. Next door to the supermarket is **Bullen's Pharmacy**. Over the road, **Patty's Deli** sells fresh bagels, quiche, cold cuts and a variety of enticing deli items and, next door, **Simply Carriacou** has a nice selection of local arts and crafts and can also offer you local travel advice. A little further down the road, along the shoreline, is the **fish market** and **Marketing Board shop** where you can buy fruits and vegetables. Continuing out of town along Main Street you come to **Millie's Apartments & Guest Rooms**, the **St Patrick's Roman Catholic Church**, and the **Carriacou Health Centre**.

The road running parallel to Main Street is Victoria Street, which is also known as Back Street. It is predominantly an area of small board houses and gardens. At its northern end Victoria Street becomes 1st Avenue where you will find Hillsborough's botanical gardens, the **Gardens Recreational Park**. Although rather small, the gardens have some interesting trees and plants and are adjoined by a small pond. From time to time cultural events take place here and you may be lucky enough to be around when there is some storytelling, traditional string band music, or perhaps even some Big Drum dancing. To find out about such events a good place to look is on the noticeboard at the **Carriacou Museum** on Patterson Street (see below) or check at **Simply Carriacou** on Main Street.

On the corner of Patterson Street and Main Street is the Vendor's Market where you can find gifts, souvenirs, and clothing boutiques. Around the corner from the Vendor's Market is a narrow road that leads to the **bus terminus** where you will also find a number of small wooden booths selling fruit and vegetables, arts and crafts. Look out for Kato Charles's very unique folk art (see box on page 215). A short distance along Patterson Street, opposite the Vendor's Market and the road to the bus terminus, is the **Carriacou Museum**.

Church Street also adjoins Main Street. There are a few stores here such as **Kim's Plaza Supermarket**, and at the end of the road to the right you will find the **Anglican Church of Christ the King**.

The Islands   WHAT TO SEE AND DO

10

217

EXPLORING SOUTHERN CARRIACOU The road south out of Hillsborough runs along the shoreline of Hillsborough Bay. Crescent-shaped and lined by a white-sand beach, the bay has three outer islands that are both visible and accessible by boat. They are **Jack a Dan Island**, **Sandy Island** and **Mabouya Island**. Sandy Island is both a yacht anchorage and the location of some interesting reefs that are popular with visiting scuba-divers.

The main road south of Hillsborough veers away from the shore and goes to **Lauriston Airport** where the road ends. It used to go across the runway to L'Esterre and Harvey Vale but the increase in both air and road traffic has meant that it is no longer considered safe to have aeroplanes, vehicles, cows, goats and pedestrians all using the runway at the same time. The road to L'Esterre and Harvey Vale now takes a more roundabout route. To get there by vehicle you must take the road from Hillsborough, opposite the Roman Catholic church, head inland a short distance and then turn off on a narrow road to Lauriston and L'Esterre. Those on foot have a more interesting option of following the beach and a pathway through the coastal mangroves of Lauriston Point to Paradise Beach (see page 228).

L'Esterre is a small village of colourful board houses. It is said that this area retains the influence of France and that some of its inhabitants still speak French Creole. At the centre of the village is L'Esterre Cross, a junction with roads heading to Hillsborough and Harvey Vale and another running through the village towards Point Cistern and Feejay Beach (see page 230).

L'Esterre's primary attraction is the stunning **Paradise Beach** that fringes L'Esterre Bay. Though no beach in Carriacou is ever crowded, in fact most are usually completely deserted, Paradise is conceivably the most popular and where

CARRIACOU MUSEUM

The Carriacou Museum was set up by the Carriacou Historical Society in 1976. It is now in its fourth home, a 19th-century cotton ginnery (that was once connected to the building next door, currently home to Osprey Lines). Its small size masks a wealth of interest, in particular the collection of Amerindian artefacts that are regularly unearthed by archaeologists along the rugged and weather-beaten Sabazan and Grand Bay coast lines. Indeed these sites are thought to be some of the largest of their kind in the Caribbean. The fascinating artefacts that have been unearthed on Carriacou include the original clay well segments that were discovered at Harvey Vale (the well appears on tourist maps but there is nothing much to see there now), a zemi stone, clay pot adornments and handles, body paint stamps, primitive tools, fertility symbols and jewellery.

There is also an informative display on African heritage, slavery, and European colonisation of Carriacou, in particular the plantation owners and Scottish boatbuilders.

The museum has a gift shop and often exhibits contemporary works such as schoolchildren's paintings (see the Camp Kayak initiative at www.campkayak.org), and the art of Canute Caliste. The Carriacou Historical Society also organises cultural events such as Big Drum dancing, string band music, poetry and storytelling. Check the museum's noticeboard.

Patterson Street, Hillsborough; ☏ *473 443 8288;* e *carriacoumuseum@gmail.com;* *www.carriacoumuseum.org;* ⊕ *10.00–16.00 Mon–Fri, 11.00–15.00 Sat; EC$5pp inc a tour.*

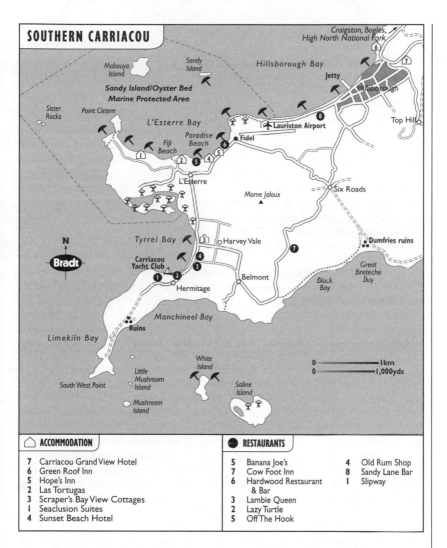

SOUTHERN CARRIACOU

Craigston, Bogles,
High North National Park

Mabouya Island

Sandy Island

Hillsborough Bay

Jetty

Hillsborough

Sandy Island/Oyster Bed
Marine Protected Area

Sister Rocks

Point Cistern

Top Hill

L'Esterre Bay

Lauriston Airport

Paradise Beach

Fidel

Fiji Beach

L'Esterre

Morne Jaloux

Six Roads

Dumfries ruins

N

Bradt

Tyrrel Bay

Carriacou Yacht Club

Harvey Vale

Great Breteche Bay

Hermitage

Belmont

Black Bay

Manchineel Bay

Ruins

Limekiln Bay

White Island

South West Point

Little Mushroom Island

Saline Island

Mushroom Island

0 — 1km
0 — 1,000yds

ACCOMMODATION

7	Carriacou Grand View Hotel
6	Green Roof Inn
5	Hope's Inn
2	Las Tortugas
3	Scraper's Bay View Cottages
1	Seaclusion Suites
4	Sunset Beach Hotel

RESTAURANTS

5	Banana Joe's	4	Old Rum Shop
7	Cow Foot Inn	8	Sandy Lane Bar
6	Hardwood Restaurant & Bar	1	Slipway
3	Lambie Queen		
2	Lazy Turtle		
5	Off The Hook		

you will actually see other people at play. Locals come here to bathe and have picnics, and private taxis often drop day-trippers here. The beach is white sand with a backdrop of sea almond and grape trees along with the occasional manchineel (see page 43). The water is turquoise and shallow along the shore making it ideal for families with young children. As it is protected, the bay attracts very few waves and little current. With colourfully painted fishing boats and water taxis bobbing sedately offshore, the image is one of serenity and relaxation. The trees at the back of the beach offer a degree of shade and there are a number of bars and eateries selling refreshments as well as meals with all the trimmings. Water taxis can be chartered at the **Hardwood Bar** to take you to the outlying islands. Sandy Island and its surrounding reef is particularly beautiful and perfect for snorkelling. It has little shade, however, so be prepared and remember that when snorkelling in this climate it is always prudent to do so wearing a T-shirt or a light wetsuit to save the skin on your shoulders and back. Located close to the Hardwood Bar along the

The Islands   WHAT TO SEE AND DO

10

roadside is **Fidel Productions**, selling a selection of unique crafts, *mojo* jewellery, and original T-shirts (see box on page 214).

There is a long, straight road from L'Esterre Cross to **Harvey Vale**, Carriacou's second-largest settlement, which is located along the shore of **Tyrrel Bay**. A natural anchorage, Tyrrel Bay and Harvey Vale are home to the 'yachties', sailing enthusiasts who have arrived in Carriacou and decided to stay, hang around for a while, or who are just passing through *en route* to their next exotic destination. With sailing boats at anchor, a yacht club and haul-out facility, and a new marina investment project well underway, Tyrrel Bay offers an interesting mix of the old, the new, the local, the international and the downright eccentric.

Dotted along the bay front road are a number of small stores, local restaurants and bars. On some tourist maps you may see a reference to an **Amerindian well**. The site is not worth seeking out. It is largely covered in manchineel trees and now set in concrete. The well casing, a series of bottomless pots, is much more interesting, however, and is on display at the Carriacou Museum. The pots were stacked above a freshwater spring, just 20m from the sea, and drinking water flowed up through them.

Harvey Vale itself is primarily residential beyond the bay road. Both Roman Catholic and Anglican churches can be found on the road heading east, which starts at the junction near Scraper's.

South of Tyrrel Bay and Harvey Vale is the small community of **Hermitage**. Hugging the cliff side, with a narrow, winding road that passes through colourful residences above the sailing boats and the yard and jetty of the **Carriacou Yacht Club**, Hermitage has a couple of very good restaurants: the **Lazy Turtle** and the **Slipway** (see page 214), both of which are definitely worth a visit. The paved road through Hermitage ends in a vehicle track which continues to the end of **South West Point**, also known as La Pointe and Smugglers' Cove (see page 228).

From Harvey Vale, the road inland leads to the small hamlet of **Belmont**. Sitting high on a ridge overlooking Manchineel Bay, Belmont has excellent views south to the Grenada Grenadines, including **White Island** and **Saline Island**. Beyond them you may also be able to make out **Frigate Island** and **Large Island**. At a junction on the main road near the Belmont Postal Station is a road heading down to the coast where there is a tiny beach along the bay. Ask at the snackettes located at this junction for information about water taxis offering rides out to White Island (Saline Island is privately owned). They run from the bay at the bottom of the steep road. White Island is beautiful and has an excellent reef for snorkelling.

Continue along the ridge past more residential houses. The road leaves Belmont above Black Bay before heading back inland to the road junction at the aptly named Six Roads. Between Belmont and Six Roads you will pass the **Cowfoot Inn**, a pleasant spot for a refreshing drink and some good local food.

South of Six Roads is **Dumfries**, where the ruins of a lime factory are located. Though the ruins themselves are very interesting, the road between Six Roads and Dumfries is not a particularly pleasant one, lined on one side by a large vehicle repair yard and on the other by the island's landfill site. An alternative and very scenic route to the ruins is via a coastal track from **Grand Bay** (see page 229). The ruins consist of factory buildings, machinery and a large brick tower. The factory was run by the L Rose and Lime Company which was established in Scotland in the 1860s. The company operated throughout the Caribbean, producing 'Rose's Lime Juice Cordial' and lime marmalade before economic and social circumstances forced it to downsize and withdraw from Grenada in the mid 1900s.

From Dumfries, **Great Breteche Bay** and **Little Breteche Bay** are to be found along the wild and windy coast of **Sabazan**, together with Grand Bay, one of the locations for Amerindian archaeological discoveries on Carriacou. Northeast of Sabazan and the very scenic **Kendeace Point** are the villages of **Grand Bay** and **Mt Pleasant**. These villages, often overlooked because of their rather remote location along the centre of the island's windward coast, have a very strong sense of community and heritage. Mt Pleasant hosts one of the island's most popular village maroon festivals and the hillside behind it is dotted with the remains of stone windmill towers that were used to drive machine works in the estates that once thrived in this area.

To the south of Hillsborough, midway to Mt Pleasant and Grand Bay, are the elevated communities of **Top Hill** and **Mt Royal**, nestled along the spine of the mountain ridge that runs the length of the island between High North and Morne Jaloux (Chapeau Carré). Mount Royal is where Carriacou's Princess Royal Hospital is located. The hospital has a particularly prominent position along this ridge and the views from its grounds down to Hillsborough Bay are definitely worth a photograph.

EXPLORING NORTHERN CARRIACOU
To the northeast of Hillsborough, along the central ridge, is **Belair**. Once a large estate, the community of Belair is one of the locations for the annual Maroon & String Band Music Festival. It also has a protected teak and mahogany forest, and the Belair windmill tower, along the northern edge of the forest, is probably the largest and most prominent of the island's windmill ruins. To the east of Belair, down the windward slopes that were once full of sugar, cotton and lime plantations, is **Limlair**, also once a large estate. On the eastern edge of Limlair, along Jew Bay, is **Tibeau**. In Tibeau there is a cemetery on the sandy shoreline that is slowly being claimed by the sea, and nearby is **Ningo Well**, a large manmade stone well that would once have been used for storing water for crop irrigation and for cattle (see page 227).

Between Limlair and the neighbouring village of Dover, you will see a large pond and a wooden cabin, the Big Pond Nature Centre, home to the Tibeau Limlair Historical Ruins Rehabilitation Project. The centre offers guided walks along the trails around Limlair. Hidden in the undergrowth in the centre of Dover are the ruins of what is thought to be the first church on Carriacou. Unfortunately the ruins are buried deep in bush and, at the time of writing, are difficult to reach.

To the north, along the coast from Dover, is the community of **Windward**. This village has a strong heritage of boatbuilding that goes back to the days when Scottish shipbuilders settled in this area. Many of the families still living in Windward have Scottish surnames, and for a while Windward was rather a closed community. In more recent times the original settler families mixed with Kayacs and cultures were shared.

The village of Windward itself is pretty and the views across the water to Petite Martinique are very scenic. It has a few small shops and bars, and numerous colourfully painted board houses that are dotted along the road and hillside above the boatyards where, it seems, there is almost always a wooden boat under construction. Customers for these boats sometimes come from very far afield. They are often built to order for overseas enthusiasts or businesses looking for a very traditional, hand-crafted boat. Some of the boatbuilders in Windward have been in this business all their lives and, thankfully, appear to be passing their skills along to younger apprentices from both Windward and Petite Martinique who are keen to inherit the talents of their seniors.

On the leeward side of the island, just to the north of Hillsborough, are the small villages of **Craigston** and **Bogles**. Craigston has become popular with overseas investors who have built holiday homes that they also rent out. Bogles is a very small village of residential houses and convenience stores. It is also the gateway to the High North National Park. Once through the village of Bogles, the paved road ends and becomes a vehicle track that is known as the **High North Nature Trail**. This trail runs through the forest along the west coast to the beautiful bay and beach of Anse La Roche and then beyond to the mangrove forest and stunning beach at Petit Carenage Bay in the north (see pages 225–6).

There are several small islands around Carriacou. North of Hillsborough is the small rocky islet of Jack a Dan and to the south of it the very pretty Sandy Island which is a favourite picnic and snorkelling spot. You can rent water taxis to Sandy Island from Paradise Beach at the Hardwood Restaurant & Bar. South of Sandy Island is the larger Mabouya Island. Off Point Cistern, to the west of L'Esterre, are the twin islets of the **Sister Rocks**. In the south, off Manchineel Bay, there are **Mushroom Island** and **Little Mushroom Island**, Saline Island, and White

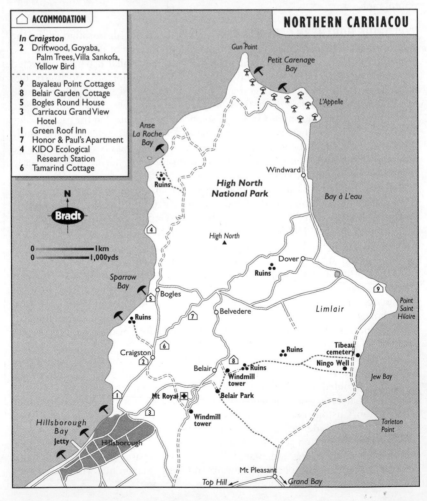

Island, which is also very popular for picnics, snorkelling and scuba diving. A little further away are Frigate Island and Large Island. You can get a water taxi to White Island from Belmont or Tyrrel Bay. To the north, between Carriacou and Petite Martinique, is the small rocky islet of **Fota**, and the larger rocky island of **Petite Dominique**.

EXPLORING PETITE MARTINIQUE When you step off the Osprey ferry you will be on the boat jetty in an area called **Sanchez**. Along the shoreline and grassy field to your left you will probably see a boat or two in the process of being built, and perhaps the boatbuilders are there working on it, hammering, sawing, measuring or just generally discussing progress on the vessel. It is a poignant and very appropriate introduction to Petite Martinique. Things are a little different here and they tend to revolve around boats.

As you walk off the jetty and down the road you will come to a junction. Welcome to the only main road on the island. To your right is the Thomas Aquinas Roman Catholic School and to your left the Petite Martinique Post Office. Turn right and walk along the main road. You will pass small businesses such as the **Mathew's Shopping Centre** and **Millennium Connection**, which has a clothes boutique, a craft and souvenir shop, an internet café and rooms to rent. On your right-hand side is the **Palm Beach Restaurant & Bar** and, a little further down, **Melodies Guest House Restaurant & Bar**. Along the shoreline of Sanchez there is a narrow strip of white-sand beach where you will see colourful fishing boats resting between trips.

The noise you cannot hear is traffic. As you would expect from an island with a single main road there are not many vehicles. People tend to walk a lot or travel by boat. Some of the young guys like to get about on all-terrain vehicles (ATVs) and you may even see an electric golf cart or two.

At a junction, a narrow road heads uphill on the left to the residential community of **Belle View**. At this junction there are some more small shops, the Petite Martinique Police Station and a couple of snackettes. Continuing from the junction you come to an area called **Moulin Vent**. Appropriately enough, you should spot the ruins of a windmill tower on the right, perched on the cliff top, overlooking the sea. After Moulin Vent the road passes above **Mang Bay**. To the left is coastal woodland and to the right is the grassy headland of Point Mion with its very isolated wooden board houses. From the communities of **Kendeace** and **Citerne** the road curves towards the southeast and the exposed windward coast of this small island. Just offshore is the rugged islet of Petite Dominique and, in front of it to the right, the smaller rocky pinnacle of Fota, both relentlessly battered by the Atlantic.

Just beyond Citerne the paved road comes to an end and is replaced by a vehicle track. Following this track takes you further around the south and east, circling the conical peak of **Piton** and finally emerging at the elevated northern community of **Sugar Hill** (see page 230 for trail details). The residences of Sugar Hill have super views of Carriacou, Petit St Vincent and the Grenadines. Below Sugar Hill, near the main road junction, is the Petite Martinique Roman Catholic Church.

ACTIVITIES AND SPECIAL INTERESTS If you can drag yourself away from one of Carriacou's beautiful beaches (yes, I know, it is difficult) then you may be surprised at just how much there is to do and to discover on the island. Be sure to look and listen out for cultural events such as boat-launchings, Big Drum and string band

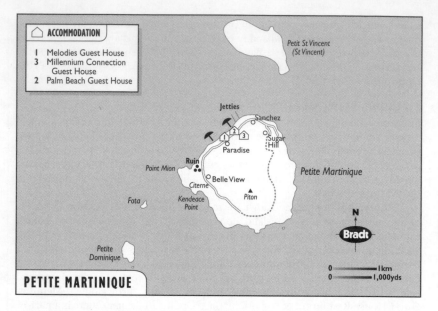

ACCOMMODATION

1   Melodies Guest House
3   Millennium Connection
    Guest House
2   Palm Beach Guest House

PETITE MARTINIQUE

performances, or village maroons and saracas during your stay (see page 204). They are definitely worth experiencing. There are numerous trails criss-crossing the island and the roads have very little traffic, making walking, hiking and biking all great options. The waters are usually calm and clear so boat trips, snorkelling or scuba-diving are also pleasant ways to spend your days here.

Snorkelling and scuba diving As Carriacou is known as the 'land of reefs' you may wish to consider dipping your head under the water to take a look around and see what is down there. There are a number of options, depending on your ability, experience and sense of aquatic adventure. If you have never tried snorkelling before, then why not give it a go? If you go to one of the dive operators in Carriacou (see page 87) they will help and advise you, and will also offer accompanied snorkelling trips. Snorkelling around White Island, Sandy Island and even Jack a Dan is very interesting. The reefs are close to the shore and in clear, shallow water. Water taxis or dive operators can take you there. Ask at your hotel for the name of a recommended water taxi. Alternatively go to the Hardwood Restaurant & Bar on Paradise Beach. Certified divers will enjoy exploring interesting wrecks and reefs. Those with more experience should definitely try the Sister Rocks and Frigate Island where strong currents attract feeding pelagics.

Boat trips Local charter boat owners and fishermen offer cruising and water-taxi services to visitors. You could take a trip around the coastline or the outlying islands, an excursion to White Island or Sandy Island where you can do some snorkelling and have a picnic, a fishing trip with a beach barbecue, a ride across to Petite Martinique, or perhaps a trip to somewhere a little further afield such as St Vincent's Tobago Cays, an idyllic desert-island setting for the film *Pirates of the Caribbean*. Local boat owners know these waters well and you are sure to have a good time.

Your hotel will probably be able to recommend someone to you as they often have relationships with boat owners and water taxis. You could also look for water taxis at Windward, Dover, and by the postal station in Belmont. **Bayaleau Point**

Using a set of solar dryers, the Sun Flavor Humanitarian Food Aid Programme makes flour from provisions and staples such as bluggo, dasheen, sweet potato, green banana, breadfruit and plantain (see page 58). The flour is packaged and donated to hospitals, homes for the elderly and school feeding programmes in Petite Martinique and Carriacou. If you find yourself in Petite Martinique then please look up Mr Osbert Felix, who is the programme founder and manager. He lives in Kendeace (his house is the one with the long black-painted solar dryers in his garden). He will be very happy to explain both the process and the programme to you. If you are not travelling to Petite Martinique but wish to support this initiative, here is some contact information: ✎ 473 443 9043; www.petitemartinique.com/humanitarian-programme.htm.

Cottages (✎ 473 443 9784; e goldhill@spiceisle.com; www.carriacoucottages.com) offers day trips on its motor launch *Mostly Harmless*. **Cinderella Yacht Charters** (✎ 473 443 7277; e beefletch@hotmail.com; www.grenada-sailing.com) offers day charters around Carriacou and the southern Grenadines.

Mountain biking Carriacou really lends itself to road cycling and mountain biking. Be sure to take a map (or this book) with you, along with sunscreen and plenty of water. The **Lambi Queen** (✎ 473 443 8162 and 473 406 4122) in Tyrrel Bay rents mountain bikes for EC$50 per day.

WALKS, HIKES AND SCENIC DRIVES There are numerous trails and farm and village tracks criss-crossing the islands. Here is a small selection.

Anse La Roche Beach from Bogles Anse La Roche Beach is one of Carriacou's most secluded and, according to many, its finest. This hike takes you there from the High North Nature Trail near Bogles. You could either walk or drive along the High North Nature Trail (a 4x4 is the better option for driving in the wet). The hike along the trail is very easy but the descent down the hillside track is a little trickier.

Starting at the bulletin board at a road junction in the middle of Bogles, take the paved road north along the coast, keeping the sea to your left and the peak of High North to your right. The road winds sharply around a couple of houses before becoming a wide dirt track. This is the start of the High North Nature Trail. Follow this pretty track around the High North National Park for about 15 minutes by car and about 45 minutes if you are on foot. It is a very peaceful walk through coastal woodland where the only sounds you will hear are the waves rolling onto the shore below, birds singing and the occasional rustle of leaves as a disturbed ground lizard or iguana runs for cover.

Look out for a path on the left marked by a boulder sporting a red blaze and a sign with a painted turtle. The track is narrow but clearly defined. It passes through some trees (be careful of thorns) and a twisted mass of cacti (be careful of spines) and comes to a fork. The path to the left is a little obscure and curls around and back towards the stone ruins of a house. You can see it from the main trail. It is well worth having a look around. Now take the right-hand path down to a second fork. Before following the trail to the right, take a diversion along the track to the left and then left again at the next fork. You will come to a steep grassy hillside where there are fabulous views down to the bay at Anse La Roche and out across the water to the northwest to Union Island, which is part of the St Vincent Grenadines. This is perhaps the best place to take photographs of the beach. Back at the main fork again, go right and follow a clear trail running along the brow of a hill and then quite steeply downwards. Keep a look out for turtle blazes on the trees if you are uncertain. At the next fork go right again through more trees. Again watch out for thorny branches. The path now becomes quite rocky and there are some steps to negotiate. Follow the trail downhill along a shallow gully. The stones and rocks underfoot are quite loose so be careful.

The path forks again around some brush – take the left-hand option. Take your time and just keep going straight down the main trail in front of you. Eventually the path will level out as you reach some tall trees. You should be able to see the beach ahead of you now. Just follow the best route through the trees to the bay.

The beach is extremely picturesque though you will probably notice that entry into the sea is quite steep and occasionally the surf is high and strong. You need to be a strong swimmer when sea conditions are like this and the waves are rolling in hard. If you do make it beyond the breakers there are some interesting reef formations and sea caves worth exploring if you have brought your snorkelling gear with you. If the sea is not stirring up too much sand, the visibility is usually good enough to see them from the surface. Take care when entering and exiting the water as both undertow and surge can be strong.

Petit Carenage Beach and L'Apelle mangrove forest
In my opinion, Petit Carenage Beach is the prettiest on Carriacou – in fact it is my favourite of all three islands. A long stretch of powder-white sand along a crescent-shaped bay with turquoise seas, rolling breakers and the skeleton hull of a shipwreck sitting on the reef at one end make it incredibly picturesque. Add to that the verdancy and tangled roots of the L'Apelle mangrove forest, with its plentiful birdlife, separating beach from road and you have a very idyllic setting indeed. Despite its apparent remoteness, Petit Carenage is actually very accessible. You can get there from the High North Nature Trail if you are coming from the west coast via Anse La Roche, or alternatively you can reach it by travelling northwards from the boatbuilding village of Windward on the east coast.

From Bogles, follow the High North Nature Trail to Anse La Roche (see page 225). From Anse La Roche, continue along the main trail for another 45 minutes or so if you are on foot, and another 15–20 minutes if you are driving (you'll definitely need a 4x4 along here). You will come to some houses and a paved road. Continue along the paved road past **Gun Point** and then downhill towards the beach and mangroves which you can see below to your left. Once at the bottom, and past a few more houses, look for a couple of wooden signs attached to a tree on your left-hand side near a telephone pole. They will read 'Petit Carenage Mangrove' and 'Mangrove Trail' and point to some concrete steps going down below the road. Follow these steps through a rather unpleasant waste area and onto a very clearly marked trail lined on each side with sun-bleached conch shells.

A ten-minute walk will take you to the beach. Before you get there, you will see a spur trail heading off to the right. This trail continues through the black mangrove forest to the point where the ship is wrecked on the shallow reef. Though nowhere near as picturesque as the main stretch of Petit Carenage Beach, it still makes for an interesting diversion.

As with Anse La Roche, bathing can sometimes be tricky at Petit Carenage. The sand shelves steeply, occasionally causing large waves to crash down on the beach.

The undercurrent can also be quite strong. In these conditions this is not really a bathing beach for families with children. In calmer conditions it is idyllic.

If you are approaching Petit Carenage from Windward, simply keep going through the village, past the boatyards on your right and then out along the coast. Follow the paved road all the way to the same signs and steps pointing towards the mangroves and the beach.

Ningo Well from Belair

This hike starts in the small, elevated community of Belair and follows a series of grassy tracks down to the windward coast and Jew Bay. Located in this area, known as Tibeau, is the impressive Ningo Well, one of the earliest and largest of the stone wells that were constructed on Carriacou.

If arriving in Belair from Hillsborough, you will reach a junction with a painted bus stop. The road to the left will pass a small playing field before rising again to a crest where there is another junction. The main road to Belvedere is straight ahead and there are rough vehicle tracks to the left and right. The track on the right is the starting point of the hike.

Follow this track for five minutes as it winds around a small peak. To the right you will see a cemetery and the teak and mahogany forest of Belair Park. To the left is the impressive ruin of the stone windmill tower of the Belair Estate. This windmill would have been used for driving machine works to crush sugarcane.

From the windmill tower continue along the track for around five to ten minutes until you reach a three-way junction. Take the trail on the left. After another five minutes or so you will reach another fork. Take the left-hand path once again. Follow the trail as it gradually makes its way downhill.

Continue down the trail and take a left at the next fork and then at the next trail junction take the track to the right. You should find yourself walking around the broken walls that once formed the perimeter of the Great House of the 140ha Limlair Estate. Continue walking around until the sea is right in front of you and a path to your left goes up above the ruined walls into the remains of the house itself. Beautiful, large agave plants border the track. Take time to explore the remains of the house that was once the residence of the Munro family. You will see the house foundations and the shell of the old water cistern.

Continue down the main trail for five minutes or so until you reach a four-way junction. Take the wide vehicle track to the right and follow it all the way down to the sea and the main, unpaved, coastal road.

You should see Tibeau Cemetery off to the left. Note how some gravestones are right on the beach and are already awash with waves. Located at the southern end of this cemetery is the broken mausoleum of Limlair Estate owner Hugh Munro and his infant son. The mausoleum dates back to the 1770s.

With the ocean on your left-hand side head south for about five minutes or so until you reach an opening on the left that goes to the sea, near an old stone bridge. Look to the left of the bridge and you should see a track heading into the trees. Follow it for a short distance until you come upon the very impressive Ningo Well. What was it used for? It was a water supply for farm animals but now seems to be cane toad city.

A 20-minute walk along the rough coastal track will take you to the settlement of Mt Pleasant. From the Mt Pleasant junction, by the primary school, you can catch a number 12 bus into Hillsborough or up to the top of the ridge near Top Hill. If you want to hike back to Belair, take a right at the four-way junction. The walk along the ridge has great views and passes a windmill tower ruin near the Princess Royal Hospital. From the hospital grounds there is a superb view of Hillsborough Bay. Continue along the road to the Belair junction and bus stop.

Southwest Point (La Pointe/Smugglers' Cove) from Tyrrel Bay

Southwest Point (La Pointe/Smugglers' Cove) from Tyrrel Bay This there-and-back hike is around 60–90 minutes each way and starts in Tyrrel Bay. It follows the road around to the coastal settlement of Hermitage and then beyond, through several livestock farms and past some ruins to the island's southwesterly extreme. Once there you will discover a sandy and remote shoreline at the western tip of Manchineel Bay as well as a remote and isolated bay good for snorkelling.

Starting anywhere along the shoreline of Tyrrel Bay, head south towards the settlement of Hermitage.

The road narrows as it climbs up through Hermitage and past the Carriacou Yacht Club. There are nice views across the bay from over the rooftops of the residential houses perched along this hillside. Keep going until the road turns into a wide vehicle track. Follow this track and soon you will have fine views of Manchineel Bay, White Island and Saline Island on your left.

Keep going straight, past cattle pens, and lots of roaming sheep and goats. On a rise to your left, near a small pond, you may see the ruins of an old estate house. Further along the track, you will come across a second pond on your right. After around 45 minutes or so from the beginning of your hike, you will reach a fork. The right-hand track heads uphill, the left heads down and around towards some farm buildings. Take this one. The track veers around to the right and passes through an open gate. Once through the gate, continue onwards and the seashore should be fairly close by on your left. After a further ten minutes or so you will reach another fork. Take the longer track to the left and keep following the shoreline until you reach a concrete structure. To the left of the building is a small beach and the waters of Manchineel Bay with views across to White Island and Saline Island, with Little Mushroom Island and Mushroom Island in between. To the right of the building there are two tracks. The left track leads to a secluded bay on the northern edge of Southwest Point (Smugglers' Cove). The bay is shingle and black sand, the waters are very clear and snorkelling is good around the rocky coastline. The track on the right runs to a desolate grassy area and a ridge. Walk up to the top of the ridge for fine views south to Grenada. Be careful as it is clearly eroding.

Paradise Beach from Hillsborough

Paradise Beach from Hillsborough Whether you are in Carriacou just for the day or perhaps staying longer, a visit to Paradise Beach in L'Esterre Bay is an absolute must. Certainly one of the prettiest beaches on the island, it is within walking distance of town thanks to a track that follows the beach and then meanders through the mangroves of Lauriston Point and the Sandy Island/Oyster Bed Marine Protected Area. It is a fun walk, along both paved road, beach and through light surf. It is a little tricky in places and you will get your feet and legs wet. Be sure to protect yourself from the sun, bring plenty of water and swimming gear.

From Main Street in Hillsborough, walk in a westerly direction out of town (if you are standing outside the exit to the jetty, turn right). Pass the St Patrick Roman Catholic Church and the Carriacou Health Centre and continue out of town. The road follows the sandy shoreline of Hillsborough Bay until it eventually veers to the left and comes to an end at Lauriston Airport. Leave the paved road on the bend and walk along the beach.

Follow the beach along the edge of the mangroves, getting your feet and legs wet as you make your way around them. Keep going around the point until you can quite simply go no further. At this point, a track through the mangroves should open up in front of you. The track is fairly obvious so if you can't see it you probably haven't walked far enough yet.

Follow the trail as it winds through the coastal mangrove forest around Lauriston Point. Occasionally the trail disappears where mangrove has fallen but take your time, look ahead of you, and keep the sea close to your right-hand side and you should be able to find your way through it. The trail emerges briefly at a small beach on the tip of the point before re-entering the mangroves again. Keep following it over a dry creek and alongside some brackish water until you come to a clearing where you may see a track off to the left. Don't take it. Instead, make your way through the mangroves to the sea on the right and wade through shallow water to Paradise Beach, which should now be in front of you.

What made all the holes in the sand? Some very large crabs.

Dumfries ruins, Sabazan and Kendeace coastline from Grand Bay This hike follows a clear vehicle track all the way along the windward coast from the Grand Bay and Mt Pleasant to the ruins at Dumfries. You do not have to go all the way, however. The view from Kendeace Point is one of the best on the island and a great place to settle down with a picnic (stock up with goodies from **Patti's Deli** in Hillsborough before you come!). If you walk to the viewpoint and back, and I recommend you do, it should take around an hour or so each way. Dumfries is a further hour away. Once you reach the ruins, and have finished exploring, you have the option of walking back the way you came or following the track up to Six Roads (about 30 minutes). This is a very unpleasant road, however, as it passes alongside (though sometimes it feels like through) the island's landfill site. I don't recommend it. A number 12 bus will get you to and from Grand Bay and Mt Pleasant from Hillsborough.

Find the paved road junction at Mt Pleasant, opposite the school. Facing the sea, go right and follow the road to a sharp hairpin. On the corner you will see a vehicle track. This is the route. The paved road continues around to the back of Grand Bay villages and comes to an end.

Follow the vehicle track to some houses. If you are driving, you could leave your car here. Take the track that runs closest to the perimeter of the houses, on the right. Stick with this main trail and ignore all spurs for the remainder of the hike. Near the beginning you will see openings in the bush with windows onto the ocean on your right-hand side. Follow the track for about 30 minutes or so and you will come to a curve where you head inland and uphill for another 20 minutes until you arrive at another junction. The track to the right is the continuation of the hike to Sabazan and Dumfries. Ignore the trail running through the hollow in the bush ahead of you. To your left is a grassy knoll. Climb up it and enjoy the view. This is Kendeace Point. Across the ocean in front of you is Petite Martinique and just behind it is PSV (Petite St Vincent). Break out your picnic and enjoy.

If you are continuing through to Sabazan and Dumfries follow the main trail as it begins to descend towards the sea. The terrain is a little more troublesome. Beware of loose rocks and stones, and also the *zouti*, a broad leaf plant with small flowers. It is a nettle with a fearsome sting.

Look to your left and you should see the ruins of an old windmill. Up to your right are further estate ruins but they have been masked by bush and scrub. Keep going until you reach sea level and the beach of Little Breteche Bay. There may be fishing boats here.

Walk along the beach and head for the prominent outcrop in front of you. The old track reappears by a small house and tyres that have been placed along the shoreline in an effort to halt coastal erosion. Walk up the hill and around the bend, sticking with the main trail through Sabazan. You should catch sight of the community of Belmont across the bay. The trail follows the coast downhill until it reaches the shore and turns sharply inland, skirting the perimeter of the ruins. One entrance is on the sea side of the ruins, the other on the inland side. They are the remains of a lime factory once operated by the L. Rose Lime Company. The track continues up the hill, past the landfill, to the six roads junction.

Feejay Beach from L'Esterre
Feejay Beach is a whisper of white sand that runs around L'Esterre Bay to Point Cistern. You could simply relax in the sun, watching fishermen repair their boats, you could bathe in the calm, turquoise waters, or you could 'water-hike', splashing your way around the margins to Point Cistern where you will find two more beaches.

At the main road junction in L'Esterre, head up the hill into the village and past **Henrietta's Bakery** until you come to a sharp curve to the left. On your right you should see two paved wheel tracks running downhill alongside a couple of houses. Walk down to the bottom, it is not far, and come to a narrow trail that follows the boundary of the residences. It can be a little boggy if it has been raining. Follow the trail to the beach where you may see nets drying and some fishing boats at anchor.

Heading left, 'water-hike' and swim along the narrow beach and shoreline as far as you can go. The water is calm, clear and shallow and the beach, where it emerges, is powder white.

Keep a wary eye on the manchineel trees (see page 43) that bound this shoreline. At the end you will discover a beach further around towards the end of Point Cistern, and another on the other side – if you decide to go that far.

Point Cistern beaches from L'Esterre
This is a relatively easy hike with just a couple of steep hills. It takes you from L'Esterre, or Paradise Beach, all the way around to Point Cistern where there are two rather nice secluded beaches and scenic views across Hillsborough Bay.

From the junction at L'Esterre Cross, take the road that goes uphill into the village. Just follow the wonderful smells coming from Henrietta's Bakery. When the road curves around to the left, take the vehicle track that runs uphill to the right of a small building (actually a church).

Follow this track as it winds up to the top of the hill and past a cemetery. At the top you will have nice views of Hillsborough Bay, Mabouya Island and Sandy Island, with St Vincent's Union Island in the distance. Follow the wide track, going straight on all the way up and then steeply down the hillside until you reach a small wooded area. Make your way to the left towards the visible shoreline and continue walking towards the point. You will pick up a narrow path through the grass that heads to the right, and around the headland. Follow it until you come to the very tip of Feejay Beach (see above). Behind the beach the track continues towards Cistern Point. Follow it through the trees until you reach a second beach, on the south side of the point. This beach is not as long but it is very pretty, running in a small crescent around a secluded cove. Both bathing and snorkelling are good here.

All the way around Petite Martinique
This is a really nice circular hike all the way around the island of Petite Martinique, starting at the jetty where the Osprey high-speed ferry service arrives and departs. The first half of the hike is along a paved road through small communities, the second a more difficult ramble along rough vehicle tracks and narrow coastal trails which are quite steep in places. Plan conservatively for the hike to take at least two hours so that you arrive back in

plenty of time for the departing Osprey ferry if you are just visiting for the day. Also take plenty of water and sun protection along with you as this island is very exposed and there is very little opportunity for shade along the way.

If you are arriving on the jetty, keep walking straight until you come to the paved road. Turn right and walk past the Thomas Aquinas Roman Catholic School. You will be walking around the island in a counter-clockwise direction.

Keep walking along the paved road, past the communities and landmarks described on page 220. Eventually, once you have passed Citerne and Kendeace Point, the paved road comes to an end and a rough but wide vehicle track continues upwards and around the coast. It should take around 30–45 minutes to reach this point from the jetty in Sanchez.

The track is rocky and quite steep for the first ten minutes or so. Be careful with your footing. Once at the top of the hill the path becomes a little easier, transitioning from rocks to grass. There are nice views of the Atlantic Ocean and the coastal cliffs below.

After another 15 minutes the path reaches a clearing where it may seem to disappear altogether. You may be welcomed by grazing sheep, goats or cattle when you arrive here. Hugging the trees to your left, walk across the clearing. Open grassland and a ridge are to your right, scrubland trees and the summit of Petite Martinique's Piton immediately to your left. At the end of the clearing you should see a path through the low trees. Follow it to a second clearing, this one much smaller and it may well be rather overgrown. The narrow trail continues at the end of this clearing and runs steeply uphill to the left. Take your time climbing as the ground may be crumbly and loose under your feet, especially in the dry season. After around five more minutes you will come to a fork. Take the trail on the right and follow it around the hillside. Take care here as the grass can be slippery underfoot and the path is narrow. Carefully cross over a small rocky slope and pick up the trail again directly opposite. Follow it uphill until you reach a wire fence. Look to your left and you should see civilisation once again.

Follow the trail downhill alongside the fence and then over a series of tall steps made of volcanic rock. This path is quite steep so take your time and, again, be careful with your footing. After five to ten minutes you will reach a fork. Take the path to the left this time and follow it up the side of a hill behind some houses. You should have good views of Petit St Vincent from here. You soon come to a junction with a wide vehicle track. Head left up to the top of the ridge on the left-hand side of a house. Look down and you will see more houses, the coastline and the jetty where you set out. Follow the vehicle track as it winds its way downhill and then becomes a concrete road. Continue down this road and you will come to the residential area of Sugar Hill and then the Petite Martinique Roman Catholic Church. At the foot of the hill you will emerge on the main coastal road again in the area of Sanchez. The Petite Martinique Post Office is on the corner opposite you. Head left towards the jetty and your ride back to Carriacou.

Appendix 1

ACCOMMODATION AT A GLANCE

ACCOMMODATION PRICE CODES Accommodation codes used in this guide are based on the price of a double room for two people per night in the high season (usually November through to April). The symbols and price ranges used are as follows:

$$$$$	US$350+
$$$$	US$250–350
$$$	US$150–250
$$	US$100–150
$	<US$10

ACCOMMODATION TYPE CODE In the following list, accommodation types are also referred to by a simple code:

Hotel	H
Hotel and self-catering	H/SC
Self-catering	SC

GRENADA

Accommodation name	Location	Type	Price Code	Page
Allamanda Beach Resort	Grand Anse	H	$$$	116
Almost Paradise	Sauteurs	SC	$$–$$$	178
Art Gallery Villa	Westerhall	SC	$$$$$	159
Barry's Country Retreat	Sauteurs	H	$$	178
Bel Air Plantation	St David's Point	SC	$$$$	159
Big Sky Lodge	Crochu	SC	$	160
Blue Horizons Garden Resort	Grand Anse	SC	$$$	117
Cabier Ocean Lodge	Crochu	H	$$	159
Calabash Hotel & Villas	L'Anse Aux Epines	H	$$$$$	114
Coral Cove Cottages & Apartments	L'Anse Aux Epines	SC	$$	118
Coyaba Beach Resort	Grand Anse	H	$$$$	115
Deyna's City Inn	St George's	H	$$	96
Epping Forest	St Paul's	H	$–$$	159
Flamboyant Hotel & Villas	Grand Anse	H	$$$–$$$$	115
GEM Holiday Beach Resort	Morne Rouge	SC	$$	118
Grenada Bay Villas	True Blue	SC	On request	117
Grenada Gold Apartments	Grand Anse	SC	$–$$	118
Grenada Grand Beach Resort	Grand Anse	H	$$$–$$$$	115
Grenada Grand View Inn	Grand Anse	H	$$	116
Grenadian (Rex Resorts)	Magazine Beach	H	On request	115

Accommodation name	Location	Type	Price Code	Page
Grooms Beach Villas & Resort	Point Salines	SC	$$–$$$	118
Ixora Villa	L'Anse Aux Epines	SC	$$$$$	116
Jenny's Place	Grand Anse	SC	$$	118
Kalinago Beach Resort	Morne Rouge	H	$$$	116
Lance Aux Epines Cottages	L'Anse Aux Epines	SC	$$$	117
La Sagesse Nature Centre	La Sagesse Estate	H	$$$	158
La Source	Pink Gin Beach	H	$$$$$	114
Laluna	Morne Rouge	H	$$$$$	114
Lance Aux Epines House	L'Anse Aux Epines	SC	$$$$$	116
Lazy Lagoon	St George's	SC	$	97
Le Phare Bleu Marina & Boutique Hotel	Petite Calivigny Bay	SC	$$$$	117
Lexus Inn	St George's	SC	$	97
Maca Bana Villas	Magazine Beach	SC	$$$$$	116
Mango Bay Cottages	Concord	SC	$$	135
Mango Palma	Gouyave	SC	$–$$	135
Moonfish Villas	Bathway Beach	SC	$$$–$$$$	178
Morne Fendue Plantation House	Sauteurs	H	$	178
Mount Cinnamon	Grand Anse	H	$$$$$	115
Mount Hartman Bay Estate	L'Anse Aux Epines	SC	$$$$$	116
Owl Cottage	L'Anse Aux Epines	SC	$$$$	117
Pelican Apartments	St George's	SC	$$	97
Petit Bacaye Villa Hotel & Restaurant	Petit Bacaye	SC	$$	160
Petite Anse	Sauteurs	H	$$–$$$	178
Rainbow Inn	Grand Bras	H	$	159
Reef View Pavilion Villas	L'Anse Aux Epines	SC	$$$$	117
Rumboat Retreat	Gouyave	H	$–$$	134
Sam's Inn	Dunfermline	H	$	159
Siesta Hotel	Grand Anse	H	$$	116
Spice Island Beach Resort	Grand Anse	H	$$$$$	114
Spicetree Suites	L'Anse Aux Epines	SC	$$	118
St Ann's Guest House	St George's	H	$	97
Sunset View Restaurant & Beach House	Grand Mal	H	$	135
The Heights	Sauteurs	SC	$$	178
The Lodge	St George's	H	$$$	97
Tropicana Inn	St George's	H	$	96
True Blue Bay Resort & Villas	True Blue	H	$$$–$$$$	115
Twelve Degrees North	L'Anse Aux Epines	SC	$$$	117
Two Bays Villa & Studio	Crochu	SC	$$–$$$	160
Valley Breeze Guest House	Grenville	SC	$–$$	160
Villa Amarillo	True Blue	SC	$$$$$	117
Villa Caribella	Westerhall	SC	$$$$$	159
Villa Heron's Flight	Westerhall	SC	$$$$	159
Willie's Court Apartments	Gouyave	SC	$	135

CARRIACOU AND PETITE MARTINIQUE

Accommodation name	Location	Type	Price Code	Page
Ade's Dream Apartment Hotel	Hillsborough (C)	SC	$	213
Bayaleau Point Cottages	Windward (C)	SC	$-$$	213
Belair Garden Cottage	Belair (C)	SC	$$	212
Bogles Round House	Bogles (C)	SC	$	213
Carriacou Grand View Hotel	Beauséjour (C)	H	$	211
Driftwood	Craigston (C)	SC	$$$	212
Goyaba	Craigston (C)	SC	$$$	212
Green Roof Inn	Beauséjour (C)	H	$-$$	211
Honor & Paul's Apartment	Cherry Hill (C)	SC	$-$$	213
Hope's Inn	L'Esterre (C)	SC	$	213
Hotel Laurena	Hillsborough (C)	H	$-$$	211
John's Unique Resort	Hillsborough (C)	H	$	212
KIDO Ecological Research Station	Prospect (C)	SC	$$	213
Kim's Plaza Guesthouse	Hillsborough (C)	H	$	212
Las Tortugas	L'Esterre (C)	SC	$$$$$	212
Melodies Guest House	Paradise (PM)	H	$	212
Millenium Connection Guest House	Sanchez (PM)	H	$	212
Millie's Apartments & Guest Rooms	Hillsborough (C)	H	$	211
Palm Beach Guest House	Sanchez (PM)	SC	$	213
Palm Trees	Craigston (C)	SC	$	213
Sand X Beach House	Hillsborough (C)	SC	$	213
Scraper's Bayview Cottages	Tyrrel Bay (C)	SC	$	213
Seaclusion Suites	L'Esterre (C)	SC	$$	212
Sunset Beach Hotel	L'Esterre (C)	H	$	212
Tamarind Cottage	Upper Craigston (C)	SC	$$$	212
Villa Sankofa	Craigston (C)	SC	$$$$$	212
Yellow Bird	Craigston (C)	SC	$$$	212

Appendix 2

RESTAURANTS AT A GLANCE

RESTAURANT PRICE CODES
Average price of a main course:

$$$	Often more than EC$75
$$	Somewhere between EC$25 and EC$75
$	Less than or around EC$25

RESTAURANT TYPE CODE In the following list, restaurant types are also referred to by a simple code:

Caribbean cuisine	C
International cuisine	I
Hotel restaurant	H
Located by a beach or water	B

GRENADA

Restaurant name	Location	Type	Price Code	Page
Aggie's Restaurant & Bar	Bathway Beach	CIB	$$	179
Ali Baba Grill & Bar (Allamanda Beach Resort)	Grand Anse	IBH	$$	119
Almost Paradise	Sauteurs	CIH	$$	179
Aquarium (Maca Bana Villas)	Magazine Beach	CIBH	$$$	119
Arawakabana (Coyaba Beach Resort)	Grand Anse	CIBH	$$$	119
B's Hot Spot Roti Shop	St George's	C	$	97
Bains Restaurant & Bar	Grenville	C	$	160
Bananas	True Blue	CI	$$	120
BB's Crabback Caribbean Restaurant	St George's	CB	$$	97
Beachside Terrace Restaurant (Flamboyant Hotel)	Grand Anse	CIBH	$$	119
Belmont Estate Restaurant	Belmont	C	$$	179
Best In Town Restaurant	Sauteurs	C	$	179
Boots Cuisine Restaurant & Bar	Woodlands	CI	$$	119
Cabier Ocean Lodge	Crochu	CIBH	$$	160
Carenage Cafe	St George's	CIB	$	97
Carib Sushi	Grand Anse	I	$$	120
Carib's Leap Restaurant & Wine Bar	Sauteurs	CI	$$	179
Charcoals Caribbean Grill	L'Anse Aux Epines	CI	$$	120

Restaurant name	Location	Type	Price Code	Page
Chopstix (Spiceland Mall)	Grand Anse	I	$–$$	120
Citrus & Spice Restaurant & Bar	St George's	CIB	$–$$	97
Coconut Beach	Grand Anse	CIB	$$	120
Creole Shack Restaurant	St George's	CI	$–$$	97
De Big Fish	True Blue	CIB	$$	119
De Graps	St George's	CT	$	98
Deliciosa (Siesta Hotel)	Grand Anse	CIH	$$	119
Dodgy Dock (True Blue Bay Resort)	True Blue	CIBH	$$	119
Fedelis Restaurant & Bar (Kalinago Beach Resort)	Morne Rouge	CIBH	$$	119
Helena's Ocean View	Sauteurs	CI	$–$$	179
Kelly's Hot Spot	Gouyave	C	$	135
La Belle Creole (Blue Horizon Resort)	Grand Anse	CIH	$$$	119
La Boulangerie	Granda Anse	I	$$	120
La Sagesse Nature Centre	La Sagesse Beach	CIBH	$$	160
Laluna	Morne Rouge	CIBH	$$$	119
Le Chateau Restaurant & Bar	Grand Anse	CI	$–$$	120
Little Dipper Restaurant & Bar	Lower Woburn	C	$$	120
Mo's Delight Restaurant & Mini Bar	Gouyave	C	$	135
Museum Bistro	St George's	CI	$$	97
New Nutmeg	St George's	CIB	$$	97
Oasis Bar & Restaurant (Jenny's Place)	Grand Anse	CIBH	$$	120
Ocean Grill Restaurant & Bar	St George's	CIB	$$	97
Oliver's (Spice Island Beach Resort)	Grand Anse	CIBH	$$$	119
Oriental Restaurant (Rex Grenadian Resort)	Magazine Beach	IBH	$$	120
Paul's Catering & Mini Restaurant	Gouyave	C	$	135
Petit Bacaye Villa Hotel & Restaurant	Petit Bacaye	CIBH	$$	160
Petite Anse Restaurant & Bar	Sauteurs	CIBH	$$–$$$	178
Pirate's Cove Terrace Restaurant (Grenada Grand View Inn)	Grand Anse	CIH	$$	120
Plantation Bar & Kitchen	Morne Fendue	C	$$	179
Poolbar Restaurant (Le Phare Bleu)	Petite Calivigny Bay	CIBH	$$	119
Rhodes' (Calabash Hotel)	L'Anse Aux Epines	CIBH	$$$	118
Rivers Restaurant & Bar	River Antoine Estate	CI	$$	179
Savvy's (Mount Cinnamon)	Grand Anse	CIH	$$$	119
Spiceisle Restaurant & Bar	Gouyave	CB	$	135
Spices Restaurant & Bar	St George's	CIB	$–$$	97
Sunset View Restaurant	Grand Mal	CIB	$–$$	135
Sur La Mer	Morne Rouge	CIB	$$	120

Restaurant name	Location	Type	Price Code	Page
The Beach House Restaurant & Bar	Point Salines	CIBH	$$$	119
The Heights Café Bar	Sauteurs	CI	$$	179
The Pizza Place	Prickly Bay Marina	CIB	$$	120
The Red Crab	L'Anse Aux Epines	CI	$$	120
Tropicana Inn Restaurant & Bar	St George's	CI	$-$$	97
True Blue Bay Restaurant	True Blue	CIBH	$$$	119
Umbrellas	Grand Anse	CIB	$$	120
Victory Bar & Grill (Port Louis Marina)	St George's	CIB	$$	97
Västra Banken (Le Phare Bleu)	Petite Calivigny Bay	CIB	$$$	119
Water's Edge Restaurant & Bar	St David's Point	CIBH	$$	160

CARRIACOU AND PETITE MARTINIQUE

Restaurant name	Location	Type	Price Code	Page
Banana Joe's	Paradise Beach (C)	CB	$	214
Bogles Round House	Bogles (C)	CIH	$$	214
Cow Foot Inn	Belmont (C)	C	$	214
Green Roof Inn	Beauséjour (C)	CIH	$$	214
Hardwood Restaurant & Bar	Paradise Beach (C)	CIB	$-$$	214
Kayak Kaffee	Hillsborough (C)	CI	$-$$	214
La Playa	Hillsborough (C)	CIB	$-$$	214
Lambie Queen Restaurant & Bar	Tyrrel Bay (C)	CIB	$-$$	214
Laurena II Restaurant & Bar	Hillsborough (C)	C	$	214
Lazy Turtle Pizzeria	Tyrrel Bay (C)	CIB	$$	214
Melodies Restaurant	Sanchez (PM)	CIBH	$	214
Off the Hook	Paradise Beach (C)	CB	$	214
Old Rum Shop	Tyrrel Bay (C)	CB	$	214
Palm Beach Restaurant	Paradise (PM)	CIBH	$-$$	214
Sandy Lane Bar	Hillsborough (C)	CIB	$	214
Scraper's Restaurant & Bar	Tyrrel Bay (C)	CIB	$-$$	214
Seawave	Hillsborough (C)	CIB	$-$$	214
Slipway Restaurant	Tyrrel Bay (C)	CIB	$$	214
Sunset Beach Bar & Restaurant	Paradise Beach (C)	CIB	$-$$	214

Appendix 3

FURTHER INFORMATION

BOOKS
Reference

Adkin, Mark, *Urgent Fury: The Battle for Grenada*, Lexington Books, 1989. ISBN 978-0669207170

Andrews, Alexis, *Genesis: Building a Traditional Carriacou Sloop*, Indian Creek Books, 2008. ISBN 978-0979011429

Anim-Addo, Joan, *Framing the Word*, Whiting & Birch, 1996. ISBN 978-1871177916

Anim-Addo, Joan, *Touching the Body*, Mango Publishing, 2007. ISBN 978-1902294230

Brathwaite, Roger, *Grenada: Spice Paradise*, Macmillan Caribbean, 2002. ISBN 978-0333801031

Brizan, George, *Grenada: Island of Conflict*, Macmillan Education, 1998. ISBN 0-333710231

David, Christine, *Folklore of Carriacou*, Coles Printery, 1985. Privately published.

Douglas, Claude J., *The Battle for Grenada's Black Gold*, Maryzoon Press, 2004. ISBN 976-8193395

Douglas, Claude J., *When the Village was an Extended Family in Grenada*, Maryzoon Press, 2003. ISBN 976-8173483

Groome, J. R. A., *Natural History of the Island of Grenada*, Caribbean Printers, 1970. Privately published.

Hawthorne, William D., *Caribbean Spice Island Plants: Trees, Shrubs and Climbers of Grenada, Carriacou and Petit Martinique: A Picture Gallery with Notes on Identification, Historical and Other Trivia*, Oxford Forestry Institute, 2004. ISBN 978-0850741629

Kilgore, Cindy and Moore, Alan, *Adventure Guide to Grenada, St Vincent & the Grenadines*, Hunter Publishing, 2007. ISBN 978-1588436245

Martin, John Angus, *A–Z of Grenada Heritage*, Macmillan Caribbean, 2007. ISBN 978-0333792520

McIntosh, Simeon C. R., *Kelsen in the Grenada Court*, Ian Randle Publishers, 2008. ISBN 978-9768167477

Sandford, Gregory and Vigilante, Richard, *Grenada: The Untold Story*, Madison Books, 1984. ISBN 978-0819143105

Sinclair, Norma, *Grenada: Isle of Spice*, Macmillan Caribbean, 2002. ISBN 978-0333968062

Steele, Beverley A., *Grenada: A History of its People*, Macmillan Caribbean, 2002. ISBN 978-0333930533

Wilkinson, Wendy and Lee, Donna, *Morgan Freeman and Friends: Caribbean Cooking for a Cause*, Rodale Books, 2006. ISBN 978-1594864247

Fiction

Anim-Addo, Joan, *Haunted by History*, Mango Publishing, 2004. ISBN 978-1902294032

Buffong, Jean, *Snowflakes in the Sun*, The Women's Press, 1995. ISBN 978-0704344235

Buffong, Jean, *Under the Silk Cotton Tree*, The Women's Press, 1992. ISBN 978-0704343177

Buffong, Jean and Payne, Nellie, *Jump-Up-And-Kiss-Me*, The Women's Press, 1990. ISBN 978-0704342439

Collins, Merle, *Angel*, The Women's Press, 1987. ISBN 978-0704340824
Collins, Merle, *Because the Dawn Breaks*, Karia Press, 1985. ISBN 978-0946918096
Collins, Merle, *Lady in a Boat*, Peepal Tree Press, 2003. ISBN 978-1900715850
Collins, Merle, *Rain Darling*, The Women's Press, 1990. ISBN 978-0704342583
Collins, Merle, *The Colour of Forgetting*, Virago Press, 1995. ISBN 978-1853818929
Ross, Jacob, *A Way to Catch the Dust*, Mango Publishing, 1999. ISBN 978-1902294087
Ross, Jacob, *Song for Simone*, Mango Publishing, 2004. ISBN 978-1902294063
Wilkins, Verna Allette, *Kim's Magic Tree*, Tandem Library, 1993. ISBN 978-0613800228
Wilkins, Verna Allette, *Toyin Fay*, Gareth Stevens Publishing, 1998. ISBN 978-0836820911

WEBSITES

www.barnaclegrenada.com Online newspaper, reviews and commentary
www.carriacoupetitemartinique.com General information on Carriacou and Petite Martinique with listings
www.gogouyave.com Website dedicated to Gouyave
www.grenadabroadcast.com Streaming news, headlines, interviews and editorials
www.grenadaexplorer.com General information about Grenada with listings and tips
www.grenadagrenadines.com The official site of the Grenada Board of Tourism
www.grenadaguide.com General business listings
www.godrenada.gd Official website of the Grenada Hotel & Tourism Association
www.grenadavisitorforum.com Conversations, news, stories and photos about Grenada
www.thegrenadarevolutiononline.com Website dedicated to the events of 1983
www.travelgrenada.com General information about Grenada with listings

NOTES

NOTES

Index

Page numbers in **bold** indicate major entries; those in *italics* indicate maps. Occasionally (C) has been used when it is necessary to indicate where an entry relates to Carriacou rather than Grenada.